TRAVEL AND DISCOVERY
IN THE RENAISSANCE

1420-1620

TRAVEL AND DISCOVERY
IN THE RENAISSANCE

1420-1620

By

Boies Penrose
Fellow of the Royal Geographical Society

HARVARD UNIVERSITY PRESS

Cambridge, Massachusetts

1952

Distributed in Great Britain by
GEOFFREY CUMBERLEGE
OXFORD UNIVERSITY PRESS
LONDON

LIBRARY OF CONGRESS CATALOG CARD NUMBER 52–5403

PRINTED IN THE UNITED STATES OF AMERICA

To WILLIAM ALEXANDER JACKSON
Who inspired me to write this book

PREFACE

The exploration and exploitation of non-European areas by Europeans during the fifteenth and sixteenth centuries form one of the greatest phenomona of the Renaissance; one that had never been previously witnessed on such a scale and one that is still of prime importance in the world today. It is curious, therefore, that this highly significant phase of human endeavor should have had no concise, adequate, one-volume treatment since the publication of Sophus Ruge's *Geschichte des Zeitalters der Entdeckungen* in 1881. Good as Ruge's book is, its value for the average interested reader is lessened by its being in German and being out-of-print; moreover, a good deal of information has come to light since Ruge wrote. True, the subject is adequately covered by the "Pioneer Histories" (London: A. & C. Black, Ltd.) but this is an uncoördinated series of ten volumes. One might also mention the publications of the Hakluyt Society, but they run to about two hundred volumes!

There is, however, for the period of geographical history ending with the rise of Henry the Navigator, a supremely great survey, Sir Raymond Beazley's *The Dawn of Modern Geography* (1897–1906); and for the period 1600–1800 there is an equally definitive example of scholarship, Edward Heawood's *Geographical Discovery in the Seventeenth and Eighteenth Centuries* (1912). But lying between these two outstanding classics is a gap of almost two centuries — from the siege of Ceuta to the death of Queen Elizabeth — not covered by any one study since the appearance of Ruge's work seventy years ago. This condition is all the more to be wondered at, since during the Renaissance period the most important geographical activity in human annals was performed. I have, therefore, in all humility set out to fill the gap with a book which I venture to hope will tell the story in concise and satisfactory form: the story not only of the great explorers, but of the lesser free-lance travelers, of cartography and navigational knowledge, and of geographical literature, as well. All these elements are closely integrated parts of the general picture, and one cannot appreciate the picture as a whole without properly emphasizing these various factors.

Nor does it appear adequate to turn aside from the subject after describing the initial discoveries in a given area. A further glance at the consolidation of footholds in strange lands and at the early efforts of colonization seem essential for the full appreciation of the subject. In other words, the theme of this book is discovery and travel merging into colonial history. It would be telling less than half the story, for instance, to leave off the Portuguese in India after Cabral's voyage, or the Spanish in South America after Pizarro.

A mere cut-and-dried account of the great voyages and their immediate results seems inadequate too: we should also describe the maps by which the explorers traveled, the types of ships in which they sailed, and the books that were written about their travels after they returned home. To put it another way, we should consider not only what the men did, but how they did it; as well as the impact of their exploits on their contemporaries and the effect of their explorations on subsequent colonial history. In this book I have attempted to do these things: if I have failed, it is not because of the subject or my intentions, but simply because of my own limitations.

It has appeared essential to begin with an introductory chapter on the classical and medieval background, without which much that followed would be imperfectly understood. At the other end of the narrative I have tried somewhat unsuccessfully to keep to the termination date of 1620, not merely because of the pretty symbolism that it was (very questionably) the bicentenary of Prince Henry's settlement at Sagres, but more especially because the heroic period of Renaissance discovery may be said to have played itself out by then. Indeed one becomes conscious of a period of stagnation in the chronicles of travel and voyaging after the first third of the seventeenth century, a period lasting for more than a generation in the case of Asia and upwards of a century and a half in Africa; in South America, aside from the Amazon valley, little was done for a great many years. In North America alone, thanks to the French, the progress of exploration was continuous throughout the years; elsewhere discovery (as against routine travel) was of a minor order for a long time to come. Viewed in this light, a terminal year, arbitrarily fixed at 1620 and adhered to with very considerable elasticity, would seem appropriate for this study. Furthermore, I have refrained from extending the narrative too far into the seventeenth century, because I have no desire to compete with Edward Heawood's book. Rather, as I have said, I would like the present volume to fit between those of Beazley and Heawood — or at least I should be flattered if, in the opinion of my critics, it is worthy of that position.

My acknowledgments happen to be few in number, but on that account they are all the more sincere. In particular, my grateful thanks go to Mr. Douglas Gordon of Baltimore; to Mr. Malcolm Letts, President of the Hakluyt Society; to Mr. Lionel Robinson and Mr. Philip Robinson of the distinguished Pall Mall firm of William H. Robinson, Ltd.; and to Dr. Lawrence Wroth, Librarian of the John Carter Brown Library, Providence, for their long-suffering patience in reading considerable portions of the manuscript, and for their invaluable criticisms and suggestions for its improvement: to Dr. Wroth especially I am indebted for innumerable courtesies. Mr. Walter Whitehill, Director and Librarian of the Boston Athenaeum was also most helpful with the section dealing with ship design. Likewise I am under deep obligations to Dr. W. G. Constable of the Museum of Fine Arts, Boston, and to Dr. Louis B. Wright of the Folger Shakespeare Library, who as chairmen of the Committee on Renaissance Studies of the American Council of Learned Societies displayed the most gracious and friendly interest in my labors. To Captain Don Julio F. Guillén, Director of the Museo Naval in Madrid, I extend my hearty thanks for his kindness in sending me a photograph of *Santa Maria III*, which he designed; to Mr. James A. Williamson, editor of the "Pioneer Histories," I record my indebtedness for information regarding the La Cosa Map; and to Mrs. James E. Duffy of the Harvard University Press I register my great obligation for her splendid services in editing the manuscript for the printer. To Mr. Robert L. Williams of the Yale Cartographic Laboratory, I am likewise obliged for his excellent maps. I also wish to pay tribute to the memory of Sir William Foster, whose never-failing and sympathetic assistance to an amateurish enthusiast like myself was always a source of inspiration. And finally I must record my deep gratitude to Professor William A. Jackson of Harvard, who suggested in the first place that I write this book and who has been a constant pillar of strength in its execution.

One final remark: the spelling of place names conforms in most instances to the usage of the Royal Geographical Society; that of personal names follows the style used in the volumes of the Hakluyt Society.

B. P.

Barbados Hill
  Devon, Pennsylvania
Columbus Day, 1951

CONTENTS

LIST OF ILLUSTRATIONS

LIST OF MAPS

TRAVEL AND DISCOVERY
IN THE RENAISSANCE
1420-1620

1

THE BACKGROUND
CLASSICAL AND MEDIEVAL

The impulse for the voyages and travels of the fifteenth century did not come into being without a background; a background, indeed, which stretched away two thousand years or more into antiquity, and which involved the medieval Venetians and Genoese, the Franciscan missioners to Cathay, the Moslem savants of the Caliphate, the seafarers and marching legions of imperial Rome, the geographers of Alexandria, and ultimately the philosophers of ancient Greece. All these groups — and many more besides — went into the making of this background, without some knowledge of which one cannot have a full comprehension of the deeds and outlook of such figures as Henry the Navigator and Christopher Columbus. In its essence, this background must be visualized as a synthetic mixture composed of three parts: theory, myth, and actuality, compounded in different proportions for the different tastes of those influenced, yet each always present. Theory was the product of the attempt of scholars throughout the earlier ages to explain the world around them (and especially the unknown world) on a basis of quite limited information; myth was the result of two millenniums of romance and fairy tale, which did duty for scientific knowledge, and which had a particular attraction for the men of the Middle Ages; actuality was what men had actually seen — in this case the experiences of such figures as the Polos and their successors in areas which were either wholly unknown or else had been unvisited by Europeans since Roman times. Such was the threefold basis of geographical knowledge when the beginning of the fifteenth century ushered in the period of the great discoveries.

THEORY

The great geographers of the ancient world were the Greeks. From their earliest period these highly intelligent and very gifted people, living in the eastern part of the Mediterranean basin, took an interest in their physical environment which was of a far higher order than that of the older cultures along the Nile and the Euphrates. Even in Homeric times, as evidenced by the *Odyssey* and the legend of the Argonauts, the Hellenes sought to learn of the world around them, while their early philosophers tried to solve the problems of the earth's origin and its place in the celestial system. By the fifth century B.C. the Pythagorean school had evolved the theory of a spherical earth; a theory which, although deduced on philosophical rather than empirical grounds, has been followed by liberal-minded students ever since. Only in the early Christian times of the Dark Ages was this globular hypothesis ruled out; and even then there were a few daring souls, who, by defying the Church, kept alive this geographical truth, which was to be of such epoch-making importance in the fifteenth century. Indeed, the inception of the spherical theory of the globe was the foundation stone of Greek geography. All geographical theory and research until the passing of the classical period flowed from this fundamental principle.

In their practical knowledge of the "world around" the Greeks by the mid-fourth century B.C. were acquainted with the Mediterranean and Black Sea littorals and had some knowledge of the Caspian Sea and (through Xenophon) of Persia. By the end of that century Pytheas of Marseilles had recorded his voyages in the outer sea as far as the British Isles, so that the Greeks also knew something of the western coasts of Europe. A good idea of their knowledge is obtained in the historical writings of Herodotus, who, although not a conscious geographer, graphically portrayed the world as the men of Periclean Athens knew it. This world became known to the Greeks as the *oikoumene*, or the area inhabited by Greeks or by men of a like nature; the limits of the *oikoumene* were not known (except to the west, in Pytheas' time), but it was felt that the land of the *oikoumene* was bounded by ocean, which covered the rest of the globe. Possibility of land outside the *oikoumene* was advanced by Plato, whose mysticism led him to introduce one of the most remarkable of all geographical fables — that of the lost continent of Atlantis, somewhere in the Western Ocean — a fable which survived through the Middle Ages and even had its measure of influence on thought in the early Renaissance.

The Greeks further made an arbitrary subdivision of the globe into zones, without regard to the distribution of the land and water areas. They envisaged two polar zones, both uninhabitable because of cold; two temperate zones, a northern (wherein lay the *oikoumene*) and a southern; and an equatorial zone, generally considered incapable of sustaining life because of its heat. In particular, the problem of the equatorial zone exercised geographical theorists until the end of the Middle Ages and was bound up with the question of whether the Antipodes could support life beyond the lifeless zone. Suffice to say that this had a decidedly

restrictive effect on geographical enterprise and research, at least until
the start of Portuguese voyaging.

Such was the state of knowledge and theory at the inception of the
Macedonian Empire; the horizon was to be greatly widened in the century
that followed. Alexander's remarkable Indian campaign (326–324 B.C.)
carried the Greeks well east of the Indus, a full fifteen hundred miles
beyond Xenophon's farthest point; while their route — eastward across
northern Persia and what is now Afghanistan, then southward down the
Indus, then westward across southern Persia, keeping generally near the
sea — had the effect of greatly extending the latitude of the *oikoumene*.

Greece was indeed fortunate in having at the same time such a man
of action as Alexander and such a man of thought as Aristotle. Although
the great philosopher left no specifically geographical work behind him,
to Aristotle must be given the distinction of founding scientific geography.
From the first he was an exponent of the spherical theory, but whereas
the Pythagoreans had adopted it through the argument that the sphere,
being the only perfect solid figure, was solely worthy to circumscribe the
dwelling place of man; Aristotle used the more modern reasoning that
only a sphere could throw a circular shadow on the Moon during an
eclipse. As for the *oikoumene*, Aristotle believed that it had a great
southward as well as a great eastward extension; but since he held that
land was heavier than water, and that the masses of each must balance,
he felt convinced that there was no other *oikoumene* outside his own.
From this tenet he concluded that the distance across the ocean from
Spain to India was not great, and that there was no land in the way.
Judged in the light of this theory, Columbus was Aristotle's direct
descendant, by way of Roger Bacon and Cardinal d'Ailly.

Aristotle's thesis of the nonexistence of other *oikoumenes* did not pass
unchallenged, for in the second century B.C. Crates of Mallos argued that,
on the principle of world symmetry, there were four great land masses, of
which the Greeks' *oikoumene* was but one. Two were in the northern
hemisphere and two (the Antipodes) in the southern; all were surrounded
by the ocean. The Cratesian theory had its champions and its opponents.
Pomponius Mela, Macrobius, and many of the medieval Schoolmen
believed in it, but it provoked the righteous indignation of the orthodox,
both in patristic times and later, as containing the seeds of heresy.
Nevertheless, in its essence the antipodal part of Crates' hypothesis finally
triumphed, for it was proved by the Portuguese that there were lands
below the Equator inhabited by human beings, and the antipodal
oikoumene passed eventually from the mysterious Southern Continent of
the Spaniards to the actuality of Australia.

Alexander's most lasting accomplishment — more enduring than his
spectacular conquests — was the founding of the city named for him in

Egypt. Alexandria quickly became a center of Hellenism and of learning (especially geographical learning) until its decline with that of the Roman Empire half a millennium later; from this center sprang a school of geographical scholars culminating in Ptolemy. These scholars were interested alike in theoretical and descriptive geography as well as in astronomy, but the problem which exercised them most was the measurement of the earth. Chief among the earlier figures of the school was Eratosthenes (276–194 B.C.). He determined the position of the Tropic of Cancer at a point approximately south of Alexandria (Syene or Assuan) by seeing the reflection of the sun in a deep well on Midsummer's Day, measured the distance thence to Alexandria, ascertained the altitude of the sun at that place by means of a gnomon, and so, by the Euclidian postulate of a known base and two known angles, computed the circumference of our planet. His result (approximately 25,000 geographical miles) was surprisingly accurate, being but little in excess of the true figure, but unfortunately for posterity his findings were supplanted by those of Posidonius (130–50 B.C.), who arrived at the much too small figure of eighteen thousand geographical miles. Eratosthenes also made some interesting calculations about the *oikoumene*, which he judged to be nine thousand miles from east to west (about one third too much), and half that figure from north to south (which was very accurate). Between the days of Eratosthenes and Posidonius lived the very practical astronomer and geographer Hipparchus (flourished about 140 B.C.). It does not appear that Hipparchus ever took a hand at measuring the earth, but posterity is indebted to him none the less; for he divided the great circle into three hundred and sixty degrees and lined the surface of the globe with parallels of latitude and meridians of longitude. His prime meridian, appropriately enough, ran through Alexandria. Hipparchus not only introduced the system of coördinates, but by inventing and developing the astrolabe (the principle of which may have been known before), he provided the way for determining latitude; indeed, his instrument was used for "shooting the sun" until the days of Queen Elizabeth.

Hipparchus, as we have said, was followed by Posidonius, noted for his erroneous measurement of the earth and for the unfortunate popularity of his opinions. Posidonius' successor in the Alexandrine school was Marinus of Tyre (early second century A.D.), who followed his predecessor in perpetuating the error of the small earth. Marinus deserves to be remembered on other counts, however, for he anticipated Richard Hakluyt by adopting the practice of interviewing homecoming mariners — thereby helping to extend practical knowledge of navigation well down the East African coast and through the Indian Ocean to the Bay of Bengal. Above all Marinus is best known as the master of the most celebrated and most influential of all classical geographers — Ptolemy. Both

Marinus and his distinguished follower lived when the Roman Empire was at its height and when its commerce and shipping were in a real sense world-wide. Merchant voyaging and practical navigation were even then important parts of the science of geography, and by the second century of our era they made the geographer's way possible. Even as far back as the fourth century before Christ a surprisingly good coast pilot of the Mediterranean and the Black Sea had appeared, known to posterity as the *Periplus of Scylax;* in Alexander's day the hero's captain, Nearchus, had sailed from the mouth of the Indus to the Persian Gulf; and by the time of the Caesars, merchant vessels were trafficking in the Indian Ocean in search of the various exotic commodities in demand in the Imperial City. A highly interesting sailing manual of Pliny's time has come down to us, the anonymous Greek *Periplus of the Erythraean Sea.* This manual not only covered the more familiar parts of the Indian Ocean, but gave indications of the lands and coasts beyond India: the Islands of Chryse (probably the Malay Peninsula); the land of Seres (Indo-China?); and, at the very end of the East, the region of Thin — this being the first mention of China in the West.

It was with this body of knowledge at his command that Claudius Ptolemaeus (active A.D. 127–160) set out to give in his writings the whole of classical geographical learning. Yet for all that, Ptolemy did not introduce much that was new. He got his measurement of the earth from Posidonius by way of Marinus; he took the idea of degrees and of latitude and longitude from Hipparchus; he obtained his catalogue of geographical names from Marinus and the Periploi, and possibly also from Strabo. On the other hand he compiled the first atlas that we have knowledge of; he saw the problem of projecting a spherical surface on a plane and in consequence developed the earliest method of map-projection; and he was the first geographer to show a realization of the bulk, though not of the shape, of the earth.

Ptolemy's fame rests on two works: his *Astronomy* (better known under its Arabic title of the *Almagest*), and his *Geography.* These books were passed across the gulf of the Middle Ages by the Arabs, to form the starting point of modern geography. It was Ptolemy's ambition to give accurate representation of the world as he knew it — a far larger world than the *oikoumene* of his predecessors. To do this he went to immense trouble to determine the latitude and longitude of all known localities. In theory his idea was sound, but in practice his information was so wide of the mark as to make his *Geography* a vast collection of errors. In the Mediterranean basin localities could be determined with some degree of truth; their latitude by the astrolabe and their longitude by dead reckoning; but when Ptolemy passed outside his immediate orbit, and tried to get the position of point A which was so many days' journey in an indeterminate direction from point B, the result is all too often ludicrous. This distortion was further accentuated by his adopting too small a figure for the earth's circumference, and in consequence giving an equatorial degree the length of only fifty geographical miles. This had the effect of bestowing on Asia a great eastward extension — the result of which was not lost on the imagination of Columbus, who saw thereby a short western seaway to India.

Ptolemy's *Geography* is in two parts: the first section is a gazetteer of place names arranged by regions, each name having its latitude and longitude; the second part is the atlas, containing a world map and many regional maps. It is easy to perceive from the world map how the old Greek *oikoumene* with the surrounding ocean has been transformed. Instead there are the continents of Europe, Asia, and Africa; while the Indian Ocean has become a greater Mediterranean, enclosed by a land-bridge which runs from East Africa to southeastern Asia. The Indian peninsula is almost wholly truncated; to the south lies the huge island of Taprobana (Ceylon), while beyond to the east is the Golden Chersonese (the Malay Peninsula), beyond this is the Sinus Magnus or Great Gulf, and beyond again is the region where the African land-bridge terminates. This latter feature gave rise to the portrayal of two Malay peninsulas in early sixteenth century cartography, while the conception of the enclosed Indian Ocean puzzled the Portuguese and other Europeans before da Gama's day. Africa is portrayed as a broad block, even broadening below the equator, but Ptolemy at least went to some pains to map the interior of the Dark Continent and showed the Mountains of the Moon and the lacustrine origin of the Nile — both features doubtless derived from accurate native information. Speculation and myth were banished as far as possible from Ptolemy's work; Plato's lost Atlantis, Crates' other *oikoumenes* and the Antipodes have all gone: only the African land-bridge remains as a definite figment of Ptolemy's imagination. For all his intellectual honesty Ptolemy paid the penalty for his errors and his fame, and the explorers of the Renaissance too often had to unlearn what he had taught them and then learn all over again, the hard way. Ptolemy was to remain, however, the most important figure in the world of geography until Marco Polo.

Compared with Greece, Rome had little to show in the way of geographical thought and literature. In fact, the only outstanding geographer associated with Rome was the Greek Strabo (64 B.C.–A.D. 20). Unlike the Greeks, the Romans were not given to contemplation of their environment; rather they were matter-of-fact generals, administrators, and empire-builders. Geographical theory was alien to them; what they wanted were useful reference books. Strabo, although not acknowledged at the time, must have supplied the need: he wrote an encyclopedic political and descriptive geography of the then known world, which remains the best thing of the sort left by the classical civilization. In essence, it is a glorified gazetteer, of the sort warranted to be invaluable for the commander of a legion or the governor of a province — no frills, just plain facts and plenty of them. Under these circumstances it is indeed curious that Strabo received no notice from the other classical geographers, though it is impossible to believe that they were wholly ignorant of his writings. In any case, he was rediscovered in the early Renaissance, when his influence was more than considerable.

Of the Latins themselves, only three may be mentioned: Pliny devoted four books of his *Natural History* to geography, in which much serious information exists alongside of mythical fictions; Pomponius Mela (*circa* A.D. 40) revived the Cratesian theory of other *oikoumenes* and wrote a slight treatise on geography which even in the fifteenth century enjoyed a popularity far beyond its deserts; Macrobius (fourth century), followed Mela in the belief in the Antipodes and like him is chiefly memorable for a surprising hold on public esteem in the Middle Ages. One must also notice the celebrated painted mural map of Agrippa, Augustus' general and adviser, done in a portico in Rome in the Ptolemaic manner, and portraying the entire world as the Romans knew it. This ends the roll of those classical geographers who are pertinent to our purpose; those few who prostituted their talents by writing about wonders and marvels will be considered under "Myth" rather than under "Theory."

With the decline of Rome and the advent of the Dark Ages, geography as a science went into hibernation, from which the early Church did little to rouse it. Strict Biblical interpretation plus unbending patristic bigotry resulted in the theory of a flat earth with Jerusalem in its center, and the Garden of Eden somewhere up country, from which flowed the four Rivers of Paradise. The chief exponent of this view was the monk Cosmas (*circa* A.D. 540), whose pious imposture is all the more grotesque as he had traveled to India and should have known better. It is only fair to state that not all writers of the Dark Ages were as blind as Cosmas, for St. Augustine and the Venerable Bede upheld the sphericity of the earth, and both Isidore of Seville and Orosius included geographical sections in their writings, which are not wholly without value. Nevertheless, geographical theory and literature of the time are hardly inspiring, and fortunately for human thought patristic geography had no influence in the days of Henry the Navigator.

A revival of the science was long in coming, and we must credit the Moslem scholars of the early Middle Ages for keeping alive the learning of the ancients. With this impetus, Christian savants from the newly founded universities of the West traveled in the twelfth and thirteenth centuries to Toledo, Palermo, and Tunis to find the knowledge of Aristotle and Ptolemy awaiting them. The introduction of classical and Islamic geography into the West is epitomized in the career of Edrisi (1100–1166), a brilliant Moor from Ceuta, who spent many years at the Court of King Roger II of Sicily. Edrisi, the most gifted of Moslem geographers, brought Ptolemy up to date, and in his exhaustive *Geography*, put before Christian scholars the best work in the field written for nearly a thousand years. In view of the Moslem regard for Ptolemy, it is quite curious that there is no record of a manuscript of Ptolemy's own *Geography* having reached Western Europe during that period, much less being translated: Christendom had to wait until the century of Columbus and da Gama for that highly important literary event. This did not apply, however, to Ptolemy's astronomical work, known to the Arabs as the *Almagest*, "the greatest"; a title which shows in what regard both it and its author were held. This book was translated from the Arabic by Gerard of Cremona, and an abstract of it, made by the Englishman John of Holywood (or Sacrobosco) in the mid-thirteenth century became the great practical manual of seamanship until the end of the Middle Ages. Sacrobosco's handy recension, under the title of *Sphaera Mundi*, grew to be one of the best known and most useful books of all time; many manuscript copies have survived, while upwards of thirty incunabula editions testify to its popularity in the Columbian period.

Of the Schoolmen themselves, it must be confessed that they did not contribute much to geographical theory, although their period witnessed a renaissance of geographical study in Christian Europe. The theory of the spherical earth came to be accepted by all save the most reactionary literalists, and along with it the Greek division of the globe into climatic zones. Albertus Magnus (*circa* 1200–1280) even argued for the possibility of an inhabited equatorial belt and the existence of populated antipodes. Roger Bacon (1214–1294) was in full agreement with him in this, and in postulating the existence of habitable land at no great distance from the coast of Spain, the Englishman put forth reasoning based on Aristotle, which was in turn repeated almost verbatim by Pierre d'Ailly, through whom it had its full effect on Christopher Columbus. It is well to remember, therefore, the link between the Schoolmen, Bacon especially, and the discovery of America.

It is strange that during the hundred years or more between Bacon's death and the beginning of the fifteenth century no geographical study of any importance was carried out; all the more strange indeed, since the first half of this period was the time of the great medieval journeys of the Polos and their successors. Perhaps it only underlines the gap between theory and practice in those days. A French churchman, Cardinal Pierre d'Ailly, Bishop of Cambrai (1350–1420), was the first geographical scholar since the days of the Schoolmen. He left two works:

the *Imago Mundi*, a comprehensive world geography written before the discovery of Ptolemy's *Geography*, and the *Cosmographiae Tractatus Duo*, written afterwards. D'Ailly was almost slavishly deferential, for there is not a single idea in his writings which cannot be traced back to some impeccably orthodox source, while his life must have been so cloistered that all knowledge of medieval travel and exploration appears to have escaped his notice. Not a single Asiatic or African traveler receives mention, although d'Ailly wrote within living memory of the missions to China. Nevertheless, by quoting Roger Bacon almost word for word on the Aristotelian view of the short westward sea passage to India, he very greatly influenced Columbus. Indeed Columbus seems to have kept the *Imago Mundi* as a favorite bedside book, and his copy of the edition printed in Louvain about 1483 (Hain 837) — still preserved in the Biblioteca Colombina, Seville — contains several hundred of his marginal annotations. Unquestionably the discoverer was impressed by d'Ailly's demonstration that the eastward length of the habitable world was even greater than that envisaged by Ptolemy, the corollary thereto being that the commencement of the Orient was not far distant from the Pillars of Hercules. For the rest, d'Ailly believed in an open Indian Ocean and an insular Africa, as well as in a habitable tropical zone. D'Ailly's second work shows the impact of the discovery of Ptolemy's *Geography*, but the Cardinal had his own methods of incorporating the classical writer's teachings, and the consequent distortion is not always for the best.

Ptolemy's *Geography* was recovered in the early years of the fifteenth century, and its translation by Jacobus Angelus in 1406–1410 was of the first importance to the learned world. It was, within its limits, convincing, authentic, and far superior to the geographies of the Middle Ages; its discovery must have created a stir then that the discovery of a missing play by Shakespeare would now. For all its errors, Ptolemy's book was stimulating rather than enslaving; culture and critical enlightenment had progressed too far for it to be a dead weight. Ptolemy's fundamental principle of geography was the accurate fixing of positions by latitude and longitude. Though he himself carried this principle into practice in a highly erroneous manner, the principle remained for those to act on who had the knowledge and the instruments. So it was that even in some of the first printed editions of his atlas (for example, the Ulm Ptolemy of 1482) his maps are supplemented by portolan-type maps, drawn on scientific lines. Even one of Ptolemy's greatest errors — the enclosed nature of the Indian Ocean — was seriously questioned by scholars of the early Renaissance. Yet, as the dean of classical geographers, he enjoyed considerable popularity in the fifteenth and sixteenth centuries, and his theories and principles continued to influence mankind.

One more writer may be mentioned in the period before the great discoveries, as having some influence on them: this was Pope Pius II, a humanist and scholar of mature culture and erudition. His *Historia Rerum Ubique Gestarum* is largely a digest of Ptolemy, but by no means an uncritical one, for Pius believed in the circumnavigability of Africa. He also incorporated information about eastern Asia and China brought home by Marco Polo and Odoric of Pordenone. Columbus' copy of this book has survived (Venice, 1477; Hain 257; preserved in the Colombina in Seville), and his marginal notes therein show a great interest in China.

This sums up geographical theory and scholarship at the eve of the period of discovery. Most of the beliefs and principles could be traced back to classical times — to Aristotle and Ptolemy, in particular. The Moslems and the Schoolmen had passed along this knowledge without adding greatly to it, and one or two scholars of the fifteenth century had brought it up to date. It was with this background, on the theoretical side, that the early Portuguese and Spanish explorers had to work.

MYTH

Reinforcing the theoretical and abstract knowledge of geography was a large body of myth and fable and fiction, which cannot be discounted in any attempt to study the minds of Renaissance voyagers. Much of this mythical lore was of classical origin, some was Biblical, some Moslem, and some simply medieval; but it resulted in a patchwork of travelers' tales and romances which had a fascinating effect on high and low alike. With a scant handful of exceptions, this mass of fable was concerned with the Orient, which held a peculiar charm for both classical and medieval men, being associated in their minds with fantastic wealth, natural wonders, and magic. Some few of the myths may actually be of Homeric origin; many of them can certainly be traced back to the writings of Ctesias, a Greek who lived for seventeen years at the Persian court (about 400 B.C.), and whose *Persica* and *Indica* form collections of many of the fabulous and marvelous tales of Oriental animals and monsters. Alexander's Indian campaign gave rise to more stories of the same sort, which in the Middle Ages grew into the Alexander cycle of romances. In Roman days Pliny passed on many geographical fictions (largely from Ctesias) in his *Natural History*, but he was completely outdone in mendacity by Caius Julius Solinus (flourished third century A.D.), whose *Polyhistor* is a collection from Pliny and other sources of marvelous tales about strange animals, monstrous races of men, and fantastic wonders of nature. Solinus' book enjoyed an almost unrivaled popularity and was used avidly by the Medieval encyclopedists and chroniclers. Even better was to come, with the accretion of Biblical and Gothic myths to classical ones; this form of geography reached its quintessence in the fourteenth-century

Travels of Sir John Mandeville, a wonderful literary fiction which must have taken the reading public of Western Europe by storm.

What men know and see they do not generally regard as mysterious; rather is it the hidden, the remote, the unknown, which gives rise to flights of the imagination. From the early days of the Greeks through the times of the Sassanians, Persia interposed an "iron curtain" between the Mediterranean world and the farther Orient. Alexander penetrated the curtain briefly by the simple expedient of beating the Persians in pitched battle, and the Romans circumvented it by sailing round the Persian domains, or by using the mysterious Silk Road across Bactria. Save for these two periods Western man did not reach central or southern Asia until the Tatar Peace of the thirteenth century. Meanwhile the fables grew to such proportions that even the travels of the Polos and their successors could not diminish men's belief in them. These fables were to a considerable degree localized in India: if the greater part of Asia was a region of fantasy, India was above all else the land of marvels. It was there that pygmies fought with storks, and giants with griffons; there lived men with dog's heads who barked and snarled, men who shaded themselves from the sun by lying on their backs and holding up a single huge foot, headless men with eyes in their stomachs, jungle folk with hairy bodies and long teeth. So wrote Ctesias and so wrote Mandeville — such was the continuity of tradition. The legend of Alexander the Great, rendered in the Middle Ages into a romance of chivalry and given a Christian slant by having that hero visit Paradise, formed a mass of fable largely laid in India. So, too, was the legend of St. Thomas the Apostle, who had a shadowy but glorious career as a missionary and martyr, and had founded in southern India an opulent and flourishing Christian colony: this myth lasted right down to da Gama's first voyage.

Other myths are more difficult to localize. With the advent of patristic geography and the placing of Jerusalem in the center of the world, Paradise was given a vague location in Asia, which varied with the whims of the various cartographers and chroniclers — to pin it down with geographical accuracy was like giving latitude and longitude to a child's fairyland. Associated with this celestial area were the Four Rivers of Paradise, which had their source in the Garden of Eden and flowed thence through the East. They were the Tigris, the Euphrates, the Pison (thought to be either the Indus or the Ganges), and the Gihon or Nile, conveniently brought to Egypt by a subterranean course under the Red Sea. Then, too, there was the fable of the giants Gog and Magog, who ruled over terrible savages in remote Asia and whose eruption on the Last Day was destined to bring about the destruction of the human race. This Biblical prophecy was combined with the story of Alexander's enclosing the giants and their minions behind great walls. Still Biblical, but of a pleasanter nature, was the legend of the fabulous land of Ophir, from which came the gold and jewels of King Solomon. Ophir was especially elusive: it was sought for by Columbus in the West Indies, by Cabot in South America, and by the Portuguese in East Africa.

In fact the confusion of localities resulting from these myths is enough to drive any conscientious geographer out of his mind. India itself is a case in point, especially in its confusion with Ethiopia. At least one medieval map bears the legends "India Egyptii" and "India Ethiopie"; and Egypt throughout the period was actually considered to be in Asia, while the extremities of Ethiopia were usually carried far to the east, and the size of the Red Sea and the Indian Ocean was minimized, so that Central Africa was placed at no great distance from India. Doubtless this confusion accounts for the transplantation of the greatest of all geographical legends — that of Prester John.

The chronicler Otto von Freising records how he met in Italy in 1145 a Syrian bishop, who related how a certain John, king and priest, dwelling in the Far East beyond Persia, had waged a successful war against the Medes and Persians and had attempted to advance westward to succor Jerusalem. This was the first news to reach the Western world of the fabulous Indian ruler, who combined the piety of an apostle with the wealth of a Croesus. If the rumor had any factual basis at all, it was that a Buddhist tribesman of Central Asia had about this time defeated the Seljuk lord of Persia near Samarkand. For more than two decades Christendom was left with this vague report; then about 1170 was perpetrated that most remarkable of all literary hoaxes — the letter of Prester John. This mysterious document, addressed variously in surviving manuscripts to the Byzantine emperor, the pope, and the Emperor Frederick Barbarossa, recounts in no uncertain terms the glories and opulence of the Prester's realm. It tells how the priest-king was superior in wealth and power to all the other monarchs of the world; how his domains included the three Indias and extended across the desert of Babylon to the Tower of Babel. His lands were four months' journey across and comprised seventy-two provinces, each of which was ruled by a king. Within the realm were the lands of the Amazons and the Brahmins, the shrine of St. Thomas the Apostle, the Fountain of Youth, and rivers that ran gold and silver and jewels. Of Prester John himself, it was written that he was descended from the race of the Three Wise Men, and that in his own person he was the embodiment of Christian virtue and devotion. Such a report as this, of a noble and magnanimous Christian monarch ruling over a Utopia of unparalleled size and incredible opulence, had a profound effect in Europe, and the quest for the realms of Prester John became a major factor in exploration down to the expeditions of the Portuguese in Abyssinia.

The center panel of the altarpiece by Nuno Gonçalves, painted about 1460. St. Vincent, the patron saint of Lisbon, is surrounded by Prince Henry the Navigator (at right, in large hat); the future King John II (boy in conical hat); and Afonso V, the African, and his queen (kneeling in foreground).

The fortress of São Jorge da Mina, with two-masted caravels and a nau in the harbor. "Once the building of this fortress was decided upon, King João ordered the equipping of a fleet of ten caravels and two urcas [hulks], to carry hewn stone, tiles, and wood, as well as munitions and provisions for six hundred men, one hundred of whom were craftsmen and five hundred soldiers." — Barros.

It is possible to trace the recurring rumors of this wonderful potentate, and the development of his legend. Thus in 1221 news filtered out of the East that a great Christian monarch was fighting the Moslems, and sweeping away their power. Of course men at first thought hopefully that it must be Prester John, but they were soon undeceived by the realization that the conqueror was the terrible, non-Christian Genghis Khan. Yet even the shattering of this delusion did not dampen the ardor of those bent on finding the domain of the priest-king. In Marco Polo's time the Prester was associated with a Nestorian king of Kerait in Central Asia, but this man, although a Christian, was an unpleasant tyrant, who did the priest-king's reputation no good. Odoric of Pordenone, who traveled to the East in the early years of the fourteenth century, put Prester John's realm fifty days' journey west of Cathay. This is the last we hear of that mysterious ruler on the continent of Asia; the next mention of him, by Jordan of Severac about 1340, placed him definitely in Ethiopia, where he was still located when the Portuguese found him a century and a half later. It is easy to see how these rumors operated on the uncritical mind; and how the quest for this mighty prince, who would prove such a valuable ally in the struggle against the Moslems, remained a ruling passion for Henry the Navigator and successive Portuguese sovereigns, as well as for Christopher Columbus.

Beside the Prester John legend the other myths seem pallid indeed, yet there are two more, which may be mentioned as having some influence upon fifteenth century enterprise. These are the fables of the River of Gold and of the lost continent of Atlantis. The first of these concerns the illusory El Dorado of the Middle Ages, the River of Gold or Rio Doro, which was believed to exist somewhere in darkest Africa. It may have been based on shadowy intelligence about the Niger or the Senegal; the river's mouth was supposed to be somewhere south of Cape Bojador; and it was said to flow through the region of Bilad Ghana (or Guinea), the wondrous land of wealth about which Edrisi had written. Probably the Arab caravans coming north across the Sahara brought rumors of it, which filtered through to Christian Europe, and inspired men to search for it. As for the second myth, the legend of the lost Atlantis goes back to Plato. It was revived in early Christian times as the story of St. Brandon, who journeyed among enchanted isles and fantastic seas to the west and northwest of Ireland. Closely related to the St. Brandon fable was the legend of the seven bishops, who fled from Moorish Spain, and sailing boldly into the Atlantic, discovered a lovely island on which they built seven cities. This tradition was fully credited in the time of Henry the Navigator; in fact a sea captain reported to the Prince that he had actually found the island. Throughout the fifteenth century, therefore, and even into the sixteenth, the islands of St. Brandon and the Seven Cities, as well as those of Brazil and Antillia figured on the maps as surviving fragments of the lost continent, and grants for their discoveries were obtained during these years from the Portuguese monarchs. In fact, as late as 1755 St. Brandon's Isle was placed five degrees west of the Canaries, while the mythical Brazil Rock, the last of these phantoms, was not removed from the Admiralty charts until 1873.

So we have a world-wide network of myth to entice the Renaissance discoverer. Ethiopia, India, and Cathay, even West Africa and the Atlantic Ocean, contributed to a mighty corpus of legend and story, which, in its illusory fashion, promised wealth and power and glory to him who had the courage and resourcefulness to seek out these phantoms. The magnetism of the myth seems to have been a constant factor in the mentality of explorers; still other legends of sixteenth-century date, such as El Dorado, the Seven Cities of Cibola, and the Empire of Monomotapa, lured men to their fate in sandy deserts and tropical jungles.

ACTUALITY

It is probable that until the middle of the thirteenth century no European had traveled east of Baghdad. Undoubtedly the Crusades had given many men some knowledge of Syria, Palestine, and even Asia Minor, while there had always been a certain amount of pilgrimage travel to Jerusalem. But the farther Orient had remained cut off, until an event, or rather a series of events, opened up literally a limitless vista to the East. Early in the thirteenth century Genghis Khan established his authority over the Mongols in Central Asia and after subduing China, embarked on a campaign of wider conquests to the West, which actually carried him across South Russia into Poland. After the first fury of the Tatar conquest had spent itself, Genghis and his successors settled down to the consolidation of their vast domains, which stretched from the Dneister to the Pacific, and showed themselves as sage in peace as they had been terrible in war. They tolerated Christians in their dominions and even welcomed European traders; while the administration of their empire was so efficient that travelers could cross the vast expanses of Central Asia with ease and safety. A phenomenon had thus come about such as the world had not seen since the heyday of the Roman Empire: that of a vast realm, tolerant and well policed, where men of all nations could come and go as they liked. Both missionaries and merchants took advantage of this situation, and for upwards of a century there followed a surprising volume of travel between Western Europe and the further Orient. In 1245 Giovanni de Plano Carpini, a Franciscan monk, was sent by the pope on a mission to the Mongol ruler at Karakorum, in a remote district of Asia between the Gobi Desert and Lake Baikal. He was thus the first noteworthy European to explore the Mongol Empire. A similar mission was undertaken, also to Karakorum, by William de Rubruquis in 1253. Some years after these ventures the Mongol rulers removed their capital to Cambaluc (Peking), which remained their principal residence during the period of the other European visits. Kublai Khan, the celebrated Oriental potentate of song and story, was ruling there when the first commercial travelers from the West reached Cathay. These courageous businessmen were the two brothers Polo, merchants of Venice, who traveled overland to China about 1256 and remained in Kublai's new capital nearly fourteen years. After an absence in Europe they were back again with young Marco — destined to become one of the greatest travelers of all time. They had spent four years on the return trip to China, journeying through Persia and the Pamirs and across northern Tibet, and they were fated to remain in China seventeen more years before returning to their native Venice. During these years Marco was admitted to the diplomatic service of the khan, and in consequence was able to travel widely through Kublai's dominions. In 1292 the Polos started homeward, proceeding by sea along the coasts of the Malay Peninsula, Sumatra, and India; they reached Venice three years later. Marco Polo was succeeded by a number of travelers, of whom ecclesiastics were the most prominent. To name but a few who made their way to China early in the fourteenth century, there were Giovanni de Monte Corvino, Odoric of Pordenone, Andrew of Perugia, Jordan of Severac, and Giovanni de Marignolli. Most of these men made protracted stays on the Indian coast on the way. Compared with them the itinerant merchants are garbed in anonymity, except for the Polos, but that there were a fair number is evidenced by the survival of a highly interesting manuscript (in the Riccardian Library, Florence) by one Francesco Pegolotti, an agent of the great Florentine house of Bardi. This is nothing less than a handbook of the route to be followed in traveling from the Levant to Peking; it includes the stages of the journey and means of transport, the most suitable articles of commerce for the Chinese trade, and the profits most likely to accrue. It further contains the comforting assurance that the road is perfectly safe, whether by day or by night.

This happy state lasted until the middle of the fourteenth century, when several events effectively disrupted it, at least as far as Cathay and Central Asia were concerned. First, the terrible plague known as the Black Death swept Europe in 1348–49 and shook the medieval world to its foundations; second, the rise of the Ottoman Turks interposed a barrier between East and West; third, the beneficent Tatar Empire ended its sway in China when the descendants of Kublai Khan were driven from his brilliant capital in 1368. In consequence, intercourse with China ended for almost two hundred years, and when at length the Portuguese reached the Celestial Empire, it was almost as if they had made a discovery similar to that of Cortes in Mexico. Yet, the memory of the medieval journeys lived

on, and the number of surviving manuscripts and incunabula editions
shows how popular this literature was in pre-Columbian as well as Columbian times. Judged on this basis, the *Travels of Marco Polo* was by all
odds the most popular and most influential book of the type, being represented by at least 138 manuscripts still in existence. Of the early printed
editions, that by Leeu of Gouda, 1483–1485 (Hain 13244), was owned by
Columbus, and is preserved in the Colombina in Seville. It was issued
as a companion volume to the same printer's *Mandeville* (Hain 10644),
which in all probability Columbus therefore had also. Second in popularity
to Polo's *Travels* was the *Descriptio Orientalium Partium* of Odoric of
Pordenone, with at least seventy-three surviving manuscript texts: it forms
a valuable supplement to Polo's book, even though the friar could not
avoid the legendary atmosphere, which Mandeville found useful in his
plagiarizing. Manuscripts remaining from the other missioners are fewer
in number; perhaps one or two apiece for each traveler. But the strategic-
religious *Crusaders' Manual* of Marino Sanuto, a Venetian statesman and
political writer, and the *Itinerario* of Ricold of Monte Croce, a hot-Gos-
peller who traveled in Persia and Iraq preaching to the Moslems in their
own language, survive in considerable quantity. From this it is obvious
that the medieval tradition of Asiatic land travel lived on, and even though
Pierre d'Ailly never heard of Marco Polo, we know that Polo's geographical information went where it counted most. Abraham Cresques used it
in compiling the *Catalan Atlas*, Henry the Navigator had a manuscript of
it, and Columbus had a printed edition.

In the Mediterranean the trade with the Orient was mostly in the hands
of the Venetians and the Genoese, whose power and prosperity had grown
enormously during the Crusades. Venice backed the Latins when they
captured Constantinople on the Fourth Crusade in 1204, and profited
greatly during the period of the Latin Emperors. Genoa, on the other
hand, supported the Byzantines, and rode into power when the Palaeologi
were restored in 1261. This had the result of making the Genoese supreme in Constantinople in the later Middle Ages. From there they extended their activities to the Black Sea, the Caspian Sea, and northern
Persia. At Kaffa in the Crimea they controlled a flourishing city the size
of Seville; at Tana near the mouth of the River Don they had a powerful
station for southern Russia and Turkestan; they were strongly entrenched
at Trebizond, where a romantic empire of the Byzantine Comneni endured until its capture by the Ottomans in 1461. Farther east, their shipping was seen on the Caspian before the end of the thirteenth century, and
they had valuable trading privileges in Tabriz, whither the Englishman
Walter Langley went in 1291 — the first of his race to reach the Middle
East. This Central Asian trade of the Genoese persisted long after the
breakup of the Mongol Empire. In Africa, too, the Genoese were active,

and there is evidence that they got up the Nile as far as Dongola in the Sudan. From their factory in Tunis they penetrated into the Sahara; Antonio Malfante in 1447 went far into the desert and wrote a description of the Niger basin. The dynamic activity of this Italian city-state even took its sailors into the Atlantic, and in 1291 two Genoese brothers, Guido and Ugolino Vivaldo, sought with magnificent daring to do at one stroke what later took the Portuguese almost a century. With the intention of reaching India by the Cape route, the brothers sailed boldly into the Atlantic — and were never heard of again. It is generally accepted, too, that Genoese-Portuguese expeditions discovered Madeira and the Azores in the mid-fourteenth century. These early Atlantic voyages seem to have been sporadic ventures, however, which were not followed up and were soon forgotten about; what evidence there is for their existence is mostly from portolan charts.

Beside the far-flung commercial activity of Genoa, the trafficking even of Venice seems rather secondary, yet the Venetians can in no way be ignored. They suffered considerably when the Latins fell and the Byzantines were restored in Constantinople, but they continued to maintain a respectable share of the Black Sea trade, with agencies at Kaffa, Tana, and Trebizond. In the western Mediterranean they were less active, sending but one fleet a year to North Africa. In fact, Venice's policy became more and more one of concentration, just as Genoa's had become more and more one of dispersion; and the Venetians established a monopoly amounting to a stranglehold on the Egyptian trade. The Adriatic, the Archipelago, Alexandria — this was Venice's life line, and she tended to pass over the possibility of trade elsewhere in order to keep this immensely valuable monopoly. The Egyptian trade was in a larger sense the trade of Southern Asia and the East Indies: cargoes came from the Spice Islands to Malacca, from Malacca to Calicut, from Calicut to Suez, and from Suez they were laden in Venetian bottoms at Alexandria. This trade supplied more and more of the bulk of Venetian activity and serves to explain why Venetian citizens like Nicolo Conti and John Cabot penetrated into the Orient in the fifteenth century.

Other Mediterranean peoples were active in those days, especially the seamen of Marseilles and Catalonia. They bore some part of the Black Sea trade and a considerable share of the North African commerce. The Catalans, in particular, made valuable contributions to nautical science, and like the Genoese were tempted by the waters of the Atlantic. An expedition, led by Jaime Ferrer, daringly set forth in 1346 to find the River of Gold. Like the venture of the Vivaldi it was never heard of again, although the *Catalan Atlas* shows Ferrer's craft heading into the unknown off Cape Bojador. Even the seafaring Normans felt the urge of discovery, and the voyage of Bethencourt and Gadifer to the Canary Islands in 1402 brings the chronicle of medieval voyaging up to the very days of Henry the Navigator.

In the same year that the French were accomplishing the conquest of the Canaries, another of their race broke fresh ground in West Africa: an adventurous citizen of Toulouse, Anselme d'Isalguier, crossed the Sahara Desert to the semibarbaric metropolis of Gao, situated on the Niger two hundred miles east of Timbuctoo. It must have been a very courageous undertaking to cross hundreds of miles of desert with hostile Moslems in the way. But d'Isalguier succeeded in doing so and remained at Gao for a full decade, finally returning to his native land in 1413 with a half-caste family and a large train of native retainers.

Certain other travelers should not go unnoticed, as knowledge of their journeyings lived after them into the Renaissance. One cannot overlook the Castilian knight Clavijo, who went on a diplomatic mission to the court of Tamerlaine at Samarkand in 1403–1405, or of the German Schiltberger, who was captured at the battle of Nicopolis (1395) and spent years as a prisoner of both Sultan Bayezid and Tamerlaine before regaining his native country.

Discussion of the discoveries of the Norsemen in Greenland, Markland, and Vinland has been omitted here because awareness of them hardly existed outside Scandinavia, while by the fifteenth century even the bare memory of them was so faint that they may be said to have had no influence on Renaissance travel. Greenland alone appears to have been remembered, but was merely regarded as an additional peninsula of Scandinavia, to the north and west of Norway. For purposes of this study, therefore, the Viking voyages may be ignored. Likewise the geographers and explorers of the fifteenth century had no thought of a western continent or New World. Fragmentary remains of the lost Atlantis might persist in the form of mythical islands, but no one expected a land mass of any size between Western Europe and the Far East.

Probably the most complete picture of geographical knowledge as it stood in the later Middle Ages is given in the celebrated *Catalan Atlas*, now preserved in the Bibliotheque Nationale in Paris (MS Espagnol 30). This series of maps, made in 1375 by Abraham Cresques, a Jew of Majorca, portrays the world in the light of the travels of Marco Polo and his missionary successors to Cathay, as well as the Venetian and Genoese merchants in the Near and Middle East and North Africa. From the British Isles to the Black Sea, including the Mediterranean, the maps are of the normal portolan type, but of a very high standard. Denmark, the southern parts of Norway and Sweden, and the Baltic Sea are all set out with some accuracy. Northwest Africa is excellent as far as Cape Bojador, but south of that latitude it is conjectural. Thus there is a large lake in the western Sahara, from which one river (the Senegal) flows west into the Atlantic, and another (the Niger) eastward into the Nile. The placing of Tenbuch (Timbuctoo) just north of the lake betrays a knowledge of the Niger basin surprising for the days of Petrarch and Chaucer, but may be the result of information received from Cresques' co-religionists in Morocco. As for Asia, the outline of the Arabian peninsula is roughly correct, although the Persian Gulf is extended too far, making a rather narrow neck of land between Basra and Suez. The Caspian appears in some detail and with considerable knowledge, and the placing of the cities of Central Asia bears witness to a wide familiarity with the writings of Polo and Odoric. India is shown in its true peninsula shape, with the Kingdom of Delhi in the north — and with the mention that Alexander the Great had built many cities thereabout. A large island with a north-south axis named Iana (*sic*) does duty for the Malay Peninsula; it may possibly be meant for Sumatra. Far to the east is the still larger island of Trapobana (*sic*), which is less easy to classify. China is especially interesting: not only is the semicircular curve of the coastline shown, but the cities immortalized by Polo are all there: Cambaluc (Peking), Zayton (Chang-chow in Amoy harbor), Kinsay (Hang-chow), and other places. Yet even with this remarkable accuracy there is mythical geography as well. Between China and India is the land of pygmies; a blunt and rounded peninsula north of China is the realm of Gog and Magog, with Alexander's wall running from the mountains to the sea (could this be the Great Wall of China?); beyond are the islands of griffons; the sea to the east and south of China is filled with a multitude of small islands, crowded so that they are almost touching. Nevertheless, the *Catalan Atlas* is a remarkable production, especially when we consider that it dates more than a century before Columbus and da Gama; there was not another portrayal of the Eastern Hemisphere as well done until the Cantino Map of 1502. It is almost certain, too, that Henry the Navigator saw this atlas or a similar one; for the son of Abraham Cresques was Jahuda Cresques, who, under the name of Master Jacome, was the prince's leading cartographer and navigational expert.

Of equal importance with a knowledge of the globe was a knowledge of navigation. There are three essentials to satisfactory navigation in the open sea: a map to determine the course, a compass to determine the position of North, and an instrument to determine the latitude by fixing the position of the sun or moon. By the year 1400 Western man had reasonably efficient equipment on these scores. In the portolan charts, examples of which date back to about 1300, he had maps of uncanny accuracy. In fact, as far as the Mediterranean coastline goes, they are hardly bettered by the most up-to-date cartography of today. As for the compass, its principle had already been known for perhaps two centuries. In its primitive form it was simply a magnetized needle thrust crosswise through a straw and floated upon a bowl of water, but by 1380 it appeared virtually in its present form, having a revolving card with a north-pointing needle attached to its underside. For position-finding, the astrolabe had been known to the Greeks, and had come down by way of the Arabs to the seafaring population of the Mediterranean. Described simply, the astrolabe consisted of a circular disc, with angles graduated on the rim, and a movable bar, pinioned at the center of the disc, along which the elevation of the sun could be sighted. The angle of the sun with respect to the horizon could then be read off and the latitude computed. A variant of this, especially popular in England, was the cross-staff, which in essence was a primitive quadrant. Tables, computed on the different declinations of the sun for each day of the year, were composed as early as the close of the thirteenth century; they were greatly improved upon by Abraham Zacuto about 1478. As for the actual knowledge of how to sail a boat, the Massiliots, Catalans, and Portuguese had all learned in the tradition passed from the Arabs to the Sicilians in the days of Edrisi, and passed on by the Sicilians to the Genoese. Thus it was that on the eve of the Renaissance, the maritime people of the Mediterranean and of southwestern Europe had more than a little knowledge of the world and a reasonably fair smattering of navigational skill.

2

SOME FREE-LANCE TRAVELERS OF
THE EARLY RENAISSANCE

The independent wayfarers described in this chapter were the living links between medieval travel of the days of Marco Polo and the Renaissance voyages of the great Portuguese; in a sense they were more medieval than Renaissance, yet they represent the first stirrings of the Renaissance mind in relation to the still little-known Orient. These men were primarily land travelers, though when necessary they did make voyages across the seas in primitive native craft. Some of them traveled on official missions, while others were traders stricken with wanderlust; but in every case the stories which they brought back stimulated interest in the mysterious lands to the east and broadened the intellectual outlook of the Renaissance.

First of these, in date if not in importance, was Nicolo Conti, a Venetian merchant of noble family, who left his native city in 1419 on what was to be a series of journeys lasting twenty-five years. His passage to Syria was too conventional to merit notice; only after staying in Damascus long enough to learn Arabic did Conti begin the experiences which he dictated years later to Poggio. From Damascus he crossed the Arabian Desert to the Euphrates valley, and proceeded through southern Mesopotamia to Baghdad. Here he boarded a native vessel and descended the Tigris to Basra, after which he sailed to Ormuz. At a Persian port in the Indian Ocean which he calls Calabatia he remained some time, learning Persian and entering into a business partnership with some native merchants. India was his next objective, and he made his way to the Gulf and city of Cambay, where he began his observations of Indian life, noticing in particular the number of precious stones and the prevalence of the custom of suttee.

From Cambay, Conti dropped down the West Coast to Mount Ely, a prominent foreland which Arab sailors used as a landfall, thence he struck across country to Vijayanagar, a hundred and fifty miles inland from Goa, and the capital of the principal Hindu state of the Deccan. This great city was destroyed by a Moslem coalition in 1565, but at the time of Conti's visit it was a mighty metropolis, as his description bears out. Conti went on to Mailapur near the present site of Madras, though whether by land across the peninsula or by sea around Cape Comorin is uncertain. Mailapur was the traditional resting place of the Apostle Thomas, and the holiest shrine of the native Christians, who, as Conti wrote, were in those days scattered all over India, as were the Jews all over E irope.

Conti must have married in this period: his wife was an Indian, and after l aving Mailapur he took his course to the East Indies, accompanied by her and eventually by four offspring as well. He refers to Ceylon at this point in his narrative, but if Conti visited it at all, he must have done so on his return journey. His description of that island as being three thousand miles in circumference may make the reader smile, but his account of the cinnamon tree is so exact as to warrant a conclusion that he did visit Ceylon at some time. Sumatra was the next region of Conti's wanderings. Here he remained for a year, gaining a good knowledge of the brutal cannibalistic inhabitants, as well as of the gold, camphor, and pepper which the island produced. After his sojourn in Sumatra a stormy passage of sixteen days took him to Tenasserim, a place near the head of the Malay Peninsula, where elephants were wonderfully plentiful. The Ganges Delta was his next stopping place, and he appears to have spent s veral months sailing up and down the river, visiting various unidentifiable cities. After calling at Burdwan on the Hooghly, Conti turned eastward into Arakan, crossed the mountains to the Irawadi, and ascended that stream as far as Mandalay. His Burmese adventures resulted in an interesting passage on the country's rich fauna, and the observant Italian discoursed on elephant hunting, rhinoceroses, and pythons, and also mentioned the native custom of tattooing. Descending the great river to Pegu, a wealthy city famed for its luscious fruits, Conti pushed on a second time into the Malay Archipelago, and made a nine months' visit to Java, his farthest point. Here he watched the native cockfights, and learned strange tales of the Spice Islands to the east; but in spite of his wanderlust he did not visit them. Having quitted Java, he sailed with his long-suffering family to Champa (probably Cochin-China), after which he is lost sight of until he turns up at Quilon in the extreme southwest of India. It is probable that his visit to Ceylon took place in the interim. The Malabar ports of Cochin and Calicut were visited next, as well as Cambay. From the latter region the tireless wanderer's way lay homeward; he touched at the island of Socotra, still mostly peopled by Nestorian Christians; and saw the rich city of Aden, with its remarkable buildings. Jidda, the port of Mecca, was another stopping place, before Conti proceeded up the Red Sea. From Suez he turned aside to visit the Monastery of St. Catherine on Mount Sinai; at the shrine Conti met Pero Tafur, a Spanish traveler who had wandered throughout Europe and the Near East and whose description of Constantinople in the days of the final decadence of the Byzantine Empire is unforgettably vivid. Conti filled the credulous Spaniard with Mandevillian travelers' tales of his own experiences at the Court of Prester John, in as brazen a piece of leg-pulling as can be imagined.

Conti could not romanticize in the same manner when he returned to Venice soon after (1444), for as a penance for his compulsory renunciation of Christianity during his travels, Pope Eugenius IV ordered him to relate his history to Poggio Bracciolini, the papal secretary. Poggio was a man of the keenest intelligence and most critical insight, and as Conti was quite obviously on his best behaviour, he gave a far more restrained account of himself than he had given the all-believing Tafur. For all that, Poggio's version is on the whole the best account of Southern Asia by any European before Varthema.

Many years were to pass before another first-hand account of India appeared in Western Europe. The travels of the Russian horse-trader Athanasius Nikitin, who was in Asia between 1468 and 1474, getting as far afield as Chaul below Bombay, need not detain us; for the Russia of that day was hardly a Renaissance country. Not until the very end of the fifteenth century did another Italian, Santo Stephano, make his way to Southern Asia; but in the meantime there were three interesting diplomatic missions from the Signory of Venice — not to India, it is true, but to Persia.

In the second half of the fifteenth century the Turkish peril was at its height; the Christian states looked on with dread as the Ottoman hordes advanced relentlessly in what appeared to be an invincible bid for world domination. Venice in particular found herself literally in the front line, while the effect of the Turkish advance on her all-important Levantine trade threatened to be devastating to the Island Republic. Yet to the east of fanatical Sunnite Turkey lay Persia, a country never regarded with the same fear and hatred as the other domains of Islam. Although Persia was a Moslem land, its subjects belonged to the Shiite sect, and in consequence the orthodox followers of the Prophet despised them almost as much as if they had been Christians. Persia, in effect, carried its Mohammedanism lightly; it tolerated a large Christian minority, and it represented the glorious traditions of one of the heroic monarchies of classical antiquity. It was only common sense and good strategy, therefore, for Venice to form an alliance with this ancient realm in the face of a common enemy. Venice in addition had a rather curious tie of blood with the ruling house of Persia. At that period the king (the title of shah did not exist until Ismail's accession in 1499) was Uzun Hasan, an adventurer of more than ordinary ability who had usurped the throne in 1468 by the very practical expedient of assassinating his predecessor. This man had married a Byzantine princess named Despina, said — after the romantic manner of the time — to have been beautiful, as well as a great lady and a true Christian. Despina was the daughter of Calo John (Comnenus), Emperor of Trebizond; her sister had married Nicolo Crespo, Duke of the Archipelago, and this sister had four daughters, all married to Venetian merchants.

One of these merchants was Caterino Zeno, a man of courage and ability, who was accordingly sent by the Signory on a mission which, it was hoped, would ally Venice and Persia against the Turks. Zeno set out in 1471, and after stopping at Rhodes, made his way across the Mameluke lands of Syria to the Persian Court at Tabriz. Here he was well received by his wife's aunt and her husband the king; in fact, according to Ramusio, "he attained such favor and intimacy with Ussun Cassano, that he even went in and out of the private apartments of the King and Queen at whatever time and hour he pleased, and what is still more extraordinary, even when both their Majesties were in bed." This intimacy bore fruit; for Zeno, being supported in his arguments by Despina, succeeded in inducing Uzun Hasan to take up arms against the Turks. In the war that followed fortune was by no means kind to the allies, although the Persians did repel a large invading army at the Euphrates. Because of the acute menace of Turkish arms, Zeno was sent back to Europe as Ambassador of the Persian monarch, with the hope of getting aid from Hungary and Poland. His route lay across Armenia to the Black Sea; thence by boat to Kaffa, the Genoese stronghold in Crimea, where he narrowly escaped being sent to Constantinople; after which he headed westward through the Ukraine. His homeward mission was hardly a success; neither Poland nor Hungary displayed the slightest interest in fighting the Turks, although Zeno was handsomely treated by Matthias Corvinus. He returned to his native Venice in 1474 and received a rousing welcome.

It was clearly felt in Venice that close relations with Persia should continue, and to this end a second ambassador was soon sent out. This person, Josafat Barbaro, had in his younger days lived and traded among the Crim Tatars of the lower Don, and this experience with Eastern peoples made him a good traveler and a careful observer. Journeying by way of Seleucia and across northern Persia to Lake Van, Barbaro reached Tabriz in the spring of 1474, after having been robbed and beaten by Kurdish tribesmen on the way. His reception by Uzun Hasan was by no means as cordial as that of Zeno had been: Persia had by this time suffered too painfully in the Turkish war, and no arguments could induce the king to meet the Ottomans in the field a second time. Yet Barbaro covered far more ground than Zeno had done, for he accompanied the monarch on a progress throughout his kingdom, visiting Sultanieh, Kashan, Isfahan, Yezd, and Shiraz. As a dutiful son of Venice, Barbaro kept his

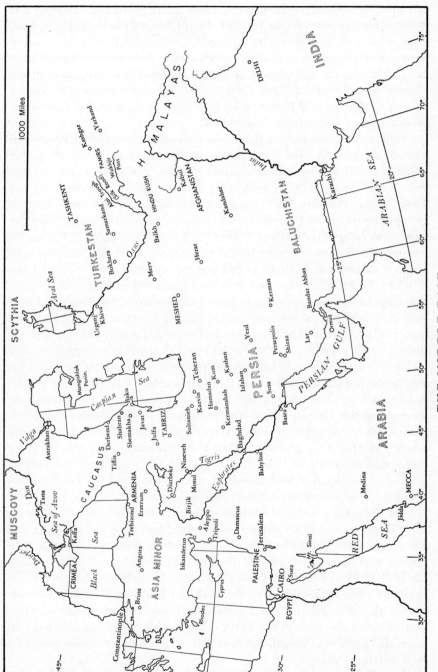

THE MIDDLE EAST

SCYTHIA

MUSCOVY

1000 Miles

TURKESTAN

HIMALAYAS

INDIA

DELHI

Kashgar
Yarkand

TASHKENT

PAMIRS
Wakhir
Ayū (Oxus) R. (SIK. Road) Pass
Samarkand
Bokhara
Khiva
Urgenj

Aral Sea

Kabul
Kandahar
HINDU KUSH
AFGHANISTAN

Balkh

Oxus

Merv

Herat

Indus

MESHED

Mongishlok
Penin.

Caspian Sea

BALUCHISTAN

Karachi

ARABIAN
SEA

Astrakhan

Volga

Baku
Shabran
Derbend
Shemakha
Javat
Julfa
TABRIZ
Sultanieh
Kazvin

CAUCASUS

Kerman

Yezd

PERSIA

Persepolis
Shiraz
Lar

Bandar Abbas

Ormuz

PERSIAN GULF

Tiflis
Derbend

ARMENIA
Erzerum
Trebizond

Diarbekr

Birjik
Mosul
Nineveh

Tigris

Euphrates

Babylon

Baghdad

Kermanshah
Hamadan
Kum
Kashan
Isfahan

Teheran

Susa
Basra

Don
Tana

Sea of Azov

Kaffa

CRIMEA

Black Sea

Angora

ASIA MINOR

Brussa

Constantinople

Rhodes

Cyprus

Iskanderun
Aleppo
Tripoli

Damascus

Jerusalem

PALESTINE

Suez
Mt. Sinai

CAIRO

EGYPT

RED SEA

ARABIA

Medina

MECCA
Jidda

Dnieper

ears open, too. Since the Persian court was the scene of much coming and going of foreign missions, he learned about China: its beautiful porcelain, its paper money, and its mighty capital of Cambaluc. Likewise he heard of the wealthy emporium of Ormuz and its traffic, and of a city "called Calicuth, of verie great fame, being, as it were, a staple of merchants of divers places." At the death of Uzun Hasan in 1478 Barbaro returned to Venice by way of Aleppo and Beirut, with very little to show for his four years' sojourn except a wealth of experiences.

Almost simultaneously, a third Venetian envoy had visited Persia and had returned during the time that Barbaro was there. Scion of one of Venice's oldest and most distinguished families, Ambrogio Contarini was sent out early in 1474, to collaborate with Barbaro in promoting the Turkish war. His way, both going and coming back, lay across Eastern Europe; he traversed Poland and south Russia, and after sailing from the Crimea to Mingrelia, reached Tabriz the following summer. After an interview with the king's son, he set out in the wake of Uzun Hasan, overtaking that monarch at Isfahan. At this historic city Barbaro presented Contarini to the ruler, and the two Venetians remained attendant at the Persian Court until the next year. In June 1475 Contarini left Uzun and Barbaro in Tabriz and set out homewards. On reaching the Black Sea at Poti, however, he learned that the Turks had captured Kaffa: this intelligence disrupted all his plans and threw him into despair, bringing on a fever which was nearly fatal. When he had recovered sufficiently, he made his way through Tiflis to Derbend on the Caspian, where he spent the winter. A hazardous passage across the sea to Astrakhan and an adventurous journey up the Volga brought him to Moscow, where he spent the following winter. He then proceeded overland to Venice, which he finally reached in April 1477. His was the last Venetian mission to Persia for many years; with the death of Uzun Hasan, and the slight easing of the Turkish peril after the death of Mohammed II, Venice refrained from seeking further Eastern alliances against the Ottoman.

Yet Venetian merchants continued to make their way into the Middle East, even as Dragon Zeno, Caterino's father, had gone to Damascus and Basra and had visited Mecca in the mid-century. Such a figure was John Cabot, who about 1480 crossed the Isthmus of Suez and penetrated to the holy cities of Islam. While in the Orient, he had seen the spice-laden caravans from far countries to the east and had heard from Arab merchants that the goods were transferred through many hands on their journey from the ends of the earth. This led him to the conclusion that since the world was round, the best way to the land of spices would be by a westward voyage.

Not all the wanderers were Venetian, however; other countries, under the stimulating influence of the Renaissance, were beginning to feel the urge for exploration. In particular there was Portugal, which although committed to the discovery of the Cape route to India, nevertheless refused to dismiss the possibilities of independent land travel through the Near and Middle East as a means of finding the realms of Prester John and the lands of Ophir and Tarshish. To this end Pero da Covilhan and Afonso da Paiva (whose travels will be described more fully below) were dispatched from Lisbon in 1487; Covilhan visited Calicut, Ormuz, and Sofala in southeast Africa, before penetrating Abyssinia. But Covilhan was not the first European to reach this remote Christian state in East Africa, for there are faint traces of travel to the land of Prester John sporadically throughout the century. There is a shadowy record of a Venetian mission under one Antonio Bartoli in 1402; about 1430 a certain Pietro of Naples had gone there and had left a brief but convincing account of his experiences. In 1482 a Franciscan delegation under Battista da Imola reached Abyssinia by way of the Red Sea, and having been received by the Negus at Aksum, accompanied that sovereign on a lengthy progress across the land to the Godjam district, south of Lake Tsana. Imola and his confreres were not well treated and met with great opposition from the native clergy. A second mission was made from Cairo the ensuing year, but its empty results led to the discontinuance of the effort. It was, however, due to a mission of Ethiopians from a monastery in Jerusalem, who reached Florence for the Church council in 1441, that the accurate knowledge of their country, so evident from the Fra Mauro Map of 1459, came to Europe.

This brings us to the last Europeans to tour southern Asia before the coming of the Portuguese. Chief among these travelers was the Genoese merchant Hieronimo de Santo Stephano, an interesting character who performed a remarkable, if unfortunate, journey. His was evidently a mercantile speculation, begun probably in 1493 or the following year, and made in company with a fellow-merchant Hieronimo Adorno. Their route took them from Italy to Cairo and then down the Red Sea, which they traversed in a flimsy native dhow, the timbers of which were sewn together with cords and the sails made of rush mats. Their voyage was leisurely; they spent two months at Massawa, the port for Abyssinia, and four months more at Aden, from which place they sailed in another very flimsy craft, with cotton sails, to Calicut. Santo Stephano has some pertinent remarks about this wealthy south Indian city, pointing out its extensive trade in ginger and pepper; the idolatry of the people, who worshipped the sun and the ox; the peculiar sort of polygamy, in which every lady has seven or eight husbands, and in which "the man never marry any woman who is a virgin; but if one, being a virgin is betrothed, she is delivered over before the nuptuals to some other person to be deflowered."

From Calicut the travelers proceeded to Ceylon, and thence to the Coromandel Coast, where they traded for seven months. Pegu was their next objective, from which they hoped to ascend the Irawadi River to Ava near Mandalay, but tribal warfare upcountry put an end to these plans. Instead, bitter misfortunes were ahead of them, for the ruler of Pegu although wealthy enough to have ten thousand elephants, was very grasping; the Genoese were compelled to sell their merchandise to the king, who in turn was so tardy in his payment that a whole year was spent in daily solicitations, amid great privations and annoyances as far as the Europeans were concerned. Adorno, never a strong man, died under the strain, and Santo Stephano himself nearly died with grief. Having finally got some compensation from the king, he sailed to Sumatra, only to have his property impounded by the ruling sovereign there. Thanks to an invoice which he had brought from Cairo, he regained some of his goods, but not without much expense and trouble. Because of this he left Sumatra as soon as he was able, on a vessel bound for Cambay, but his ill-luck proved worse than ever. For six months he was detained by stress of weather at the Maldive Islands, and after he was well on his way again, his ship was struck by a squall and foundered with all his worldly possessions. By clinging to a plank for a whole day the poor man preserved his own life, and in the evening was picked up by a vessel bound for India. When he reached Cambay his luck did begin to turn slightly for the better, for he fell in with a merchant from Damascus, who took the wretched Genoese into his service. Santo Stephano was thus sent as supercargo to Ormuz, from which he made his way across Persia by the Shiraz-Isfahan-Tabriz route to Aleppo and Tripoli; where in September 1499 he penned his pathetic narrative.

The German pilgrim-traveler Arnold von Harff made a noteworthy journey to the Levant in 1497-1499. After a stay of some duration in Cairo, von Harff went on to the monastery of St. Catherine on Mount Sinai, and then instead of proceeding directly to Jerusalem, he relates that he joined a caravan for Mecca. If his account be true (which is questionable), he was able to penetrate into the holy city, and he states that he continued south from there through Yemen to Aden. According to his narrative, he then sailed to India and Madagascar, but this part of his odyssey is regarded as apocryphal, though he may have gone as far afield as Socotra and Magadoxo in Somaliland. His return to Cairo by way of the Mountains of the Moon would also appear a figment of his imagination: what is more interesting because of its obvious veracity is his journey overland across Asia Minor, from Adana to Brusa and Constantinople, which he performed on his return route.

Another independent traveler of the early Renaissance — a man whose fame in his own lifetime rivaled that of Columbus and Magellan and

who even now must win our admiration by his courage and resourcefulness — was Ludovico di Varthema, a gentleman of Bologna in Italy,
whose sprightly narrative was so popular in the sixteenth century that
his name must have been a by-word throughout Europe. Varthema
was unquestionably one of those whose love of travel was a ruling
passion, and he must too have been a man with a taste for languages,
like George Borrow, and with an actor's capacity for playing strange
roles. Little is known of him aside from his travels, but he was probably
a young fellow when he started on his way in 1502; so we may place his
birth about 1475 or a very few years later.

Varthema left Venice towards the end of the year 1502, and after
visiting Alexandria and Cairo, proceeded up the Syrian coast to Tripoli.
At this point he went inland to Aleppo and Damascus, staying long
enough at the latter city to learn Arabic. He adopted Moslem dress as
well, took the name of Yunus (Jonah), and enlisted as a Mameluke
guard in a caravan of pilgrims bound for Mecca. Of course this meant
his pretending at least to become a Mohammedan, but such was the
traveler's uncanny flair for languages and his speed in mastering Moslem
ritual that he made the truly astonishing journey without arousing suspicion. (Von Harff, in contrast, had gone to Mecca with a commercial
caravan and as an admitted Christian, which was something very different from taking the Hajj). As was usual in pilgrimages, Varthema's caravan was a large one — he says forty thousand persons. There were sixty
guards for its protection. The route lay across Transjordania to the head
of the Gulf of Akaba, near which Varthema and his Mameluke colleagues
fought a valiant two days running battle with wild Arabs and saved the
vast caravan by their bravery. The pilgrims pushed on rather aimlessly
across desert and mountain to reach Khaibar, an ancient Jewish city
north of Medina. Three days more brought the caravan to Medina, of
which Varthema gives a good description; and on May 22, 1503, the
pilgrims, including Varthema, arrived safely in Mecca. Varthema was
thus the first Christian of whom we have knowledge to take the Hajj, a
journey which was then and for many centuries after a highly dangerous
undertaking for anyone who was not a True Believer. Besides von Harff,
other Christians, such as John Cabot, had reached Mecca before Varthema, but they had merely gone inland from Jidda in a purely private
capacity. If there be any possible predecessor of Varthema, it would be
Pero da Covilhan; but the exact circumstances of his visit to Mecca are
little known.

Varthema went through the conventional rituals of the pilgrims while
in Mecca, and his account of them and of the town itself is long and
extraordinarily accurate — all the more so considering that he had no
European sources to guide him, and no particular knowledge of Arabic

literature. His sojourn in Mecca was about three weeks; he was impatient to continue his travels, so he quite calmly and casually deserted the Syrian caravan and joined a band of Indian pilgrims returning from Jidda by sea. This duplicity involved his hiding all day in a mosque, covered up and groaning as if in pain, but he was able to get safely aboard a ship and so make his escape. On the voyage, however, his true status as a Christian was for the first time discovered, and a prison cell awaited him in Aden, where the local ruler was livid with rage against all Christians, because of the recent Portuguese depredations in the Indian Ocean. After two months of imprisonment Varthema and a Moslem fellow-prisoner were sent to the sultan's palace about sixty miles to the east. There one of the sultan's wives proceeded to fall desperately in love with the European unbeliever. Owing to her intercession and to his feigning madness, he was released from his captivity; but instead of requiting her affection, he ungratefully made his way back to Aden as fast as his legs could carry him. However, he found that the next ship bound for India would not sail for a month, so to keep out of danger and to while away the time as well, he set out on a walking trip through Yemen, which took him as far as Sana. His wanderings in this corner of Arabia have been estimated at six hundred miles, and as the terrain in the southwestern part of the peninsula is rugged and very mountainous, one cannot but admire his endurance.

After a day in Aden, spent as in Jidda by concealing himself in a mosque, Varthema sailed for the Indian Ocean. His ship stopped at Zeila and Berbera on the African coast before steering for Gujarat. Having reached India, Varthema inexplicably back-tracked, and sailed again for Arabia. He touched at Dhofar and Muscat and then went up the Persian Gulf to Ormuz. In fact, he spent a large part of the year 1504 in southern Persia; he landed at Bandar Abbas and journeyed to Shiraz, where — having exhausted his supply of money — he had the good fortune to run across a Persian merchant whom he had known as a fellow-pilgrim in Mecca. This man lived at the town of Herat near Shiraz (not to be confused with Herat in Afghanistan); he took Varthema home with him, and together they planned a trip to Samarkand. This venture never materialized, but Varthema spent his time pleasantly enough in unofficial wedlock with his friend's niece.

In company with the Persian, Varthema reached India a second time in the autumn of 1504, calling first at Cambay and then coasting along the Ghats. He landed at Goa in order to make a journey inland to Bijapur, the capital of the Deccan, and from Cananor he made a still more extensive journey upcountry to the great city of Vijayanagar, which he saw at the close of its glory. It was Calicut, however, far more than any other city in India, which took his fancy, albeit his first visit there was brief,

since the Persian merchant had to push on for reasons of trade. As Varthema said, Calicut had been ruined by the king of Portugal, for the
merchants who used to come there were not there, neither did they
come. Matters looked more hopeful on the other side of the peninsula,
on the Coromandel Coast; to this end Varthema and the Persian rounded
Cape Comorin, and after touching at Ceylon, landed at Pulicat, near the
present site of Madras. They then crossed the Bay of Bengal to Tenasserim, and then quickly doubled back to the Ganges Delta. Pegu was
their next objective, and they finally reached Malacca in the spring of
1505.

Now follows a very controversial part of Varthema's itinerary — his
trip to the Spice Islands. By his own testimony he would have us believe
that he sailed as far eastward as Ternate and Banda, but his time-table
as set by Sir Richard Carnac Temple allows only two months for the
trip, including a retrograde lap to Pedir in Sumatra, and a fortnight's
stay in Java, which would mean impossibly rapid traveling. So great
an authority as Dr. Armando Cortesão roundly denies the voyage and
even states that Varthema never got east of India. So Varthema's voyage
to the Moluccas should at best be taken with a grain of salt. His own
account nevertheless states that he returned to India from Malacca in
the summer of 1505, and after this his credibility need no longer be
doubted.

Even after he had reached Calicut on his return, Varthema continued
to play the part of a devout Moslem, sleeping in the mosque and pretending to be a saint: "and happy was he who could kiss my hand and
some my knees." Yet his nostalgia must have preyed upon him, for a
chance meeting with two Milanese jewelers who had come out with the
Portuguese fleet prompted him to drop the role of impostor. He therefore
abandoned his kindly and loyal Persian companion in what appears to
have been a very cavalier manner and proceeded to Cananor, where he
entered the Portuguese service. This led to his appointment as a factor
in both Calicut and Cochin, in which capacity he served for a year and
a half. During this time he apparently became intimate with the Viceroy
Almeida and was an eye witness of the Portuguese attack on Ponnani,
a port south of Calicut. His account of this engagement (November 24,
1507) is the last record of his sojourn in the East: before the year was
out he had sailed for Europe by way of the Cape, and with the completion of his voyage home his travels ended and his fame as a traveler
began.

Like Marco Polo, Varthema was fortunate in his publicity. His book
·"caught on" as soon as it was published (1510) and went through many
editions all over Europe. Yet Varthema deserved his reputation, for he
was a daring traveler who (especially in the Middle East) covered new

ground; he was the first traveler to reach India by the Red Sea and to return around the Cape of Good Hope; and he was the last of a goodly line of free-lance travelers who spanned the gap between the followers of Polo and the Portuguese conquerors.

Throughout the late fifteenth century and even into the first years of the sixteenth, the pilgrimage to the Holy Land continued to be popular in all Christendom, and although such journeyings were of but slight geographical consequence, the pilgrims did return with a vastly wider mental horizon, which undoubtedly bore fruit in the popular interest in Renaissance exploration. In plan the pilgrimage was quite standardized: the pilgrim sailed from Venice on a special pilgrim ship, which touched at various Greek islands and put him ashore at Jaffa. From there he made his way to Jerusalem, visited the Dead Sea and other Biblical sites, and then usually went south across the Sinai Desert to the Monastery of St. Catherine. After that he would go to Cairo, descend the Nile to Alexandria, and sail back to Venice. Many of those who made the pilgrimage left accounts of some merit, which cannot be overlooked in the travel literature of the time. Among these men one might mention William Wey, a Fellow of Eton, who made two pilgrimages (1458 and 1462); Hans Tucher (1479), the Nürnberg brewer and friend of Dürer; Felix Faber (1480 and 1483), a Dominican whose record is perhaps the most elaborate; Sebastian Brandt (1490), the celebrated humanist, who afterwards wrote the *Ship of Fools*; and Sir Richard Guildford, Master of Ordnance under Henry VII, who died at Jerusalem in 1506. Most pictorial of all accounts, however, is that of Bernard von Breydenbach, Canon of Mainz and companion of Faber, whose trip resulted in the *Peregrinatio in Terram Sanctam*, the most lavishly illustrated travel book of the fifteenth century (Mainz, 1486, and later editions).

After the second decade of the new century, however, the popularity of the pilgrimage declined sharply. In 1517 the tolerant Mameluke dynasty of Egypt, which hitherto had ruled the Holy Land, fell before the all-conquering Ottomans, and Palestine passed under repressive Turkish control. Rhodes, the stronghold of the Knights of St. John and long the eastern outpost of Christendom, was won by Suleiman the Magnificent in 1522. In Europe itself the Reformation followed soon thereafter, and the combination of events caused pilgrimage travel to the Near East to reach the vanishing point.

3

HENRY THE NAVIGATOR AND THE AFRICAN VOYAGES

The House of Avis	Reigned
John (João) I, "the Great," illegitimate son of Pedro I	1385–1433
Edward (Duarte), son of John I	1433–1438
Afonso V, "the African," son of Duarte	1438–1481
John II, "the Perfect," son of Afonso V	1481–1495
Manuel, "the Fortunate," cousin of John II	1495–1521
John III, son of Manuel	1521–1557
Sebastian, grandson of John III	1557–1578
Henry, son of Manuel	1578–1580

The epic figure in the first phase of Renaissance discovery was noble and lofty-minded Prince Henry of Portugal, the fifth son of King John I and his queen, the English Princess Philippa of Lancaster, daughter of John of Gaunt. Surnamed "the Navigator" though he never traveled farther than Morocco, this prince has left a truly great name in the history of geography. He was in every sense a "maker," and it was his vision and his determination alone which launched Portugal on a century of voyaging, discovery, and conquest such as the world had never seen. In appearance a tall, blonde, muscular Englishman, he embodied the best qualities of the two great seafaring nations from which he sprang; brave in heart, keen in mind, and noble in spirit, he was a man with a vision before him, and with a passion for doing deeds which would redound to the glory of Portugal and of Christendom.

In 1415, when Henry was but twenty-one his father led an expedition against the Moslem stronghold of Ceuta on the northern tip of Morocco, in which Henry participated. Seldom has such an event been so decisive a turning point in history, insignificant though it must have seemed to men of other nations at the time — if indeed they ever heard of it at all. Yet the capture of this North African port, in which Henry distinguished himself by his bravery, gave the young prince the inspiration which was to mold his whole life and that of his nation. To a man of Henry's temper-

ament — at once visionary and practical — this event was a powerful
tonic and stimulant: it brought him face to face with the Moslem world,
it pointed the way down the African coast, even around Africa to India,
and it filled his mind with the limitless possibilities awaiting his countrymen, if only they had the leadership to take advantage of their opportunities. On the day that Ceuta fell, Portugal ceased to be a trivial state
on the western edge of the Iberian Peninsula with little or no experience
in seafaring (beyond local coasting and fishing, and probable participation in the shadowy Genoese ventures to the Azores and Madeira in
the mid-fourteenth century), and entered into a fantastic career which
was destined to take her flag to the ends of the earth. It is not too much
to say that this career was very largely due to the energy and brains of
Prince Henry.

In Ceuta the impressionable young prince learned from Moorish
prisoners of the caravan routes from Tunis to Timbuctoo, of the River
Senegal or Western Nile, of the rich trading center of Cantor on the
Gambia, and of the Gold Coast. In the light of this knowledge Henry
realized that he must outflank the great western shoulder of Africa to
reach Guinea; that he must outflank Guinea to reach the southern end
of Africa; and that he must outflank Africa itself to reach the Indies —
and finally that just as India was the great prize, so the Gold Coast was
the reward of the initial successes. Thus it was that Henry's African
voyages and the subsequent exploitation of Guinea were the immediate
consequences of the conquest of a lesser outpost of Islam on the Straits
of Gibraltar.

There seems little reason to doubt that Henry's long-term objective
was the discovery of a passage to India; not only for the sake of the new
knowledge itself, but also for the power which that knowledge would
give. Likewise he hoped to add to the greatness and wealth of Portugal,
for the India trade was the prize of the world, and the riches of the
East — certainly in the eyes of ordinary men — were the plain and primary reason for exploration. Naturally, therefore, with this objective in
mind, any incidental trade on the way to India would be pure gain. Then,
too, Henry had the true Christian spirit of a crusader: he wanted to deal
a body-blow to Islam, and he wanted to convert the heathen at the same
time. Until his death, he hoped to find the land of Prester John, the fabulous priest-king of the dim Orient and Ethiopia, so long cut off from
Christendom by the minions of the Prophet, and by doing this he might
seize the Mohammedan world in a gigantic pincers.

Before Henry's time discovery had been a casual occupation: voyages
into the unknown had been sporadic, unplanned, and occasional; their
records had been either scanty, mendacious, or simply nonexistent.
Likewise the geography of the day was (as we emphasized in the first

chapter) good in spots, but all too often Ptolemaic and Mandevillian. Beside his forerunners Henry stands out like a beacon, for it was he who for the first time in history laid down a definite geographical policy: he made a systematic and continuous campaign of exploration; he made discovery an art and science; and he made voyaging a national interest. Stated broadly, Henry first of all sought to know the world we live in and teach men the new knowledge; second, his more material aims were those of his time and nation, but they were no less a part of his life.

In 1418 Henry was back in Ceuta a second time; the Moors had made a valiant attempt to capture the town, but the arrival of the prince with reinforcements caused the siege to be raised. On his return to Portugal the following year his father made him governor of Algarve (the southern province of Portugal). Henry established himself at Sagres on the southwestern tip of the province, and there, on the Sacred Cape with Atlantic rollers coming in on three sides, he built a small palace, an observatory (the earliest in Portgual), a chapel, and a village for his workers and attendants. For the rest of his life Sagres was to be the headquarters for his work. History is indeed the poorer for our ignorance of the specific activities of his academy there. As it is, scholars have to depend on a few facts, a vast amount of conjecture, and the actual results of Henry's voyages. It is known, nevertheless, that Henry did surround himself with a group of cosmographers, astronomers, and physicians, many of them Jews and some even Spanish Moors, chief of whom was Master Jacome, a Jew from Majorca, whose father, Abraham Cresques, was the author of the celebrated *Catalan Atlas* of 1375 (see Chapter I). With these scholars around him, Henry immersed himself at Sagres in the study of cosmography and mathematics; here he selected his captains and pilots; had them instructed and had his charts brought up to date with each fresh discovery; here in fact was the focal point from which the impulse for discovery emanated.

Two great improvements may be traced directly to the Sagres academy; the first in the art of map making, the second in the art of shipbuilding. Although no Sagres charts have survived, there is evidence from Portuguese chronicles and from the works of Italian portolan makers that much activity in this direction was carried on. As for shipbuilding, the Venetian Cadamosto, writing in Henry's later days, stated that the caravels of Portugal were the best sailing ships afloat — in fact there is evidence that their design originated at Sagres. However, the full proof for the accomplishment of the School of Sagres lies in the Henrician voyages and in the colonial development to which they gave rise.

Henry's first enterprise was the conquest and colonization of the Atlantic islands. As we have seen, the Canaries were known to antiquity, while the Madeira group and the Azores were probably discovered by the Genoese in the mid-fourteenth century, but to Henry was due the effective discovery and colonization of the two latter archipelagoes. In no sense, therefore, was the voyage of João de Trasto to the Grand Canary in 1415 one of discovery, yet his report of a strong current between the islands caused Henry to send out Gonçalo Velho the following year to find out the reason for it — the first scientific expedition of the kind recorded. More fortuitous was the rediscovery of Madeira. In 1418 two squires of the prince's household, João Gonçalves Zarco and Tristão Vaz Teixeira, anxious to distinguish themselves, set out in search of the land of Guinea, but a storm drove them to the island of Porto Santo, forty miles northeast of Madeira itself. They returned to Portugal with such an enthusiastic report that Henry sent them in 1420 to colonize the island, and on the voyage they reached and settled the main island of Madeira. The colonization of Madeira received an initial setback by a destructive forest fire (said to have raged for seven years!), but after this disaster Malmsey grapes were introduced from Crete and the future of Madeira was assured; when Cadamosto visited the island a generation later he was able to describe the vineyards as the finest sight in the world.

Following this exploit, Henry dispatched Fernando de Castro in 1425 to conquer the Grand Canary. Resistance of the natives and lack of provisions led to the abandonment of the campaign, and a subsequent expedition two years later failed for similar reasons; but these voyages did have the result of giving Portuguese mariners a thorough knowledge of the Canary Islands and the surrounding waters.

It is impossible to give an exact date for the effective discovery of the Azores, although the event certainly took place between 1427 and 1432 — the latter year being most generally accepted. At that time Gonçalo Velho sailed westward under Henry's orders in search of islands which were believed to exist there, and by so doing discovered St. Mary's. At this point the narratives vary. According to the local historian Antonio Cordeiro (in his *Historia insulana*) no further discoveries took place until 1444 when Velho, on another expedition, explored St. Michael's; a year or so later Terceira, "the third island," was first sighted. Prince Henry's servant, Diogo Gomes, however, related that Velho found St. Michael's, Terceira, Fayal, and Pico on the same voyage on which he fell in with St. Mary's. This would seem more likely, because in 1439 the king granted Henry the right to settle seven islands in the group, and Azurara states that by 1445 colonization was well underway. In a sense, nevertheless, any hair-splitting over dates is rather superfluous, inasmuch as the three island groups — Canaries, Madeiras, and Azores — were well explored by the time that the African voyages got fairly started.

From the time of his early settlement at Sagres, Henry had been sending ships every year along the African coast; probably timid and minor ventures of one or two vessels that sailed by day and anchored each night and probably seldom got below Cape Juby, directly across from the Canaries. South of Cape Juby lay the formidable Cape Bojador, which man had never sailed beyond — a barrier very inconspicuous on modern maps and so low and sandy that it is visible only for a short distance. Yet it is a barrier that because of treacherous currents and reefs, and more particularly because of the mythical terrors beyond it, proved to be wholly impassable; Henry's crews invariably turned back before it and contented themselves with raiding Moorish settlements along the coast to pay their expenses. Beyond this terrible cape lay the Sea of Darkness, the mere thought of which had frozen the blood of the Arab geographers; and beyond too, lay the torrid zone, in which white men would become black. Gil Eannes, one of Henry's most skillful captains, felt this haunting fear when in 1433 Henry sent him into the unknown, and he got no further than the Canaries. In the next year the prince ordered him to make a second attempt: Eannes tried again and this time succeeded. Cape Bojador was doubled, and the first hurdle on the way to India was cleared. Compared with the voyages of da Gama and Columbus, Eannes' exploit seems quite tame and trivial, but this bold Portuguese was a pioneer, sailing into the frightening unknown, and the importance of his act cannot be overrated.

In 1435 Henry sent out Eannes again, with the royal cupbearer Afonso Baldaya. They cleared Cape Bojador without difficulty and even sailed fifty leagues to the southward, reaching Gurnet Bay (25° N). When they rowed ashore at this place they saw footprints of men and camels and concluded that an inhabited region was not far off. Henry was enthusiastic about following up this clue, and in 1436 he sent out Baldaya again. This time the bay of Angra dos Cavallos (24° N) was reached, and Baldaya sent two cavaliers ashore, who rode seven leagues upcountry through the desert. They were set upon by a band of savages armed with assagais and galloped back to shore for safety. Like the rounding of Cape Bojador, this incident was slight in itself, but symbolically this earliest landing of Christian knights on the coast of unknown Africa was indeed a prophecy of the future conquests of Christian Europe in the new worlds it was in search of. Pushing on from Angra dos Cavallos, Baldaya passed the coast of Rio do Ouro, and continued south to a large rock named Galha Point, just short of Cape Blanco (Branco in Portuguese), and four hundred miles beyond Cape Bojador. Portugal had thus carried her flag beyond the belt of the Moslem world, and had begun to touch the wider world outside.

In spite of this brilliant beginning of the rounding of Africa, there was a lull of four or five years during which nothing further was done in the way of exploration. This may be accounted for by the fact that Henry had other distractions during the period: in particular, the tragic expedition to Tangier in which Henry himself took part and in which his brother Fernando was captured. The shock of this failure was largely responsible for the death of King Edward in 1438, and this in turn brought great discord to the realm, so that — as Azurara expressively put it — Henry clean forgot all other matters, and for the time sent no more ships to Africa.

It was not until 1441 that Henry dispatched another expedition — an expedition memorable for inaugurating an insidious traffic which was to plague the civilized world for the next four centuries. In that year two of the prince's captains, Antão Gonçalves and Nuno Tristão, proceeded to the Rio do Ouro, where they sent landing parties ashore and made the first captures of African natives. Gonçalves returned home with the cargo of slaves, but Tristão, having orders to proceed as far as possible, careened and repaired his vessel, keeping his tides as if he were in the Tagus — an act of boldness never before done outside Portugal and one which caused great wonderment. When the repairs were done, Tristão sailed to Cape Blanco and discovered the Bay of Arguim, destined to become the headquarters of the slave trade for the next few years.

In its immediate effect on Portuguese maritime enterprise, the start of the slave trade had both good and bad results. It supplied a powerful incentive for gain, and thus by arousing the commercial part of the population, made maritime enterprise a national interest. On the other hand, it distracted mariners from Henry's grandiose plans of exploration, so that expedition after expedition, which the Prince hoped would sail ever southward into the unknown, merely wasted their efforts in the Bay of Arguim. It is of course impossible to palliate slavery as an institution, but is would appear that the victims of these early raids were well treated as soon as they reached Portugal; they were baptized, given some education, and eventually absorbed into the general body of the population. In the first five years of the trade it is estimated that almost a thousand slaves, who had been either captured or bought from the coastal chiefs between Cape Bojador and Arguim, were brought to Portugal.

For the next few years, therefore, Portuguese endeavor was confined to slaving voyages to Arguim, led by Gonçalves, Tristão, and Gil Eannes. A chaotic, cut-throat traffic resulted, which was finally regularized by Prince Henry with the construction of a fort at Arguim in 1448 — the first European settlement on the West African coast. However, the period

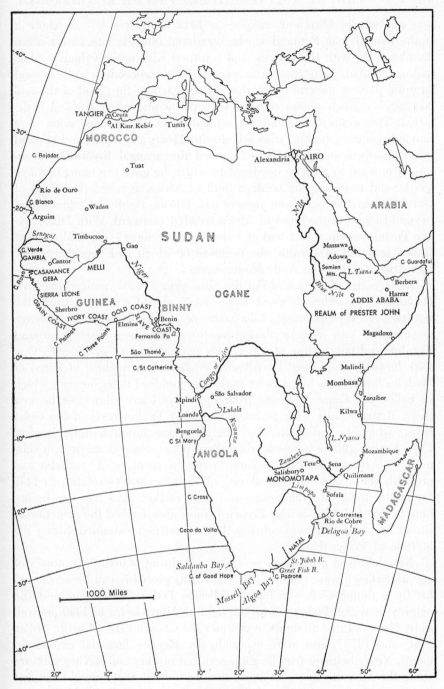

AFRICA

was not wholly barren of results; in 1444 Gonçalves left on shore a squire named João Fernandes, who wandered into the interior for seven months, lived with the natives, and returned with much valuable information. Probably in the same year Tristão proceeded well beyond Arguim, passing the end of the desert and reaching the "land of the real Negroes," a green region covered with palms and other tropical vegetation. This venture inspired the emulation of Dinis Dias, scion of a famous seafaring family, who sailed with Henry's blessing in 1445 and never dropped anchor until he reached the Senegal River. Dias continued onward to a green headland to which he gave the name of Cape Verde, and rounding the western limit of Africa, reached the island of Goree across the bay from present-day Dakar, rightly convinced that beyond this point the coast of Africa trended eastward. With Dias' voyage Portuguese mariners had at last reached Guinea — the fabled Bilad Ghana or Land of Wealth, the tradition of which had been kept alive by Edrisi and the later Arab geographers.

A large armada was sent out the same year (1445), under Lançerote Pessanha, and although great hopes were placed in the venture, the results were disappointing. Like some of its predecessors the voyage degenerated into a mere slaving venture: there was fighting around Arguim, and only a few of the vessels pushed on to Cape Verde. One ship, however, captained by Alvaro Fernandes — a nephew of Zarco of Madeira fame — reached a point perhaps a hundred miles beyond, which he called the Cape of Masts, from the many bare palm trees he saw there. Better results were to follow: in 1446 Tristão reached the Geba River, which he called the Rio Grande, three hundred miles beyond Cape Verde; although he was slain there by a poisoned arrow in a skirmish with the natives, this voyage marks the memory of one who was probably the ablest and most daring of all the prince's captains. In 1447 Fernandes made another cruise and went farther than any one before him; he coasted what is now French Guinea and reached the present-day site of Konakry. This was actually the farthest point attained during the lifetime of Prince Henry.

Now followed a hiatus of several years, during which no ventures of any importance were undertaken. The hiatus probably can be accounted for by a minor civil war between Prince Pedro the Regent and the nobility in which Pedro fell on the field of Alfarrobeira in 1449, as well as by Henry's three attempts to conquer the Canaries from Castile (1450, 1451, and 1453), and more especially by Henry's financial embarrassments. Nevertheless it may be supposed that raiding and slaving ventures along the African coast continued, such as the one that brought the first live lion to Lisbon (1447) and the tragic voyage of Vallarte the Dane to Cape Verde in 1448.

It was not until 1455 that another noteworthy expedition along the African coast took place, that of the intelligent and observant Venetian Alvise da Cadamosto, the first of a distinguished line of Italian captains in the service of other states, and hence the precursor of Columbus, Vespucci, and the Cabots. Cadamosto covered no new ground on his voyage, but he appears to have explored the coast more intensively than had been done previously, and his narrative is perhaps the most vivid picture of West Africa in the period that has come down to us. Sailing first to Madeira for victuals (a practice which earlier voyages started, and one which testified to the good results of Henry's colonization), Cadamosto continued via the Canaries to Arguim. While there he learned much of the interior: of the rich caravan center of Oden (Wadan); of the Tegazza region, famous for its rock salt; and of the empire of Melli to the south, a land of unbearable heat, but of much gold. Cadamosto passed on from Arguim to the Senegal, and stayed for weeks as a guest of the king of the Jaloff Negroes at a place between that river and Cape Verde. Later he proceeded to the Gambia and would have sailed upstream, but skirmishes with the natives discouraged his men, and they bade him return after he had progressed a few miles. While in this region, however, he made stellar observations, using the Southern Cross, this being the first occasion that such a thing had been performed.

Evidently the Gambia had fired Cadamosto's imagination, for in 1456 he departed on a second voyage thither, with another free-lance Italian named Antoniotto Usodimare. After passing Cape Blanco they were blown off their course by a storm, and by this trick of fate discovered the Cape Verde Islands. Passing on to the Gambia, they found the natives more friendly than on the previous visit and were able to sail up the river to the residence of the local ruler, a full sixty miles from the open sea. Here they remained some days, doing a roaring business in barter. Cadamosto describes this part of the river graphically: the luxuriant vegetation, the hippopotomi and elephants, and the picturesque river life, with its innumerable small craft, and the cotton-clad warriors in their war-canoes. An outbreak of fever among the men caused Cadamosto to leave the Gambia; but before returning to Portugal, he explored the coast as far south as the Geba, about a hundred and fifty miles beyond.

After Cadamosto's two voyages came the two voyages of Diogo Gomes, but his narrative, dictated in his old age to the German geographer Martin Behaim, is so vague and full of inconsistencies that extreme accuracy in the matter of routes and dates is impossible. His first voyage, made either in 1456 or 1458, took him to the Geba and beyond; on his return he ascended the Gambia even further than Cadamosto, reaching the fabled city of Cantor (the present Kuntaur), two hundred miles inland as the crow flies, where he met men from Timbuctoo and from Kukia, a great city to the southwest noted for its abundance of gold. As in Cadamosto's case, the unhealthy climate sickened most of Gomes' men, so that he had to abandon any further expedition inland and return to the sea. On his second voyage, undertaken in 1458 or 1460, he only got as far as Cape Verde, but while steering for Portugal he fell in with the Cape Verde Islands and later put forth claims as their discoverer.

A fitting climax to the work of a generation was made in the last of the Henrician voyages — that of Henry's squire and Cadamosto's friend, Pedro de Sintra. Although the prince had died before the voyage took place, one nevertheless feels that his spirit motivated the enterprise. De Sintra went with two caravels three hundred and fifty miles farther down the coast than any Portuguese before him; he explored the shoreline from the Geba to Sierra Leone, frequently landing and bartering with the natives. Beyond the present site of Freetown he discovered and named Cape Santa Anna, coasted on to the point of Mesurado, where Monrovia now stands, and reached his farthest point some little way down the Liberian coast. Altogether it was a memorable expedition.

In 1458 Henry had taken part in his fourth campaign against the Moors of North Africa, and in spite of his sixty-four years he distinguished himself in the capture of Alcacer, near Ceuta. But he had spent himself too strenuously for many years past and the addition of the active military service was too much. The man who was the heart of Portuguese voyaging for nearly half a century died quietly on November 13, 1460, at Sagres. Though many great heroes will appear in these pages, his like will not be met again.

The voyages undertaken at Henry's direction pointed the way for his successors, for by de Sintra's cruise the great western bulge of Africa had been almost rounded, and the ground work for the subsequent "Grand Voyages" had been thoroughly laid. To Prince Henry the human race is indebted in large measure for the maritime exploration within a single century of more than half the globe; this accomplishment is a sufficient monument to his greatness. Rightly did Sir Raymond Beazley say: "If Columbus gave Castile and Leon a new world in 1492, if da Gama reached India in 1498, if Dias rounded the Cape of Tempests in 1486 [*sic*], if Magellan made the circuit of the globe in 1520–22, their teacher and master was none the less Henry the Navigator."

For seven years after de Sintra's return, exploration languished — a vivid proof of the void caused by Henry's death. In 1469, however, King Afonso V (Henry's nephew) made a five-year agreement with one Fernão Gomes, a wealthy citizen of Lisbon, who in exchange for certain trading rights undertook to discover a hundred leagues of coast each year. This arrangement proved very satisfactory, and since Gomes chose competent men, a rapid advance was made. Little is known in detail about the Gomes voyages, undoubtedly because of the so-called "conspiracy of silence," which kept news of the African discoveries on a high-security level within the circle of the king and his advisers. What is known comes from a brief mention in Barros' *Decades*, and an historian, therefore, must content himself with a mere catalogue:

1470 Soeiro da Costa rounded Cape Palmas and reached the Camoe River on the Ivory Coast.
1471 João de Santarem and Pero de Escolar reached the site of Elmina on the Gold Coast. They probably pushed on to Lagos and may have discovered the islands of São Thomé and O Principe.
1472 Fernando Pó followed the coast of Benin to the Cameroons, discovering the island which bears his name.
1473 Lopo Gonçalves crossed the equator.
1475 Ruy de Sequeira reached Cape St. Catherine (2° S) and visited the islands of São Thomé and O Principe.

In 1474 the Gomes contract lapsed, and the king gave the rights to his son John. Then ensued another of those lulls which seem to characterize Portuguese maritime activity. Gomes and his captains deserve all praise for their splendid accomplishments, about which we know all too little, for in five brief years they had discovered as much coastline as Henry's mariners had done in thirty; but then they had behind them the great traditions and knowledge so painfully won in the Navigator's time. Undoubtedly Gomes' men must have been distressed at discovering the southward turn of the African coast at the Cameroons; this put another obstacle in the way to India, and may account for the relative inactivity of a decade.

But if India was the ultimate prize, Guinea was the immediate one, and the Portuguese early began to reap the wealth of West Africa. Trade centered in four commodities: pepper, ivory, gold, and slaves. They were gathered from parts of the coast that still bear the terminology of these products — the Grain Coast (southern Sierra Leone and Liberia), the Ivory Coast (Cape Palmas to Cape Three Points), the Gold Coast (Cape Three Points to Cape St. Paul), and the Slave Coast (Cape St. Paul to Benin). In the treaty following the war with Castile (1475–1479) Portuguese possession of Guinea was officially confirmed; but in spite of her attempts to control the trade monopoly, Spanish interlopers began trespassing on Portugal's chosen preserves. In 1482 the most celebrated Portuguese fort on the African coast, Elmina, was founded largely because of this threat: it was built by a picturesque old warrior named

Diogo de Azambuja, who was its governor for the first years of its existence. Elmina fully justified that existence: its name means "the Mine," and situated as it was in the center of the Gold Coast, it turned out to be in a rich auriferous district. One of its earliest visitors, who may in fact have accompanied Azambuja on his founding voyage, was a young Genoese captain named Christopher Columbus, whose experiences on the Coast made a profound and lasting impression on him. With its satellite gold-producing localities of Samma and Axim (both just to the west), the fortress of São Jorge da Mina was destined to be the principal focus of European activity in West Africa for a century to come.

Portugal's second factory in Guinea was at Benin, founded in 1486 by Afonso de Aveiro, but abandoned a few years later because of the site's unhealthiness. At least one highly important consequence stemmed from its creation. Aveiro returned from Benin with the envoy of the local king, who related that twenty moons' march from the coast there lived a mighty monarch named Ogané, who was held in the same reverence by his subjcts as the Pope was by the Christians. So anxious were the Portuguese to locate and find Prester John that they jumped to the conclusion that he and Ogané were one and the same. King John's cosmographers reckoned twenty moons' march as three hundred leagues, and concluded that Ethiopia would then be reached. In view of this intelligence, King John resolved to send out two more expeditions — to be described later: one by the Mediterranean route, and the other around Africa, with the dual object of finding Prester John and reaching India. The first was entrusted to Pero da Covilhan and Afonso de Paiva; the second to Bartholomew Dias. But this is to anticipate.

King John II, who succeeded his father Afonso V in 1481, proved to be almost as great an influence in exploration as his great-uncle Henry had been — in some respects he was even greater, for he had the resources of the royal treasury behind him, and he was a harsher task-master than the Navigator. At the beginning of his reign, his driving power was evident; Elmina was founded, and expeditions were sent into the interior of Africa as well. Among these were the mission of Pedro de Evora and Gonçalo Eannes to Timbuctoo; also an embassage to the ruler of the Mandinga country, far in the hinterland of Sierra Leone. King John was very interested too in cosmography and astronomy, and he had a committee of experts — the Junta — headed by the brilliant Jews, Joseph Vizinho and Abraham Zacuto, to work on the problem of position-finding at sea. Zacuto had written in Hebrew in the previous decade his *Almanach Perpetuum*, the most advanced work yet to appear on the subject, and one containing full tables of the sun's declination. But its technical nature, coupled with the fact that it was written in a language little understood by the average skipper, rendered it quite impractical. Vizinho

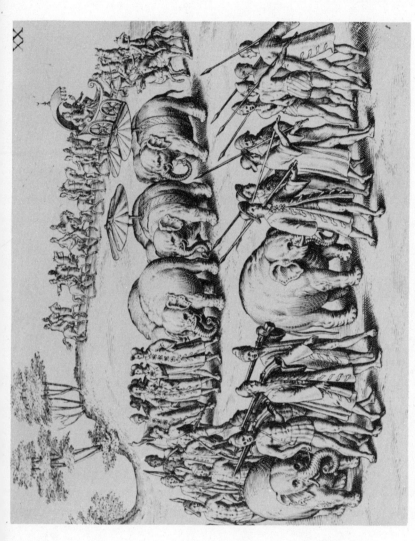

The King of Pegu with his elephants in solemn procession. "He is a great lord, who possesses more than ten thousand elephants." — Santo Stephano. "The King rideth on a triumphal cart all gilded, which is drawn by 16 goodly horses: this cart is very high with a goodly canopy over it, behind the cart goe 20 of his Lordes and nobles." — Cesare Federici.

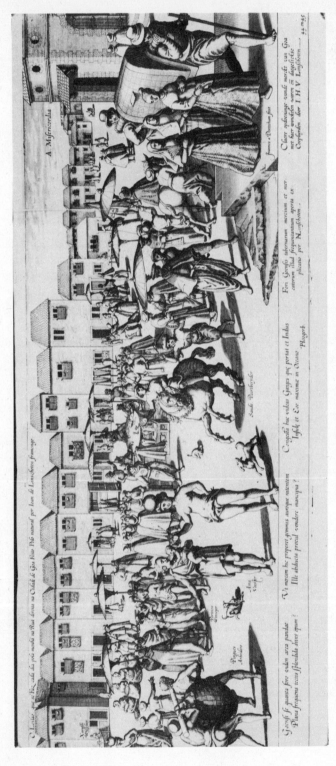

The Market Place in Goa. "The great market, which is held all along the great straight street, the one end whereof touches the Misericordia, and the other the palace of the Viceroy. This street is very handsome and broad, full of shops of jewellers, goldsmiths, lapidaries, carpet weavers, silk mercers, and other artizans. While this market is afoot, there is so great a crowd in the street that one can hardly pass. In short, one sees there the wealth of the Indies in all kinds, and jewels the finest that can be seen." — François Pyrard.

therefore translated it into Latin (printed at Leiria, 1496; Hain 16267) and later made an abridged version, which he combined with a recension of Sacrobosco under the title *Regimento do Estrolabio e do Quadrente* (printed *circa* 1509). One result of this technical research was the voyage of Vizinho in 1485 along the Guinea coast as far as Fernando Pó for the purpose of determining the declination of the sun throughout Guinea. It is now regarded as possible that among Vizinho's companions on this expedition was the Nürnberg geographer Martin Behaim. The observations made by the Vizinho expedition led to the introduction of graduated sailing charts into Portugal. But events of even greater importance were taking place in these years, for Diogo Cão was on his voyages.

Cão, a practical navigator of humble birth, with experience in the Guinea trade, was sent out to continue the exploration of the African coast. He sailed in June 1482, taking with him large stone pillars called *padrões*, to be set up as marks of discovery. His course took him first to Elmina; from there he sailed straight to Cape Lopo Gonçalves, and then coasted southward, passing Cape St. Catherine (the farthest point previously reached), and continuing close inshore until he came to a mighty river, on the north bank of which he erected a pillar. The river was therefore christened the Rio do Padrão, although the natives who lived along it were called the Mani-Congo. Later the Portuguese renamed it the Zaire, a corruption of the native word *nzadi* meaning "river," but modern readers know the great stream as the Congo. Cão is said to have stayed some months at or near the mouth, and he even sent some of his men upcountry on a mission to the local potentate. Continuing his voyage southward, Cão stood out to sea until the westward trend of the coast brought him in sight of the high land around Benguela, and he did not turn back until he had reached Cape St. Mary (13° S), where he erected his second pillar. On returning to the Congo, he found that his mission had not come back from the king, so he seized four Negro chieftains as hostages and sailed home to Portugal. He dropped anchor in the Tagus in April 1484, after an absence of almost two years. King John was so delighted with the results of the expedition that he knighted Cão, and gave him a liberal pension. But the King was so anxious for the exploration to be continued that Cão was vouchsafed but a few brief months ashore.

Early in 1485 Cão was sent on a second voyage, in company with Pero de Escolar, one of Gomes' old pilots, who lived to accompany da Gama to India. In spite of the statement in the *Nürnberg Chronicle* it is unlikely that Martin Behaim, the constructor of the famous globe, was along; rather, as suggested above, is it more probable that he went with Vizinho or Aveiro to Guinea. On this voyage Cão penetrated still farther into the unknown, and put up two pillars, one at Monte Negro near Cape St. Mary, and the other at Cape Cross in Damaraland (22° S). On his return trip, he called at the Congo and collected the men left on his previous voyage, who — wonderful to relate — were safe and sound. Contemporary carvings on a rock near the junction of the Mposo River show that he ascended the main stream at least a hundred miles. These carvings include an inscription recording that the ships of King John of Portugal arrived there, Cão and his companions are named, and further names with crosses and Masonic symbols occur on another part of the rock. This would indicate that Cão took his ships through the whirlpool known as Hell's Cauldron, where the stream surges through a passage half a mile wide at ten knots an hour, a feat of seamanship which shows what consummate navigators the early Portuguese were. Cão then proceeded to Portugal, taking with him a native prince named Caçuta as ambassador from the Mani-Congo. The expedition reached Lisbon in the first half of 1487, and Cão on his two voyages had revealed more than fifteen hundred miles of the coast of the Dark Continent. Full details of his two voyages are lacking, however; thanks again to the "conspiracy of silence."

History is reticent about the subsequent career of the gallant Cão (Barros says he returned; the Martellus Germanus Map states that he died on the African coast), but the record of what became of Caçuta is of considerable interest. With his companions this native chief was instructed in Christianity, baptized with great ceremony as João da Silva, and taught Portuguese. About 1490 he was sent back to the Congo in company with Gonçalo de Sousa, John II's ambassador, and this mission led to the creation of the semibarbaric Christian Kingdom of Congo, which, under strong Portuguese influence, endured throughout the sixteenth century.

Before de Sousa and Caçuta had left Portugal, however, the last and greatest of the classic African voyages had taken place. This voyage far more than all its predecessors opened the way to India — although here again posterity is handicapped by the "conspiracy of silence." In August 1487 Bartholomew Dias left Lisbon with two caravels and a storeship, his captains being the indefatigable Pero de Alamquer, a veteran Guinea pilot destined to go with da Gama, and João Infante, a knight of the royal household. It is probable that Dias steered straight from Cape Palmas to the Congo, and then coasted close in to the southward, naming all natural features on the way (as was the custom of the period) after the saints' days on which they were sighted. Like Cão, he carried a number of pillars; he also had with him several Negroes brought from the Congo on Cão's voyages, who were to be landed at various parts of the coast to advertise the coming of the Portuguese in such a way that the news thereof might reach the ears of Prester John. Two of the Negroes were landed at Port Alexander (16° S), well dressed and supplied with samples of gold, silver, and spices, but it is highly doubtful if tidings of their arrival ever reached the Court of the Priest-King of Ethiopia.

At Cabo da Volta (present-day Lüderitz), Dias put up his first pillar. After leaving there he was beset by storms, blown far off his course, and in consequence quite unwittingly carried around the Cape of Good Hope, to have his next landfall at Mossel Bay, almost two hundred and fifty miles eastward. Very pleased to observe the eastward trend of the coast, he sailed to Algoa Bay, and at Cape Padrone he set up another pillar. But at the very moment when the expedition stood at the threshold of the Indian Ocean, events took an unfavorable turn. The crews were worn out by their trials and exertions, the storeship had been lost, food was running short, and the ships had suffered from the rough weather. In a manner almost mutinous the men besought their leader to steer for Portugal, and Dias had to yield. At the mouth of the Great Fish River, about fifty miles beyond Cape Padrone, the little fleet turned back; it is recorded that when passing the pillar on Cape Padrone on the return, Dias cried with as much sorrow as if it were a son condemned to perpetual exile. Nevertheless his work was done; the trend of the land was now unmistakably to the northeast, and the perservering captain must have realized that he had accomplished his task.

On the way back, the fleet sighted the great cape which they were seeking. Dias christened it Cabo Tormentoso (the Cape of Storms) because of the weather he had experienced, and he landed to erect a pillar, dedicated to St. Philip. After that, Dias cruised northward, falling in with his missing storeship and calling at the island of O Principe and at Elmina, and finally reached the Tagus in December, after an absence of more than sixteen months. Of Dias' reception at Court and the reward for his services the record — in keeping with Portugal's secretive policy — is naturally silent, but his voyage indeed did give realization to the Passage to India; and King John, foreseeing the fullfilment of his long-sought desires, rechristened the Cape of Storms with the stimulating and enduring name of the Cape of Good Hope.

4

THE PORTUGUESE IN THE ORIENT

D*ias had rounded the Cape* and sailed into the Indian Ocean, but he had failed in his attempt to reach either India or the mysterious realm of Prester John. Better luck was in store for the other mission which King John II sent out simultaneously, which as a piece of advance reconnaissance was brilliant and far-reaching in its effects. This mission was undertaken by two men, Pero da Covilhan and Afonso de Paiva. Both of them were intelligent, well traveled, and in every way qualified for their task; Covilhan in particular had had wide experience in North Africa, for he had gone on missions to Fez and Tlemcen, and he spoke Arabic fluently. Of Paiva less is known, but as he has connections with the Canary Islands, it is likely that he knew Morocco as well. Nothing was left to chance in preparing for the journey; the travelers were thoroughly briefed by the royal chaplain Diogo Ortiz, who was an expert cosmographer; by the learned Jew, Master Rodrigo, who was the royal doctor; and also by the distinguished Joseph Vizinho. Their instructions were that one of the travelers was to go to Prester John, while the other was to determine the possibility of sailing around Africa to the Eastern seas. In sending Paiva to Ethiopia, King John's purpose was not so much to seek an ally against Islam, as the Navigator had done, but rather to find through the prester's domains an avenue for Portuguese expansion.

In May 1487 the two venturers had a farewell audience with their sovereign and shortly afterwards turned their backs forever on their native country. Their route took them across Spain to Barcelona, where they embarked for Naples and Rhodes. Doing some buying and selling on the way, they eventually reached Alexandria, where they both fell desperately ill with fever and had their goods confiscated by a hopeful official who expected them to die momentarily. Receiving some indemnity upon their recovery, they bought a fresh supply of goods and proceeded to Cairo. This experience with the mercantile class of Egypt was very useful in widening their acquaintance with Moslem traders and Eastern commerce; it was natural for them therefore to join a party of Moorish merchants and sail in an Arab dhow down the Red Sea to Aden in the spring of 1488. At Aden the wanderers parted company, and Paiva went alone in the direction of Ethiopia, with the intention of returning from there to Portugal on the completion of his assignment. Covilhan on his part embarked on a "Mecca ship," as the Portuguese called it, and in a month's time reached the port of Cananor on the Indian mainland, being thereby the first of his countrymen ever to set foot on the land which Portugal had sought so long and so tenaciously.

From Cananor, Covilhan made his way down the Malabar coast to Calicut, which in those days was the richest port in all India, with its large colony of Moslem merchants, who monopolized the spice trade and carried on an extensive traffic with ports in the Red Sea, the Persian Gulf, and the East African coast. Covilhan kept his eyes open in Calicut, and learned not only about its commodities but also how the traders took advantage of the monsoon wind, sending ships laden with spices, gems, and porcelains to Arab lands in February, and receiving their return cargoes in August and September. After a sojourn of some little time in Calicut, Covilhan went northward to Goa, a city destined for greatness in the following century but in 1489 chiefly notable for its trade in horses, brought there from Arabia to supply the martial and ceremonial needs of the various Indian rulers. At length Covilhan, a strange, solitary figure a decade in advance of Portuguese expansion, quitted India and crossed the sea to Ormuz, the emporium of the Persian Gulf. By the end of 1489 he was on the move again; he took ship down the long coasts of Arabia and East Africa to Sofala (21° S), a town in Negro-land (Portuguese East Africa), inhabited by Arabs who brought gold from the interior. The purpose of his journey was clear: to find out whether a seaway existed around Africa to the Orient. Having satisfied himself affirmatively on this point, and having learned of a great island to the eastward (Madagascar), known to the Arabs as the Island of the Moon, he made his way north to Aden and Cairo, with the intention of going on to Portugal to reveal his discoveries to his sovereign. But at Cairo, which he reached towards the end of 1490, he found that his colleague Paiva had died, leaving no record of his wanderings whatsoever, except that in the last stages of illness he had reached the Egyptian capital. In place of Paiva, however, Covilhan encountered two Portuguese Jews, sent by King John to find him, and whatever hopes the weary traveler had of a speedy return to his native land were dashed by the royal commands to get through to Prester John at all costs. Before setting out again, Covilhan wrote a full report of his travels, and sent it back to Portugal by one of the Jews, Joseph of Lamego; this report was destined to be of inestimable value in the planning and execution of da Gama's voyage, and hence is of decisive importance in the whole stream of Portuguese history. It might be added that some skeptics in the past have doubted the existence of this report, but historians are now generally agreed on its authenticity and importance.

In company with the other Jew, Rabbi Abraham of Beja, Covilhan proceeded to Ormuz, which the rabbi had orders to visit. Covilhan left Abraham there, who after his mission returned to Portugal, while the indefatigable Christian retraced his steps to the Red Sea, and dressed as a Moslem taking the Hajj, made his way to Mecca. This perilous visit was not warranted in his instructions and can only be ascribed to Covilhan's love of adventure. Even this did not satiate his curiosity, for he went on to Medina, and thence to Mount Sinai, where in the Monastery of St. Catherine he heard his first Christian service in five years. Finally in 1493 he reached Prester John's land, and his travels ended forever; even though he survived for another thirty years. He did in fact meet the mighty emperor of Ethiopia, but he was not allowed to leave the dominions of the Negus. When Rodrigo de Lima made his embassy to Abyssinia in 1520, Covilhan, by then an elderly, Africanized exile, was on hand to give assistance and to tell his life's story.

At the court in Portugal the news of Covilhan's journey to India, coupled with Dias' report of rounding Africa, must have had a considerable effect on the inner circle of royal advisers, and one can only wonder why several years elapsed before anything further was done. Possibly the delay was due to the king's prolonged attack of dropsy, which made him an invalid and eventually caused his death (1495). John the Perfect Prince was succeeded on the throne by his cousin Manuel the Fortunate, a young man of twenty-six, possessed of all the old king's enthusiasm and drive, and filled with desire to win through to India at all costs. Hence, the project nearest Manuel's heart was taken immediately after Manuel's accession; the fitting out of a fleet which was to revolutionize the history of the Orient was entered upon in thorough and methodical fashion.

Four ships were constructed under the supervision of Bartholomew Dias: the square-rigged flagship *São Gabriel*, the square-rigged *São Raphael*, the lateen-rigged caravel *Berrio*, and a large storeship. Bishop Diogo Ortiz supplied the fleet with maps and books, and Abraham Zacuto provided astronomical instruments, made tables of declination, and trained the ships' officers in the art of taking observations. Equal care was given to the selection of personnel: among the pilots were such men as Pero de Escolar, who had sailed for Diogo Gomes and had accompanied Cão, and Pero de Alemquer, who had been with Dias on the voyage to the Cape. Like Alemquer, many of the crews were veterans of Dias' voyage. Supreme command was vested in Vasco da Gama, a man of unrecorded experience at sea, whose selection for the post instead of the more obvious one of Dias, was fully justified by the success of the venture. Da Gama, a gentleman of the Royal Household, had been born in the year of Henry the Navigator's death (1460), the son of an official in the coastal town of Sines in southern Portugal; that he was chosen for so important a position would indicate that he had had considerable naval experience as well as strength of character.

After a dramatic farewell, the fleet left the Tagus on July 8, 1497, and proceeded down the African coast to the Cape Verde Islands, where the first call was made. Bartholomew Dias accompanied the expedition in a caravel until the bulge of Guinea was cleared, when he steered for Elmina, and the fleet itself held a circular course far out into mid-ocean to the southwest, to escape the doldrums and currents in the Gulf of Guinea.

Da Gama's passage from the Cape Verdes to South Africa was far and away the greatest feat of navigation done up to that time. Columbus' passage from Gomera to the Bahamas was twenty-six hundred miles, sailed before a fair wind; in contrast da Gama's course was thirty-eight hundred miles, on a seaway which took him almost across the South Atlantic, where great circle sailing was impossible because of currents and contrary winds. Columbus took five weeks; da Gama three months — and it was not until November 8 that he cast anchor in the Bay of St. Helena in the land of the Hottentots, about a hundred and thirty miles north of the Cape itself. Even da Gama's crews were conscious of their wonderful accomplishment; as they approached the shore they put on their best clothes, fired off bombards, and dressed the ships with bunting. The fleet remained at this bay for eight days while the ships were careened and wood and water were taken on. But the natives proved unfriendly, and in a skirmish da Gama himself was wounded by a javelin. Leaving the anchorage November 16, the fleet doubled the Cape six days later and made its next call at Mossel Bay, where it hove to for a fortnight to dismantle the storeship.

Amid violent storms and an attempted mutiny, the Portuguese passed Dias' farthest point, and on Christmas Day they sighted a fair coast which they christened Natal. No pause was made here, the explorers pushed on northward until they reached the Zavora River, between the mouth of the Limpopo and Cape Correntes. At this place they were well received by the natives; they observed that the women far outnumbered the men, and as the principal commodity was copper, they named the stream the Rio de Cobre. At Quilimane, the next port of call, they remained over a month, careening and refitting the ships. They got on amicably with the natives, but the visit was marred by an outbreak of scurvy. From Quilimane the fleet proceeded to Mozambique, and the minarets and white houses showed da Gama that he had left behind him the country of primitive savages. He had now made contact with the Mohammedan world, and had at least reached the commercial perimeter of the Indian Ocean.

At first the Moslems were friendly, for they believed that the newcomers belonged to the same creed; but when they were undeceived they became angry and even plotted to seize the Portuguese vessels. In retaliation da Gama bombarded the town, and having filled his water casks, sailed on his way. Mombasa was the next port of call, and here the fleet had an even worse reception than at Mozambique. On the night of its arrival a hundred men armed with cutlasses sought to board the *São Gabriel*, and when this failed, the Moors tried to entice the ships close to the town in order to capture them. Quite fortuitously a slight collision obliged the *São Gabriel* to anchor, and thus the plot was thwarted. On another occasion armed swimmers tried to cut the cables of the Portuguese vessels, but this also was discovered in time. Da Gama patiently faced this intense hostility for six days, in the hope of getting a pilot, whose services were essential in the prosecution of the voyage to India. Frustrated in this plan, the admiral led his fleet to the next port along the coast, Malindi, which was reached on Easter Eve. As at Mombasa the people were Moslems; but strangely enough the Portuguese received a rousing welcome, from the local sultan and his subjects alike, so that the visit of ten days must have been the happiest interlude in the entire voyage. The trim, white-washed town with its houses lining the shores of the bay reminded the sailors of towns at home, such as Alcochete on the Tagus above Lisbon. We have a pleasant picture of the sultan being rowed out to the *São Gabriel*, dressed in his best, seated in a bronze chair with a crimson umbrella held above him, and accompanied by native musicians making frightful discords on massive instruments of elephants' tusks. Here, too, the Portuguese saw the first Hindus, whom they uncritically but joyfully believed to be Christians, probably because they mistook the sound of "Krishna" (the second person of the Hindu Trinity) for "Christ." At length da Gama secured the services of a Gujarati named Ibn Majid, who was probably the best pilot in the entire Indian Ocean and was the writer of several high-sounding works in Arabic on the science of navigation. With this expert at the helm the fleet left Malindi on April 24 and headed across the Indian Ocean toward the goal of Portuguese hopes. The passage was uneventful; on May 18 Mount Ely in the Ghats hove in view, and two days later (May 20, 1498) the fleet dropped anchor off Calicut. After seventy or more years of effort the Great Enterprise was accomplished.

Da Gama reached India twenty-eight years before the Mogul conquest. There were petty Moslem dynasties in the north and in the northern part of Deccan, but in South India at this time the ruling power was the Hindu Empire of Vijayanagar, which exercised an ill-defined sovereignty over the lower part of the peninsula from the fourteenth to the sixteenth century, representing in fact the last stand of the national faith against all-conquering Islam. Within this sovereignty were a number of local rulers, who asserted their independence by squabbling with each other. Such a ruler was the Samuri (Zamorin) of Calicut, whose fortune it was to encounter the Portuguese. At the same time, commerce, and the export trade

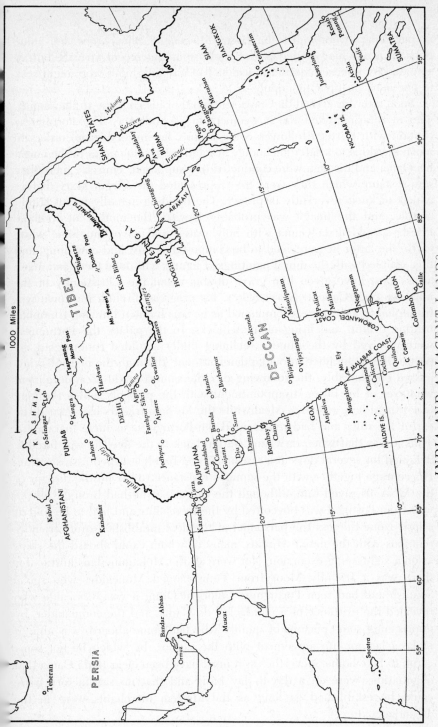

INDIA AND ADJACENT LANDS

in particular, were in the hands of Moslems — some Arabs and some Persians, some long settled in India and some but recent arrivals; but all actuated by intense hatred and jealousy of any interloper who might seek to encroach on their monopoly.

Soon after his arrival da Gama sent word of his embassy to the samuri, who in return invited the newcomers to an audience. The Portuguese captain with thirteen followers went ashore, having first given orders to move the ships to a safer anchorage at Pandarani, some miles to the north. Da Gama and his men were conducted to a supposed "church"; there they saw a statue which they were told represented the Virgin Mary, before which all knelt reverently in prayer. The building actually was a Hindu temple, and the image was probably Devaki, the mother of Krishna. Priests sprinkled da Gama with holy water, and gave him some white earth; the latter he perceived to be composed of dust and cow-dung, and this, coupled with the mural paintings of figures with long teeth and many arms, must have given him grave doubts about the Christianity of the inhabitants of Calicut. Nevertheless, his progress through the town was triumphal to a degree, accompanied as he was by men blowing trumpets, beating drums, and firing off matchlocks. In the palace the Portuguese were received by the samuri, reclining under a gilded canopy and expectorating betel juice into a golden spittoon. Although the first interview passed off amicably, the following day the samuri made no concealment whatever of his bitter disappointment with the presents which the king of Portugal had sent him. Meanwhile the Moslem traders had gained the ear of the ruler and had represented the Portuguese as mere marauders. Thus it was that when da Gama started back to the fleet he was forcibly detained for several days at a rest-house and barely escaped assassination. His courage together with the samuri's resistance to the hostile designs of the Moslems saved him, although the cargo that he had brought all the way from Portugal was boycotted by the merchants and had to be sold at a loss. None the less the personnel of the fleet established quite friendly relations with the native Hindus, many of whom came aboard the ships as on a sightseeing excursion. Nor were all the Mohammedans hostile, for there was a friendly Moor from Tunis named Monçaide, who spoke Spanish and had seen Portuguese sailors at Oran; it was Monçaide who revealed the existence of a plot to kill da Gama, and the commander, by imprisoning some persons of quality who had come aboard, was able to make a last-minute agreement with the samuri, by which he got some cargo to take home. Nevertheless it must have been clear to da Gama that negotiations were on a day-to-day basis and that no satisfactory trade could be established as long as the Moslem merchants were in the ascendancy.

After a stay of three months, the fleet set sail for Portugal at the end of August; it carried Monçaide, whose life was now unsafe at Calicut, and also several Hindus as an offering to King Manuel. Steering north along the coast, da Gama put in at the island of Anjediva below Goa for a refit, and here he took aboard a much-traveled Jew, whom he baptized as Gaspar de Gama. The passage across the Indian Ocean was long and tedious; it took almost three months, and the ravages of scurvy were terrible. At length the African coast at Magadoxo was sighted, and on January 7, 1499, the fleet entered the friendly port of Malindi. By this time the crews were so decimated that da Gama did not have enough sailors to man three vessels, so the *São Raphael* was broken up, and her men distributed among the *São Gabriel* and the *Berrio*. This respite among a friendly population was salutory, and the passage down the African coast was free of incident. Zanzibar was passed, and a momentary stop was made at Mozambique to erect a pillar. Ten days were spent in refitting at Mossel Bay, and on March 20 the *São Gabriel* and the *Berrio* rounded the Cape together. A month later the ships were parted in a South Atlantic storm, and the *Berrio*, captained by the gallant Nicolas Coelho, held her course for Portugal, to drop anchor in the Tagus on July 10, 1499, after an absence of two years and two days. Da Gama put in at the Cape Verde Islands and then proceeded to Terceira in the Azores, where his brother Paul died as a result of the exertions of the voyage; Vasco then sailed on to Portugal and reached Lisbon on September 9.

Nine days later he had his triumphal entry into the city. It was triumphal indeed; for while his diplomatic mission had failed because of Moslem intrigue, he had found India and the seaway thither, he had brought back samples of its gems and spices, and he had performed one of the three or four greatest voyages in recorded history. But since the first step is always the most difficult, what he had accomplished could again be repeated — meanwhile, owing to his skill and courage, the fabulous wealth of the Orient lay open to his countrymen.

One thing, however, was clear to da Gama and the more thoughtful of his colleagues: that Portugal could not gain the full benefit of this trade until she had wrested the commercial control of the Eastern Seas from the Moslem merchants, who held the monopoly throughout the Indian Ocean. That trade had been long established, so that by the end of the fifteenth century there existed from the Red Sea to China a well-organized commerce which was almost entirely in the hands of Mohammedans. Calicut, where the eastern flow of trade met the western flow, was the center of the whole system. Far to the East lay Malacca, also under Moslem control, where junks from Canton and spice-laden craft from the islands of the East Indies transshipped their cargoes. To the west of Calicut lay Ormuz and Aden, each on its own thoroughfare to the Occident. From

Ormuz, goods passed through the Persian Gulf and up the Euphrates to Aleppo; from Aden the more important of the two routes lay up the Red Sea to Suez and Alexandria. In each case the eventual destination was Venice. At the base of the whole system was the monsoon, which made easy transit — westbound in winter, eastbound in summer. It was a system, too, which had the effect of enriching everyone along the line, and so such potentates as the sultan of Turkey, the sultan of Egypt, and the doge of Venice were alike vitally concerned in its preservation. Little Portugal had taken on more than she had bargained for, when da Gama sailed for India!

As a result of da Gama's voyage, therefore, Portugal adopted a policy which for the next fifteen years she pursued in a fashion wholly ruthless and relentless until she had gained her ends, and that policy was the complete elimination of Moslem dominance in the Indian Ocean. In the light of that policy, one can understand and even sympathize with the hostility of the Moslems, and such incidental unfriendliness as that of the samuri of Calicut.

It was natural that Portugal's second voyage to India should have been on a far larger scale than her first: thirteen ships instead of four, and those thirteen armed to the gunwales and filled with twelve hundred men. Command of the expedition was vested in Pedro Alvares Cabral, a young aristocrat of no particular experience, who nevertheless turned out to be a capable and courageous leader. Under him were some of the most skillful mariners to be found in Europe: Nicolas Coelho; Bartholomew Dias; his brother Diogo Dias, who had sailed with da Gama as supercargo; and Pero de Escolar, who had been on almost every voyage of importance during the past thirty years.

On March 8, 1500, the fleet set sail from Lisbon on the first commercial voyage to India. With good winds their progress was rapid; in a week they were among the Canaries, and in a fortnight they had passed the Cape Verde Islands. They held their course south-southwest for another month and signs of land became evident. On April 22 Mount Pascoal on the Brazilian coast (17° S) was sighted. The following day a landing was made; the first landing of any Portuguese within their sphere of American soil. Natives came down to greet them; strange people with painted and tattooed bodies, whose only garments were capes of brilliant feathers. That night there was a storm, and as the open roadstead was unsafe, the ships moved a few miles northward to a harbor which Cabral called Porto Seguro, a name which it still retains. Cabral remained here until May 2; then sending a ship back to Portugal to announce the discovery of the Brazilian mainland (or Terra de Vera Cruz, as he called it), he led the fleet across the South Atlantic. Cabral's discovery of this stretch of the Brazilian coast has long divided geographers into two schools of thought;

one holds that the discovery was accidental and merely the result of holding a westerly course which was taken solely for purposes of navigation; the other maintains that it was a deliberate attempt to find land, the existence of which was at least suspected. In all humility, I submit that I favor the latter view, but it is at best a question where dogmatism is difficult.

Crossing the South Atlantic well below the Tropic of Capricorn, the fleet ran into a tempest so terrible that it nearly ended the entire venture then and there. Four ships foundered with all hands, while the rest were scattered to the four winds, and were badly battered. The gallant sailor, old Bartholomew Dias, was among those who perished; no Portuguese mariner ever performed greater services than he. His brother Diogo, who commanded one of the vessels which was separated from the others, proceeded on his way alone, on what became a voyage of considerable geographical significance. Not until mid-July did the seven other surviving ships join forces at Mozambique, where they remained some days for repairs. The members of the expedition found the local ruler far more tractable than two years previously; he evidently had taken da Gama's bombardment very much to heart. A cooler welcome awaited them at Kilwa, the wealthiest and most important city in East Africa. Da Gama had not called there, so the Portuguese had no terrors for the ruling Moslems. Cabral hoped to make a trade agreement, but ill will towards the Portuguese was so apparent that he sailed away empty handed. Mombasa, in view of its hostility, was studiously avoided, but Malindi was as friendly as ever, and here pilots were easily secured for the crossing of the Indian Ocean.

The fleet reached Anjediva near Goa by the end of August 1500, after a voyage of only six months, in spite of the visit to Brazil and the hurricane. This time was to remain the standard of a good passage to India until the days of steam. From Anjediva, Cabral dropped down the coast to Calicut, and the business end of the voyage began. After taking the precaution of securing hostages, Cabral and his officers had an interview with the samuri, which resulted in arousing the bitter opposition of the Mohammedan merchants. The Portuguese, in consequence, were able to conclude an agreement with the samuri only after a long delay. The agreement allowed a Portuguese factory to be established on shore, with a staff of seventy men under the chief factor, Ayres Correa. This first step in Western imperialism in India was destined to be tragic and short-lived. Provoked by Cabral's capture of one of their ships (which he took in order to secure an elephant as a present for the samuri), the Moslems stormed the factory and slew fifty of the Portuguese, including Correa. Cabral in vengeance burned ten Arab ships with their crews and then bombarded Calicut with all his ordnance. This was the first step of active war against the Arab merchants in India; Calicut was badly damaged, and the samuri quite naturally became from that day forward an implacable enemy of the Portuguese.

With nothing further to be gained at Calicut except casualties, the fleet proceeded southward to Cochin. News of the warfare at Calicut had preceded them, and the local king, partly through fear of Portuguese artillery and partly through joy at the humbling of his more powerful neighbor, received the strangers cordially. Here and at Craganore, a nearby town on the backwaters, a large cargo of spices was taken aboard. An equally favorable reception awaited them at Cananor, to the north of Calicut, where the king insisted on furnishing Cabral with everything he might need. His ships now well laden, Cabral set his course for Portugal. His return voyage was uneventful, save for the fact that he put in at Sofala, the southernmost Arab town in East Africa — which Covilhan had seen, but which Portuguese ships had not previously visited. After rounding the Cape the ships proceeded separately. The first to reach Lisbon, arriving June 23, 1501, was the Italian-owned *Anunciada*, captained by the same Nicolas Coelho who had been first home on da Gama's voyage.

Diogo Dias, who lost the rest of the fleet during the great storm, was swept around the Cape in so wide an arc that he found himself coasting the eastern shores of Madagascar, thereby discovering that island. A landing was made on the northern extremity. Holding a course northwest, Dias fell in with the African coast near Magadoxo and followed it around Cape Guardafui to Berbera in the Gulf of Aden, thereby revealing to the Renaissance world the long coast line all the way to Ethiopia. With the triple discoveries of southern Brazil, Madagascar, and Somaliland, Cabral's voyage was indeed of the first importance from a geographical standpoint. Economically its influence was even greater, for the fleet brought back a magnificent cargo of Oriental commodities. Before the year 1501 was out, spices from Portugal had reached Antwerp, and shortly thereafter German and Italian bankers began to arrive in Lisbon in considerable numbers. In Venice, where the tidings of da Gama's voyage had been greeted with rather bored indifference, the news of Cabral's return was hailed as a calamity — "the worst news the Venetian Republic could have had," as the diarist Priuli put it. The commercial balance had indeed begun to shift.

Even before the first of Cabral's ships had returned, King Manuel dispatched another fleet to India, thus inaugurating the practice of annual voyages. The fleet of four ships, under the command of João da Nova, was not strong enough to face the opposition of Calicut, so it went direct to Cananor. Its progress seems to have been prosperous; it took on a good cargo and dispersed a fleet which the samuri sent against it; but it is of geographical interest chiefly because of the discovery of the island of St. Helena on the way back.

In consequence of Cabral's report, King Manuel determined to send out a large fleet to avenge the massacre of the factory garrison at Calicut. Cabral was appointed to command it and for eight months was busily engaged in the preparations — only to be superseded at the eleventh hour by Vasco da Gama. This change has never been satisfactorily explained, but it obviously caused bad blood between the two men, and Cabral went into retirement, never to be employed again. With the title of Admiral of India, da Gama sailed in February 1502 with fifteen ships — to be joined later by his brother Stephen with five more. On the way out, da Gama stopped at Kilwa, where he extracted a sizable tribute from the local sultan, and then proceeded to Calicut, where he bombarded the city and destroyed a fleet sent out against him. Da Gama is said to have treated the inhabitants of Calicut with a savagery too horrible to describe, but his brutality may be explained (though not excused) by the fact that the Portuguese were but a few men, far from home, surrounded by many thousands of enemies, who, for safety's sake, had to have the fear of God put into their hearts. Da Gama's second voyage was not entirely one of vengeance, however, for he established factories at Cochin and Cananor and left a squadron to protect them and to intercept Moslem ships bound for the Red Sea. He sailed for Lisbon, with ships fully laden, in September 1503.

Portugal's greatest hero now first appears in the Orient. Contrasting with the relative youth of such men as da Gama and Cabral, Afonso de Albuquerque was a grizzled veteran of fifty with a distinguished record of service in Africa when, in company with his cousin Francisco, he sailed to the East in 1503. His fleet proceeded direct to Cochin, arriving just in time to save its friendly rajah, whose territories had been invaded by the angry samuri. The rajah in return allowed Albuquerque to erect a fort at Cochin for the protection of the Portuguese factory and the Cochinese themselves. The building of a fort was the first step toward dominion; the foundation-stone of Portugal's empire in the East. It turned out to be a measure fully justified by events, for no sooner had Albuquerque sailed for home than the samuri was back with fire and sword. It was his fate, however, to be opposed by a man of invincible courage. The commander of the Cochin garrison was Duarte Pacheco Pereira — a sailor and writer on navigation who had come out to India with Cabral and had been in Guinea in the days of Cão and Dias and who was to become known as the Portuguese Achilles. With a small force which included the first Sepoys ever used by Europeans, Pacheco defeated the samuri in seven battles at the fords of Cochin, and in the last battle the samuri himself was slain. As if that were not enough, the brave Pacheco gathered what shipping he could and dispersed a large fleet from Calicut.

During these eventful years wealth in the form of exotic commodities was beginning to flow from India to Lisbon, where Oriental freight was transshipped to Antwerp and other towns in Northern Europe. In 1504, for example, the first cargo of Eastern goods for England came from Lisbon to Falmouth. It was not long before Venice and Egypt began to feel the effect of the Cape route, and the Republic early dispatched envoys to Cairo to engage the sultan of Egypt to take measures for the protection of their mutual interests. With Oriental guile the sultan first tried his hand at blackmail, and he threatened to destroy the Holy Places in Jerusalem, unless the Portuguese abandon their Indian voyages. To this end, Frei Mauro, prior of the Monastery of St. Catherine on Mount Sinai, was sent to Rome, to plead with the pope. When King Manuel heard of this mission, it only strengthened his resolve; and by the time the prior had progressed from Rome to Lisbon, Manuel had already sent out Francisco de Almeida as Viceroy of India, at the head of a large fleet.

This appointment of a high-ranking nobleman to viceregal status was another very definite step in Portuguese domination, and it proved a sound choice, as Almeida was an excellent man for so responsible an office. Perceiving clearly the necessity of conquering the Moslem strongholds, he captured and fortified the hostile ports of East Africa — Sofala, Kilwa, and Mombasa on his way out (1505), and Mozambique two years later. That he did his work well is evident from the survival after four and a half centuries of the original fort built by his able underling, Pedro d'Anaya, at Sofala; at Kilwa he constructed a fort "so strong that it would keep even the King of France at bay"; and the ever-hostile town of Mombasa he was compelled to sack and destroy. His son, Lourenço Almeida, led an expedition to Quilon, near Cape Comorin, which he bombarded in retaliation for the murder of a Portuguese factor. After that high-handed act Lourenço sailed on to Ceylon and was the first of his race to visit an island which Portugal was to dominate for the next hundred and fifty years.

It is easy to follow the steady march of Portuguese imperialism in the decade after da Gama's initial landing at Calicut. Those who suffered from the consistent and relentless policy of expansion saw that the hour of resistance would soon be too late; that a counter-blow, if launched at all, must be launched immediately. With the collusion and support of the Venetians, the sultan of Egypt decided to fight, and in 1507 he equipped a large fleet, manned by a motley crew of Levantines, Turks, and Arabs, which sailed for the Indian coast to annihilate the European infidels. A confused and indecisive action took place in March 1508, off Chaul, in which Lourenço Almeida lost his life, gallantly fighting his few ships against heavy odds. Not only the reputation of the Portuguese but their very existence in the Orient depended on a decisive victory, and the elder Almeida set out to inflict a terrible punishment on the Islamic forces. With all the ships he could muster, he sailed north from Cochin, burning Goa and Dabul and destroying every Moslem ship he encountered. Off Diu, in February 1509, he finally sighted the Egyptian fleet, strengthened by a hundred vessels; and, like Nelson undaunted by the terrific odds against him, Almeida attacked boldly and completely destroyed the Mohammedan navy. This victory was nothing if not final, and for many years to come the Indian Ocean was completely under Portuguese domination.

In view of these immense services, Almeida's end seems little short of tragic. He returned in triumph to Cochin, only to find Albuquerque there with a commission to supplant him (Albuquerque's rank being governor of India, not viceroy). For a few months the elder held out against the claims of his rival, but in November 1509 he was compelled to yield, and sailed for home shortly thereafter — only to be killed in a skirmish with the Hottentots when his ship touched at the Cape.

Yet if Almeida was cast in the heroic mold, even more so was Albuquerque; once again the choice of a leader was justified. Albuquerque had returned to the East in 1506 along with Tristão da Cunha, on an expedition which coasted Madagascar and then, in alliance with the king of Malindi, waged war on the coastal towns of southern Somaliland. After subduing these places and also the Arab towns on the Oman Coast, Albuquerque sailed to Ormuz (September 1507), which he captured and held for several months, simultaneously with da Cunha's occupation of Socotra. Circumstances prevented Albuquerque from keeping Ormuz: he reluctantly abandoned it and continued his way to Cochin. When he first revealed his commission as Almeida's successor, he was cast into prison, but as soon as the unlucky viceroy had sailed for Portugal, Albuquerque speedily showed the energy and determination of his character. Moslem sea power had been crushed by Almeida's victory, but Albuquerque saw that Portuguese ascendancy had to be secured with land bases as well — if only a few key strongpoints, strategically situated, which would enable a small but determined European nation to control the vast perimeter of the Indian Ocean. Four such points would suffice; one in the east, two in the west, and one in the center. With the foresight of a genius Albuquerque selected Malacca, Ormuz, Aden, and Goa as the four pillars to support the far-flung empire of Lusitania. Goa, hitherto a secondary port midway up the Malabar Coast, was his first objective; he stormed and occupied it in February 1510; only to be driven out three months later by sixty thousand fanatical Moslems. In November of the same year Albuquerque was back with a larger armament, and overcoming desperate resistance, he recaptured the city and put the Mohammedans to the sword. Henceforth this was to be his capital, and the great monument to his governorship. It was the first territorial possession of Portugal in the East, intended from the first to be a colony and a naval base, in contrast with the fortified factories previously established at Cochin and Cananor. Goa was indeed the keystone of the arch formed by the perimeter of the Indian Ocean. Its situation and its trade gave it a century of prosperous, romantic, and dissipated brilliance; and even after the passage of nearly half a millennium it remains Portugal's principal colony in the Orient.

Malacca was Albuquerque's next objective. Situated on the west coast of the Malay Peninsula, at a point where the Straits between the mainland and Sumatra are at their narrowest, Malacca was a settlement of prime importance in the Moslem commercial system, since it was the port not only for China but for the whole of the East Indies as well. Most of the spices so greatly in demand in Europe were transshipped there; its geographical position made it at once the eastern anchor of whatever power might dominate the Indian Ocean and the gateway to the Spice Islands besides. A fleet under Diogo Lopes de Sequeira had visited Malacca in 1509, but had been thwarted in plans of trade and exploration by a treacherous plot of the Moslem merchants, which was fortunately revealed before harm could be done by a young officer named Fernão de Magalhães, or as we would call him, Ferdinand Magellan. Sequeira thereupon departed for Portugal, leaving a number of his countrymen as hostages in the hands of the local sultan. When Goa had been put in order as a Portuguese base, Albuquerque led a fleet to Malacca, and after two assaults (July–August, 1511) the place fell, and the Portuguese prisoners were released. A colony patterned along the lines of Goa was set up, and Malacca remained one of the most vital links in Portugal's Eastern economy until the Dutch finally captured it in 1641.

From Malacca, Albuquerque sent an expedition under Antonio de Abreu to explore the East Indies (1511–12). The expedition was of prime geographical importance, but unfortunately too little is known about it. Francisco Serrão was second-in-command, and Ferdinand Magellan was one of the officers. As far as is known, the fleet sailed along the eastern shore of Sumatra to the Straits of Sunda; surveyed the north coast of Java; gained some knowledge of Bali, Madura, Sumbawa, and Flores; and proceeded by way of Buru, Amboyna, and Ceram to the Banda Islands. Serrão was shipwrecked on the Lucipara islets near Banda, and was taken by native craft to Ternate in the Moluccas, where he remained several years, giving assistance to the native sultan in his wars against the rival ruler of nearby Tidore. Some of Serrão's companions are said to have made their way to Mindanao; if so, they were the first Europeans to reach the Philippines. Abreu's return followed much the same course as his outward passage, and it appears unlikely that he sighted either Celebes or Borneo. This expedition led to important results: when news of it reached Spain, King Ferdinand concluded that the islands lay within his sphere under the terms of the papal Bull of 1493 setting up the Line

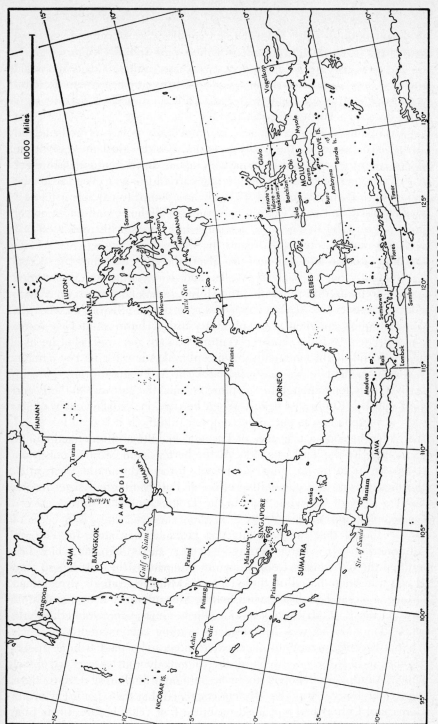

SOUTHEAST ASIA AND THE EAST INDIES

of Demarcation. Thus Magellan's circumnavigation was a direct consequence; while the Portuguese, on their part equally jealous to assert their claims, sent out a second fleet to Ternate (1514). This island during the next few years became the center of Portuguese activity in the entire archipelago; a regular traffic with Malacca was established, and the native ruler became a Portuguese vassal.

Meanwhile Albuquerque had continued his policy of consolidating Portuguese power in the Indian Ocean. Hostile Moslem vessels were swept from the seas, and such native craft as dared venture forth did so with Portuguese licences. Albuquerque carried the war even farther into the enemy's domains and in 1513 made an attempt to capture Aden. This was repulsed, but such was the governor's confidence and ambition that he sailed into the Red Sea. At this stage in his career his mind was filled with the most extravagant dreams; he thought of digging a canal from the Nile into the Red Sea, so as to divert the river and thus ruin Egypt; he thought, too, of sacking Mecca and carrying away Mohammed's coffin — to be used in ransoming the Holy Land. A fiery cross, seen by the Portuguese over the African coast, was regarded as a favorable omen, but Albuquerque's common sense plus pressure of business at Goa caused him to return to India, and the venture was not renewed. Had he lived, he would no doubt eventually have captured Aden, for its key situation was soon evident to his masterful intellect. As events fell out, however, he lived only long enough to recapture Ormuz, the gateway to the Persian Gulf and the Euphrates valley. When he died in 1515 his chain of strategic strongpoints was not quite complete, although it is only fair to add that Aden became a tributary of Portugal in 1524 and remained so until its capture by the Turks in 1538. At the hero's death Moslem power was so beaten as to be no longer a menace, for many years at least; rather the menace was the cumulative effect of Portugal's small size, the now familiar story of the white man in the Tropics, and the overextension of the colonial empire.

Yet for all that the next hundred years held in store for Portugal, Albuquerque left a noble heritage gained with the heroism which fully entitled the old warrior to be known to posterity as the Portuguese Mars. It was a heritage based on three factors. First, the strategic strongpoints; Ormuz, Goa, and Malacca; with Sofala, Mozambique, Kilwa, and Mombasa on the East African coast, and Diu in Gujarat to bolster the Portuguese dominion, as well as subsidiary trading centers under their protection. Second, suzerainty over native rulers, who paid tribute to King Manuel and his successors. Third, the colonization of the territory of Goa, which Albuquerque hoped to make into a little Portugal beyond the seas. Gone forever was the Moslem commercial system against which da Gama and Cabral had run head on but a few years before; in its place was the Portuguese Empire. A truly magnificent achievement for a remote nation of probably less than two million inhabitants, situated on the southwestern extremity of Europe!

This, the first European supremacy in the Orient, was fundamentally the work of Albuquerque and the greatest monument to his genius. Portugal had produced great men in those days — Dias, da Gama, Cabral, Pacheco, Almeida — but the master of the lot was Albuquerque. His name is still the greatest, not only in the history of Portugal in the East, but in all the long annals of the Indian Ocean. After his death, we feel a sense of anticlimax; it is even more a breath of the past to read of da Gama's return to India as viceroy in 1524. But the conquest was now over and there was less history to make. Portugal consolidated her gains and reaped her reward — the wealth of the Indies. Decline did come, but it came slowly and is hardly noticeable until mid-century.

Around the whole perimeter of the Indian Ocean, Portuguese seamen and traders carried the banner of Christendom. Albuquerque's successor as governor of India, Lopo Soares de Albergaria, conducted an abortive and costly campaign up the Red Sea in 1516, being turned back by various circumstances at Jidda. He followed this two years later by a more fortunate expedition to Ceylon, during which he surveyed the coasts of the island and founded a fort at Colombo. Simultaneously the Coromandel Coast was explored and settlements made at Mailapur (1517) and Pulicat, near Madras (about 1522). Further north, the coasts of the Bay of Bengal seem to have been relatively neglected by the Portuguese, possibly because they had little to offer, but a certain João Coelho visited the Ganges Delta about 1516. Three years later the Portuguese opened trade with the Kingdom of Pegu, and shortly thereafter João da Silveira led a party north along the shore to Akyab and Chittagong, "the City of Bengalla." Thus the entire eastern half of the Indian Ocean as far as Malacca became revealed; and even beyond, for in 1511 and the following year a mission under Antonio de Miranda and Duarte Coelho had made its way to Siam.

China remained to be reached: China, known from the writings of Marco Polo and the missionaries of two centuries before. Chinese merchants were conspicuous figures in Malacca, and their awkward-looking junks had been noticed (and laughed at) by Portuguese mariners ever since Sequeira's visit in 1509. In this sense the opening of intercourse with China can hardly be called a discovery — it was rather the culmination of a hundred years of voyaging by men whose romantic moods must have conjured up visions of far Cathay. It was therefore but a question of time after the capture of Malacca for the initial Portuguese venture to make contact with the Celestial Empire. To Jorge Alvares is due the distinction of being the first European since the fourteenth century to reach the ancient realm. At the end of 1513 he made a voyage which took him to Lintin Island at the mouth of the Canton River, but was not permitted to proceed to the city itself. Two years later one Raphael Perestrello (who from his name may have been a relative of Columbus' wife) made his way to the Canton River in a native junk, together with some other Portuguese. On his return with a rich cargo, he bore the news that the Chinese were a good people, anxious to gain Portuguese friendship.

These tentative expeditions were followed by an official embassy, led by Fernão Peres de Andrade and Tomé Pires, which departed from Malacca in 1517. From the start the mission was hampered by Chinese procrastination and nonsensical formalities, and it was only after considerable altercation that the Portuguese reached Canton. Having at last received privileges of residence and trade, Andrade sent Tomé Pires overland to Peking for an audience with the emperor — an audience never granted, in spite of Pires' long journey. Andrade in Canton displayed much tact and skill in dealing with the Chinese and was able to take back a valuable cargo — only to have his work ruined by the bad behavior of his successor (his own brother, Simão) in the next expedition (1519–20), who so alienated the Chinese that the hard-won trading privileges were forfeited and the Portuguese were expelled in 1522. Poor Pires was imprisoned on his return to Canton and was kept in prison until his death years later. Not for four more decades were the Portuguese able to gain a permanent foothold in China; only in 1557 did they settle at Macao, which, immortalized as the residence of Camoens, still lives under the flag of Lusitania.

Temptation was strong, however, for conducting an illicit trade with a land as wealthy as China, and in 1542 three men, Antonio da Mota, Francisco Zeimoto, and Antonio Peixoto, sailed from Siam with a cargo for Chincheu. A typhoon of terrific intensity drove them far off their course, and after a fortnight their battered junk reached an unknown island, where the survivors were greeted by short, friendly, and intelligent men. Such were the fortuitous circumstances of the first European landing in Japan. This initial journey was soon followed by others, both for trade and missionary work, with the Jesuits fervently carrying the banner.

Persia was another of the classical Oriental monarchies affected by Portuguese enterprise. The Persians, as we have pointed out, although Mohammedans, were Shiites and not the orthodox Sunnites; hence they were the natural enemies of the Arabs and Turks around them. Nor did Persian and Portuguese interests often conflict as Arab and Portuguese interests had done. Albuquerque, who wished to have Persia as a powerful ally, sent a mission under Miguel Ferreira in 1513 to the Court of Shah Ismail. This embassy was received by the Sophy at Shiraz and later crossed the country northward to Tabriz. After its return in 1515 a second envoy was sent to the Shah, one Fernão Gomes de Lemos, who made his way to Isfahan, to be badly received by the ruler, angered because of the capture of Ormuz. Nevertheless, relations between Persia and Portugal were on the whole amicable throughout the sixteenth century, and Portuguese traders and priests came and went freely in the Shah's dominions. A particularly distinguished journey was that of Antonio Tenreiro, who crossed the whole of Persia from Ormuz to Tabriz, and in 1528, having worked back to Basra, made his way up the Euphrates valley to the Mediterranean — the first of his nation to do so.

FOUR FAMOUS WANDERERS

With the opening up of Persia, China, and Japan, Portuguese enterprise had reached its full flowering. Portugal was destined to enjoy three quarters of a century more of monopoly, if not of prosperity, in the East; but the picture becomes increasingly static as the epic years between Vasco da Gama's first voyage and the death of Albuquerque recede into the background. There were occasional recurrences of the old heroism, primarily in the gallant defenses of Diu and Malacca against the Moslems, and in the defense of Goa itself (1570). Moreover, much interesting travel continued to be done. Four men made especially notable wanderings: João de Castro, Francis Xavier, Fernão Mendes Pinto, and Luis de Camoens.

Mention of the sieges of Diu instantly brings to mind the name of Portugal's universal Renaissance genius and Admirable Crichton — Dom João de Castro. Soldier, sailor, scientist, humanist, man of letters, this brilliant aristocrat excelled in every field in which he entered; and during the course of his life he entered most of them. As a colonial administrator he ranks second only to Albuquerque; as a general he became one of Portugal's greatest heroes; as a navigator, a hydrographer, and a skilled observer of terrain he remained unsurpassed up to the time of Barents and John Davis. He embodied sixteenth century greatness and versatility, even to the same extent as did Sir Walter Raleigh and Sir Philip Sidney.

From the time in 1518 when as a youth he ran away from home in order to fight in Morocco, he displayed a swaggering Renaissance determination to live dangerously. His military service took him to North Africa on no less than six campaigns, as he tells us; later he turned sailor and cruised against the famous Moslem corsair Khair ed-Din Barbarossa in 1535, when the Christian fleet captured Tunis. After that he returned to Portugal, a man entering middle age with a comfortable home and a growing family. This period with his books and his children did not last long, for in 1538 his brother-in-law, Garcia de Noronha, was appointed viceroy of India, and de Castro seized the opportunity of accompanying the ruler, evidently with a somewhat unofficial roving commission.

The outward voyage in 1538 gave Dom João a chance to indulge his gifts as a geographer. As a voyage it was uneventful — a fortnight's call at Mozambique was the only episode of note, but the experience of the long passage resulted in the first of de Castro's three *Roteiros*. The *Roteiro de Lisboa a Goa*, a useful pilots' handbook, is filled with all sorts of observations and with much of the awe and wonder of the half-year's voyage over the watery wastes.

De Castro reached India at an exciting time. A powerful Turkish fleet, sent out by Sulieman the Magnificent, had just begun the investment of the fortress of Diu on the coast of Gujarat, thus constituting a major threat to the whole position of the Portuguese in the Orient. The new viceroy and his brother-in-law soon found themselves equipping a relief expedition; but as matters fell out this was not needed, for the small Portuguese garrison of Diu defended the fort with such heroism that the Turks raised the seige after two months. Noronha's fleet nevertheless sailed for Diu after the siege was over, in order to reëquip the fort. De Castro was aboard, and the cruise gave him an excellent chance to indulge his enthusiasm for the scenery of the Indian coast. It resulted in his *Roteiro de Goa a Diu*, a book which in appreciation of the tropical landscape rivals Columbus' *Journal*. The author tells us that to get his information he dived below the ship, climbed hills, followed the creeks around the swampy shores, and scrambled up headlands overgrown by jungle. He visited Dabul, Chaul, Bombay, and Bassein, and on the island of Elephanta indulged a humanist's passion for archaeology. From Diu he returned to Goa, then made an important mission to Calicut; but for the bulk of 1540 he was relatively inactive. On the last day of that year, he embarked on the most daring of his voyages, a voyage up the whole length of the Red Sea to Suez. This venture involved an enormous risk: the Red Sea was an unconquered Moslem preserve (no Portuguese fleet had ever sailed beyond Jidda, where Lopo Soares had gone in 1516); and if a Christian fleet should fail to pass the Straits of Bab-el-Mandeb before the monsoon turned, it would be benighted with no hope of deliverance. De Castro and Estevão da Gama sailed the whole length of the sea, until they were within gunshot of the Turkish fleet in Suez harbor. The presence of many soldiers made them decide against a landing, but they had the satisfaction of being aboard the first Portuguese fleet to penetrate the inner sanctum of Islam's defenses. It was also on this voyage that the expeditionary force under Cristovão da Gama was landed at Massawa, to help the Abyssinian monarchy in its struggle against the Mohammedans. On the basis of the voyage de Castro wrote the third and greatest of his *Roteiros*, the *Roteiro de Goa ate Soez*, which is not merely a

superb coast pilot but also a wonderfully vivid record of a hazardous
venture.

In 1542 de Castro returned to Portugal. After further service against
the Moslem pirates and a brief year of home life, he went back to India
in 1545 as governor, to arrive shortly before the event with which his
name will always be associated — the second siege of Diu. Invested by
the armies of the King of Cambay in April 1546, Diu was stoutly defended
by a heroic garrison under João Mascarenhas. Governor de Castro forthwith sent his two sons to take part in the defense: one was slain, the
other became a heroic defender. Meanwhile Dom João had prepared a
large armament; in November seven months after the siege began, he
landed at the hard-pressed fortress with reinforcements. A week later
he led the devoted garrison in a furious attack that completely defeated
the Moslems and broke up the siege. Now followed the best known
episode in de Castro's career: the enemy had been vanquished, but the
condition of Diu was deplorable. Money had to be raised for the emergency, and the governor, having no other resources, managed to negotiate
a loan with the merchants of Goa with his beard as security! Equally
typical of the Renaissance was his triumphal, if ostentatious, return to
Goa, an event appropriately commemorated in the magnificent series of
tapestries now preserved in the Kunsthistorisches Museum in Vienna.
This was indeed de Castro's hour of triumph. A further spell of campaigning up and down the coast was too much for Dom João and in a little
over a year after his return from Diu the great hero had been named
viceroy and was dead. Yet he had lived long enough to deliver Portuguese
India from a mortal threat, and enabled it thereby to enjoy another generation or more of relative security.

De Castro's most devoted friend in his later days was an even greater
traveler, St. Francis Xavier. The Apostle of the Indies was sent out to
the Orient by Ignatius Loyola in 1541; sailing from Lisbon in the spring
of that year, he wintered at Mozambique, and reached Goa the following
May. He then journeyed southward to the Fishery Coast of Travancore,
where he labored for fifteen months among the heathen pearl-divers,
founding, it is said, no less than forty-five Christian settlements. This
feat is all the more remarkable inasmuch as Francis by his own confession
was a poor linguist, who, when interpreters were lacking, was obliged to
fall back on sign language. After a brief return to Goa, he was off on his
missionary travels again, visiting Ceylon and the shrine of St. Thomas at
Madras, and then crossing to Malacca in the late summer of 1545. From
the latter place he wrote to the Portuguese sovereign, urging him to set
up the Inquisition in Goa — a suggestion which was eventually followed
and which was ultimately to have serious repercussions in Portuguese
influence in the Indies. St. Francis sailed eastward from Malacca and

spent a year and a half in the Spice Islands, during which time he visited Amboyna, the Moluccas, and other places in the Malay Archipelago. Then he went back to Goa, where he comforted the dying de Castro, and again to Malacca, where he met a Japanese exile, who fired him with zeal for the conversion of Japan. With this companion, originally named Yajiro and baptized Paul of the Holy Faith, he sailed to Japan in 1549, reaching Kagoshima in mid-August of that year. He remained in the land of Nippon until 1551, suffering during that period great privations: one winter he was forced to make a two months' journey on foot to Kyoto in order to see the emperor, a walking-trip which turned out to be entirely futile. He did, however, eventually receive permission to preach Christianity, and was able to make hundreds of converts before his departure.

In February 1552 the dauntless missionary was back in Goa with his head full of schemes about converting the Chinese. He persuaded the viceroy, Afonso de Noronha, to send an embassy to China, in whose train he might enter, despite the law which then excluded foreigners from the Celestial Empire. The mission was duly dispatched, but fell to pieces at Malacca because of friction between the envoy and the local governor. St. Francis was obliged to proceed independently, and sailing in a Portuguese craft by way of Singapore, he eventually reached St. John's Island below the mouth of the Canton River, which, before the acquisition of Macao, served as the port for Europeans, not then admitted to the Chinese mainland. Doubtless he hoped to proceed from this point in an unofficial if not clandestine manner, but he was stricken with fever before he was able to realize his ambition of reaching the Chinese seaboard and died December 2, 1552. So perished one of the greatest of travelers; one who had the real traveler's ability of getting on in the friendliest fashion with the rough sailors and pirates with whom he was thrown. Although his aim was Christianity rather than geography, he nevertheless covered the Portuguese Indies and the lands beyond them as few men have done before or since.

In sharp contrast with the saintly Francis Xavier was Fernão Mendes Pinto, who was probably the greatest adventurer in Portuguese history. In the course of twenty-one years he traveled, fought, and traded all the way from East Africa to Japan, being several times shipwrecked, thirteen times a captive, and seventeen times sold into slavery. His bouyant and courageous spirit — as well as an iron constitution — brought him through every peril, and he lived to return to Portugal to write a wonderful account of his fabulous adventures.

Born near Coimbra in 1509, Pinto sailed for the East in 1537 in the fleet of Pedro da Gama, one of the numerous sons of old Vasco. Once he reached Goa, he was not long in taking up his highly interesting career of soldier and sailor, merchant and doctor, missionary and ambassador.

His earlier travels took him to Abyssinia, or at least as far as the Ethiopian coast, while subsequent adventures brought him as a prisoner to southern Arabia and Ormuz. Eventually regaining Goa a free man, he became a soldier and went off to Malacca, in the service of the governor of that place. From there he visited Sumatra, and had a hair-raising escape at Kedah on the Malay Peninsula. During this period he fell in with a privateering merchant named Antonio de Faria, with whom he set off on a commercial venture up the Gulf of Siam. They were robbed off Ligor, half way up the Malay Peninsula, and won a desperate battle against Lascar pirates off Patani. But in the pursuit of the pirate leader, Koja Achem, Pinto, and Faria tended to become more and more piratical themselves, and what had started as a merchant voyage degenerated into a buccaneering cruise.

Nevertheless, this voyage of Pinto's resulted in opening up Indo-China to Europeans; he and his companions went to Pulo Condore, an island off the mouths of the Mekong River, then sailed to the mainland of Cambodia, where they learned of the great mineral riches of the land. They coasted to Turan, the center of the overland trade to China by way of the Mekong; Pinto also visited the great island of Hainan. Still with Faria and his adventurers, Mendes Pinto then sailed to Ning-Po in China, defeating Koja Achem and sacking a seaport named Nouday on the way. At Ning-Po the Portuguese heard of an island called Calempluy, where seventeen Chinese monarchs had been buried in tombs containing great treasure. Pinto and Faria, nothing loath, sailed across to the island and plundered the place, but they had the misfortune to be wrecked in the Gulf of Nanking on their return, so that their reception on the Chinese mainland was by no means favorable. Pinto and his fellows were ducked in a pond full of leeches, given a series of floggings, and sent to Peking in chains. Still Pinto was able to observe his surroundings and give an animated account of the two great cities, Nanking and Peking, as well as a vivid picture of the colorful life along the rivers and canals that he traversed. After an interlude among the Tatars, he gained his freedom and made his way to Japan but a short while after the first Portuguese had reached it. Among other things, he is said to have performed the curious service of introducing the musket into that country.

Pinto's return from Japan was adventurous even by his own exacting standards. He was shipwrecked on the Lu-chu Islands, enslaved in Burma, shipwrecked again off Cambodia, and involved in an exciting campaign in Siam. A second visit to Japan was followed by his meeting with Francis Xavier in Malacca in 1547. The swashbuckling adventurer came so much under the spell of the great missionary that he resolved to enter the Jesuit order and devote the not inconsiderable money he had gained in the East to the evangelization of Japan. He became a novice in the order but eventually left it, possibly because it was alleged that he was partially of Jewish extraction, although a more likely reason was that he was temperamentally unsuited for a monastic life. Nevertheless, the viceroy sent him on an official mission to Japan in 1554, with Father Belchior Nunes; his embassy there is said to have represented a notable service for Christianity and civilization. In 1557 he returned with Nunes to Goa, and the next year sailed home to Portugal, where the story of his travels made him famous. His celebrated book, however, was long suspected of being made up of fictions, and the author became scornfully known as Mendax Pinto, but in the light of present-day knowledge of the East, he is on the whole vindicated as having been a careful observer and a truthful narrator.

The wanderings of Portugal's greatest poet were as picturesque as those of the adventurous Mendes Pinto. Luis de Camoens left his native land in disgrace in March 1553, a common soldier condemned to five years' service in the Indies. On the long voyage out he began to form the idea of the *Lusiads*; in fact, at least two of the cantos appear to have been composed before he reached Goa. His stay at Goa was brief; for the closing months of 1553 saw him on an expedition to the Malabar Coast. The next year he participated in a campaign along the shores of Arabia to suppress piracy; after reaching the Red Sea the fleet cruised to Ormuz and Basra, taking prizes, and as usual inspiring the Muse in Camoens: "in one hand the sword, in the other the pen." In 1555 he was off on another pirate chase, and after six weary months off Cape Guardafui, he paid a visit to Mombasa before he returned to Goa. Partly because of a satire he wrote on the viceroy and partly because of the call of military duty, he left Goa in 1556 for an extensive period in the East Indies. There he fought and wrote poetry for two years, visiting, Ternate, Banda, and Amboyna. In 1558 he took part in the military occupation of Macao in China, and although by now his five years' enlistment was over, he stayed on many months, writing the bulk of the *Lusiads* in the grotto which still bears his name. When he did set out for India, it was under arrest for an intrigue, but his ship was wrecked off the Mekong in Indo-China, and the poet saved his life and his precious manuscript by swimming ashore, holding the pages of his poem above his head. After wandering naked about the Cambodian coast he somehow got to Malacca, and from there finally reached Goa, still a prisoner, in June 1561.

His release from prison took place three months later, and for the next six years he led a life of pleasant and easy poverty in Goa, surrounded by a coterie of wits and littérateurs. At length in 1567 he accompanied Pedro Barreto, the newly appointed captain of Mozambique, to East Africa. He reasoned that this was on the way home, but he found himself so impoverished and so much in debt that he was forced to remain in Mozambique for two years, until some friends came to his rescue. He did not reach Lisbon, therefore, until April 1570, exactly seventeen years after his departure. His tribulations during this period had indeed been many, but they resulted in his giving mankind one of the noblest of epics — the *Lusiads*.

SOME REFLECTIONS ON THE DECLINE
OF THE PORTUGUESE EMPIRE

The decline of the Portuguese Empire was not as spectacular as its rise, but it is just as striking a phenomenon in history. It set in gradually: it was barely noticeable before 1550, and its progress was slow but of increasing intensity between then and 1600. After the latter date there could be not doubt about the decline whatsoever. No one cause was responsible for this decline, although there indeed was a major reason — Portugal's small size — and several minor reasons, which interacted with eventually calamitous results.

Chief of all the reasons for Portugal's decay in the East was the small size and small population of the home country, which led to a fatal over-extension of Portuguese manpower and resources. This was the fundamental cause of the infirmity of the realm that Albuquerque had established. Perhaps if the other causes had been inoperative, Portugal might have carried the white man's burden indefinitely; but with the other causes to aid the major one of overextension, the resulting decay was inevitable. This overextension is all too evident from the estimate that Portugal's home population dropped from almost two million to hardly more than one million in the course of the sixteenth century. Not only was Lisbon repeatedly devastated by plagues, but year after year the flower of the nation went to India as soldiers, sailors, and officials. Few of these ever lived to return to their native land, with the inevitable result that their loss was not replaced. Linschoten, the Dutch observer, reckoned that of those who went out to the East, not one in ten returned to Europe. To this must be added the dysgenic slaughter of the Portuguese nobility at Alcazar-Kebir in 1578. In short, Portugal was simply too small to support such a far-flung empire; and the nation that had sent out da Gama, Cabral, Almeida, and Albuquerque, one after the other, was eventually bled white. By the end of the sixteenth century she was having great difficulty in producing able men, or even tolerable leaders — though there were exceptions, of course. That this decline was hardly paralleled in Spanish America is doubtless because the sister kingdom had more than eight million people at the close of the sixteenth century and had the manpower to weather the strain.

Meanwhile a cause closely allied to Portuguese overextension was operating in India itself: the racial degeneration of the descendants of the conquerors. Very few Portuguese women settled in the East, and there was no strong color prejudice among the white men who had come out. Albuquerque's opportunist policy of intermarriage with the natives resulted in the creation of a half-caste population with the weaknesses of both races and few of their better qualities. When the grand generation of the original Portuguese had died out, their place was gradually filled with a half-native, half-European race. Even those Portuguese who refrained from interbreeding seemed all too often to undergo an unhappy metamorphosis, owing no doubt to climatic and environmental conditions. The effect of this degeneration is nowhere better seen than in the decline of Portuguese seamanship: because of the scarcity of manpower from home, ships were manned by unskilled half-castes; there was growing carelessness in buoyage and pilotage; and the number of shipwrecks as the century drew to its close threatened the very command of the Portuguese sea lanes to India.

Allied to the degeneration of the Portuguese race in the East was the widespread dishonesty and corruption throughout the colonial government. Officials from the viceroy downwards all too often took their jobs for the sole purpose of feathering their own nests, and most forms of what in our own days is known as "racketeering" were practiced on a large scale. There are only too many examples of nepotism, the farming of taxes, private speculation, and the like, which were all the easier to manage when the home government was months away, and a poor example was set by those in power.

Not only was the canker bureaucratic; it was ecclesiastical as well. It cannot be gainsaid that Goa, in its later days, grew into a theocracy. From the start of Portuguese dominion the conquerors had displayed remarkable obtuseness in the matter of native religions, and their intolerance was wholly alien to the traditional tolerance of the Hindus. The introduction of the Inquisition and the development of the government into an official proselytizing agency fostered an unfortunate degree of religious bigotry and ecclesiastical corruption, while the churches and religious houses of Portuguese India absorbed a very high proportion of the wealth of the colony. The Church as a church was an enormous power for good in the East, but it was a tragedy for all concerned when its secular aspects outgrew their proper functions.

Another very potent reason for the decline of the Portuguese empire in the Orient was the constant unrest of the native peoples, which sorely strained the Portuguese administration, and its resources in men and money. During the Renaissance period there was a strong recrudescence of Moslem power in southern and southeastern Asia, which was aggressively militant in character. Not only was the Mogul Empire established in north India, but the powerful realm of Vijayanagar in the Deccan fell to all-conquering Islam in 1565, by which all southern India came under

Moslem rule. Thus from de Castro's time there was continuous strife in India, accentuated by this growth of militant Mohammedanism in India and Malaya. Between the death of de Castro and the coming of the English, Malacca was besieged no less than six times, Colombo three times, Cananor and Chaul both twice, and Ormuz, Daman, and Goa itself each once — this in addition to the burden imposed on the Portuguese of conducting punitive expeditions against pirates on sea and against brigands on land. Portugal had indeed conquered an empire in the East, but she had to fight to keep it, even with her dwindling resources. The climax was reached in the years 1570–71 with the almost simultaneous sieges of Goa, Chaul, and Malacca, engineered by a powerful coalition of Eastern princes determined to extirpate the Portuguese from India. In each case the attacks failed, but at the same time Portugal's valor meant loss of Portugal's life-blood, and the toll was taken which sooner or later made itself felt. Portugal was unable to keep up the pace indefinitely; and as she grew weaker, her enemies multiplied.

Last, and perhaps most obvious among the causes of the decline, was Portugal's absorption by Spain. In 1578 King Sebastian fell before the Moors on the field of Alcazar-Kebir in Morocco, to be succeeded by the idiot Prince Henry, who died eighteen months later. Such was the tragic end of the great house of Avis, founded by John I of Portugal and the daughter of John of Gaunt. The Portuguese awoke one morning to find themselves the subjects of Philip of Spain. Now the outlook was changed: from a nation whose destiny had been in the East, Portugal was dragged into the maelstrom of European politics, and when at last she found herself a free and independent state (1640), the sceptre of the Indies had passed irrevocably to Holland and England.

Yet no sooner have these generalizations about Portugal's decline been made than they demand many qualifications, for no conclusion could be wider of the mark than to suppose that about the year 1600 the Portuguese Empire dissolved in fragments. The decline that set in after the days of João de Castro, was gradual and was punctuated by surprising instances of resilience; and it seems time to revise the theories of the traditional historians about the complete and comparatively sudden disintegration of Portuguese power in the East. For example, the threefold threat to Goa, Chaul, and Malacca in 1570–71 was met with a heroism and determination not exceeded in the sieges of Diu, under the skillful and courageous leadership of the Viceroy Luis de Ataide, a man worthy to rank beside Albuquerque and de Castro.

In 1606 the Portuguese beat off the Dutch in the desperate four months' siege of Malacca, and the following year they repelled the Dutch in the valiant two months' defense of Mozambique. At Macao, on midsummer's day of 1622, they handed out to the attacking Hollanders the most overwhelming defeat in the course of Dutch colonial history. Even in their naval defeats at the hands of the English (Captain Best's action, 1612, and Captain Downton's action, 1615), the Portuguese fought boldly and stubbornly, and as late as the 1630's they had as a viceroy the Conde de Linhares, an able administrator and a far-sighted statesman who would have been a credit to any government. In short, they were still to be reckoned with throughout the earlier part of the seventeenth century, while their trade, especially as middlemen in inter-Asiatic commerce, continued to bring in large returns. Nevertheless, Portugal's star was waning, and the capture of Ormuz by the English in 1622 destroyed one of Albuquerque's key points, on which the whole edifice of Portuguese power rested. This was followed by the martyrdom and expulsion of the Portuguese from Japan in 1638–1640, which put an end to the lucrative trade of Macao, and in 1641 the fall of Malacca to the Dutch robbed Portugal of another of Albuquerque's strong points. But the total eclipse of Portuguese power did not come until the decade 1656–65; in those years Bombay was ceded to the English, and Quilon, Cochin, and Cananor fell to the Dutch, as well as the strongholds in Ceylon and on the Coromandel Coast, and from that period only can it be said that Portugal no longer was a power in the Indian Ocean to be feared and respected. But the final tragedy of Portugal's decline must not make us lose sight of her supreme accomplishment in the creation of her Eastern Empire; that accomplishment is not alone Portugal's noblest heritage — it is the heritage of the human race.

Columbus' Santa Maria, *conceived as a caravel, in Alicante harbor. Built from the designs of Captain Julio Guillén, this realistic reproduction of a square-rigged caravel* (caravela redonda) *has the following dimensions: 120 tons; length from stem to stern, 84 feet; length of keel, 61 feet; beam, 25 feet; draught, 7 feet; height of mainmast, 92 feet. The early Portuguese caravels were of the same hull design but were usually lateen-rigged and without a bowsprit.*

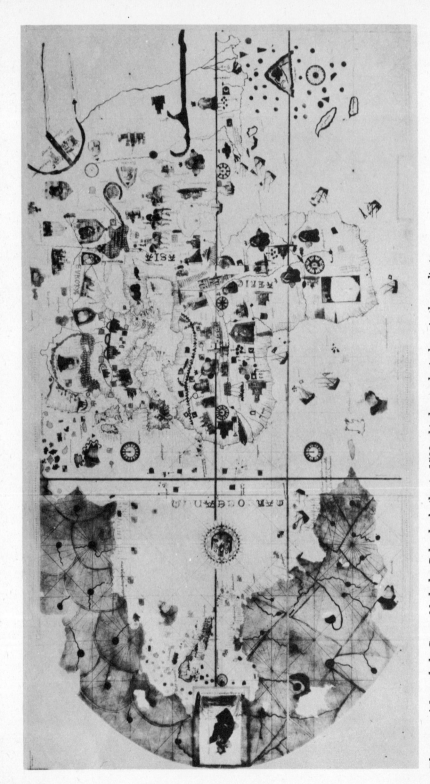

The map of Juan de la Cosa. Made by Columbus' pilot in 1500, this large planisphere is the earliest map known to portray the lands discovered by Columbus. The voyages of the Cabots and V. Y. Pinzon are also noted for the first time, as well as the arrival of da Gama in India.

CHAPTER

5

THE COLUMBIAN VOYAGES

*A*s the second half of the fifteenth century wore on, discovery was more and more in the air; the quest for the Indies inspired men throughout Europe, and Portugal's powerful neighbor entered the lists, to embark on a career of exploration and conquest which was destined to have even greater consequences in the stream of world history than the epic exploits of the Portuguese. Spain had hitherto taken little part in overseas expansion, but she was not wholly without nautical experience and had in fact at least a modicum of maritime tradition behind her. Those harbors between Gibraltar and the Portuguese frontier face the Barbary Coast and the Atlantic Islands; they look southwestward across what the early chroniclers called the Ocean Sea. A hardy seafaring population grew up in these parts of Andalusia, men who at first indulged in local coasting and fishing, later voyaged to the Canary Islands, and conducted a number of expeditions to Guinea, especially during the so-called War of the Castilian Succession (1475–1480). In this sense the first Columbian voyage was by no means a novel or an isolated venture, but rather a further achievement, stemming from the West African navigation of experienced and adventurous men, who were at home on the sea. Columbus therefore was not involving himself with a nation wholly amateurish when he sought to interest the Spanish crown in a trans-Atlantic course to China; he was on the contrary associating himself with a people who had fished and traded along the coasts between the Bay of Biscay and the Gulf of Guinea.

So it was that circumstances were fortuitous; Spain had sailors and, in Andalusia at least, some experience of the sea, while Columbus had a vision and intense enthusiasm. How long Columbus had the vision no one knows, but in 1474 the future discoverer, a young man of twenty-three still living in his native Genoa, began a very serious correspondence (once questioned, but now generally accepted as genuine) with Paolo Toscanelli about the possibility of reaching the Orient by a westward passage. Toscanelli was a celebrated Florentine scholar whose profession was medicine and whose hobby was geography; he admired Marco Polo in particular and accepted his theory that the Asiatic land mass extended much

farther to the eastward than even Ptolemy had argued. At the same time
Toscanelli held with the Ptolemaic measurement of the Earth, which gave
the circumference as eighteen thousand geographical miles. This resulted
in the figure of a mere five thousand miles between the Canaries and
Kinsay (Hangchow) — which Columbus, with hopeful enthusiasm, further
reduced to thirty-five hundred miles. Obviously then, Toscanelli would be
a hearty exponent of the western route to the Indies, and his conviction
was not lost on his young disciple, whose ideas, too, were fundamentally
Ptolemaic and who was strongly influenced by the *Imago Mundi* of Pierre
d'Ailly, to say nothing of Marco Polo and Sir John Mandeville. This curious medievalism in Columbus' thought was balanced by the practical
side of his nature, such as his superb skill as a navigator; but these two
sides of his character must always make him a problem for the psycholo-
gist and a puzzle for the historian.

To sum up, Columbus believed the world to be a sphere; he greatly
underestimated its size; and he overestimated the extent of the Asiatic
continent — concluding that the further Asia extended eastward, the
nearer it came to Spain. His plan, early determined on and adhered to
with unshakable tenacity, assumed that between the Azores and the eastern shores of Asia there were no lands to be discovered, and accordingly
that there was no other course except to cross the Atlantic Ocean by as
direct a route as possible. This perfectly reasonable forecast, and the
firmness with which he held to the plans based on it rank among the most
conspicuous indications of Columbus' greatness.

His experience as a sailor dated for the most part from his earlier years.
As a young Genoese he had gone on one or more trading voyages in the
Mediterranean, probably getting as far afield as the Greek Archipelago.
In 1476 he had embarked on an enterprise for England, but the fleet was
set upon by a hostile Franco-Portuguese armada off Lagos, and the future
discoverer of the New World made his landing in Portugal by swimming
ashore after his ship had gone down. Because of this accident he passed
into Portuguese service, and late in the same year he took part in a voyage to the British Isles and quite possibly to Iceland. (The latter venture
is by no means unlikely, inasmuch as there is known to have been a lively
trade between Iceland and such ports as Bristol and Galway in the later
Middle Ages.) The last of these early voyages, and the one which made
the most lasting impression on Columbus, was an expedition to Elmina
on the Guinea coast in 1482 or the following year, in which he obviously
served in a responsible capacity; moreover, sailing with skilled Portuguese
pilots down the West African coast must have greatly improved his seamanship. Another influence on Columbus' vision must have been his
residence during most of these years in Madeira and nearby Porto Santo,
he had gone to the islands about 1479 as a result of his marriage to Felipa

Perestrello, the sister of the captain of Porto Santo, and until his wife's death about five years later his headquarters were in the romantic archipelago which in effect pointed the way westward into the unknown.

After his African voyage Columbus gave himself entirely to "the enterprise of the Indies," and devoted the better part of a decade in studying the problem, in planning, and in attempting to secure the backing of a royal patron. To convince rulers of his mission in life was not easy; he first tried King John II of Portugal, but that sovereign thought him (according to Barros) "a big talker, and boastful in setting forth his accomplishments, and full of fancy and imagination with his Isle Cypango [Japan], than certain whereof he spoke." Yet John was fair enough to appoint a commission to examine Columbus' proposals, and it was largely because Columbus' price was so high that negotiations fell through. In 1485 Columbus went to Spain to lay his schemes before Ferdinand and Isabella; and to have more strings to his bow, he sent his brother Bartholomew to France and England in a vain attempt to interest Charles VIII and Henry VII in outfitting a westward expedition to Cathay. Columbus' dealings with the Spanish Court were unbelievably tedious and tantalizing. It was touch-and-go almost to the last minute, and only the loyal backing of the queen made Columbus' voyage possible. Thus Christopher Columbus, after five long years of dancing attendance at court as a poor suitor while the Royal Commission examined his project, was empowered by Queen Isabella to equip a fleet which was destined to revolutionize the course of history. Reasons for this delay are not far to seek; Spain was engaged in unifying herself and in expelling the Moors — it was, as Professor Morison says, as if a polar explorer had tried to interest Abraham Lincoln in the conquest of the Antarctic about the time of the Battle of Gettysburg. And yet in a larger sense, the conquest of America can be viewed as a continuation of the *reconquista* of Spain, as a fresh adventure of expanding dominion and crusading zeal — as well as of lucrative enterprise. To her everlasting credit, Queen Isabella viewed the project in this broader light.

Armed with the royal mandate, Columbus proceeded in the spring of 1492 to Palos, a small port on the Rio Tinto near Huelva, which was to be his base. This choice proved a happy one; Palos had an active part in the Guinea voyages, and its shipping was largely controlled by a family of shipowners and sea captains named Pinzon. Columbus won over the head of the family, Martin Alonso, to his project, and the latter, by engaging crews and procuring caravels, put the enterprise fairly on its feet. Three vessels were chartered for the voyage: the lateen-rigged *Niña* of approximately sixty tons; the square-rigged *Pinta* of about the same size; and the flagship *Santa Maria*, a square-rigger classed as a small ship or *nao*, rather than a caravel, and with perhaps twice the tonnage of either of her smaller consorts. On the *Santa Maria*, Columbus was captain, Juan de la Cosa (not to be confused with the cartographer of the same name) was master and owner, and Peralonso Niño was pilot; on the *Pinta*, Martin Alonso Pinzon was captain and Francisco Pinzon master; on the *Niña*, Vincente Yañez Pinzon was captain, and Juan Niño, pilot and owner. All these men were sailors of skill and experience, and at least two of them (Peralonso Niño and V. Y. Pinzon) later undertook important voyages on their own account.

At dawn on August 3, 1492, the little fleet left Palos on what was the most important single voyage on record. Columbus had hoped to reach the Canary Islands as his first port of call, but three days out the *Pinta's* rudder broke, and the other two vessels proceeded to Gomera alone, arriving on August 12. A delay of three weeks or more ensued, during which the missing *Pinta* was found at Las Palmas and her rudder repaired, and the lateen rig of the *Niña* was changed to a square rig. On September 6 the ships set out westward into the tractless wastes of the Atlantic. The weather was fine, the wind was favorable, and the morale was generally high. For perhaps half the voyage Columbus clung to the twenty-eighth parallel as if he were a tight-rope walker; after that he gradually made his southing. After a month of very fast sailing, signs of land became evident, and at two in the morning on October 12 Rodrigo da Triana, on lookout on the *Pinta's* forecastle, shouted "Tierra! Tierra!" — the New World had been sighted. This land turned out to be San Salvador or Watling's Island in the Bahamas, a coral island about thirteen miles long and six across, which had a picturesque and volatile native population. Columbus spent three days there, and then steered southward through the archipelago; he anchored at Rum Cay, explored Long Island, and spent four days at Crooked Island. From the friendly natives he learned of a rich and beautiful land to the south; hopeful that this was the land of the Grand Khan, he hastened southward and sighted the Cuban mountains on October 27. For the next five weeks or more he explored the northeastern coast of Cuba. His first anchorage was at Bahia Bariay; the following day he coasted westward to Puerto Padre, some forty miles, and then retraced his course as far as Puerto Gibara. At this anchorage he remained eleven days, even sending an embassy upcountry to find the Grand Khan. Futile as this mission was, his stay was not without one highly important result — it initiated Europeans into the craft and mystery of tobacco smoking. From Puerto Gibara the fleet coasted eastward and the admiral employed himself in taking various lunar and stellar observations.

All was not well in the discipline of the higher officers, however, and on November 22 Martin Alonzo Pinzon sailed away in the *Pinta* without even a by-your-leave from his commander. Columbus, thoroughly exas-

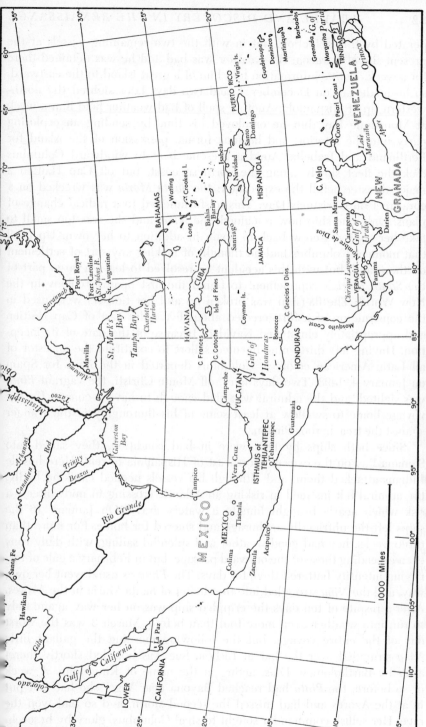

CENTRAL AMERICA AND THE WEST INDIES

perated by this defection, put in with the two remaining vessels at the present site of Baracoa; the weather was bad and he was detained there for a week. Native information told him of a great island to the eastward, so he made sail on December 4, and two days later sighted the northwestern tip of Hispaniola. Another spell of bad weather held him a week at Moustique Bay, but he employed his time by sending an exploring party into the interior, and he took formal possession of the island for Ferdinand and Isabella. Amid a tiresome beat to windward Columbus took the fleet slowly along the northern coast, but off Cap Haitien a major disaster befell the expedition: the *Santa Maria* was wrecked on a coral reef on Christmas Day. This misfortune led to a radical change of plans. Only one ship now remained, the *Niña*, and she was too small to take her consort's crew back to Spain in addition to her own. Up until that moment Columbus had no thought of making any sort of settlement on the island, but with this accident he resolved to leave a large part of the *Santa Maria's* complement to found the first Spanish colony in the New World. The flagship was broken up and her timbers were used in the construction of a fort, erected about five miles east of Cap Haitien and appropriately christened Navidad, because of the date of its inception. Having left thirty-nine devoted sailors to constitute the ancestor of all Latin American colonies, Columbus departed in the *Niña* for Spain on January 4, 1493. Two days later, off Monte Christi, the vagrant *Pinta* was sighted, and the admiral was glad enough to have a consort for the voyage home to swallow at least some of his thoroughly justified anger against the treacherous Pinzon.

Since both ships by now were in bad condition, they sailed into Samana Bay on the extreme northeast of Hispaniola to refit. Here hostile Indians attacked them, and although his vessels needed caulking badly, the admiral felt justified in risking an Atlantic crossing in midwinter — a risk which nearly brought him to a watery grave. On January 16 the ships left the unfriendly anchorage and steered for home. For more than three weeks they had good weather and splendid sailing, with daily runs even exceeding those of the outward passage, but in February a gale of terrifying intensity battered them for days. The *Pinta* as usual went her own way, and the *Niña* struggled into the shelter of Santa Maria in the Azores. After a respite of ten days the crippled ship was on her way again, only to run into weather even more foul than before. March 3 was the worst day of the entire voyage, but the following morning the gallant little *Niña* struggled over the bar at Lisbon. She was boarded shortly thereafter by Bartholomew Dias, acting in the name of King John. A week or so before, the *Pinta* had reached Bayona near Vigo; she had not put in at the Azores and had missed the second storm, and so had won the race. Her selfish commander sought to steal Columbus' glory by beseeching an audience with his sovereigns, but he rightfully received a complete snub. He sailed the *Pinta* down to his native Palos and died almost immediately, probably to the benefit of, all concerned.

So ended Columbus' crowning achievement; his three subsequent voyages seem anti-climatic in comparison, for his five weeks' passage from the Canaries to the Bahamas did indeed prove the turning point in man's slowly progressing knowledge of the globe. News of his wonderful — if misunderstood — discoveries was joyfully received in Spain. He had not found what he sought, but he was convinced that he had found it. But he had discovered regions whose tropical beauty and luxuriant fertility beggared description, and when in April 1493 Columbus, accompanied by a group of quaintly clad, red-skinned Indians, was received in Barcelona by the sovereigns of Aragon and Castile — to be named Admiral of the Ocean Sea and Viceroy of the Indies, with all the prerogatives and privileges set forth in the capitulation — that indeed was the most glorious moment of his career.

Elsewhere in Europe knowledge of Columbus' discovery spread quickly; his own account (the famous *Columbus Letter*) was published not only in Barcelona but in Rome, Paris, and Basel as well, and a petition was sent to Pope Alexander VI for a confirmation to the Spanish crown of the newly discovered islands, in order to obviate possible Portuguese claims. This led to the issuance of the famous Bull instituting a Line of Demarcation running from north to south a hundred leagues west of the Azores, to the west of which the Spaniards were authorized to explore, and to the east of which the Portuguese received the monopoly of discovery. This line was later adjusted to three hundred and seventy leagues west of the Cape Verde Islands, this being chosen as a half-way mark between the Azores and the newly discovered lands; thus it was that the bulge of Brazil was brought within the Portuguese sphere.

Columbus now had the wholehearted backing of the Spanish throne, and during his audience at Barcelona it was decided to equip and send out a second voyage as soon as possible. Whereas his first venture was undertaken with a handful of men in three ships small even by the modest standards of the time, the admiral now found himself in command of a mighty armada of seventeen ships, carrying fifteen hundred men — sailors, artisans, colonists, officials, and churchmen, who had flocked to his standard in the hope of sharing in the riches of the Indies. Many figures destined to fame enlisted to serve under him, such as Alonso de Ojeda, who became one of Columbus' most daring successors; Juan de la Cosa, chartmaker and explorer; Ponce de Leon, the discoverer of Florida; Diego Columbus, the admiral's younger brother; Dr. Diego Chanca, the surgeon of the expedition and also its historian. After Columbus' experience with insubordination on the First Voyage, the Pinzon family were passed over, but various of the faithful Niños appear as masters and pilots. In truth, it was the Grand Fleet.

On September 25, 1493, the imposing squadron sailed from Cadiz, calling at the Canaries for fresh supplies, and leaving Ferro for the main crossing on October 13. Fortune favored Columbus even more than it had the previous year; amid glorious weather a steady wind blew the fleet across the ocean in the remarkable time of three weeks. On November 3 the landfall was made at Dominica, after which the admiral steered northwestward, keeping just inside the beautiful Leeward Islands. A stop of six days was made at Guadeloupe, where a shore party was lost in the tropical jungles. The search for it, though ultimately successful, delayed the voyage. In consequence Columbus pushed on quickly, discovering the many lovely isles of the group and giving them names which in most cases have survived to this day. Anchorages were made at Nevis and Saint Croix, and the fleet put in for several days at the southwestern tip of Puerto Rico. They finally sighted Hispaniola and coasted its northern shore, but when they reached Navidad on November 27, they found that the entire colony had been wiped out by the Indians. The admiral then proposed a new site for the colony, and a place to the east of Monte Cristi was selected, as being near the reputed gold mines of an interior district called the Cibao. Here, about seventy miles from Navidad along the coast, the settlement of Isabela was founded in the opening days of 1494, named appropriately for the puissant sovereign whose patronage had made the discovery of a New World possible.

Having established this infant township and made a reconnaissance inland to the Cibao, Columbus set forth on what, without too much facetiousness, might be called the first West Indies cruise. With him were picked men and three small vessels suitable for inshore navigation, including his old favorite *Niña*. In late April the ships left Isabela, and after coasting the now-familiar shores of Hispaniola, steered for Cape Maisi, the eastern tip of Cuba. Columbus was still keenly on the trail of the Grand Khan and Prester John. His course lay close inshore along the ironbound south coast of Cuba, past Guantanamo and the site of Santiago to Cabo de Cruz at the western end. As he cruised along, he learned from natives of the existence of a rich and beautiful island to the south, so he stood away from Cuba and sighted the gorgeous coast line of Jamaica on May 5. His first port of call was St. Ann's Bay, which he was to know only too well in the period of his deepest distress years later. From there he proceeded westward as far as Montego Bay, thinking the land "the fairest island that eyes have beheld."

On May 13 he returned to Cabo de Cruz and then sailed to explore the whole southern coast of Cuba. As Columbus made his way among the archipelago of small islands which lies to the south of the Cuban mainland, his mind harked back to Sir John Mandeville, who had written that there were five thousand islands in the Indies, and the ever-elusive Orient seemed near at hand. Columbus, with poetic felicity, named these islands El Jardin de la Reina, or the Queen's Garden. His course led him to the western knob of Cuba near Cape Frances. This was his farthest point, and concluding that the land beyond was the Golden Chersonese, he set sail eastward. He coasted the Isle of Pines, beat to windward to Cabo de Cruz, then held his course a second time for Jamaica. From Montego Bay he proceeded counter-clockwise around the island, anchoring every night and trading with the natives who came alongside in their huge seagoing canoes. Sailing direct from Portland Bight to the Blue Mountains, he missed Kingston Harbor, and having cleared Morant Point, he steered for the south coast of Hispaniola. His course took him right around that island, past Cape San Rafael, past Las Flechas where he had harbored with Pinzon on the First Voyage, to Isabela, which he reached the end of September, after an absence of five months.

Much had happened at the little frontier outpost since his departure; the history of Isabela during those months was one of sickness, death, scarcity, threatened mutiny — and endless trouble with the Indians. His youngest brother, Diego, and an incompetent wastrel named Margarit had been left in charge during his absence; they had been wretchedly unequal to the job and the colony was foundering. Columbus' middle brother, Bartholomew, had come out from Spain that summer; he was a strong man and an administrator of some ability, though given to cruelty. Still, his presence seemed to promise hope for better things. The following year a royal commission arrived, who assumed arrogant authority, and six months later Columbus — a weary and discouraged man — returned to Spain in the faithful Niña, leaving Bartholomew in charge. Bartholomew very wisely abandoned the ill-fated and unhappy settlement of Isabela, and transferred the colonists to a more propitious site on the south coast, which as Santo Domingo (or currently Ciudad Trujillo) remains today as the oldest town of European origin in the Western Hemisphere.

Before taking leave of the explorations during the period of Columbus' second visit to America, we might notice one narrative which is at least more circumstantial than hypothetical. There is plausible evidence from the celebrated Sneyd-Thacher Manuscript in the Library of Congress that five ships sailed southward from Hispaniola in the autumn of 1494 and fell in with the South American coast near Margarita, to follow it as far as Panama or beyond. The existence of this voyage has by no means met with universal acceptance, but if it did take place, that would mean that the American mainland was discovered four years earlier than the date usually assigned: August 1, 1498, on Columbus' Third Voyage.

Columbus' reception at court was all that could be expected; he brought with him an Indian king decorated with a heavy gold chain, and he announced that he had found Solomon's Ophir — and he received a generous welcome from his sovereigns, along with a fresh confirmation of privileges. But no eager crowd of volunteers flocked to his standard, for the enthusiasm of 1493 had vanished. For two years the wearied visionary struggled to get a new fleet together, and at last in the spring of 1498 (almost to a week of da Gama's arrival in Calicut) he sailed from San Lucar at the mouth of the Guadalquivir with only six ships. On the Third Voyage the fleet called first at Madeira before proceeding to the usual jumping-off point, the Canaries. From Gomera three vessels were dispatched direct to Hispaniola, and the admiral with the three that were left continued down the West African coast to the Cape Verde Islands. Columbus did this because he had been impressed by the opinion of the Portuguese king that a large land mass lay athwart the Equator, somewhere in the Western Ocean, and he therefore wanted to discover lands lying south of the Antilles. In charting a course for this venture, Columbus anticipated the rule-of-thumb navigation of West Indian skippers of a later date: "South till the butter melts, and then due west."

His outward crossing, however, was the poorest so far. He encountered many calms and blistering hot weather, and it was not until the last day of July that his lookouts sighted the triple peaks of Trinidad. Columbus' intuition was justified, for he had found the southern land mass, as the low shores of Venezuela hove in view off the port bow. His course took him through the Serpent's Mouth into the Gulf of Paria; he spent some days in exploring the Paria Peninsula, which he claimed for Spain, and then leaving by the Dragon's Mouth, he sailed past Margarita to Hispaniola. From the great volume of water flowing from the mouths of the Orinoco, he rightly concluded that the land must be of continental dimensions, since no island could have such a watershed. But even here his perverse medievalism destroyed his rationalization, for he was convinced that the Orinoco flowed from the Terrestrial Paradise. This curious presumption he reached by holding that the earth was in fact not a true sphere, but was slightly pear-shaped; that a projection like the stem of a pear rose toward Heaven at the Equator, and that the Earthly Paradise lay at the top of this projection. From this premise he argued that he had reached the End of the East. Be that as it may, Columbus' discovery of Venezuela and Trinidad was a substantial one, but it was to be the only geographical contribution of the third voyage.

Affairs in Hispaniola were in a parlous state when he arrived, for even his brother Bartholomew had failed to govern the mutinous and starving colonists, who when not fighting the Indians had been fighting each other. Such bad accounts indeed had filtered across the ocean that the king and queen had sent out a commissioner named Bobadilla, who in October

1500 packed off all three Columbus brothers to Spain — in chains. Although Columbus had failed as a colonial administrator and had consequently lost popularity throughout Spain, he never wholly forfeited the confidence of his sovereigns — Queen Isabella in particular — who realized his uncanny skill as a navigator and his ability as a discoverer. The queen therefore released him from his chains and consented to send him out on another venture, to be devoted to exploration, and thus one for which the admiral was perfectly suited. This final voyage is notable in the annals of discovery; as Columbus had been the first to reach the Antilles in 1492 and the Spanish Main in 1498, so was he now the first to explore the coastal region of Central America — and he was also the first to come into contact with the remarkable Indian civilization of the Mexican periphery.

In the spring of 1502 Columbus sailed from Seville with four fair-sized caravels, and after putting in at Arzilla on the Moroccan coast to relieve a Portuguese garrison besieged by the Moors, he continued his course to the Canaries. His ocean crossing was the best he ever made: twenty-one days from Grand Canary to Martinique, which was sighted (and discovered) on June 15. A run down the chain of the Leeward Islands brought his ships to Santo Domingo by the end of the month, where, however, he was forbidden to land by the governor. There was a large fleet in the harbor of Santo Domingo, ready to sail for Spain. Columbus, with his uncanny flair as a navigator, had an almost psychic hunch that a hurricane was in the making and sought to persuade the leaders to put off their departure. But these men, who had no love for the admiral, refused to listen to his advice, and shortly after their departure Columbus had the cold satisfaction of learning that most of the fleet, including his old enemy Bobadilla, had gone to the bottom. Columbus rode out the storm off Santo Domingo; it was a terror but his ships survived, and under the circumstances he was allowed by the governor to repair his damaged vessels. It would seem that at this time he met some of the crews of Rodrigo de Bastidas' expedition, just returned from a cruise along the Spanish Main as far as the Isthmus of Panama, and their information must have enlightened him considerably about the lands to the south.

He left Santo Domingo in mid-July, passed Jamaica to the south, and steered by the Cayman Islands to Honduras. At the island of Bonacca off the Honduras coast he encountered a great canoe laden with merchandise; its well-built cabin was filled with people dressed in dyed cotton, who had weapons and domestic utensils of copper. They said they had brought these things from the west, that is, Yucatan. Here was Columbus within sight of the culture of the Mayas and the Aztecs, but instead of being drawn westward by these evidences of wealth and ingenuity, he persevered in his original intention of following the land in the other direction. Ironically, therefore, this was to be his only glimpse of the wonders which awaited his successors.

Perhaps he later regretted his decision; at all events his passage along the northern shoulder of Honduras must have been a soul-destroying piece of navigation — beating to windward in the teeth of a never-ending rainy gale and making good a run of less than two hundred miles in a month. Only the admiral's iron determination to seek a strait to nearby India and China kept the fleet going throughout this ordeal. Once around the cape, thankfully named Gracias a Dios by the admiral, the expedition had better going, and after coasting along Nicaragua, Columbus put in for a few days at the present site of Puerto Limon, Costa Rica, to give his exhausted crews a well-earned rest. The fleet next explored the Chiriqui Lagoon, ever hopeful that it would be a short-cut to the tantalizingly elusive Orient. They then coasted Veragua, where some gold was found and evidences of more gold, and pushed on amid wet and tempestuous weather past the future site of Nombre de Dios. Still, the land seemed unrewarding and the Indians hostile, so the admiral decided to return to the gold mines of Veragua. They spent Christmas at what is now the entrance of the Panama Canal, and early in January 1503 Columbus selected a site for a settlement at Belem, about fifty miles to the west. Rather more than three months sufficed to mark the rise and fall of this colony; the natives were furiously hostile; they ambushed and massacred to a man a party sent to fill the water-casks, and on another occasion Bartholomew Columbus, the governor of the new settlement, was severely wounded. After much danger and suffering, as well as anxious delay owing to stormy weather on the surf-beaten coast, the survivors were taken on board and the enterprise was abandoned.

The expedition was by no means out of danger, as the ships had been cruising for a year under the hardest possible usage, so that the crews were literally "at sea in a sieve." Two of the four ships were abandoned on the Central American coast and the remaining two were actually falling apart; yet there was nothing for Columbus to do but struggle back to Hispaniola. At length, having got as far as the northern coast of Jamaica, it became evident that the ships could not stay afloat more than a few hours longer. The admiral ran the two vessels ashore at St. Ann's Bay, which had been his first anchorage in the island nine years previously. Here Columbus was fated to be marooned for an entire year and to face a full-scale mutiny, while one of his devoted followers, Diego Mendez, paddled a canoe all the way to Hispaniola for help. At last, in June 1504, help arrived, and Columbus and his surviving seamen were delivered from their island prison. Well might the gallant Mendez, in his dying days, direct that a canoe be carved on his tombstone!

Broken in body and spirit, Columbus reached Spain for the last time shortly before the death of his great patron, Queen Isabella (November 24, 1504). Although he was only in his mid-fifties, his exertions, mental and physical, had aged and exhausted him before his time. In May 1506, while the court was at Valladolid, he died there — the greatest of all discoverers, but probably convinced to the last that the lands he had discovered were Asiatic. Although in his later years he had been treated with injustice and unfairly deprived of his rights, he was by no means indigent, as he received a fair share of the royal dues from the West Indian revenues. His sons, Diego and Fernando, were educated as pages at court, and Diego was destined to become not only admiral and viceroy but also to marry a relative of the king.

Of the rights of which Columbus was deprived, none galled him more than a royal decree of 1495 which permitted any subject to obtain (albeit under strict conditions) a licence for western exploration. Although he protested vigorously against this, his protests had no effect; at least five expeditions sailed for America at the turn of the century, all of which were to make considerable contributions to geographical knowledge. Ruge appropriately refers to their leaders as "die kleinen Entdecker."

In the spring of 1499 two of Columbus' former officers, Alonso de Ojeda and Juan de la Cosa — from whose map we learn much of the discoveries of the Columbian period — sailed on a course intended to reveal the coast below the farthest point of Columbus' Third Voyage. They fell in with the South American mainland near Surinam, and after exploring the shores of Guiana and Venezuela ("the queer little Venice") they continued westward as far as the Gulf of Maracaibo, enlivening their passage with piracies and kidnapings. One of their captains, a Florentine named Amerigo Vespucci, seems to have had a roving commission; there is evidence that he left the rest of the fleet, visited the mouth of the Amazon, and continued eastward toward Cape São Roque before doubling back to follow the course of his commander.

Columbus' Third Voyage had revealed the presence of pearl fisheries in the Gulf of Paria and near-by waters; this undoubtedly explains the reason why these five voyages of Columbus' followers took place in the short order they did. It was like the Klondike gold-rush. Close in Ojeda's track, sailed Peralonso Niño, who had piloted the *Niña* on the First Voyage, in company with Cristobal Guerra. They arrived off the coast of Paria a few days after Ojeda had left it, and proceeding westward to the island of Margarita, loaded their small craft with a valuable cargo and arrived in Spain in April 1500 "so laden with pearls that they were in a manner with every mariner as common as chaff."

If Niño's venture had been a brilliant financial success, the next voyage was to be as great a commercial failure, although its geographical significance is greater. This expedition, led by the Vincente Yañez Pinzon who had captained the *Niña* on the First Voyage, sailed from Palos with four vessels toward the end of 1499. Pinzon's course was very southerly, and he fell in with the Brazilian coast about where Pernambuco now stands. Then, reversing his course, he rounded the bulge of Brazil, and cruised along the coast, exploring the Amazon Delta and sailing through the Gulf of Paria to the pearl fisheries. Bad luck was in store for him, however; for he lost all he had risked on the venture and led back to Spain but a few exhausted survivors of tempest and shipwreck. Yet inasmuch as Vespucci's cruise along the northern shoulder of Brazil is at best open to question, to Pinzon must go the palm of having discovered both Brazil and the Amazon and of having revealed the coast from about 8° S. This is not to discredit Cabral's discovery; Pinzon reached Brazil in February, Cabral in April. Word of the latter's landfall was transmitted immediately to Europe, while news of Pinzon's was brought by him on his return in September — and the land which Cabral had found was about six hundred miles below Pinzon's farthest south.

A lesser known expedition is that of Diego de Lepe, who left Palos shortly after Pinzon and pushed still farther south along the Brazilian coast, before retracing his course to the Gulf of Paria. To the loss of posterity there is little record of this voyage, for a full account of it would probably fill several gaps in our knowledge.

The last of these post-Columbian voyages was undertaken in October 1500 by Rodrigo de Bastidas, a notary of Seville, in company with Juan de la Cosa. They sailed from Cadiz to Venezuela and proceeded to explore the coast to the westward very thoroughly. Stopping frequently to trade with the natives, they passed Cabo de la Vela and explored the mouths of the Magdalena River, the harbor of Cartagena, and the Gulf of Darien. However, they were unsuccessful in their search for a strait to the west, and after sailing along the coast of Panama as far as Nombre de Dios, they started back for Hispaniola. The ships by this time were so badly wormed that Bastidos lost them both near Santo Domingo, but his men carried away enough treasure to make the voyage most profitable. They reached Santo Domingo on foot as Columbus' fleet arrived there, outward bound on the Fourth Voyage.

In little more than a decade, therefore, the four Columbian and five post-Columbian voyages had revealed the coast line continuously from Honduras to Pernambuco and even beyond, and every island in the West Indies of any importance, except Barbados, had been discovered. Not all the captains and navigators who sailed these seas in the early days could have possessed the warped Medievalism of Columbus; and many, more critical than he, must have realized that these lands were not Asiatic but were part of a New World. However, it remained for

Amerigo Vespucci to go on record as saying so. After Ojeda's expedition Vespucci passed into Portuguese service, and in 1501 he was sent on a voyage to extend Cabral's discoveries of the preceding year. This mission took him down the Brazilian coast from Cape São Roque; it is said that he reached the mouth of the River Plate, and may have continued down even as far as Patagonia. It was this voyage, as well as his earlier venture with Ojeda, that caused the geographer and humanist Martin Waldseemüller to regard him as the true discoverer of the Western Hemisphere, and so prompted that scholar to bestow on our continents the name AMERICA.

The natural sequel of the Columbian cycle of voyages was seen in the conquest, colonization, and consolidation of the Greater Antilles. For many years Hispaniola was not merely Spain's most important colony: it was Spain's *only* colony, and the settlement at Santo Domingo remained the political capital of Spanish America for half a century. During the early years of its existence as a colony Hispaniola went through stages of great hopes, great despair, and finally of moderate revival. Columbus had set out on the Second Voyage with a great following of enthusiastic colonists, hungry for gold, but these men were speedily disillusioned when cast loose in a savage wilderness. The dark days of the unfortunate settlement at Isabela mark the nadir of the enterprise. When Bartholomew Columbus moved the settlers to the new site at Santo Domingo, the way pointed to better prospects; but even for some years after matters were desperate.

Affairs began to pick up only in 1502, when the ruthless but able Nicholas de Ovando was sent out as governor; from then on a reoriented policy became evident, and the undisciplined horde of gold-seekers gradually settled down to the more prosaic occupation of agriculture. These years, too, witnessed the gradual extinction of the native population, thanks to the cruelty of the Spaniards as well as to the diseases which they introduced. From a humanitarian point of view this cannot be palliated, but economically it led to beneficial results; for the Indians had neither the stamina nor the willingness of the African slaves, who were soon imported in large quantities to take their place. Gold had proved a disappointment, but the settlers found two less spectacular sources of wealth — sugar and pigs. Sugar cane, introduced from Spain, flourished exceedingly, and the swine, brought over in 1493, increased enormously. Since bacon was a big element in provisioning ships and land expeditions as well, pig-farming became very profitable. Hispaniola therefore soon became a field for the industrious planter and stock-raiser, and the ambitious spirits in search of a golden fortune had to look elsewhere for their conquests. Along the forest path from Santo Domingo to the North Coast four or five tiny villages sprang up, and the Cibao district soon attracted farmers. The capital itself became a cathedral see and the seat of a colorful little court.

This maturing of colonial policy became evident in Spain itself. A Colonial Office was taking shape, to be formed afterwards into the famous Council of the Indies; and the Casa de Contratación (or Department of Commerce), to deal with trans-Atlantic trade, was established in Seville in 1502.

Second in importance to Hispaniola was Cuba, which was circumnavigated and explored with a view to settlement by Sebastian de Ocampo in 1508. Three years later Diego Velasquez and Panfilo de Narvaez landed at Baracoa, near the eastern tip of the island, and began the task of conquest — a task completed in 1514, thanks to the dashing raids of Narvaez on the hostile natives, as well as to the statesmanlike qualities of Velasquez in consolidating what had been won. Shortly thereafter most of the principal settlements of the island were founded: Havana, Santiago (the early capital), Puerto Principe, Sancti Spiritus, and Trinidad, while legends of wealth drew many immigrants to the island. Cuba had got off to a good start.

Not so Puerto Rico, inhabited by savage Indians, and settled by equally savage Spaniards. Ponce de Leon first explored the island in 1508, and was made temporary governor the following year, at which time his companions established the settlement of Caparra, near the present-day San Juan. Later Ponce was superseded, but he waged a minor civil war against his successor, and put down an Indian rising with such revolting cruelty that the native population was almost wiped out. San Juan was founded in 1520 to supplant unhealthy Caparra as the capital, and an episcopal see was established; but the island remained under-populated, badly administered, and given over to lawlessness.

Jamaica, the fourth of the Greater Antilles, had the least theatrical and least important early history. An expedition under Juan de Esquivel sailed in 1509 to occupy the island; they had comparatively little difficulty in overcoming the aboriginal inhabitants. No gold was found, although Esquivel saw the great possibilities of cattle raising, and established several big ranches, which flourished in the plains suited to the industry. The original settlement was made on the north shore, but in 1534 Santiago de la Vega (the present Spanish Town) was founded as being healthier and more convenient for shipping. Jamaica, however, never attracted a large Spanish population, and little attention was paid to intensive planting.

With the settlement of the Antilles, the first chapter of the history of Europeans in the New World comes to an end, and a second phase, even more spectacular, begins — the conquest of the native empires of the mainland.

6

THE CONQUISTADORES

In a sense the Columbian cycle of voyages comprises an almost self-sufficient phase in the history of exploration. After Columbus' Fourth Voyage, there was a pause of several years in the progress of discovery, during which the Greater Antilles were exploited and settled, but during which no effort was made to penetrate the mainland of Central and South America. By the end of the first decade of the new century, however, the logical sequel of the development of the Islands reveals itself, and Spanish enterprise embarked on a second phase even grander, and more heroic than the first — the conquest of the barbaric empires of the New World. This period lasted almost until mid-century and may be divided into four stages: the conquest of the Central American Isthmus, 1509–1519; the conquest of Mexico, 1517–1525; the conquest of Peru, 1530–1548; and the conquest of New Granada, 1535–1539. It might be argued that the conquests belong more to history than to geography; actually the men who undertook them were primarily conquerors and only incidentally explorers, yet many thousands of square miles of territory were for the first time traversed by Europeans, and man's knowledge of the globe was immeasurably increased by the wanderings of these unprincipled adventurers.

The men who performed these mighty feats have become known to us as the Conquistadores, and they indeed embodied much of the best and much of the worst of which the human soul is capable. Their courage was peerless, their cruelty revolting; their endurance was heroic, their lust for riches despicable; their devotion to their leaders was often the personification of fidelity, but the treachery of the leaders to one another was often beneath contempt. As John Fiske well put it: "The Spanish adventurers in America need all the allowances that charity can make for them." Another historian of the conquests, Sir Arthur Helps, asks the reader to picture to himself "what his own nature might have become, if he formed one of such a band toiling in a fierce new clime, enduring miseries unimagined by him before, gradually giving up all civilised ways, growing more and more indifferent to the destruction of life — the life of animals, of his adversaries, of his companions, even his own —

retaining the adroitness and sagacity of man and becoming fell, reckless, and rapacious as the fiercest brute of the forest." Yet for all this, one cannot withhold admiration from these little bands of Renaissance Spaniards, whose dauntless courage enabled them to overthrow mighty kingdoms defended by huge armies. Truly the conquistadores were men of superlative extremes.

THE CONQUEST OF THE CENTRAL AMERICAN ISTHMUS

Spanish enterprise on the mainland began in 1509. In that year the crown granted two licences: one to settle the Isthmus of Panama and lands to the westward and the other to settle what is now the north coast of Colombia. Diego de Nicuesa commanded the Panamanian enterprise, but it turned out to be a miserable failure; in a few months nine-tenths of the settlers were dead, and the colony was abandoned. Alonso de Ojeda, the veteran of many voyages, was the leader of the Colombian venture, with the cartographer Juan de la Cosa as his second-in-command. This expedition left Hispaniola in November 1509 and seemed destined to share the same miserable fate as Nicuesa's.

Landing at the present site of Cartagena, Ojeda and his men had a bitter fight with the Indians, in which la Cosa and many others were struck by poisoned arrows and died raving. Ojeda thereupon sailed westward and made a settlement on the Gulf of Uraba, a move which hardly promised better things. The company diminished daily through hunger or poisoned arrows. Ojeda himself was wounded, but survived to sail to Hispaniola for help; however he did not return to the struggling colony. In his absence a brave but unprincipled soldier took charge, one Francisco Pizarro, who was able to hold the settlement together until Ojeda's official successor, Martin Fernandez de Enciso, at length arrived with welcome reinforcements and provisions. Enciso was hardly a man for so difficult a task as commanding a company of starving and desperate adventurers in a savage country; he had been a lawyer in Hispaniola and was of an impractical, mild, and studious nature. Fortuitously enough, his fleet had brought along a stowaway, one Vasco Nuñez de Balboa, a man who had sailed with Bastidas along the Spanish Main years before, but who at this juncture was forced to flee his creditors at Santo Domingo. Balboa proved to be the one man who could save the colony and quickly rose to be its unofficial leader. His first act was to move the colony to a site on the western side of the Gulf of Uraba, where there was food but no poisoned arrows, and by general consent Balboa became alcalde of the newly founded "city" of Darien. His next act was to get rid of Enciso, who was deposed and packed off to Spain, there to tell his story at court, much to Balboa's ultimate detriment. None the less Enciso deserves to be noted; he was a man of learning and an accomplished cosmographer, whose *Suma de Geographia* (Seville, 1519) is not only a cornerstone in the history of navigational literature, but the earliest printed American coast pilot as well.

Balboa, now in complete command and reinforced by the survivors of Nicuesa's colony, proceeded to make his settlement a reasonably successful one. His were the natural qualities of a leader: he was ever in the forefront in toil and danger, he was scrupulously fair in the division of spoil, and he was considerate and thoughtful in the care of his men. Toward the Indians he could be — and sometimes was — cruel, but never unnecessarily so; he used forced as a last resort and preferred to depend on conciliation and diplomacy. On all counts he was the best of the conquistadores. In addition to putting the colony on its feet, he ranged the coast in his ships as far as Nicuesa's abandoned post at Nombre de Dios, and made incursions inland in search of food, gold, and slaves. In this way he learned that Central America was an isthmus, beyond which lay the great South Sea, a piece of intelligence that led to his famous discovery.

His expedition to the Pacific Coast probably crossed the River Chuqunaque to the Gulf of San Miguel, many miles to the east of the present canal; where, according to Indian information, the isthmus was narrowest. Balboa had with him a large party of Indians and Spaniards, including Francisco Pizarro; they fought their way through swamps and tropical jungles and over broken hilly country, twice forcing their passage through ranks of hostile Indians. As they neared the last summit on September 25, 1513, Balboa advanced alone, and from the height looked down on another ocean spread before him. Thus he solved the main secret of the new lands. This event, just twenty-one years after Columbus' First Voyage, is the second great landmark in American discovery. Indeed, Balboa rightly regarded it as such, for his actions upon making the discovery were ceremonious and ritualistic to a degree. He waded into the water clad in armor and with drawn sword, and standing breast-deep he raised aloft the banner of Castile. More practical was a brief venture on the broad waters of the Pacific in frail canoes, which led to the discovery of a rich pearl fishery: this with the acquisition of some gold on his journey made his venture a profitable one.

Beside the subsequent triumphs in Mexico and Peru, the conquest of the Central American Isthmus must seem rather tame; only the fact that it was the first campaign on the mainland, coupled with Balboa's discovery of the Pacific, puts it in competition with the accomplishments of Cortes and Pizarro. There were no large native kingdoms, nor was there an advanced native culture; the Spaniards merely encountered tribal life in tropical jungles. Nevertheless Balboa's administration presaged the state of things to come, and the early history of Spanish America cannot be written without mention of the deeds of a hard-pressed band of settlers in the Isthmian region in the period between the arrivals of Columbus and Cortes.

Even as Balboa had accomplished his great discovery, trouble was brewing for him in Spain. Enciso had told his story of Balboa's usurpation, and the king had sent out a new governor, Pedro Arias de Avila, better known as Pedrarias; he sailed in 1514, with Enciso and Oviedo y Valdes, who became one of the great historians of the Spanish discoveries. Pedrarias was a hard, cruel man, who observed the letter of the law but ignored its spirit. Balboa was not wholly deprived of power; he was made Adelantado of the South Sea and of the provinces bordering on it. But it was inevitable that there would be trouble between Balboa and Pedrarias. For two or even three years there was harmony at least on the surface, but Balboa was revolted by Pedrarias' needless cruelty to the Indians, and discouraged by the conviction that his work was being undone by the brutality and ruthlessness of the new governor. During this period Balboa was intent on continuing his work of exploring the lands bordering on the South Sea, and to this end he conveyed materials across the Ithmus to construct vessels. Four ships were almost completed when Balboa was arrested by Pedrarias' orders, taken across the Isthmus, and executed. This cruel act was one of the greatest calamities that could have happened to South America, for the discoverer of the Mar del Sur had developed from a mere adventurer into a statesman, and had he lived, a humane and judicious man would probably have been the conqueror of Peru instead of the savage and ignorant Pizarro.

As for Pedrarias, he continued to pursue his ruthless course. When the terrible old man died in 1530, after sixteen years of tyrannical rule, he had been, according to Oviedo, responsible for the death and enslavement of two million Indians. However, the name of Pedrarias merits remembering on less sinister grounds, since he extended his sway to Nicaragua, and since in 1519 he founded the city of Panama, the oldest existing European settlement on the American mainland. From that day to this, the highway across the Isthmus — whether mule-track or canal — has been one of the most important thoroughfares in the world.

THE CONQUEST OF MEXICO

For the first quarter-century after the discovery of the New World the economic results were frankly disappointing. Some pearls had been found, it is true, and some gold as well; but the compensation did not in any way balance the expenditure in men and money on the part of the mother country, and successive colonies tended to revert to a very unromantic agrarian economy. Fortune was soon to be kinder, and as always was to favor the brave. The twenty-fifth anniversary of Columbus' landfall saw Spain on the threshold of conquests which would bring in wealth undreamed of even by the Hapsburgs.

In the northern part of the Central American mainland flourished the wealthy and powerful state of the Aztecs, a warlike but able people who had succeeded to the barbaric civilization of their kinsmen the Toltecs, when they migrated to the Valley of Mexico about two centuries before the coming of the Spaniards. In the island marshes of Lake Tezcuco the Aztecs in 1325 erected their impregnable capital of Tenochtitlan, from which, through their superior military organization and political capacity, they were able to extend their control across Mexico from sea to sea. At the time of Montezuma's reign Tenochtitlan was a city of some sixty thousand householders, and the Aztec Empire comprised perhaps five millions of subjects. The government was centralized, with an elective monarch, and a very close-knit and powerful priesthood, which developed one of the most extensive systems of human sacrifice that ever existed. In the arts and sciences, the Aztecs had attained a considerable degree of development in engineering, architecture, mathematics, and astronomy. Their buildings were of stone, mortar, and stucco; their agriculture was well advanced; and they had a body of tradition, history, and poetry which was transmitted both orally and through picture writing. But their methods of governing were stern and cruel; many of the subject peoples were restive under their domination, while in the mountains to the east of Lake Tezcuco there existed the independent republic of Tlaxcala, which regarded the Aztecs with implacable hatred. It followed that these conditions created a situation very favorable to Cortes and his Conquistadores. Nevertheless the Aztec Empire was at the height of its power in the early sixteenth century, and its able and intelligent ruler, Montezuma, lived in the midst of a barbaric pageantry that dazzled the conquerors.

We have seen how Columbus had a fleeting glimpse of Mexican civilization when he overtook the boatload of Mayans off the Honduras coast on the Fourth Voyage, and Balboa and Pedrarias must certainly have heard tales of the fabulous empire "up north." Yet these rumors remained travelers' tales for many years, largely waiting on the development of the colony of Cuba, which needed to grow to sizable proportions before it could become a base for so vast a project as the conquest of a mighty realm.

All the Spanish conquests began with preliminary reconnaissances, and the conquest of Mexico was no exception. Determination to solve the riddle of the rumors of a wealthy empire was largely due to the vitality and drive of the governor of Cuba, Diego Velasquez, who in 1517 dispatched Francisco Fernandez de Cordoba on a westward journey of discovery. This voyage no sooner scratched the surface than it met with disaster. Cordoba reached Yucatan at its northeastern corner and probably coasted as far as Campeche; he and his men found people in dyed cotton clothing cultivating cornfields, and they saw monstrous idols and a towering city of masonry so wonderful that they christened it Grand Cairo. But the natives were everywhere bitterly hostile, and after several battles Cordoba returned to Cuba to die of his wounds. A few battered survivors of his crews returned with him.

This reverse only whetted Velasquez's appetite. The next year he sent out another expedition, three times as large, commanded by his cousin, Juan de Grijalva. This venture was indeed memorable; Grijalva reached Yucatan near Cape Catoche and sailed southward into the Gulf of Honduras. Then, retracing his course, he rounded the Yucatan peninsula, and made the discovery of Mexico itself. Grijalva was cautious and prudent; he had read the lesson of Cordoba's failure too well to try any excursions inland, and he took great care to avoid hostilities. Even then he had a bloody skirmish at Campeche, in which thirteen Spaniards were killed, but elsewhere on his long coasting voyage his caution and diplomatic mein won him a friendly reception. His course extended as far as Tampico, and he returned to Cuba with tales of the Aztec Empire, whose ruler Montezuma lived in a great city in a mountain lake — with tales also of Mexican picture writing, and of the runners, who brought word of the white men to Montezuma even while Grijalva's vessels were still off the coast — and best of all with tales of gold.

Grijalva was too cautious and too obedient to his instructions to satisfy the aggressive Velasquez, who expected much more than a mere coasting voyage; so a third expedition was prepared. Its command fell to Hernando Cortes, who had come to Cuba as Velasquez's secretary; a man distinguished among the Conquistadores for being a university man (he had attended Salamanca), and no less distinguished for his numerous affairs of gallantry, which brought him on one occasion to prison and on another to unintended matrimony. Yet he was to show himself neither a scholar nor a Casanova, but as a fearless, ruthless, determined, and insubordinate man of action. Velasquez, perhaps too late, realized this strain in Cortes' character and revoked the appointment, but Cortes had the intuition to anticipate him, and sailed from Santiago to western Cuba before the governor could act. Cortes was temporarily at least beyond the governor's reach, and along the coast he proceeded to gather recruits and collect stores, for which he could not pay. Whatever his other failings, Cortes must have been an inspiring leader, for he quickly gathered around him as devoted a gang of desperadoes as ever engaged in a desperate venture: Alvarado, Olid, Sandoval, Bernal Diaz, and even the governor's own nephew, Diego de Velasquez, later to be slain during the retreat from Tenochtitlan on the *Noche Triste.*

With this picturesque following, Cortes sailed in early 1519, before the irate Velasquez could lay hands on him. His course took him along the coast from Yucatan to Tobasco, where he landed and had a desperate battle with the natives — his first, but by no means his last. He then moved farther up the coast to a point which native information revealed as the harbor nearest to the Aztec capital. Landing there on Good Friday 1519, Cortes set up a municipality with all the high-sounding officials and elaborate organization of a Spanish town, and he christened the new-born metropolis Vera Cruz. Four months were spent there, during which Cortes consolidated his position, won the allegiance of the coastal regions, and planned his daring campaign upcountry. Then, with a profound touch of the dramatic, he had his ships burned and set off in mid-August with four hundred Spanish infantry to pit his strength against unknown odds. The march to Mexico took nearly three months, although the air-line distance is but two hundred miles. But savage tribes had to be vanquished and mountain passes negotiated. As the Spaniards ascended the barrier between the tropical shores of the Carribean and the lofty Valley of Mexico, they entered the territory of the Tlaxcalans, a warlike race, the traditional enemies of the Aztecs. Three times the great hordes of Tlaxcalans attacked the Spaniards, as often to be repulsed with great slaughter; then, and not until then, did the Tlaxcalans yield. In winning the peace Cortes gained a mighty ally, for the Tlaxcalan state became from then on a loyal friend of the Spanish vanquisher. Without their help Cortes could never have overthrown the empire of Montezuma.

After the Tlaxcalan campaign, Cortes pursued his way to Mexico City (Tenochtitlan), which he reached early in November. One of his soldiers, Bernal Diaz del Castillo, wrote of the Conquistadores' approach through the Valley of Mexico: "When we saw so many cities and villages built in the water and other great towns on dry land and that straight and level causeway going towards Mexico, we were amazed and said it was like the enchantments they tell of in the legend of Amadis, on account of the great towers and *cues* and buildings rising from the water, and all built of masonry. And some of our soldiers even asked whether the things we saw were not all a dream . . . I do not know how to describe it, seeing things as we did that had never been heard of or seen before, not even dreamed about. . . Gazing on such wonderful sights, we did not know what to say, or whether what appeared before us was real, for on one side, on the land, there were great cities, and in the lake ever so many more, and the lake itself was crowded with canoes . . . and in front of us stood the great City of Mexico, and we — we did not even number four hundred soldiers!"

Cortes and his men entered the city peaceably and amid much ceremony. But within a few days Cortes, by an arrant bit of treachery, had seized the person of Montezuma and held him in honorable, but none the less close, captivity among the Spanish soldiery. With the ruler in his possession, Cortes was able to amass a huge amount of gold and silver, and most of the winter was spent in collecting treasure from throughout the Aztec lands. With the spring (1520) came bad news from the coast; Velasquez had sent an expedition from Cuba under Panfilo de Narvaez to arrest Cortes as a traitor. Leaving a garrison under Pedro de Alvarado in Tenochtitlan, where the unfortunate Montezuma was still in custody, Cortes returned to the coast and decisively defeated Narvaez. Most of Narvaez's men thereupon joined Cortes' force, which immediately returned to the capital. Cortes found that things had taken a very serious turn in his absence; the whole populace was in rebellion against the Spaniards, provoked by the needless slaughter of some Aztec nobles during a ceremonial dance — a deed as tactless as it was cruel. In the hope of quieting the populace, Cortes made Montezuma show himself to his subjects, but when the ruler declared himself a friend of the Spaniards, one of the stones hurled by the angry mob struck his head, and the poor Montezuma, refusing any treatment, died of his wound as well as of a broken heart soon after.

This tragedy was a bitter blow to Cortes' plans, for as long as Montezuma lived, he was a powerful instrument in the Spaniards' hands. With his removal, there was but one course left for the isolated group of invaders in the hostile city: to get out as soon as possible. This was accomplished with tremendous losses in one of the most difficult operations in military annals: a night march over the western causeway to the mainland, during which the Spaniards and their Tlaxcalan allies were beset every foot by fanatical foes; a night so terrible that it has been known ever afterwards as the *Noche Triste* (June 30, 1520). Hopeful of annihilating the hated invader, the Aztecs pursued closely, but in the desperate Battle of Otumba the Spaniards defeated the natives and were able to get through to Tlaxcala. There, among a population of loyal friends, they spent many months regaining their strength.

The following spring (1521) the Spaniards advanced again on Mexico City, with fresh reinforcements and a large number of Tlaxcalan warriors. The resulting siege of the city of Mexico (May-August) was the triumphant climax of the conquest. The invaders by skillful use of locally constructed war vessels on the lake were able to overcome the heroic defense of the Aztec populace, and with the fall of the capital, organized resistance ceased throughout the land. Compared with the subsequent history of Peru, the Conquest of Mexico was speedy and complete; the conquerors' rule was harsh, and every vestige of the Aztec monarchy and religion was swept away; Spanish rule and Spanish institutions became all-powerful and universal. In the brutality and tyranny of the times, however, it is pleasant to recall that Cortes, in gratitude to his allies, never allowed a Tlaxcalan to be sold in slavery and persuaded Charles V to exempt them forever from tribute.

With the subjugation of the Aztec realm exploration and expansion followed a natural course. A great deal of Mexico had of necessity been revealed during the conquest; the terrain between Vera Cruz and the Valley of Mexico had been crossed and recrossed, and even Popocatepetl, Mexico's highest peak, had been scaled by a daring mountaineer in the first recorded American ascent. With the country now at his feet, Cortes was not slow to push his triumphs southward to Central America and westward to the Pacific. In 1523 he ordered his lieutenant Alvarado to Guatemala and that doughty warrior, proceeding overland through mountainous country, captured the native capital of Utitlan, and then founded the first city of Guatemala (1524). Simultaneously Cristobal de Olid was sent by sea with an expedition to Honduras to make a colony on the north coast. Olid, when left to his own devices, was not slow to disavow Cortes' authority, and Cortes felt obliged to chastise him. To this end Cortes led a party eastward across the base of the Yucatan peninsula — a daring march through unknown country, and one rendered all the more bizarre by the ostentatious way in which Cortes traveled, accompanied by musicians, jugglers, and captive kings. Olid had been slain before Cortes reached Honduras, and the rebellion quelled, but the expedition remained a very great achievement, in which Cortes' iron will and resourcefulness alone saved his men from perishing in the tropical jungles and among precipitous mountains.

This venture must rank as Cortes' only great blunder; he returned from Honduras broken in health (1526), to find that all was confusion in Mexico City. For the next few years, therefore, he was unable to give proper attention to exploration, especially since he returned to Spain for an extended visit. In 1533, he was able to turn his activity to the Pacific coast, and in that year he sent out a fleet which discovered Lower California. Accompanying a voyage in person in 1536, he founded the town of La Paz on the southeastern part of the peninsula. It remained for Francisco de Ulloa four years later to explore the Gulf of California completely; he sailed close inshore up one side and down the other, going to the head of the gulf. Ulloa followed the Pacific shore as far as 30 degrees North, convinced that the land was not an island, but a peninsula. These voyages were made possible by the development of the Pacific port of Acapulco, destined to play a major part during the next two centuries in the trade between New Spain and the Philippines.

Ulloa's expedition was the last undertaken at Cortes' direction, for the great captain left for Spain in 1540 to plead his interests with the Emperor Charles V. He died in 1547 near Seville, never again having set his eyes on the land of his glory. Yet the impetus which he had started continued, and after his departure much exploration was done from Mexico as a base. As these later journeys took place mostly to the north of the Rio Grande, they will be described in the section dealing with the discovery of North America.

THE CONQUEST OF PERU

Mexico was not the only barbaric monarchy of the New World, for an even richer domain lay far to the south, high up in the Andes. The Inca Empire, with its capital at Cuzco, extended at the time of the Conquest from Ecuador to northern Chile, and from the Pacific coast to the eastern slopes of the Andes. Its expansion had been especially rapid during the fourteenth and fifteenth centuries, and one of the greatest of the empire-builders, Huayna Capac, had actually lived until seven years before Pizarro's arrival. This empire, with a population of six to eight million, was governed on more humane lines than that of the Aztecs, and was in effect a most thoroughgoing and paternalistic socialism, in which each individual had his fixed place in society, and the state benignly provided for the welfare of the subject. Over all was the Inca, who in his own person embodied the supreme secular and priestly offices, as absolute ruler and as representative of the Sun Deity. Under the rule of this welfare state technics had reached a higher development than they had under the Aztecs; and in engineering, architecture, textiles, and ceramics, the Peruvians were ahead of their Mexican cousins, while the system of post and military roads, extending to all parts of the empire, commanded the admiration of the Spaniards. Although they had no writing, the Incas used a device called a *quipu*, a series or combination of strings and knots, by which ideas could be expressed and facts recorded. Politically the Incas appear to have been the most advanced of all the pre-Columbian peoples; they had also developed commerce and coastal navigation; and in gold-working they had reached a high degree of skill. For a scant handful of Spaniards to attempt the conquest of such a realm might seem an obvious impossibility, but fortuitously Pizarro arrived during a disputed succession for the office of Inca: old Huayna Capac had left two sons, one legitimate and one the offspring of a concubine, and a civil war for the throne was raging.

Rumors of this mysterious kingdom first reached the ears of the Spaniards in 1515, when Francisco Pizarro made a filibustering expedition from the Isthmus of Panama to the Pearl Islands; confirmation of these rumors came in 1522, when Pascual de Andagoya, an experienced captain, sailed from Panama to what is now the coast of Colombia. As an enterprise, the conquest of Peru promised to be far more difficult than that of Mexico; the remoteness of the Inca realm, its mountainous terrain, the

SOUTH AMERICA

intervening tropics, all combined to render the scheme terrifying to ordinary mortals. But the champion of its possibilities was no ordinary mortal. Francisco Pizarro, the bastard son of an Estramaduran squire, was a man of the greatest possible courage, determination, and physical strength — qualities which, in spite of his ruthlessness, his cruelty, and his selfishness, must command our admiration. Pizarro was convinced of the existence of a semi-civilized land of wealth amid the Andes, and he was convinced that he could conquer it. Never has man had greater faith in himself and in his ideas, and Pizarro's faith was justified by events, as well as by his own courage and brutality.

Pizarro was by this time an old veteran of the Panama colony who had served with Ojeda, Balboa, and Pedrarias; he had always been a capable officer, but he had yet to rise to the top. Among his colleagues were Diego Almagro, an illiterate adventurer who had attained some standing in Panama, and the priest Fernando de Luque, who served as schoolmaster of the cathedral. These three men formed a close partnership with a single aim — the conquest of Peru. In a sense they must have been like promoters of a wildcat mining scheme in our own day. Their proposition was a will o' the wisp in which they had implicit faith, but they had an uphill fight to convince their neighbors of the wealth which only awaited the taker. And it was veritably an uphill struggle, because the early reconnaissances were privately financed and privately organized, and the more that ill-success dogged Pizarro's footsteps, the harder it was to get men and money to go on with. Only the almost superhuman determination of this little band of brother adventurers enabled the enterprise to succeed.

Pizarro's first expedition, in 1524–25, was a complete failure. His small fleet beat its way against winds for a hundred leagues down the coast; he led his men inland through swamps and rain-soaked forests in search of food, only to be assaulted by hostile Indians. Crippled by seven wounds, Pizzaro somehow got his surviving companions back to the ships. Almagro had gone his own way with about the same luck and had lost an eye in a fight with the natives, an accident which by no means improved his naturally uncomely countenance. When the miserable adventurers returned to Panama, they had a sorry tale to tell, and they had spent all the money they had on the futile venture. Yet such was their faith in the project that they were anything but discouraged.

Somehow, by hook and by crook, they raised enough funds for a second attempt, and early in 1526, having with the greatest difficulty got together a hundred and sixty men and two ships, Pizarro and Almagro sailed from Panama for the Colombian coast. Pizarro, having landed to sack an Indian town, sent Almagro back for reinforcements, and dispatched the other vessel to the south, under her pilot, Bartolomé Ruiz. This skillful seaman, henceforth famous in the annals of discovery, did his work well; he touched at several places on the coast of Ecuador and crossed the Equator, finding everywhere increasing evidences of civilization. His return, therefore, was indeed welcome to Pizarro, who by this time had received Almagro's reinforcements which enabled the expedition to renew its southward course. But friction between the leaders and mutinous behaviour on the part of the men nearly finished the whole enterprise by the time they had reached the Island of Gallo, two degrees north of the Equator. Here among ceaseless tropical rain, swarms of mosquitoes, and acute shortage of food, Pizarro dramatically traced a line in the sand and bade all loyal volunteers to step across it. With the few faithful one who did, Pizarro crossed to the nearby island of Gorgona, where conditions were slightly better, and Almagro returned again to Panama for more reinforcements. For seven months Pizarro and his thirteen devoted followers endured starvation and tropical rain in Gorgona before Almagro appeared from the north; then with one ship and a handful of men the expedition was renewed. Guided by the skillful Ruiz they sailed straight for the Gulf of Guayaquil, and at last reached the Peruvian coast at the town of Tumbez. Here, amid signs of a very advanced culture, they had a good reception, and after a brief, satisfactory visit continued on to a point 9 degrees South. Everywhere they were struck by the solidity of the buildings, the arts of the people, and the reports of the wealth and power of the Inca; and when at length they returned to Panama, they indeed had glowing tales to tell of the riches of the strange lands they had visited.

Notwithstanding all this, Pizarro's magnificent reports got no hearing whatever in Panama, for the colonists there had been told these tales once too often and were decidedly skeptical in consequence. Pizarro, more determined than ever to see the matter through, proceeded to Spain, to lay his proposition before the Emperor Charles V. In the late summer of 1528 he appeared at Court at Toledo, where, largely because of Cortes' successful conquests, he received a favorable hearing. By the following summer (1529) a capitulation had been signed on the emperor's behalf. By this Pizarro was appointed governor of Peru for life, in return for which, according to Gomara, he "promised great wealth and kingdoms: in order to attract men, he announced more riches than he knew of, but less than the reality."

After leaving court, Pizarro found time to visit his native town of Trujillo in Estramadura, where he persuaded various brothers and other relations to join his enterprise. With these and other volunteers he returned to Panama, where he lorded it over Almagro in a manner which boded ill for future harmony. Finally toward the end of 1530 the expedition got under way and proceeded to a place called Coaque near the Equator, where rather unaccountably half a year was spent. Having received more men from Panama (which played the role in the conquest of

Peru that Cuba did in that of Mexico), Pizarro sailed to Tumbez and made his classic landing on Peruvian soil. Here more time is consumed while the town of San Miguel was founded. It was not until the early autumn of 1532 that Pizarro, at the head of sixty-two horse and one hundred and six infantry, began his daring and perilous march over the Andes. After many hardships in ascending the freezing heights, and in threading precipitous defiles, the little band at length reached the camp of the Inca Atahualpa at Cajamarca.

Pizarro's star was in the ascendant when he reached Cajamarca, and fortune was indeed kind to the Spaniards. In the civil war caused by the disputed succession between the legitimate Inca Huascar and his illegitimate brother Atahualpa, the latter had but recently overthrown Huascar's army and was ruling in uneasy state from Cajamarca, rather than from Cuzco, the traditional capital. Pizarro now proceeded to take a leaf out of Cortes' book and by a daring, unscrupulous act caused the person of the Inca to be seized. In the subsequent battle the natives were routed with great slaughter, and Pizarro was completely master of the situation. Later events continue the parallel with Cortes and Montezuma. Months were spent assembling the Inca treasure, while the captive monarch was kept in luxurious but very close confinement. When the unfortunate Atahualpa had served his purpose as a puppet, Pizarro had him strangled (August 29, 1533). After this treacherous and despicable crime, the Spaniards took their way along the wonderful Inca Road to Cuzco, which they entered in November.

So far Pizarro had had a much easier and much less bloody time of it than Cortes, but the establishment of his rule was to prove infinitely more difficult and time-consuming, for the civil wars of Peru began where the conquest had left off. News of Pizarro's triumphs traveled north on the wings of the wind, and even reached Guatemala, where Cortes' erstwhile lieutenant Pedro de Alvarado was brooding over his rather empty conquest. That worthy, entirely on his own initiative, set forth on an expedition down the Pacific to Ecuador and marched inland to conquer Quito. Almagro was sent north from Cuzco to head him off, and by joining forces with a rough soldier named Belalcazar, was able to frustrate Alvarado before Quito in 1534.

Many of Alvarado's men joined Almagro, and in 1535 this band was sent on an exploring mission to Chile, which lasted two years. This expedition, hopeful of finding another golden Peru, was an epic of hardship, endurance, and mortality, but was distinguished throughout by the splendid leadership of Almagro. Its route lay along the western shore of Lake Titicaca, across the highest and bleakest part of the Bolivian plateau, then across the Andes, to reach the sea at Copiapo after a terrible passage through the mountains, in which fifteen hundred of the accompanying

Indians perished. From Copiapo, Almagro pursued his way along the coast beyond the site of Santiago; then, finding nothing that pleased him, made his way northward back to Peru, an operation which involved traveling the whole length of the dreadful Atacama Desert. Almagro's journey, in spite of all sufferings, was apparently profitless, but it was the prologue of Valdivia's conquest of Chile three years later, and it provided Almagro with a band of followers who were soon to be a thorn in the side of the Pizarros.

Such unprincipled and grasping men as Francisco Pizarro and Diego Almagro could not live peacefully side by side indefinitely, and in 1538, the year of the latter's return from Chile, the first of the classic Peruvian civil wars broke out. This struggle, called the War of Las Salinas from the field of the decisive battle fought among the salt-pans outside Cuzco, resulted in the capture and execution of Almagro. His followers, though beaten, were not destroyed, and after nursing their grudges for several years they accomplished the murder of Francisco Pizarro in 1541. Then, with Diego Almagro, the half-caste natural son of their old leader, at their head, they engaged in the War of Chupas against the surviving Pizarro brothers. In the gory battle of Chupas (1542) fought in the mountains a hundred and fifty miles west of Cuzco, the Pizarrists were again victorious, and the hopes of the Almagro faction were at an end. In this war the Pizarrists had the official backing of the Spanish government, and the new royal governor, Vaca de Castro, had taken a valiant part on the bloody field of Chupas. De Castro was an able and intelligent man, and it was a sorry day for Peru when he was recalled in 1544, to be succeeded by the stubborn and unimaginative Nuñez de la Vela.

Within the same year Nuñez and Gonzalo Pizarro were at each others throats, and the third civil war — the War of Quito — had begun. After months of maneuvering, the rivals came to grips in January 1546 at Quito in Ecuador, and Gonzalo routed the royal troops and beheaded the governor. By this act Gonzalo had literally become an outlaw, and official vengeance was not long delayed. A new governor, Pedro de la Gasca, was speedily sent out, and after gathering a considerable body of troops, he brought Pizzaro to bay near Cuzco in March, 1548 and routed his army in an engagement which was rather a wholesale flight than a battle. With the subsequent execution of all but one of the remaining Pizarros, the civil wars came to an end, and under Gasca's able government Peru passed from the stage of discovery and conquest to that of colonization.

Yet even during the difficult times of the civil wars exploration had progressed, and valiant Spaniards had gone north, east, and south from Peru into the wilderness. In fact, after the foundation of Lima in 1535, Francisco Pizarro's policy was firmly oriented in the matter of discovery, Almagro's expedition to Chile being a case in point. These journeys fall into three groups; those eastward into the Montaña, in search of the Land of the Cinnamon; those northward into Colombia; and those southward, into Chile. The journeys into the Montaña involved crossing the Andes and entering the upper watershed of the Amazon, in search of a land which, the natives said, was overflowing with spices. This search later took the form of a quest for El Dorado and also for a lost kingdom of the Incas. Several expeditions were made, all in the teeth of heart-rending hardships, and all doomed to disappointment. In 1538 Pedro de Candia, a stalwart Greek gunner, went southwest from Cuzco, crossing the freezing heights of the Andes to the tropical jungles of the Madeira Valley. Later in the same year one Peranzures traveled east from Cuzco, only to be forced back by starvation and exposure. More successful was Alonso de Alvarado, who in 1539 crossed the Andes east of Cajamarca, reached the headwaters of the Amazon and founded Chachapoyas. In one of the most terrible journeys known to human annals Gonzalo Pizarro set out from Quito in 1541 in search of the Land of Cinnamon and El Dorado, and with incredible hardships made his way down the Coca River to its junction with the Napo, and then returned to Ecuador up the course of the latter (the exploits of his lieutenant Orellana concern Eastern South America, and so will be described in a later chapter).

In the north, the picturesque Belalcazar made his way through the mountains to Popayan, and penetrated into Colombia, where, after founding the towns of Cali and Cartago, he met Quesada, the conqueror of Colombia, on the Plains of Bogota (1539). From there he proceeded down the Magdalena River to Cartagena, having thus gone overland from Peru to the Caribbean.

To the southward, too, it was the same story of courageous exploration. Undeterred by the fruitlessness of Almagro's journey, Pedro de Valdivia entered Chile in 1540, keeping to the coastal route. After eleven months on the march, which included traversing the Atacama Desert, Valdivia reached verdant regions, and founded Valparaiso and Santiago. Peaceable settlement was delayed, for the Indians turned out to be ferocious savages, who fearlessly assaulted the white men wherever they saw them — the decade 1540–1550 is therefore one of almost continuous warfare. By the latter date, the natives, except for the belligerent Araucanians in the far south, were subdued, and Chile soon began to attract settlers from Peru and from Spain as well. The town of Valdivia, named in honor of the explorer, was founded five hundred miles below Santiago in 1551, and two years later a ship traversed the whole of the Chilean coast and actually entered the Straits of Magellan from the Pacific side. Thus in less than thirty years the entire Pacific slope of South America had been revealed.

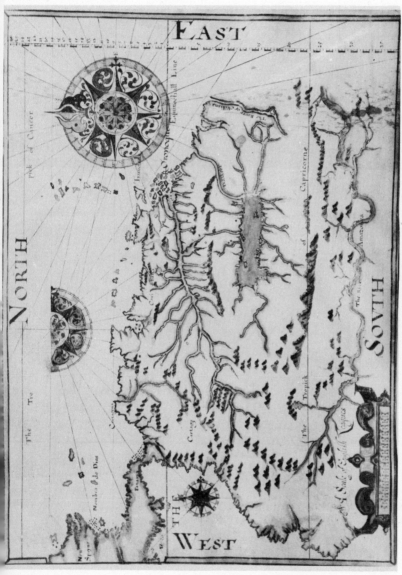

An English manuscript map of northern South America. Besides the Orinoco and the Amazon, it shows the mythical Lake of Parima, in the realm of El Dorado, on the shores of which the fabulous city of Manoa was supposed to stand. Since Captain Keymis explored the Essequibo (Desakebi) River in 1596 and concluded that it was the outlet of the lake, the map must date from that period. It very probably was prepared by Thomas Hariot under Sir Walter Raleigh's direction for presentation to the "Wizard Earl" of Northumberland.

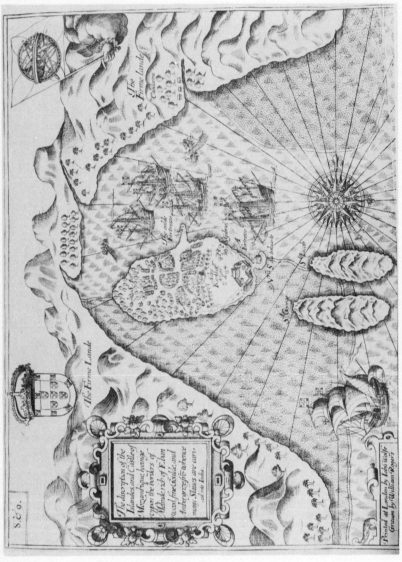

Mozambique. "The Ile of Moçambique is above halfe a league long, and but a quarter broad. At the entry of the Barre is the Fort with a Portugall Captaine and Garrison. This is one of the chiefe Forts of India; built by a good Architect, An. 1558. The Iland is drye, and without wood: the water they fetch three miles without the Barre. It was at first sickly, but now by Gods goodnesse is proved health-full." — Dos Santos.

THE CONQUEST OF NEW GRANADA

After Balboa moved the survivors of Ojeda's colony across the Gulf of Uraba to the Isthmus of Panama in 1510 no further exploitation of what is now Colombia took place for many years. Rather did the attractions of the Isthmus itself, of Mexico, and lastly of Peru prove too strong for an additional effort of colonization to be made in a region which in the first attempt had been so unpromising. But after Mexico, Peru, and Central America had been explored, the possibilities of a vast area athwart the northern collar of South America began to tempt the hardy Spaniards, in the hope that there too might be found a realm as wealthy as those of the Aztecs and the Incas. A beginning was made by the foundation of Santa Marta on the north coast in 1524, and the more important and subsequently far more historic city of Cartagena was established in 1532. These were merely two coastal settlements; the interior still remained an unaccepted challenge — forest-covered, mountainous, and forbidding. Not until 1535 did the conquistadores venture to meet this challenge, and then they went only far enough to realize the difficulties ahead. In that year Alonso de Lugo, son of the governor, led a party inland from Santa Marta, which failed completely because of the unscrupulous rapacity of the leader, who fled to Spain after robbing the natives, his father, and his sovereign with equal impartiality.

Lugo's lieutenant was a man of different metal, and was chosen in 1536 to lead a large expedition to lands of wealth upcountry, which native information had led the Spaniards to believe was another Mexico. This figure was Gonzalo Jimenez de Quesada, a young lawyer fresh from Spain, who like Cortes and Pizarro was possessed of an indomitable will and an uncanny gift of leadership. His expedition was faced by obstacles different from those which faced Cortes and Pizarro, but no less formidable in their own way. The conquerors of Mexico and Peru had better terrains to traverse and a reasonably good climate for campaigning; their enemies were human — the armies of mighty, barbaric empires. For Quesada the human element was infinitely less troublesome; he was confronted, it is true, by tribes of hostile Indians whose weapons were poisoned arrows, but they were a nuisance rather than a menace. For his expedition the threat was environmental — the steaming climate, the tropical jungle, the rugged and pathless hillsides, the plagues of insects, as well as all the tropical diseases that one can catalogue.

Undismayed by this prospect Quesada led nine hundred men from Santa Marta in April 1536. This party, one of the largest yet seen in America, divided into two groups — one going up the Magdalena River in small brigantines, and the other going overland and keeping the river to its right. Total failure was in store for the river party, and after a series of gales, wrecks, and Indian massacres, a few disheartened survivors returned to Santa Marta. Quesada with the overland party had almost as bad luck, but his courageous spirit won out. After fighting his way through forests and swamps in the midst of the rainy season, he did eventually reach the land he was looking for. Eight months after leaving Santa Marta he had progressed as far as the Indian town of Tora on the Magdalena, a scant three hundred miles south of Santa Marta as the crow flies, thus making his rate of march little more than a mile a day! A year after leaving the coast he had reached Velez, perhaps a hundred and fifty miles beyond Tora on a tributary stream, and here he reviewed his army of one hundred and sixty-six men, the pitiable and starving remnant of the original nine hundred.

Quesada was now above the tropical forest, and amid upland plains and valleys, cultivated by a milder and more settled people. Yet his authority could not be established without a struggle, and the Indians of the region had several petty monarchs, who though far less powerful than the dynasties of Mexico and Peru, still had to be reckoned with. One of these, the King of Tunja, a man of enormous corpulence, was captured in a skirmish in August 1537, and shortly thereafter Quesada brought his colleague the King of Bogota to bay and slew him in battle. Quesada was now in control of the upland country, and the rewards for the horrible tribulations of the march began to come in — gold and emeralds were found in considerable quantities, particularly in the Savanna of Bogota. Here in this favored spot Quesada laid out his capital, originally called Santa Fe, after the city founded by Ferdinand and Isabella during the siege of Granada, but now known by the name of the plain in which it stands.

It was fortunate for Quesada that he was able to establish his sway over the Colombian uplands, for there were other adventurers who had designs on the wealth of the region. By one of history's freaks, Belalcazar, coming north from Quito, and the German Federmann, coming west from Venezuela, met Quesada at Bogota in February 1539 — all three having been hitherto completely ignorant of each other's existence. Quesada's authority happily was so well established that the two newcomers did not even attempt to unseat him, and everyone parted company as friends, Belalcazar and Federmann going down the Magdalena to the sea. Quesada shortly afterwards returned to Spain, but his services were ignored, and the dishonest Alonso de Lugo was made governor of New Granada — an unfortunate appointment. This was more the pity as Quesada had shown himself to be more of a Balboa than a Pizarro, a man fundamentally humane, honest, and far-sighted. His conquest, at least in one respect, differed sharply from those of Mexico and Peru, for he was completely cut off from the outside world for nearly three years. During that time he received no reinforcements, or weapons, or provisions of any kind, and he finished the conquest with the gallant survivors of his original nine hundred.

Some emphasis should be given here to the major economic consequences of the Spanish conquests: the flood of gold and silver that was to overwhelm all other Spanish interests in the American colonies and was in addition to have profound and widespread effects throughout Europe. As soon as Cortes reached Mexico, the royal treasure of the Aztecs was seized, and the Inca hoard was taken when Pizarro got to Peru. From that time on, throughout the Renaissance, huge annual shipments of bullion were carried across the Atlantic on the famous plate fleets. Most of the metal was silver, cast into great ingots. Production soared after the discovery of the fabulous vein of silver at Potosi in the Bolivian highlands in 1545, and it is estimated that twenty million kilograms of silver were sent across the ocean between that date and the end of the century. The influx of this silver transformed the economy of Europe; since the fall of the Roman Empire more than a millennium previously there had been a shortage of coin — but now the money market was flooded with Spanish wealth. Consequently prices rose steadily, and governments were completely nonplused by this new and very disturbing phenomenon. Of all Europe, Spain was naturally the most effected, and Philip II's government, incapable of dealing with the new situation, defaulted three times during the second half of the very century that saw the establishment of the Spanish colonial empire and the realization of dreams of the New World's untold treasure.

7

EASTERN SOUTH AMERICA, 1500-1600

The exploits of the Conquistadores' colleagues and contemporaries on the eastern side of the South American continent, in the lowlands of jungle and pampas, were generally less successful and less spectacular than the conquests of Peru and Mexico. There were at least three areas of exploitation in eastern South America: first, the forest district between the Amazon and the Caribbean, where the futile search for El Dorado was carried out; second, the Brazilian littoral, where Portuguese and French attempted colonization; and third, the Plate Valley, where the seeds of South America's most prosperous state were painstakingly laid. These three areas and the part they played in Renaissance discovery have very little in common; far less in fact than the lands which the Conquistadores invaded, but for geographical convenience this grouping into one chapter seems logical.

THE QUEST FOR EL DORADO

While the conquests of Cortes and Pizarro — and even of Quesada — seemed fantastic to their own generation (as indeed they do to ours), yet these men, by their own observation or that of their immediate predecessors, or else by reliable native information, did have something to go on when their expeditions started. Quite different were the journeys made in the Venezuelan jungles in search of that elusive will o' the wisp, the Gilded Man, who lived in the golden city of Manoa on the shores of the fabled lake of Parima. This was a truly glorious myth, the American equivalent of the Prester John legend, and it continued to draw treasure-seekers for almost a century, until Sir Walter Raleigh's second, and fatal, expedition. Nor does the similarity to the Prester John legend end in the stories of the monarch's wealth and power, for just as Prester John's whereabouts were gradually transferred during the Middle Ages from Asia to Ethiopia, so El Dorado was gradually moved from the neighborhood of Bogota to the mysterious region of the Venezuela-Guiana borderland. Just as there was some factual foundation for the existence of Prester John, so was there some for El Dorado; and in both cases fact was elaborated into fiction in the most unblushing fashion. For many years the legend had been current among the Indians, and it seems to have come to the ears of the Spaniards about 1530. In essence it was historically true and referred to a religious rite practiced at the sacred lake of Guatavita near Bogota. The rite had ceased with the conquest of the Guatavita region by another tribe about 1480, but the legend lived on, transmuted strangely to a distant region far to the east of the Andes.

An authority, Colonel Joseph de Acosta, has described the rite as follows: "When the chief of the Guatavita was independent, he made a solemn sacrifice every year . . . which was the origin of the belief in El Dorado. . . On the day appointed, the chief smeared his body with turpentine, and then rolled in gold dust. Thus gilded and resplendent, he entered the canoe, surrounded by his nobles, whilst an immense multitude of people, with music and songs, crowded round the shores of the lake. Having reached the centre, the chief deposited his offerings of gold, emeralds, and other precious things, and then jumped in himself to bathe. At this moment the surrounding hill echoed with the applause of the people; and when the religious ceremony concluded, dancing, singing, and drinking began."

With the migration of the legend from Bogota to the Orinoco jungles, the imagination of the legend-bearers took flight. El Dorado from a native chief became a mighty potentate like Prester John, and the Indian town on Lake Guatavita became the fabulous city of Manoa, the streets of which were paved with gold. Even for the belief in Lake Parima there appears to have been some justification, inasmuch as the plains in the upper watershed of the Guiana rivers are frequently flooded in the rainy season. Such, in brief, was the legend, which implausible though it was, continued to attract not only Spaniards, but also Elizabethan Englishmen, who certainly were nobody's fools.

The exploration of the Venezuelan region is remarkable too in that it is the only instance of geographical enterprise on the part of the Germans during the Renaissance. Reports of the riches of South America had reached Central Europe, and the Welsers, who rivaled the Fuggers as the merchant princes of Augsburg, took the initiative in overseas enterprise. Having obtained a patent from the Emperor Charles V, these bankers sent out an agent named Ambrose Alfinger (in German, Ehinger), who in 1531 led an expedition inland from Coro on the eastern side of Lake Maracaibo. Alfinger pushed over the mountains into Colombia and eventually reached the Magdalena River, having left a trail of murder and devastation in his wake. After a year of prospecting in this region he set out for Coro, but his return journey was terrible to a degree; the Indians, everywhere enraged at his brutality, showed his men no mercy. Alfinger himself was killed, and only a few exhausted stragglers reached Coro in 1533, to tell the horrifying story of their hardships.

Two years later a second German, George von Speier (also known as George Hohemut or George of Speyer), set out. By this time the El Dorado myth was fully current and gave the Germans an incentive which even Alfinger's failure could not dampen. Judged by its objective, von Speier's expedition was just as futile as Alfinger's, but his men did not suffer so terribly and they covered much more ground. Going south from Coro, they kept east of the Andes, crossed the rivers Apure and Meta, and reached their farthest point on the Papamene, or Japura, near the Equator. At the large village of La Fragua they found a temple of the sun, a discovery which made them feel hot on the scent of El Dorado and thus inflamed the ardor of many subsequent adventurers. They crossed the savannahs of upper Brazil, where they had constant brushes with the Indians, and finally got back to Coro, after covering fifteen hundred miles of unknown country.

Meanwhile Nicholas Federmann, a subordinate of von Speier's whose duty was to follow the main party with supplies and reinforcements, disobediently chose to set off on his own initiative. After three years in the Meta headwaters, he led his men across the Andes to Bogota, where he had the weird meeting with Quesada and Belalcazar, described in the previous chapter.

Last of the Germans was a knight named Philip von Hutten, who had accompanied von Speier on his journey. In 1541 this man set out with a large following, making his way south from Coro to La Fragua and the Papamene district, but near the Guaviare River he had a sanguinary battle with the Omagua Indians when he sought to attack their town, rumored to be filled with golden idols. Von Hutten was badly wounded in this engagement, and the survivors of the party returned to Venezuela. This ended the little cycle of Germanic expeditions to South America.

While the Germans were exploring the western part of the El Dorado country, the Spaniards were seeking to penetrate it from the east. In 1531 Diego de Ordaz, a hardened veteran of Cortes' army, sought to find the golden realm by way of the Amazon. Shipwreck caused him to change his plans, and having proceeded to the mouth of the Orinoco, he resolved to enter the interior by way of that river instead. He made his way slowly and with great difficulty upstream to the junction of the Meta, and ignoring the natives' suggestions to ascend this great tributary, he pushed on to the cataract of Atures, which effectively barred his way. Thereupon he turned back to the coast, having, however, explored a thousand miles of virgin country, and having thus paved the way for subsequent journeys in the Orinoco valley. Ordaz's lieutenant, Alonso de Herrera, traveled up the Orinoco in 1533 and ascended the Meta for a considerable distance. On this stream Herrera encountered Indians of a much higher culture than the savages of the Venezuelan jungles, but his death by a poisoned arrow led to the return of the expedition in 1535.

Thereafter, for at least two generations, there were so many ventures in quest of El Dorado from Peru, from Colombia, and from the East Coast that it is impossible to chronicle any but the most important. Pizarro's men were early in the quest; in 1536 Gonzalo de Pineda set out from Quito across the mountains to find the Gilded Man, and in so doing discovered the Land of Cinnamon; in 1539 Gonzalo Pizarro embarked on his terrible journey related in the previous chapter. Gonzalo's venture gave rise in turn to one of the truly epic and most remarkable voyages in the annals of exploration — Orellana's descent of the Amazon.

After Gonzalo Pizarro and his followers fought their way across the Andes to the Coca River, they had a brigantine built, and Francisco de Orellana was sent off in her with fifty men to find the junction of the Coca and the Napo, where the Indians reported a land well supplied with provisions and rich in gold. It seems only fair to acquit Orellana of treachery; the current of the river was strong, and the further downstream Orellana proceeded, the more difficult it was to return to Pizarro's hard-pressed band. As a result, the body of the expedition was left in the lurch, to make its painful way back to Quito, while Orellana sailed with the current down the mightiest of rivers. His voyage, though a marvelous achievement indeed, was not an eventful one. After being carried along some five hundred leagues, which would have brought him somewhere near the mouth of the Rio Negro, he stopped for a considerable period to build a second brigantine. At the mouth of the River Trombetas (56° W) there was a skirmish with Indians, and the presence of women in the hostile ranks brought to Orellana's mind the Scythian female warriors of antiquity and caused him to bestow on the tribe and on the river the misnomer which has survived through the centuries. At last, on August 26, 1541, eight months after parting with Pizarro, he reached the open sea, and after a perilous voyage along the coast, the two brigantines — with rigging made of grass, blankets for sails, and "without either pilot, compass, or anything useful for navigation" — struggled into port at the island of Cubagua. Thus was the great central artery of the continent traversed for the first time. But Orellana had not found El Dorado.

Once the development of Colombia was under way, search for the elusive realm of gold began to take place from that quarter. In 1541 Hernan Perez de Quesada, younger brother of the conquistador, led an expedition from Tunja, near Bogota, across the Andes and marched southeast as far as the Papamene. But he lost half his men in the process, without ever laying eyes on the Temple of the Sun. A year after he set out, he was back in Bogota with a sorry tale to tell.

Six years later the best known of the Spanish seekers of El Dorado made his first journey, like Quesada crossing the Andes from Tunja. This romantic figure was a young and handsome Navarrese nobleman named Pedro de Ursua, whose only faults were lack of judgment and inability to rule turbulent subordinates. In the period 1548–1550 he crossed the mountains to the land of the Musos Indians, with whom Ursua had so many battles that he was forced to return whence he came. In 1560 he undertook his second search for El Dorado. Against friendly advice he insisted on taking his mistress, a beautiful young widow named Doña Inez de Atienza, and as if this were not foolish enough, he included in his company a certain Lope de Aguirre, one of the most blood-thirsty and homicidal maniacs in all human annals. Indeed the expedition had all the elements of high tragedy in the best scenario manner — an attractive woman accompanied by a chivalrous knight, traversing a tropical wilderness with a band of desperadoes incited by a hideously dangerous criminal.

This time Ursua started his journey from Peru — from historic Cajamarca, — crossed the Andes to the Huallaga and proceeded down stream to the Amazon. At the mouth of the Putumayu the party encamped for some time; dissention had reached a high pitch, and on New Year's Day 1561 Aguirre had Ursua murdered. The heroic Doña Inez, "who forsook not her lord in his travels," was killed shortly afterwards, for Aguirre said she took up too much room in the boat. Ursua's puppet successor, Fernando de Guzman, was next assassinated, and Aguirre, revelling in the name of traitor, renounced his allegiance to Philip of Spain and slew all of the expedition who refused to do likewise. From then on, the journey was a holocaust of murder among the Spaniards themselves and of every sort of outrage and atrocity among the unfortunate Indians. Yet, in spite of so ghastly a voyage, important and extensive discoveries were made. Aguirre and his Marañones (for so he christened them) followed Orellana's course down the Amazon to its junction with the Rio Negro, and ascending the latter passed through the Cassaquiari Canal to the headwaters of the Orinoco, and descended that river to its mouth. This voyage took six months from the time of Ursua's murder and involved a thorough exploration of the two great river systems of northeastern South America — truly a wonderful accomplishment. Yet it was not enough for the bloodthirsty Aguirre, who as soon as he got clear of the Orinoco Delta, captured the island of Margarita, and led a party into Venezuela with the intention of conquering both it and Colombia. Only his death at the hands of the royal governor put an end to his fiendish career.

In the years following the Ursua-Aguirre journey, adventurers from everywhere sought the elusive land of the Gilded Man; it would be tedious and useless to chronicle their names or their wanderings, though it is fitting to mention Don Pedro Malaver de Silva, whose various expe-

ditions made between 1565 and 1576 had the effect of localizing the back-
lands of Guiana as the favorite site for El Dorado. In turn de Silva went
into the interior from Peru, from western Venezuela, and finally from
what is now British Guiana — to be slain by ferocious Caribs.

After the failure of de Silva's final expedition, enthusiasm for the
golden myth waned among most potential seekers, but in one quarter
it glowed brighter than ever. Antonio de Berrio, a grizzled old veteran
in his sixties, who had fought valiantly in Italy and North Africa and
who had married a niece of Jimenez de Quesada, was so completely won
over to the idea that at an age when most men think seriously of retirement he brought his family to the New World to embark on the most
hazardous of adventures. Berrio's journeys were three in number. On
the first (1584–85) he went from Colombia by way of Tunja to the Orinoco, crossing and recrossing the various tributaries of the Meta on the
way. But the fever-laden swamps proved so unhealthy that he was forced
to return to Tunja instead of continuing down the main stream. His
second journey took almost three years and carried him from Colombia
to the mountainous region east of the Orinoco. For two hundred leagues
he explored the Sierra Parima and its western foothills, attempting to
find the pass which would give him entry to El Dorado; failing this he
went back to the Orinoco to build vessels to explore the river, but a
mutiny interrupted his plans and ended his second venture.

In March 1590 Berrio, now invested with the title of Governor of
El Dorado, set out from Tunja on his last and greatest journey. His course
took him down the rivers Cacanare, Pauto, and Meta into the mighty
Orinoco. His progress was leisurely; for many months he descended the
river, fruitlessly exploring a tract of country thirty or forty miles deep
along the right bank, but never finding a break in the hills. Very
unwisely, he spent the rainy season in the marshes, where his men
suffered badly from fever; his canoes were lost in the swirling eddies
and on the sharp rocks of the upper Orinoco, and it seemed as if his
entire party would perish in the wilderness. At this critical juncture,
however, Berrio showed real leadership. Having learned from the natives
of the existence of a tributary stream (the Caroni) which came through
the mountains from the upland plains beyond, he pushed his plans with
a new enthusiasm. Four boats were built, and the survivors with their
gallant leader descended the Orinoco to the Caroni — only to find that
a great waterfall near the mouth of the latter stream barred their entry
to the promised land. A costly brush with the Indians rendered further
exploration impossible; Berrio with a handful of Spaniards struggled
into Trinidad in September 1591, after a truly remarkable journey from
the Andes to the Atlantic.

Though Berrio had made his final journey, his enthusiasm was still keen, and in April 1593 his protegé Domingo de Vera set out with thirty-five men to explore the Caroni. Vera did succeed in ascending the river for a considerable distance, only to find — as was usual — that El Dorado was always "just around the bend." Friendly Indians told him of a great lake, wealthy cities, and civilized inhabitants further on, but his men were sickly and exhausted, and even with the mirage seemingly within his sight he was compelled to return to Trinidad.

At this point a new element enters the story of El Dorado. Vera's official account was sent to Spain on a vessel which fell into the hands of one of Sir Walter Raleigh's captains, and Raleigh, improvident and adventurous as always, was quick to make use of it. In fact, Raleigh seems first to have heard of El Dorado from Pedro Sarmiento de Gamboa, a celebrated Spanish navigator, who had been captured by the English and imprisoned in London (1583–1588). Raleigh had consequently sent Captain Jacob Whiddon to Guiana on a voyage of reconnaissance in 1594. But Vera's report was much more informative: it gave Raleigh the type of information he wanted and the latest news at that. Sir Walter's expedition was not long in the making, and in the spring of 1595 he appeared before Trinidad and captured Berrio, from whom Raleigh was able to get a wealth of first-hand information. It did not matter if many of Berrio's statements were deliberately false, for Sir Walter was as uncritical as he was enthusiastic, and Berrio's poetic licence only made the Englishman keener. Disappointment of course awaited Raleigh, as it had his predecessors; he reached the Caroni, found his way blocked by the waterfall and returned to the Orinoco to find it furiously in flood. Thereupon the expedition was abandoned, and the Englishmen, having painfully made their way back to Trinidad, sailed for home.

Not daunted, Raleigh in 1596 sent out another voyage, this one under his captain, Lawrence Keymis. The expedition found that Berrio had built a fort at the confluence of the Orinoco and the Caroni, which kept them from ascending these streams; but they did accomplish some original exploration on the River Essequibo, which they concluded to be the outlet of the Lake of Parima. Other rivers, such as the Wiapoco (Oyapock), Marowine (Maroni), and Corentine (Courantyne) were likewise explored, but El Dorado remained just as far away as ever.

Many years elapsed before Raleigh was again able to respond to the challenge of El Dorado; after his long imprisonment in the Tower he was made admiral at last and was sent out to Guiana in 1617, with his old captain, Keymis. Raleigh stayed in Trinidad while Keymis went up the Orinoco, and ran head on into Berrio's old fort at the mouth of the Caroni (by this time renamed San Thomé), and in the ensuing fight Raleigh's son and many of his colleagues were slain. Keymis thereupon committed suicide, and Raleigh returned to England to face the executioner on Tower Hill. Such was the pathetic ending of the quest for El Dorado.

THE GENESIS OF BRAZIL

The Brazilian littoral, as we have seen, was discovered by Vespucci (possibly) in 1499, and by Pinzon and Cabral on their respective voyages the following year. In 1501 Vespucci had coasted the whole region, so that the outline of the shore had been well determined by the very beginning of the new century. But of the hinterland and its possibilities nothing was known; its mineral wealth was unsuspected, and its jungles, inhabited by poor and barbarous tribes, offered but few attractions to a government which was reaping the wealth of Guinea and India. In consequence, the early history of Brazil is vague and nebulous; there were no conquistadores, no Inca Empires — in fact no lure whatever, so that a generation elapsed between discovery and any serious attempt at colonization.

The only one of the land's natural productions to tempt Europeans was brazilwood, which produced a dye of commercial importance. It is said that in 1503 a converted Portuguese Jew obtained the rights to cut and export this commodity. Several other "New Christians" are rumored to have come to Brazil in the ensuing years, to join in the trade and to escape the rigors of the Holy Office, which demanded their conversion or emigration. Vessels of other nations occasionally touched at the coast: a French ship from Honfleur was reported as early as 1504 and on a long shoreline not too far removed from the trade route to India there were of course castaways. Two of these solitary individuals deserve mention, for they played their part in the subsequent colonization of the country. One, named Diogo Alvares, was wrecked near the present site of Bahia in 1505. He was adopted by the Indians, grew to great power in their tribe, and came to live like a Biblical patriarch amid his wives and children. After many years a French vessel in the brazilwood trade took him and his favorite wife to France, from whence he communicated with the king of Portugal about the possibilities of his adopted home. Another brazilwood ship took him back, and he was on hand when the first group of colonists landed at All Saints' Bay. A strikingly similar instance took place near present-day Santos, where a mariner named João Ramalho was washed ashore about 1510, to be found some twenty years later by the first colonists, living with his tribe of native friends and half-breed children.

These two figures fortuitously paved the way for the initial colonization, which took place in 1531–32 under Martim Afonso de Sousa. Settlements were made near Bahia in the north and Santos in the south, and the country was divided up into hereditary captaincies of fifty leagues of coast apiece, a scheme which on a smaller scale had been found to work well in Madeira and the Azores. Along with the rest of the coast, the Bay of Rio de Janeiro was thoroughly surveyed by de Sousa, but another quarter century was to elapse before a settlement was made on this superb harbor. Nevertheless, in a slow, unspectacular fashion, the seeds of a great nation were sown, and gradually the coast line between La Plata and the Amazon became studded at intervals with Portuguese settlements, based on an agricultural economy, in contrast to the Spanish colonies of the mainland. This was marked by widespread negro slavery, and the growth of great sugar estates from Bahia northward. The appointment in 1549 of Thomé de Sousa as governor general with his seat at Bahia may be said to mark the coming-of-age of the colony.

Doubtless the most vivid account of early Brazil that has come down to posterity is the narrative of Hans Staden of Hesse, a German gunner, who in the years 1547–1555 made two voyages to the country. While serving with the garrison of Santos on his second visit, he was taken prisoner by the Indians, and in consequence he spent several years of adventurous captivity among the natives of the São Paolo region. His story, so graphically illustrated by de Bry, gives a horrible but realistic picture of the cannibalism and barbarity of the aborigines.

In addition to the towns of Bahia and Santos, settlements had been formed at São Paolo and Olinda (Pernambuco), but it remained for another nation to plant a colony in the most logical spot of the entire land. Rio de Janeiro was first settled by a large and respectable body of French Huguenots in 1555, sent over by Admiral Coligny under the leadership of an able but treacherous seaman, Nicholas Durand de Villegagnon. Included in the group were André Thevet, the geographer royal, and Jean de Lery, both of whom left accounts of the expedition. Villegagnon, although outwardly a Calvinist, was a Catholic at heart, and as soon as he felt secure in his power, he began to oppress and persecute his fellow colonists by every means he could devise. This needless tyranny started the break-up of the colony; many of the settlers returned to France, and Villegagnon, finding his force greatly reduced, sailed home for more recruits. In his absence, the Portuguese attacked and drove out the remaining French (1560). For some years the plucky Huguenot survivors kept up a bush war in the hinterland around Rio, and on one occasion they actually recaptured the place, but the Portuguese were too strong, and in 1567 the original colonists were finally liquidated.

THE WINNING OF THE PLATE VALLEY

The discovery of the River Plate (Rio de la Plata) and its watershed stemmed from the Spanish desires to find a salt-water route around South America to the Pacific. As in the case of Brazil, colonization was a secondary thought and did not follow the initial explorations for many years. Rather was it a desire to circumvent the Line of Demarcation between Spanish and Portuguese possessions that led to attempts to reach the East Indies by sailing across the Western Ocean.

First of these expeditions was that of Juan de Solis, which sailed late in 1515 with instructions to enter the South Sea and sail northward along the Pacific coast to the Isthmus. In February 1516 de Solis arrived at the great estuary of the Plate, named by him El Mar Dulce, "the Freshwater Sea," which appeared to offer the hoped-for passage. But de Solis had the misfortune to be slain by hostile Indians when he rowed ashore on the Uruguayan coast, and the expedition — distinguished from all other Spanish ventures of the time by its lack of courage — thereupon sailed back to Spain. Nevertheless it resulted in an important discovery, although had the enterprise succeeded, it would have anticipated by more than a decade the Pacific explorations of Pizarro.

A reconnaissance of a similar nature was made four years later by Magellan on his voyage of circumnavigation; he spent two days sailing up the estuary in the hope of finding a westward passage. Having satisfied himself that this did not exist, and having sighted and named the present location of Montevideo, he left the river without landing, to sail down the Patagonian coast to the Straits that bear his name.

It remained for an expedition with a strong English flavor to make the first thorough exploration of the great river system. Sebastian Cabot had in 1519 left the English service for that of Spain and had received from Charles V the post of pilot major formerly held by de Solis. With a view of determining the Line of Demarcation and of laying claim to the Spice Islands, he was dispatched in 1526 with the very extravagant commission "to discover the Moluccas, Tarsis, Ophir, Cipango, and Cathay, to barter and load his ships with gold, silver, precious stones, pearls, drugs, spices, silks, brocades, and other precious things." Among Cabot's colleagues were Roger Barlow, the supercargo, and Henry Latimer, the pilot; and since Cabot himself had lived in Bristol since early childhood and since Robert Thorne was a driving force in the inspiration, the venture has a distinctly Tudor character, foreshadowing the classic Elizabethan voyages to South America. But Cabot, a better geographer than a captain, was not made of the stuff of Drake, and when the flagship struck a rock off the Brazilian coast, the commander was the first to leave the vessel.

It may have been due to this accident that Cabot lost sight of his primary objective of reaching Tarsis and Ophir; in any case a chance meeting with some castaways of de Solis' party on the Uruguayan coast helped divert Cabot's attention from the duties contained in his commission, and he determined to look for treasure along the Plate instead.

It was not the first or the last time that an expedition had completely dropped its solemn instructions. However, much valuable exploration was accomplished, for de Solis' men told Cabot of the mineral wealth of the interior, where they had heard rumors of a populous empire, and thereby stimulated him with the ardor which was to take him a thousand miles into the continent. This rumor seemed justified, for waterside Indians let him have some objects of silver, which caused him to bestow on the river the high-sounding misnomer of Rio de la Plata (River of Silver).

After building a fort on the Uruguayan shore, Cabot pushed up-stream, entering the River Paraná. Some thirty miles above present-day Rosario he constructed another fort, which he called Sancti Spiritus. Continuing upstream, he got more silver from the natives. When asked where it came from, the Indians pointed westward and talked of "the White King" (the Inca); the silver was in fact Peruvian, and was there-fore the first lot of Inca treasure to reach Europe. In spite of skirmishes with the Indians, Cabot ascended the Paraná as far as the Rapids of Apipé, and finding his course barred in that direction, he explored the River Paraguay as far as its junction with the Bermejo. At this point his party was furiously assaulted by Indians, so that Cabot did not think it advisable to continue northward. None the less, his exploration of these immense waterways, which lead into the innermost recesses of the con-tinent, blazed the trail for further discovery and colonization, and as his farthest point was close to the present capital of Paraguay, about a thousand miles upstream, a glance at the map will show the extent of his travels.

Two unforeseen events, led to the humiliating return of the expe-dition to Spain. One was the arrival of another party under Diego Garcia, a man distinctly in competition with Cabot; the other was the capture of the fort of Sancti Spiritus by the Indians and the massacre of its garrison. At the end of 1529, therefore, after three years in the country, Cabot sailed for Spain, with little to show for his efforts except the ruins of his fort, which, known as Gaboto's Tower, long remained a land-mark for travelers in that flat country.

Conditions after Cabot's return were ripe for the colonization of the Plate Valley, for his expedition did have the effect of awakening the Spanish government to the possibilities of the district. But the conquest and settlement of this part of the New World was destined to be a slow and arduous process, resembling in this respect that of the English col-onies along the North American seaboard in the next century. Yet the hopes of the exploiters were certainly high enough in the beginning, and when Pedro de Mendoza sailed for the Plate in 1535 with fifteen hundred colonists, he led the greatest expedition to be sent out from Spain to America since Columbus' Second Voyage. Mendoza's venture may be considered a failure, although the tenacity and adaptability of the survivors enabled a lasting Spanish area to be settled in the Plate Valley. Having sailed into the Estuary, Mendoza made a settlement on the south bank of the Plate, which he called Buenos Aires from the salubrity of the climate. That soon came to be regarded as the only good thing about the place by the early colonists; water and provisions were scarce, the Indians were savage, and Mendoza himself became incapacitated by a severe attack of syphilis — an ailment to which the Conquistadores appear to have been particularly subject. By 1537 his disease had become so malignant that Mendoza sailed for Spain, only to die en route. Meanwhile affairs had become so critical that the resourceful second-in-command, Juan de Ayolas, built eight vessels of shallow draft, and took most of the colonists upstream with him. His navigation took him even farther than Sebastian Cabot had penetrated, and after defeating the Guarani Indians and making a treaty of friendship with them, he founded the town of Asuncion (1537) on the banks of the Paraquay River, almost eight hundred miles above Buenos Aires. A German soldier, Ulric Schmidt — or Schmidel, to give his name the Spanish rendering — served throughout this enterprise and enriched posterity by an excellent account of the adventures of the settlers.

Asuncion thus became the principal Spanish town in the Plate Valley and was the place from which the second and successful settlement of Buenos Aires was made; it remained the capital of the whole region until 1620. Its founder, Ayolas, had the misfortune to be killed while on an exploring expedition to the north, and his lieutenant, Martinez Irala, was elected governor in an unofficial way and as a temporary expedient. Nevertheless, Irala had all the characteristics of a true South American dictator, and he entrenched himself in absolute power, maintaining an iron grip on the colony until his death in 1557.

Not knowing of any of these developments, except of Mendoza's death, the Spanish crown appointed an official governor. This man was Alvar Nuñez Cabeza de Vaca, the survivor of an epic journey from Florida to Mexico after eight years of strange adventures. With this experience in fighting his way through a wilderness, Cabeza da Vaca decided to take a short cut to Paraguay, and having landed on the coast of Brazil below Santos, he made a four months' march overland through unknown country to Asuncion. This extraordinary achievement was accomplished with the loss of only one man, drowned accidentally, but Cabeza de Vaca's leadership was of small avail, for after a year of conflict with Irala, he was arrested by Irala's followers, confined in a mud hut for many months, and finally shipped back to Spain as a prisoner. Nevertheless, his overland route between Brazil and Paraguay was developed, and was used by Schmidel on his return to his native Straubing in 1555.

This was not the only route developed in those years, for in 1547 settlement from the Atlantic came in touch with the Peruvian conquests, when a party from Asuncion, having traversed the Chaco forests and the Andes, reached Cuzco on a mission to Gasca. Almost simultaneously a party led by Diego de Rojas and Felipe de Gutierrez crossed the Andes from Chile, and reached Cabot's Tower on the Plate, where its leaders were astonished to hear of the presence of Spaniards in that region. Exploration and settlement thus reached the Argentine from north and west, rather than from the logical direction of Spain itself. Peruvian settlers crossed the Andes to found Santiago del Estero, the oldest town in the Argentine, in 1549, Chilean settlers crossed the mountains to establish Tucuman and Mendoza; and finally, when time was propitious for a successful refounding of Buenos Aires, this was done by Juan de Garay, coming downstream from Asuncion (1580). What is now the continent's largest city was the very unspectacular creation of some sixty Spaniards and several hundred friendly Guarani Indians, but its prosperity was far in the future. When Buenos Aires was an infant hamlet at the close of the sixteenth century, the largest city in the Western Hemisphere was Potosi, now a forgotten ghost-town high up in the Bolivian Andes, but then a booming city of a hundred and fifty thousand persons, prospering from the fabulous silver mines nearby.

CHAPTER

8

AFRICA IN THE SIXTEENTH CENTURY

The position of Portugal's African enterprises in the sixteenth century may be likened to that of the large islands in the West Indies at
the same period. In each case they were the lands initially discovered
and exploited, and in each case it came about that they were passed by
when far richer areas beyond them were reached. Guinea was won before
India; Cuba before Mexico; and both Guinea and Cuba were by-passed
by the main streams of human avarice when the larger goals were
attained. Yet in neither case did the Antilles nor the African littoral
become complete backwaters: the islands which Columbus discovered
turned to quite a prosperous agricultural economy, while Portugal
throughout the century was able to wring a substantial proportion of
her imported wealth from West Africa and Angola. In other words, both
the Columbian islands and the lands discovered under the impetus of
Henry the Navigator remained in the picture on a thoroughly respectable secondary level. This, however, inevitably led to some stagnation
as far as enterprise for exploration and discovery in the Dark Continent
was concerned, although there was at least one expedition (Barreto's in
Mozambique) which rivaled those of the Conquistadores in the New
World, and there were a number of military campaigns in Angola and
Abyssinia, as well as much missionary enterprise (largely unsung).

Throughout this period Portuguese influence continued to be predominant everywhere south of Moslem North Africa. That influence had
four main areas: West Africa and the Guinea Coast, including the island
of São Thomé; the region south of the lower Congo, including the kingdom of Congo and contiguous Angola; the coastal strip along the Indian
Ocean, comprising present-day Mozambique or Portuguese East Africa;
and finally Abyssinia.

GOLDEN GUINEA

Three phases of development are distinguishable in the history of
West Africa during the first century of European influence: the initial
period of exploration, lasting perhaps until 1480; half a century of pros-

perity, settlement, and monopoly from 1480 until 1530; and gradual decline after 1530, largely due to the activities of interlopers of other nations. This decline gained speed and momentum as the period passed the middle of the sixteenth century, so that within a hundred years of the foundation of Elmina, the Portuguese monopoly, in spite of active and intelligent countermeasures, was broken beyond repair.

But in the year 1500 Portuguese influence was at its height, and no signs of decay were manifest. The threat of Spanish interlopers, active two decades before, had ended, and Guinea enjoyed a vigorous life, separate from Portuguese enterprise to the Orient, and based on an economy of gold, pepper, ivory, and slaves. Trade was formalized by what became known as the "Guinea season," for only between September and early May were conditions suitable for traffic with the home country. Four months in the summer were too hot and too unhealthy for man or beast, and it was early learned that in this humid period the miasmic littoral of West Africa was indeed "the White Man's Grave."

Of Portugal's fortified trading posts, the oldest and the first to be reached on the Guinea voyage was Arguim, situated on an island in a bay of the same name, between the broad Atlantic and the endless sands of the desert. In spite of its dour situation, Arguim shared in the importance of the West African trade, especially in the earlier part of the period. It tapped the wealth of the Western Sahara and was the entrepôt for trade as far south as Cape Verde, besides being the starting point for numerous unrecorded excursions into the interior. Some gold reached Arguim in those days, and many slaves, but after 1540 its importance declined.

For the great western bulge of Africa, the main Portuguese station was Santiago Island in the Cape Verde archipelago, more than three hundred miles from the mainland, but strategically located at the crossroads of the shipping lanes: Portugal–Guinea–Brazil–East Indies. Santiago thus early became the base of trade between Upper Guinea and Portugal, and the men of that island sent their vessels far up all the rivers along the coast. In this way, little enclaves of Santiagians sprang up well in the interior of the mainland, along such streams as the Gambia, the Casamance, and the Geba, as often as not filled with jailbirds, fugitives from justice, and similar characters, who may have been picturesque as individuals but who were scarcely good ambassadors of Western civilization. Under these conditions, it is hardly surprising that the Portuguese efforts to convert the native chiefs to Christianity were not uniformly successful. Most flourishing of the Santiago settlements was Cacheo on the river of the same name, which had a trade extending south to Sierra Leone. Trade in these parts, as well as elsewhere throughout West Africa, became the chief medium of Portuguese influence, and the factor came to play a far more important role in colonial affairs than either the missionary or the slave dealer.

The keystone of the arch of Portuguese dominion between Barbary and the Equator was the fortress of São Jorge da Mina on the Gold Coast, dominating the entire littoral from Sierra Leone to Benin, and controlling the gold-producing lands of the interior. A castle and a town comprised the dual organism; the castle a royal stronghold, garrisoned under the governor and run on the lines of military discipline; the town a sort of self-governing republic, inhabited by natives of a superior type, known as Mina Blacks, who were organized into a formidable fighting force by their white masters. Famous names appear on the roll of governors. Duarte Pacheco Pereira, whose doughty deeds in Indian had gained him the title of the Portuguese Achilles, was governor from 1520 to 1522; he was recalled in disgrace on charges of peculation but was subsequently exonerated. His successor was Braz Albuquerque, illegitimate son of the great conqueror and editor of the hero's *Commentarios*. Like Pacheco he found himself in trouble, for he brutalized the Mina Blacks. He is said to have been succeeded by João de Barros, the Portuguese Livy, who is known to have been in Guinea in this period. It seems ironical that both Barros and Braz Albuquerque, two of the great historians of their country's conquests in the Orient, never got nearer India than this out-of-the-way spot on the Gulf of Guinea.

From 1500 until at least 1530 the Mina trade was very prosperous, and there was but little trouble with the natives. Here as elsewhere, the trader was more important than the missionary, and even among the garrison of the fortress we have evidences of religious apathy and of far more interest in wine, mulatto women, and profits from gold. A brisk trade was carried on with Benin, and in spite of the unhealthiness of the district a station flourished at Gwato on the Niger delta in the first two decades of the century. Other Portuguese settlements followed trade along the coast, and with the growing threat of interlopers, subsidiary forts were built at Sierra Leone, Axim (the western end of the gold region), Samma near Elmina, and Accra, at the eastern end of the Gold Coast. Even with the coming of the interlopers, and even after the assault of the Fetu savages (1570), Elmina remained a post of great importance throughout the whole period, flourishing as it did on gold and slavery.

Portugal had one other settlement of prime importance in the Gulf of Guinea, the island of São Thomé. Lying athwart the Equator and one hundred and fifty miles from the coast, this island rises to a height of seven thousand feet and therefore comprises a variety of climates, so that in spite of its equatorial position, Europeans can live there in relative health and comfort. It early became a settlement for Jews and convicts, and during the years of the factory at Gwato in Benin, São Thomé rose to prosperity with its trade (largely in slaves for America). In fact it would seem that the island became the principal clearinghouse for the slave traffic on all this part of the coast. From about 1540 for at least a generation the prosperity of the island attained even greater heights by the rise of the sugar industry, which flourished enormously on the very suitable soil and enabled the planters to live on a grand scale, anticipating the way of life of the British planter aristocracy in the West Indies by two centuries. From this period of quite amazing prosperity the island fell into a decline, brought on by several causes. A rising of the slaves in 1574 crippled production; Antwerp, whither most of the sugar had gone, was beset by the revolt in the Netherlands; and the trans-Atlantic slave trade passed about the same time to the newly founded port of Loanda in Angola.

If São Thomé experienced prosperity until the latter part of the century, the areas of Portuguese influence on the mainland began to go down hill from about 1530. This retrogression can be for the most part explained by one factor alone — the coming of foreign interlopers to the Coast. French sailors from Dieppe and other ports in Normandy were the most important. These adventurous seamen, partly traders and partly pirates, were quick to see the possibilities of illegal traffic; their first voyages appear to have been made in 1530, later their ventures became regular, and after 1540, particularly numerous. These Frenchmen went chiefly to Malagueta on the Grain Coast (modern Liberia); they seldom got as far as Elmina and never reached Benin. Their trade was almost exclusively in pepper, and their activity was such as to disorganize completely the Portuguese pepper market. They soon saw the advantages of a triangular traffic and would sail from France to Guinea for pepper, and then across to Brazil for brazilwood. Of these hardy adventurers few are remembered by name, but history records a Portuguese renegade named João Affonso, who, sailing as the French pilot Jean Alphonse, was especially active in the field. Illicit trade was by no means the only occupation of these men; they fought and plundered every Portuguese ship they could, and thereby added insult to injury in their incursions into forbidden waters.

West Africa was the proving ground on which the navigators of Western Europe first tested their skill. The Portuguese under Prince Henry, then the pre-Columbian Spaniards, then the Norman French in the days of Francis I, and finally the most enduringly successful of the lot, the English: all these nations had in West African waters their first experiences in navigating "off the beaten track." As for the English, there is some slight documentary evidence of one or more pre-Tudor ventures between Bristol and Guinea, late in the reign of Edward IV, but of these attempts so little is known that there is no indication that they ever got beyond the planning stage. A half century later, in 1530, old William Hawkins, the progenitor of the famous brood of seamen, sailed from Plymouth to the River Sestos on the Grain Coast, where he took on a load of ivory; from there he proceeded to Brazil, to return eventually to England with a Brazilian "king" whom he presented to Henry VIII at Whitehall. Two years later Hawkins repeated the voyage, to take the King back to his native heath. In 1540 either Hawkins or his captain, John Landye, sailed on another triangular voyage, returning with "elephants' teeth" and brazilwood; but after this voyage at least a decade intervened without definite record of an English voyage to Africa.

In 1551 trade between West Country ports and Barbary got a fresh start, which rightly promised a period of considerable activity. In that year Thomas Wyndham or Windham, a Norfolk gentleman having affiliations with Somersetshire, made a highly profitable voyage to the coast of Morocco. A successful repetition of this in 1552 emboldened him to extend his ventures as far as Guinea, and in 1553 he departed for the Gulf with a renegade Portuguese pilot named Antonio Pinteado. Like many another experiment this venture had both heavy losses and encouraging gains. The English, trading and plundering as they went, proceeded by way of Madeira to the Grain Coast; thence to Elmina, where, avoiding the fortress, they traded on either side of the town; and finally to Benin. In spite of the fact that the Guinea season was now over and the summer heat had begun, Wyndham, a very stubborn and headstrong man, determined to push up the Niger to Gwato. This was done, and the English were received in the city and court of Benin; but the result was inevitable. Fever broke out, Wyndham died, Pinteado died (not, however, before he had been made the scapegoat), and the crews died in such numbers that the enfeebled survivors were filled with the sole desire of getting away while there were still enough hands to work the ships. After a harrowing homeward voyage, forty survivors reached Plymouth. They did none the less bring home with them a hundred and fifty pounds of gold in addition to much other merchandise, so that the promoters of the voyage reaped a rich reward.

A second voyage was sent out that autumn (1554), under John Lok, a member of a family interested in overseas trade. Lok profited by Wyndham's experience; he got a good start and sailed straight to the Grain Coast, going from there to Elmina, but like Wyndham steering clear of the fortress. Being careful to avoid his predecessor's criminal delay at Benin, Lok did not go east of Accra, and after leaving a young officer named Martin Frobisher as a hostage with the Portuguese, he proceeded back to England. His voyage was an unqualified success, for he returned with a splendid cargo, and with the loss of but a handful of of men. Doubtless this success led to the annual ventures that followed, differing as they did from the French voyages of the Norman freebooters in that they had a high-echelon backing of the moneyed magnates of the City of London. (Earlier voyages had also been promoted by the Duke of Northumberland, the real ruler of England in Edward VI's time.) These men found an able captain in William Towerson, who took three expeditions to Guinea (1555, 1556, and 1558); on his second voyage he joined forces with a French fleet and had a running fight with the Portuguese off Elmina; on his third voyage he made Wyndham's mistake of staying too late in the year, and after vicissitudes — including a call at São Thomé — he reached England with very depleted crews.

Portugal tried hard to combat these interlopers — by fortifying more positions on the Coast, by instituting armed convoys, and by protesting through diplomatic channels at the courts of France and England — but their efforts were futile, and after the 1550's their monopoly was broken forever. In the 1560's the English often made several voyages a year. Robert Baker, the ancient mariner whose wonderfully graphic poems in the 1589 Hakluyt edition anticipate Coleridge's *Rime*, sailed in 1562 and again the following year, at the same time that John Hawkins, son of William, began his slaving voyages between Guinea and the West Indies. Hawkins made three of these cruises; on the last (1567) he was accompanied by Francis Drake, then a young dare-devil in his mid-twenties. However, the tragedy that befell the third voyage at San Juan de Ulúa (an island in the harbor of Vera Cruz, Mexico), when Hawkins' ships were treacherously and furiously attacked by the Spaniards, meant the closing of the West Indies to English slavers, with the result that this branch of traffic fell off sharply after 1570. But England's Guinea voyages had left their mark; they had ended the Portuguese monopoly and they had given English mariners invaluable experience, especially in sailing in tropical waters.

THE KINGDOM OF CONGO

The embassy of de Sousa in 1490–1491 resulted in the introduction of Christianity into the region south of the Congo and in the conversion of its rulers, who took the names of João and Leonor, after the King and Queen of Portugal. Their capital was the town of São Salvador, situated on a lofty hill a hundred and fifty miles due east of the mouth of the Congo, and some miles south of the river, which at that point takes a northeastern course. At this barbaric metropolis, Christianity of a sort flourished and quite an active intercourse was carried on with Lisbon. There was much missionary endeavor, and many young Congoese were sent to Portugal to be educated, not always with gratifying results. Dom João was succeeded by his son, Dom Afonso I, who reigned for over

thirty years (1509–1540) and fell so completely under Portuguese influence that he introduced the titles of duke, marquis, and count among
his chieftains, and in a valiant attempt to be Europeanized waded
through six bulky volumes of Portuguese laws. He thus became unwittingly a complete vassal of Portugal, while it is to be feared that Christianity never got more than skin-deep in his domains. No greater mistake could have been made by the Portuguese than to suppose that a
series of wholesale baptisms would result in a devout population, for
native cults and superstitions continued to exist, and such were the native
clergy that a priest on one occasion tried to assassinate the king after
Mass.

It may have dawned on the king, however, that the white men had
not come solely for the purpose of saving souls, for the Portuguese sought
to develop mining in the region and gave so many other evidences of
their control that the patience of the native ruler must have been sorely
tried. After Dom Afonso's death there followed two decades of short
reigns, and then a period of anarchy, during which many Portuguese
were slain, while the invasions of the fierce and dreaded Jaggas from
the interior brought on the decline of the region. None the less, the
rulers continued in São Salvador, nominally Christian and observing
many of the superficial fictions of Portuguese civilization.

Until the second half of the century, therefore, the Portuguese do not
appear to have reaped much wealth from the Congo. They had a factory
at Mpindi, at the mouth of the river, where they annoyed the natives by
levying heavy duties, but their schemes for mining and for exploring
the interior always met determined opposition. However, successful trade
by the islanders of São Thomé with the lands to the south pointed the
way to better opportunities, and the ambitious Dom Sebastian determined to conquer the region of Angola, a district under the sovereignty
of the Congo rulers. To this end Paolo Dias, a grandson of old Bartholomew, was sent out in 1560 to reconnoitre. Taking a party of Jesuits and
adventurers, he sailed to the mouth of the Kwanza and then went sixty
leagues upcountry to the chief's residence. After helping the chief suppress a revolt, he departed for Portugal — leaving the priests, however,
for the spiritual welfare of the inhabitants. Considerable delay then
ensued, and it was not until 1574 that Dias was sent out to make a settlement and open up trade, but this time he built on firmer foundations.
His first act was to found the seaport of São Paolo de Loanda, which is
still today the capital of the colony; he then divided up the coastal zone
as far south as Benguela into seigniorial estates, as had been done with
success in Brazil, and he humored the native chiefs with aid in their
wars. But after a few years both the king of Congo and the native chiefs
woke up to the fact that Dias was taking over their lands, and years of

warfare followed between the Portuguese and the Africans, during which Dias campaigned up and down the country. His marches were chiefly along the course of the rivers Kwanza and Lukala, and after a long and active career the gallant soldier died in the field at Masanganu on the Kwanza. His successor, Luis Serrão, carried the war to the headwaters of the Lukala, only to be defeated on a remote battlefield two hundred miles from the coast.

Still the natives were never strong enough to threaten the Portuguese position along the sea, and Loanda grew to be a fine town, the center of a prosperous and important district. From the start of the colony, Angola had much in common with Brazil. Not only was its agricultural economy modeled on Brazilian lines, but there was close commercial intercourse between the two lands. Their interdependence was most conspicuous in the slave trade. Loanda early displaced São Thomé as the chief African slave market, and as a ready sale for Negroes was found in the sugar districts of Brazil, slaving voyages from Loanda to Bahia were the rule.

It was in consequence of these voyages that two Englishmen reached Angola: Andrew Battell and Anthony Knivet. Battell was shipwrecked off Brazil about 1589 and taken as a prisoner to Angola. After participating in coastal trading voyages which took him as far as the Loango, north of the mouth of the Congo, he fell into the hands of the savage Jaggas, in whose company he traveled extensively through Angola. In eighteen years' time he got back to England, and was able to give an account of his adventures, which came to the notice of Samuel Purchas. Knivet, a survivor of Cavendish's second expedition, escaped from bondage and made his way from Brazil to Loanda in 1597; he sailed up the Kwanza and spent some months trading around Masanganu, before he was arrested and sent back to Brazil. Like Battell he lived to return to his native land, and to have his narrative included in Purchas' collection. More celebrated than the accounts of Battell and Knivet, however, was that of Duarte Lopes, a Portuguese colonist in São Salvador. This man was sent on a mission to Rome, and his description of the country, taken down by Pigafetta, the papal chamberlain, gives an excellent general account of the region; it contains much accurate information, as well as some interesting remarks on the source of the Nile. It was translated into English at Hakluyt's suggestion by Abraham Hartwell in 1597 under the title A Report of the Kingdome of Congo.

In short, then, as São Salvador and the northern part of the area declined, Angola, with its connection with Brazil, prospered. In spite of the interference of the Jesuits, who sought to create a theocratic government, Loanda flourished; the episcopal see was transferred there from São Salvador, and expeditions — which came to naught — were planned to cross the continent to Abyssinia and Mozambique. In 1606 an attempt was even made to open up a route to the Zambezi. Congo's royal dynasty lingered until 1888, and even now Angola is Portugal's largest colony, larger than all the rest of the Portuguese Empire put together, the homeland included.

THE EMPIRE OF MONOMOTAPA

From Angola around the tip of Africa until far past Zululand there was no Portuguese settlement; not until the present bounds of Portuguese East Africa had been reached did the chain of fortified places begin, to extend around the periphery of the Indian Ocean to Malacca. It might seem strange that the Portuguese made so little of the Cape, but it would appear that they never got over the massacre of Almeida and his men on the shores of Table Bay, and the impression of this tragedy was so profound that ever afterwards the Portuguese avoided the region as they would shun the plague. A valiant nation who fought and conquered heathens and infidels all over Asia and Africa was put to fright by a band of poorly armed Hottentots!

It has been told earlier how the Portuguese, in the first flush of their Oriental conquests, established fortified posts along the coast of East Africa. Of these settlements, Mozambique, with its strategic situation with regard to Moslem fleets coming from the north, with its fine harbor, and with its convenient location as a port-of-call on the route to India, was considered the most important and became the seat of the governor of the district. Kilwa, to the north, had been a prosperous Arab port, but the Portuguese had no luck with it — as a result it had the curious distinction of being the first Portuguese post in the Orient to be abandoned (1512). To make good the failure of Kilwa, the Portuguese founded an excellent station at Sofala, south of the Zambezi delta, which far more than even Mozambique throve on local trade with the hinterland; so that, if Mozambique dominated the political map of the area, Sofala dominated the economic one. In consequence, the story of travel in sixteenth-century East Africa is largely dependent on the influence of Sofala and its surroundings, as well as on the Zambezi itself, which the white men soon perceived to be a thoroughfare into an interior rich in promise.

Rich in promise indeed it was, for there were romantic traditions that the fleets of King Solomon had sailed thither, to get gold for his temple, as well as diamonds and rare spices and ivory. Tradition had it too, that this land was the fabled Ophir of the ancients, and the rumors of magnificent ruins in the interior lent color to this belief. A mighty sovereign was said to live in the mysterious hinterland, called the Monomotapa, whose wealth, power, and barbaric luxury put him in a class with Prester

John and El Dorado. All these traditions had some factual basis, but as so often happened were wildly exaggerated. Asiatic traders (probably Sabaeans from southern Arabia) had possibly penetrated the interior, but at a far later date than King Solomon's day — say, in early Moslem times. There were also some remarkable ruins, such as those of Zimbabwe, which have been shown by archaeologists to date only from the fifteenth century; and there was a native king called the Monomotapa, who was neither better nor worse than many another chieftain in darkest Africa. But Renaissance discovery was made up of a series of futile searches for fabulous myths — and this was no exception, even though the myth has continued into our own day in the fiction of Rider Haggard.

As a consequence of this powerful incentive, therefore, exploration proceeded apace both along the coast and in the interior, but with the inevitable result of heavy loss of life due to the deadly climate, a disappointing harvest of riches, and eventual discouragement, made all the deeper by inroads of warlike savages.

The pioneer explorer in the East African hinterland was the little-known Antonio Fernandes, who in 1514 made two journeys up country from Sofala. His route is obviously conjectural, but it would appear that he kept south and west of the Zambezi and that he probably penetrated no less than four hundred miles into the interior, passing through Mashonaland into the Monomotapa's domains, and finally returned to the coast, bearing tales of goldfields in the Manika country two hundred miles inland from Sofala. Fernandes' report shows him to have been a very shrewd and highly intelligent explorer, with a true geographical instinct; in fact, on every count he must be rated as one of the greatest of all African travelers. It is indeed history's loss that so little is known about him.

Along the shores of the ocean, too, much exploration was done, both by accident and plan. In 1544 Lourenço Marques and Antonio Caldeira proceeded southward from Sofala, and after inspecting the lower course of the Limpopo, where they saw the possibilities of copper mining, they made a thorough survey of the great Bay of Delagoa, even penetrating well up the three rivers which flow into it. On their return, Marques reported favorably on the possibilities of the ivory trade in the region of the bay, with the result that an annual traffic sprang up with Mozambique, and Marques remained for years stationed in the bay, in charge of the trade. The next exploration was fortuitous. In 1552 the great galleon *São João*, homeward bound from India, ran aground off the St. John's River south of Natal, and the passengers and crew struck out along the coast for the nearest white settlements. Their story was one of profound suffering and tragedy, and only eight haggard Portuguese were picked up in Delagoa Bay by a chance vessel almost a year later. Hardly had they finished their painful trek, when another homeward-bound Indiaman was wrecked on the coast. This was the *São Bento*; she came to grief in April 1554 at the mouth of the Umtata River, fifty miles south of the St. John's. Her survivors had almost as grim a time as their predecessors. The passage of the Tugela River in Natal was especially terrible, but their officers were resourceful and intelligent, and fifty-six Portuguese reached Delagoa Bay, after three months of hardship, to be taken back to Mozambique on the annual ivory vessel.

The marine disasters shook the confidence of the Portuguese, and the authorities decided that steps must be taken to prevent their recurrence. Accordingly, instructions were issued to Manuel de Mesquita Perestrelo, one of the surviving officers of the *São Bento*, and a member of a family famous in the annals of Portuguese expansion, to make a thorough survey of the coast from Cape Correntes north of the Limpopo to the Cape of Good Hope. So strong had the Iberian principle of "mañana" become, that it was not until 1575 that this experienced seaman left Mozambique. In spite of this tardy start, Perestrelo did his work well; the coast as far as Delagoa Bay was fairly well known, but to the south he conducted what was probably the most thorough and most scientific coastal survey of East Africa made up to that time. Proceeding along the shore almost as far as the Cape of Good Hope, Perestrelo took soundings and made stellar and lunar observations with the crude instruments of the day, besides charting the whole coast with the greatest possible care. Many of his latitudes and distances were of course incorrect, but the value of his work is evident from the fact that wrecks on the coast are said to have decreased sharply, although this later period was one in which Portuguese marine disasters elsewhere were all too frequent.

After the journeys of Antonio Fernandes, exploration of the interior, stimulated by the desire to find the Monomotapa and King Solomon's mines, followed the course of the Zambezi. In 1535 the Portuguese had established factories at two places well up the river: Sena, a hundred and fifty miles from the sea, and Tete, as far again in the interior. To assist in the resulting trade, the station of Quilimane was founded in 1544 on the northern arm of the Zambezi delta, and by means of these places a brisk trade was carried on with the subjects of the Monomotapa. Of this trade, ivory was the most important item, followed in turn by gold, ambergris, pearls, gum, and wax. The commerce was sufficient to sustain some prosperity, but it must have seemed disappointing to the hopes of the treasure-seekers who fancied themselves on the threshold of Ophir.

As for the Monomotapa, he was as elusive as he was overrated, but he was finally run to earth in 1560 by a party of missionaries, who reached him by going southwest from Tete. His savage capital seems to have been near the present city of Salisbury in Southern Rhodesia; it was situated on a mountain called Faro, which from the sound of its name seemed to give some color to the legend of Ophir. The initial success of the Jesuits was astounding, and they baptized the Monomotapa and many of his followers. The effect of these wholesale baptisms was not lasting. On the contrary, some Moslems persuaded the Monomotapa that the Christians were sorcerers; so with fine impartiality, the Negro chieftain first had the Jesuit leader, Gonçalo da Silveira, strangled and then executed his accusers. This effectively finished the mission, but one priest, André Fernandes, was able to return to the coast after considerable hardships, and the barbaric and impulsive Monomotapa reverted to the religion of his fathers.

In spite of the failure of this undertaking, which might well have disillusioned more rational souls, the youthful monarch of Portugal, Dom Sebastian, saw in the realm of the Monomotapa a fabulous land of opulence and luxury. This strange but heroic character, gloomy, mystical, willful, and brave as a lion, resolved to create a vast dominion south of the Zambezi, which would rival in wealth and importance the Spanish dominions of Mexico and Peru. He determined to gain sovereignty over the Monomotapa and all other native chieftains who dared oppose his arms, and to this end he pushed the preparation of a large and well-equipped expedition. The choice of leader fell to Francisco Barreto, a high-ranking officer who had been governor of India. In 1569 Barreto sailed from Portugal at the head of a thousand soldiers, half of them of gentle birth. But magnificent though the expedition was, it was from the start dogged by delays and bad luck. It took over a year to reach Mozambique, after which Barreto was ordered to undertake a naval campaign along the coast above Malindi, and when the army finally reached Sena, they had to wait seven months while an envoy journeyed to the Monomotapa to bring him to terms. It was not until 1572 that the campaign actively began, and the Portuguese, now reduced to six hundred and fifty men, struck out upstream from Sena. It appears that a powerful tribe called the Mongasi, under a ruler of that name, lived between the Zambezi and the Monomotapa's country, and there was constant warfare between the two. After Barreto's force had turned southwest up the valley of the tributary Mazoe, the Portuguese ran head on into these savages; in the sanguinary battle that followed, with no quarter asked and none given, the white men were victorious, but they were already decimated by fever, and they had suffered such losses in the engagement that they could not go on. Having penetrated only about fifty miles inland from the Zambezi, the exhausted soldiers straggled back to Sena. This spelled the failure of the expedition on which so much time and care had been lavished, and poor Barreto, after being summoned to Mozambique, returned to Sena, to die as much of heartbreak as of fever.

His successor, Vasco Fernandes Homem, thereupon evacuated the fever-stricken survivors to Mozambique, where the force was reorganized for another venture. Homem then took his men down the coast to Sofala and marched them westward into what was known as the Manika country, a region reputedly rich in mineral resources. But disappointment still pursued the Portuguese, and Homem found the native mines to be poor and unproductive. A return to Sofala was then made, and Homem, ever hopeful, went up the Zambezi again, with the lure of more gold in his thoughts. Past Sena, however, the natives cut off the bulk of the Portuguese force and slaughtered them to a man — an action which effectively ended these disastrous military expeditions into the interior.

Indeed, the sands of Portuguese sovereignty in East Africa were running low, for the final decades of the century witnessed a dreadful wave of war and destruction over the lands north of the Zambezi. Hordes of savages, pressing from the interior of the continent, pushed on to the Indian Ocean, committing the most frightful ravages. Mozambique, being on an island, was not attacked, but the inhabitants suffered severely from famine caused by the devastation of the mainland. Flowing northward, the tide of war swept along the coast. Kilwa was wiped out, Mombasa was sacked, and the progress of the cannibal horde was stopped only at the gate of Malindi, where a few Portuguese and their Moslem allies, under the brave leadership of Mendes de Vasconcellos, inflicted a crushing defeat on the savages. Thus the traditional friendship between the Portuguese and the Mohammedans of Malindi paid good dividends, for this victory alone saved the white man's precarious toe-hold on the eastern side of the continent.

A good account of Africa in those difficult days has come down to posterity in the writings of João dos Santos, a humane and intelligent Dominican friar, who lived almost ten years in Sofala (1586–1595). His mission took him upcountry, and he visited Sena and Tete, where he witnessed the horrors of native warfare. Fortunately, however, he was safely back in Sofala when in 1592 the savage Mazimba tribe slaughtered the Sena garrison and the following year heavily defeated a retaliatory force — events which for a time, at least, practically ended Portuguese influence in the Zambezi Valley. Dos Santos' book, *Ethiopia Oriental*, was published at Evora in 1609, at a time when, thanks to her hold on the important coastal points, Portugal in East Africa had had a slight recovery from the humiliating and disastrous setbacks of the last quarter of the sixteenth century.

Meanwhile, fruitless search for precious metals continued, as well as attempts to establish close relations with the Monomotapa, but none of these ventures led to any new contributions to geography. It was not until the seventeenth century was well under way that new ground was broken; in 1616 Gaspar Bocarro, desiring to take some specimens of silver ore from the Zambesi to India, set out across country from Tete in a northeasterly direction, and after passing around the southern extremity of Lake Nyassa, eventually reached the Indian Ocean at Kilwa. Nyassa was thus the only one of the great African lakes definitely known to have been discovered by the early Portuguese. There are plausible reports that Tanganyika was visited by missionaries, but I have encountered nothing to substantiate the rumors that Victoria Nyanza was ever seen by white men before the days of Speke and Grant; nor is it likely that Victoria Falls were visited before Livingstone. But the Monomotapa continued until comparatively modern times to exercise his influence on the cartography of southern Africa, to the exclusion of accurate knowledge.

THE REALM OF PRESTER JOHN

Relations between Portugal and the mysterious land of Abyssinia continued intermittently throughout the sixteenth century, mainly on an amicable basis, but conducted with glacial slowness because of geographical barriers and mutual proclivities of procrastination. Abyssinia had but one port, and that was Massawa, far in the Red Sea. Albuquerque had never conquered Aden, and the Red Sea remained in Moslem control — a control all the more aggressive because of its importance in protecting the pilgrimage traffic. This is not to say that the Portuguese could not have swept all before them had they so desired, but such a campaign would have required ships and men, and for want of protection the occasional single vessels which made their way to Massawa were under the handicap of running the gauntlet. Portuguese energy was required elsewhere, and the wonder of it is that Portugal did go to the efforts on Abyssinia's behalf that she did, rather than the reverse.

As a return for Covilhan's mission (see Chapter IV) the African ruler dispatched an Armenian named Matthew to serve in the capacity of ambassador to his brother monarch in Lisbon. This man left Abyssinia in 1510 and after many vicissitudes reached Portugal by way of India four years later. In 1515 he set out homeward with an official Portuguese embassy, most of the members of which perished of fever in the Red Sea. Matthew and a few survivors made their way back to India, and it was not until 1520 that a new expedition, improvised but enthusiastic, sailed from Goa. In fact there was no decision to make an embassy of the party at all, and not until Massawa was reached did Rodrigo de Lima receive instructions accrediting him as ambassador to the court of Prester John. Included in the party was a quarrelsome secretary named Jorge d'Abreu;

there were also two clerics, one of whom, an erstwhile barber named João Bermudez, lived to take an active part in Portuguese-Abyssinian relations for many years; the other, Francisco Alvares, played the part of peacemaker between Lima and Abreu, and after returning to Portugal, he wrote the official history of the embassy. The much traveled Matthew died on the march into the interior, but the rest of the party pushed on across the mountain wall, and after various delays at the hands of local officials, met the emperor at Adowa in the latter part of 1520. For the next five years Lima and his men were attendant on the barbaric court of Lebna Dengel Dawit (David), who far from allowing the Europeans to leave, made them follow his royal progresses throughout his domains. The aged Covilhan was on the hand to greet his countrymen, whom he assisted in a number of ways, but the mission proved disappointing because of the wayward casualness of Lebna Dengel and the squabbles between Lima and Abreu. There were misgivings, too, about the heresies of Abyssinian Christianity, although the tolerant and liberal Alvares took it all in his stride and worshiped in the native churches without a qualm. It is difficult to follow the wanderings of the Portuguese, but it would seem that they traversed the whole eastern side of the land as far south as the circular course of the Blue Nile. After years of this detention, the mission was finally dismissed and reached Portugal by way of Massawa and Goa in 1527.

Shortly after the departure of Lima's embassy the domains of Prester John were harried by a fanatical horde of Mohammedans from the south, led by a very able soldier called Mohammed or Ahmed Granyé (the Left-handed). This man, probably a Somali or a Galla, came up from the low country around Harrar, and his wild tribesmen overran the kingdom to such an extent that Lebna Dengel had to take refuge in the mountain fastnesses. Portugal was called upon for aid, and in 1535 the priest Bermudez, who had remained in the country, was sent to Europe for armed help. Bermudez traveled by way of Egypt and the Mediterranean; a very risky journey, but he reached Rome in 1536 or 1537 with a whole skin, and as a result of his appeal, an expeditionary force was sent out. This was led by Cristovão da Gama, a younger brother of the governor of India, Estevão da Gama, and a son of the famous Vasco. So slow was intercourse between Abyssinia and Europe, and so tardily had action been taken, that by this time it was 1541. Lebna Dengel had just died, to be succeeded by his son Galawdewos (Claudius), and Granyé was running wild throughout the realm. The Portuguese had only four hundred and fifty men, but they were trained and disciplined soldiers, and their arrival instantly changed the face of the war. In two bitterly contested engagements in April 1542, they worsted the savage Moslems, but in the desperate battle of Wofla, fought in August, the Portuguese were defeated by sheer numbers. Dom Cristovão was captured in the retreat and was beheaded by Granyé himself. At this juncture Granyé showed the weakness characteristic of barbarian leaders; he did not follow up his victory. His troops melted away, and he let most of the Portuguese escape without serious pursuit. This gave Galawdewos an excellent chance to rally his forces, which that monarch was not slow to do. With a revived army, he met the Moslem hosts in two bloody encounters, fought the following February among the Semien Mountains north of Lake Tsana. In both battles the Christians were victorious; in the second, decisively so. A battalion of Turkish match-lock men formed the spearhead of the Moslem attack, but the Portuguese literally wiped them out; Granyé was slain, and the wreck of his army scattered to the four winds. In this wise did Portugal save Prester John. Most of the gallant band of Portuguese never saw their native land again, but settled in Abyssinia by force of circumstances — to be eventually absorbed into the native population. Two men did get out, however, both of whom wrote accounts of the campaign. One was the soldier Miguel de Castanhoso; the other was the irrepressible Bermudez.

In spite of the defeat of Granyé, conditions in the unhappy country continued to be chaotic, and fanatical Moslems kept up their incursions. Galawdewos was killed in repelling one of these raids, and his brother and successor was likewise slain a few years later, while the Portuguese survivors of da Gama's army played their part as bravely as they had in the past. A further element of discord was introduced in the persons of the Jesuits, who first came to Abyssinia in 1555, and who established a large mission two years later under Bishop André de Ovieto. These zealots lacked the broad tolerance of Father Alvares, and they were horrified by the schismatic condition of the Ethiopic Church. Finding it riddled with errors, they set out to suppress all heresy, with the result that they met with a very cool reception. For forty years, however, the mission was maintained at Fremona near Adowa; its members were not actively persecuted but were merely shunned and ignored. A revival of the mission took place early in the following century, in the person of Pedro Paez, who resided in the country from 1604 until his death in 1622, during which period he traveled through the various provinces in the emperor's suite. Later Jesuits continued to traverse the land. Two of these bear mention: Antonio Fernandez, who in 1613–14 penetrated far into the Galla countries south of Shoa; and Jerome Lobo, whose wanderings became familiar to English readers through Dr. Johnson's *Rasselas*. Unfortunately, the Jesuits had provoked the enmity of the ruler and native clergy alike, and in 1633 the mission was liquidated by martyrdom and expulsion. With this event, Portuguese intercourse with Abyssinia ceased; in fact with the decline of Portuguese enterprise generally, travel and exploration everywhere in the Dark Continent languished. Until the revival of the impulse for African discovery in the latter part of the eighteenth century, conditions were admirably parodied in Dean Swift's jingle:

So Geographers in Afric-Maps
With Savage-Pictures fill their Gaps;
And o'er unhabitable Downs
Place Elephants for want of Towns.

9

THE EARLY EXPLORATION
OF NORTH AMERICA

Compared with Central and South America, the area comprised in the present-day United States and Canada had but a meager history in the annals of Renaissance exploration. There were doubtless several reasons for this; the climate was harsher, the eastern half of the continent was clothed in an impenetrable primeval forest, precious metals were not readily accessible, the natives were ignorant and savage, and there were no wealthy empires such as those of the Incas and Aztecs. All these factors combined to make the North American continent a relative backwater during the sixteenth century as far as discovery and colonization were concerned. Nevertheless, there is still something to chronicle, and that something all the more valuable, since it is the foundation of our national heritage. Three different fields of endeavor may be included in this survey: the coastal voyages of the early mariners; the Spaniards in the Gulf region and the southwest, coming up from the West Indies and Mexico; and the French in the St. Lawrence Valley.

THE EARLY COASTAL VOYAGES

Did the Portuguese undertake any pre-Columbian expeditions to America? There are elusive scraps of evidence here and there, which have been argued, especially by Portuguese historians, as proof that such voyages may have occurred, but it is doubtful if the question will ever emerge from the stage of controversy. Evidence for one of these apocryphal voyages is adduced from the Bianco Map of 1448, which portrays an island to the southwest of Cape Verde, with the enigmatical inscription "Isola Otinticha xe longa a ponente 1500 mia," which has been translated as "Genuine Island, 1500 miles distant to the west." On the strength of this, a discovery of the northeast corner of Brazil has been suggested; a theory quite lacking in demonstrative evidence, however possible in itself. The records of the Azorean, Diogo de Teive, known to Columbus, indicate that he cruised in North American waters in 1452, although he is said to have turned back before sighting land. From this, the theory has been suggested that Teive discovered the Grand Banks. Another apocryphal undertaking was that of João Vaz Corte Real, an Azorean and the father of the noted Corte Real brothers of the next century. In company with two Danish seamen, Pining and Pothorst, he sailed at the command of King Afonso in 1473 to "Terra Nova dos Bacalhaus," or the New Land of Codfish, thought to be either Newfoundland, Labrador, or Greenland. The fact that the younger Corte Reals a generation later sailed in these waters is certainly suggestive that their father may have blazed the trail, but at the present time the safest conclusion about this and the other fifteenth-century Portuguese ventures across the Atlantic is: not proven. The same happily cannot be said about the English voyages; the proof is there, even though the details are lacking.

The false dawn of English colonial enterprise appeared in the closing years of the fifteenth century, anticipating by half a dozen decades the true sunrise of Britain's glorious day of overseas expansion; the impetus was there, but it was weak and it soon played itself out — to lie dormant until its tremendous awakening in the days of Good Queen Bess. Yet the cycle of voyages from Bristol to North America is among the most significant if mysterious of maritime ventures.

Throughout the Middle Ages, sailors of Bristol had navigated the North Atlantic, to the West Coast of Ireland and even to Iceland, trading in fish and salt. Rumors of the mythical islands of Atlantis were current along the quays of the Avon, and as early as 1480 a certain John Jay financed an expedition to find the Island of Brazil, far to the west of Ireland. This venture, although a failure, led to almost annual voyages, especially in the 1490's, so that the way was prepared, by tradition and experience, for the ventures of the Cabots.

No voyages are at once so well-known and so little-known as the Cabot voyages. That they did result in the discovery of North America is beyond dispute, though what parts of the coast they saw will always be a matter of conjecture. John Cabot, of Genoese origin and Venetian nationality, was a man well versed in seamanship, who had worked out the problem of a westward voyage to India from his own experience as a trader in the Levant. That he knew of Columbus' discoveries seems highly probable; the *Columbus Letter* in one or more of its numerous editions must have circulated in so marine-minded a port as Bristol, while trade between the West of England and Spain would have further resulted in the spread of the new knowledge. Be that as it may, Cabot had enough confidence in himself and in his ideas to apply to Henry VII for a patent for discovery, which was duly granted him in 1496. In May of the following year, he sailed on the small bark *Matthew* with a crew of eighteen Bristol mariners, and probably with his subsequently famous son, Sebastian, who was then a young boy of twelve or thirteen. Cabot was away three months, and he did sight land; that much is definite. But as to his course, one cannot dogmatize. Perhaps the least controversial theory is that he had his landfall at Cape Breton Island, and that he doubled northeast and coasted the southern shores of Newfoundland. There is some probability that he may have seen Nova Scotia, and considerably less probability that he sighted Labrador, but the report that he followed the coast for three hundred leagues is an obvious exaggeration, as the time of his absence from England would not have permitted it.

Cabot returned home convinced that he had reached Asia, but that the habitable parts of that continent lay to the south of his explorations. A second voyage was justified by the success of the first, and Cabot was off again in 1498. This venture is even more shadowy than its predecessor; one can only guess that he steered south and southwestward after his landfall in the hope of reaching Asiatic civilization. Possibly he followed the coast as far as the Delaware Capes or even Hatteras, for contemporary maps, such as the La Cosa Map, convey the impression that Cabot sailed far enough south to excite the apprehensions of the Spaniards in the West Indies. At best, however, this second voyage was a failure, since the wealth of eastern Asia was not revealed. Cabot's only material benefit was the discovery of the Grand Banks off Newfoundland, which soon attracted fishermen of many nations. After this, John Cabot fades out of the picture, to be robbed of his proper place in history by the mendacity of his garrulous and unreliable son. Yet his contribution to geography is a magnificent one: he discovered North America.

After these Cabot voyages, a curious link appears between the Portuguese and the Bristolians. A farmer in the Azores named João Fernandes became interested in the northern seas even before the Cabots; he received a patent from the king of Portugal in 1499 and turned up in England in 1501, when with three Bristol merchants he got from Henry VII official permission to explore this quarter of the globe. Evidently he boasted about his position as a husbandman, for the Portuguese word for his status (*Labrador*) was given on his behalf in succession to Greenland and Labrador. Fernandes and his Bristol companions probably sailed to the northwest in 1501 and 1502, and there are faint traces of voyaging to America for several years thereafter. By this time the barrier of a thinly populated and meager North America shifted men's thoughts from exploiting it to finding a passage around it.

Fernandes was not the only Portuguese who originally viewed the northwestern Atlantic as having possibilities: his fellow Azoreans, the Corte Reals, were doing the same thing simultaneously. Gaspar, the elder of the brothers, sailed on his first voyage in 1500, to rediscover Greenland. His second voyage, the following year, took him from Greenland along the eastern coast of Newfoundland; from Cape Race he sent two ships

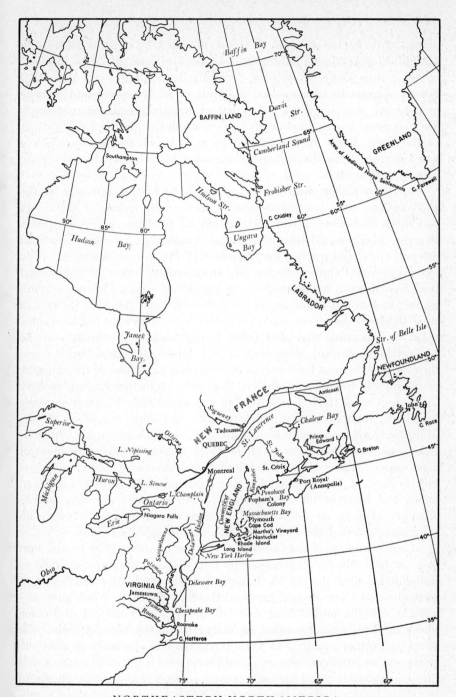

NORTHEASTERN NORTH AMERICA

home, while he sailed away to the southwest to disappear forever. In 1502 his brother Miguel went out to look for him, but had the bad fortune of going down with his ship off Newfoundland. One of Miguel's other vessels appears to have entered the Gulf of St. Lawrence and to have worked her way along the west coast of Newfoundland; she may even have returned by the Straits of Belle Isle. From the period of the voyages of the Corte Reals, Newfoundland grew to be known as Baccalaos, a word derived from the colloquial name for codfish used by the Mediterranean fisher-folk.

Sebastian Cabot, who does not appear to have taken part in the 1498 voyage, soon became convinced of the true nature of the North American continent, and in 1509 he set off to discover the Northwest Passage, which would take him around America to Asia. It was a bold attempt, for Cabot reached the latitude of 67 degrees north and may even have penetrated Hudson Straits into Hudson Bay, before he was turned back by ice and a mutinous crew. In his old age, when Cabot was reminiscing to Richard Eden, he confused the 1498 and the 1509 voyages to such an extent that geographers ever since have been hard put to unravel them. It is possible that after being turned back in the Arctic seas, he proceeded southward along the Atlantic seaboard. His failure to win through to Asia must have been a painful disappointment to the shipping community in Bristol; nevertheless, there are two further English voyages to be chronicled. In 1527, while Cabot was in the Plate Valley serving the Spaniards, John Rut sailed northwest with two ships, one of which, the *Mary Guilford*, apparently turned up near Santo Domingo in the Caribbean — the first English craft in the West Indies. A later expedition of 1536 under "Master Hore of London" had degenerated into cannibalism on the coast of Newfoundland before a French fishing vessel happened along and brought off the survivors. Both of these ventures are so shadowy as to be almost mythical, even though Rut's ship, by her calm arrogance, worried the Spaniards with well-founded forebodings.

A more important coastal voyage was made about 1520 by the Portuguese João Alvares Fagundes, who traced the southern coast of Newfoundland, sailed up the St. Lawrence River, and after attempting a settlement on Cape Breton, explored the Bay of Fundy. Even more significant was the undertaking sent out in 1523 by Francis I of France under the Florentine Giovanni da Verrazano, in the hope of finding for France a northern passage to Asia. Verrazano was obviously an able surveyor and an intelligent observer, and his account is the most accurate and the most valuable of all the early coastal voyages that has come down to us. From his landfall on the shores of North Carolina he turned north; although he missed the entrance of the Chesapeake Bay, he sailed well into New York harbor, an event which is appropriately commemorated by his statue at the Battery. Continuing eastward, he surveyed Block Island, spent fifteen days in Narragansett Bay, rounded Cape Cod, and ran along the New England coast to Maine. Shortage of supplies compelled his return, and he reached Dieppe in July 1524. His voyage led to one persistent and erroneous theory, for the Hatteras sand-spit prompted him to report a narrow neck of land separating the Atlantic from the Pacific, a feature which as the "Mare de Verrazano" found its way into maps for years afterwards and caused endless speculation. In 1524–25 the Spaniard Estevan Gomez (the same who had so basely deserted Magellan in the Straits) made a similar survey in the reverse direction, beginning at Nova Scotia and working down to the Carribbean. His voyage led to no important discovery, though it convinced the Spaniards that there was no truth in Verrazano's Pacific.

Such were the early coastal voyages; which indeed were nothing but coastal voyages. No serious attempts at colonization were made, nor was any penetration of the interior accomplished. A fair coastal survey was the sole result — nothing more — but at least men saw that the present area of eastern United States and Canada had nothing to offer in the matter of long hoped-for gold and silver.

THE SPANIARDS IN THE SOUTH AND SOUTHWEST

When Gomez returned from his coastal voyage, he wrote very enthusiastically about the future United States; the lands being "agreeable and useful countries, corresponding exactly with our latitude and polar degrees." "But what need have we of what is found everywhere in Europe?" replied Peter Martyr bitterly, thereby reflecting the predominant attitude of the great majority of Spanish explorers. Far more, then, than potentially fine agricultural lands were needed to draw the Conquistadores to our country, and the lack of more obvious incentives explains why, after a few painful expeditions of reconnaissance, the Spaniards left the territory alone. Such few parties as did explore the Gulf region were drawn thither in the hope of finding a northern passage to the Pacific, or else by myths of the El Dorado variety.

Such a myth was the tall story of the Fountain of Youth, which reached the ears of the Spaniards in the Antilles in the early days of the settlement. In a mysterious land to the northward was rumored to be a spring, the magic waters of which bestowed the mental and physical powers of young and virile manhood on the senile. This challenge was taken up by Ponce de Leon, veteran of Columbus' Second Voyage and conqueror of Puerto Rico, and in 1513 he sailed north from Cuba on his voyage of discovery. After threading the Bahamas, he struck the Florida coast near Palm Beach, and followed it northward to the St. John's River. There was no sign of the Fountain of Youth, and the natives were everywhere hostile, so Ponce, unaware that Florida was part of the mainland, turned back and retraced his course. Keeping close inshore, he rounded the southern tip of Florida, and proceeded up the West Coast above Tampa Bay. By that time he was disillusioned in the fountain, so he returned to Cuba; but in tracing most of the coastline of Florida he had performed a noteworthy geographical service. Rumors of the fountain continued, and it was eventually localized in the island of Bimini, but Ponce had no successors in its search.

Hope of finding the Northwest Passage inspired the next expedition, led by Alonso de Pineda in 1519. No passage was found, but a good coastal survey was made between Key West and Tampico, for Pineda sailed along the whole northern perimeter of the Gulf. He even entered the mouth of the Mississippi, and remained six weeks in the Delta region, inspecting the many large Indian villages there, from whose inhabitants he heard rumors of gold upcountry. These rumors led to the later expeditions in the area, while Pineda's voyage had the further result of settling for all time the geography of the northern shore of the Gulf.

Almost simultaneously another Northwest Passage expedition was setting out; in 1520–21 Lucas Vasquez de Ayllon, a prosperous man in Santo Domingo, sent his captains along the Atlantic coast as far as South Carolina. Unlike the bulk of his countrymen, Ayllon was filled with the desire of colonizing the coast; with the dual aim of settlement and finding a passage, he was able, after many delays, to sail in person in 1526 with a considerable number of colonists. After coasting the Carolinas, he entered Chesapeake Bay and founded his settlement — probably near the future site of Jamestown. But the venture was short-lived, for Ayllon soon died, and the riddle of the Northwest Passage remained unsolved. Thereupon the discouraged colonists returned to the West Indies, to leave Virginia unsettled until the coming of the English.

A more pretentious and more ill-starred undertaking was made in 1528 by Cortes' old rival Panfilo de Narvaez. With the very large number of four hundred colonists, this incompetent and unfortunate leader landed on the shores of Tampa Bay in the hope of reaching the gold districts that Pineda had heard of. Through carelessness, the ships were lost, and the colonists marched north along the Gulf to St. Mark's Bay, hopeful of finding gold but on the verge of starvation. At the latter place five boats were built (the one commendable example of coöperation in the expedition), and in September 1528 the now desperate colonists — reduced to about two hundred fifty — set out for Mexico. Four of the boats were lost with all hands off the mouth of the Mississippi; only eighty survivors under the leadership of Alvar Nuñez Cabeza de Vaca were cast ashore in the remaining boat near Galveston. Fifteen were alive the following spring.

It was the further misfortune of Cabeza de Vaca and his men to be thrown with impoverished and nomadic Indians, who always lived on the very edge of starvation. Cabeza de Vaca's survival for the next six years was no mean accomplishment, but he proved a resourceful and intelligent man, able to adapt himself to his unfortunate lot. Becoming first an itinerant trader and later gaining a reputation as a healer of the sick, he lived among the Indians all this while, wandering through southern Texas and along the Rio Grande Valley, but never abandoning hope of reaching Mexico. With him was the ever-diminishing handful of survivors of Narvaez's band of four hundred, eventually reduced to Cabeza de Vaca himself, two other Spaniards, and Estevan, a Moorish slave. At length in 1536, after years of prolonged and intense hardships, these four men who had clung to life with such grim determination fell in with a Spanish raiding party in northern Mexico. Seldom has sheer will to live been more impressive.

In spite of his exertions, Cabeza de Vaca was full of the inevitable rumors of wealth; this time of seven golden cities — the Seven Cities of Cibola, lying vaguely to the north of the poverty-stricken lands that he had traversed. His report had the effect of arousing adventurers and gold-seekers to look for this new El Dorado and led thereby to much exploration of our southwest. Cabeza de Vaca had meanwhile returned to Spain, where he met a stout soldier who had served with Pedrarias in Darien and with Pizarro in Peru — Hernando de Soto. From Cabeza de Vaca this cavalier received a glowing account of the Seven Cities, as well as tales of the great wealth of the Mississippi Valley generally — all of them exaggerated either by mendacity or enthusiasm. De Soto saw his chance to emulate Cortes, so with a royal commission as governor of Florida in his pocket, he embarked for America. After equipping a large expedition in Cuba, he landed in Charlotte Harbor, May 30, 1539, at the head of six hundred soldiers — to set out on a relentless, courageous, profitless march, which was to last four years and to take his men over 350,000 square miles of unexplored North America. Following the route of Narvaez, de Soto proceeded north along the coast and spent his first winter at Narvaez's old camp on St. Mark's Bay; he then struck inland and marched north across Georgia to the Savannah River, which he ascended to the Blue Ridge. His progress in these parts was rendered pleasant by a friendly nation of Indians, ruled by a genial queen of great corpulence.

Beyond the mountains the people were not so agreeable, and during his descent of the Alabama River de Soto had to fight a desperate battle at Mavilla (probably near Camden, Alabama), in which much equipment was lost as well as many Spaniards. Pushing on in a northwesterly direction, the army spent the winter of 1540–41 near the Yazoo River in

Mississippi. Early the next spring they were on their way again, urged on by reports of a people to the westward so rich that they went into battle wearing golden hats. De Soto's route now took his men to the banks of the Mississippi, which they crossed a few miles south of modern Memphis. The Spaniards appear to have betrayed no awe whatever at the size of the river; to them it was merely an awkward military obstacle, which put them to a month's hard work making barges for its crossing.

De Soto and his robust band pushed on through the Ozark Mountains and across northern Arkansas, to reach their farthest point west at the confluence of the Arkansas and Canadian Rivers in eastern Oklahoma. A third winter was spent among considerable hardships in this locality, with the Seven Cities as far away as ever. By the spring of 1542 the company was in desperate straits, so the almost naked men marched southeastward along the Arkansas, hoping to reach the Gulf. Instead they struck the Mississippi hundreds of miles above the sea; here de Soto, fever-stricken and bitterly disappointed, drew his dying breath — and was ceremoniously buried in the great river. His subordinate, Luis Moscoso de Alvarado, took charge of the party, and in a valiant attempt to reach Mexico overland, led them across the Texas plains to the Brazos River. When hope for this route vanished, Moscoso reversed his march to the Mississippi, where the fourth and most dismal winter was passed. In the spring of 1543 the survivors rallied to the emergency and built seven barges, in which they floated down the Mississippi to its mouth, and then made their way along the coast to Mexico. It is a commentary on the hardihood of these early Spaniards that of the six hundred who landed in Florida in 1539 over three hundred survived four years of great privation and Indian fighting, with enough of their innate Castilian bravado left to be scornful of the poverty of Tampico, where they finally landed. A great piece of exploration had been accomplished, but de Soto's soldiers had nothing more material to show for their wanderings.

Simultaneously with de Soto's travels, search for the Seven Cities had been in progress from the southwest, and several expeditions had come up from Mexico into the Rocky Mountains and the Great Plains. In 1539 a French ecclesiastic from Provence, one Friar Marcos, accompanied by Cabeza de Vaca's Moorish slave, Estevan, passed through eastern Arizona to Hawikuh Pueblo, on the Little Colorado River, which Friar Marcos was sure must be one of the Seven Cities. A good reconnaissance was made, and it is a pleasing thought that traditions of Estevan remained in Zuni folklore down to our own times. In 1540 Melchior Diaz looked for Cibola along the eastern shores of the Gulf of California, even going up the lower course of the Colorado River; and in the same year Francisco Vasquez de Coronado set out on a journey, which, when taken with that of de Soto, spanned the continent from Georgia to Arizona.

Coronado followed Friar Marco's road northward through eastern Arizona, and then turned eastward, to winter near the future settlement of Santa Fe. From this point he sent out parties in all directions in search of the Seven Cities, and one of these groups, under Lopez de Cardenas, discovered the Grand Canyon. In the following year (1541) Coronado led his party southeast across the Texas plains, and then turning north, crossed Oklahoma to reach his farthest point in eastern Kansas. This penetration of the Kansas prairies was inspired by rumors of another realm of wealth, called Quivara, which proved just elusive as the Seven Cities. After experiencing nothing but disappointment, Coronado returned in a more direct route to the Santa Fe district, and then made his way down the Rio Grande Valley to Mexico.

Like de Soto's travels, Coronado's journey was barren of any lucrative result, but when combined with de Soto's it was of far-reaching importance in giving Europeans an insight into the hitherto unknown vast interior of North America, and in forming thereby the foundation of the region's cartography. Likewise, it brought to light the pueblo dwellers of the southwest, the buffalo-hunting Indians of the Plains, and one of nature's greatest marvels — the Grand Canyon of the Colorado.

Some valuable exploration by sea along the Pacific Coast was also done in these years. Following Cortes' captains, whose exploits in the Gulf of California have been recounted in an earlier chapter, Hernando de Alarcon, on an expedition integrated with Coronado's, sailed in 1540 to the head of the Gulf of California in the hope of finding a waterway to the Seven Cities. Alarcon even made the Indians drag his boats up the lower course of the Colorado for fifteen days; then, satisfied that the river provided no passage to Cibola, he shot downstream with the current in two days. More significant was the voyage of Juan Rodriguez Cabrillo in 1542 along the coast of California. Cabrillo, having discovered San Francisco Bay, died off Point Conception, and his successor, Bartolomé Ferrelo, took the ships the following year well up the coast of Oregon, an extraordinary feat of navigation with two flimsy Pacific-built vessels.

De Soto's failure dampened the enthusiasm of the Spaniards for exploration east of the Mississippi. Consequently, only two journeys in this region in the second part of the century deserve mention. In 1559–60 Tristran de Luna, an old captain of Coronado's, ascended the Alabama River and made his way westward toward the Mississippi, and in 1566–67 Juan Pardo and José Boyano explored the southern Appalachians. In the Southwest, however, there was much coming and going, especially in the upper Rio Grande Valley (first ascended by Rodriquez in 1581). Most noteworthy of these excursions was that of Bernardino Beltran and Antonio de Espejo in 1582–83, which followed the course of the Pecos to northern New Mexico, took a diversion right across Arizona, and returned to Mexico down the Rio Grande. Espejo's account of this highly important expedition early became known to English readers, as it was translated in 1587 under Hakluyt's direction, with the title *New Mexico, Otherwise the Voiage of Anthony of Espeio*. Although the Seven Cities of Cibola declined in sordid reality to mere squalid pueblos, the Spaniards from Old Mexico realized that its young namesake had enough future to warrant the foundation of a permanent settlement at Santa Fe about 1605.

THE FRENCH IN CANADA

Compared with the efforts of Spain and Portugal, France's entry into the field of overseas expansion was timid and half-hearted, but under the stimulus of the pleasure-loving humanist and virtuoso, Francis I, some voyaging was accomplished. Thus Verrazano made his fine coastal survey, interlopers sailed to West Africa and Brazil, and even one or two highly apocryphal ventures may have been made to the East Indies; there were also fishing voyages to the Grand Banks, and piratical cruises on the high seas. In all these ventures the ports of Dieppe and St. Malo played the leading role, with other Norman and Breton ports doing their share. From the first, however, France showed more interest in north-eastern North America than in any other land overseas, doubtless for the triple reasons of fishing, colonization, and the Northwest Passage. The creation of Canada was the result of this tenacious policy.

With the financial backing of his sovereign, Jacques Cartier, a substantial sea captain of St. Malo, set out across the Atlantic in April 1534. His reasons for this voyage may have been to find a passage to the Pacific or merely to search for gold; nothing is certain, although references in his narrative to his disappointment at not finding the "passage" would imply the former motive. After calling at the east coast of Newfoundland to repair his ships, Cartier sailed through the Straits of Belle Isle and held his course southwest across the Gulf of St. Lawrence to Prince Edward Island, a lovely spot, where the expedition spent several days and where everyone was delighted with the fruitfulness and fertility. After they left this island, their hopes ran high for discovering a passage, as the open sea appeared to lie before them, but their delusion was the greater when they found they had run up Chaleur Bay to its head. So they worked back around the Gaspé Peninsula, coasted Anticosti Island, and sailed home through the Straits of Belle Isle.

Cartier reached home without wealth and without having found the passage, but he brought several Indians with him, as well as rumors, stories, and reports of the St. Lawrence region. In particular, he was able to tell of three native kingdoms; that of Hochelaga (around Montreal), that of Saguenay (on the Saguenay), and that of Canada (around

Quebec). Although Cartier was by this time probably convinced that the St. Lawrence was not a strait, but merely a river, yet the existence of these three kingdoms, each one of which might be like Mexico, seemed to warrant a thorough exploitation of the new-found lands.

In the following year, 1535, Cartier sailed on his second voyage to North America, using his captive Indians as guides to take him to the mysterious kingdoms of the St. Lawrence Valley. With the methodical thoroughness which was characteristic of him, Cartier circumnavigated the gulf, surveying the shores from Newfoundland to Gaspé, and then proceeded up the river to the large Indian town of Stadacona, on the site of modern Quebec. Here the French were well received by friendly Indians, who sought by diverse means to discourage them from going on to Hochelaga. But delighted though Cartier and his men were with the fertility of the land, and especially with the abundance of grapes, the hope of riches in the more remote kingdom caused them to sail on. By early October the French reached the impressive, palisaded Iroquois village of Hochelaga (Montreal), where they were given another rousing welcome. Doubtless the reasons for these repeated gestures of friendship were that the Indians wanted to obtain tools and implements of European manufacture, that they realized that the strangers could cure diseases, and that, unlike the Indians with whom the Spaniards had come in contact, they had not yet seen the white man at his worst.

In reaching the site of Montreal, Cartier had traveled about a thousand miles from the Atlantic, only to find that the interminable river still led into the hinterland a whole summer's journey by the Iroquoian calendar. Nor was the superb view from the top of Mount Royal more conducive to hope, for the continental land mass stretched away as far as the eye could see. In particular, the much-touted kingdom of Saguenay proved especially difficult to localize, and its site fluctuated from the river of that name all the way to Ottawa, and even farther westward. Under these circumstances, and also because the year was getting late, Cartier decided to winter across the St. Charles River from Stadacona. This experience convinced him that the Canadian climate was not as idyllic as the early autumn days at Stadacona had led him to believe; the cold seemed endless, his men were much beset with scurvy, and the Indians pilfered every piece of hardware they could find. As soon as the ice went out of the St. Lawrence, Cartier sailed for home, and after rounding Cape Race and crossing reached St. Malo in the early summer of 1536.

In spite of the discomforts of the long winter, Cartier was still full of enthusiasm, and he visited the court of Francis I in company with an Iroquois chief named Donnacona, in the hope of interesting Francis in a full-blown colonial undertaking. But war with the Holy Roman Empire and the subsequent diplomatic negotiations forced the king to put aside the project for some years, and it was not until 1541 that Cartier was able to realize his voyage of colonization. In the spring of that year, Cartier sailed with a thoroughly equipped expedition and with an adventurous nobleman, Sieur de Roberval, prepared to follow him as military commander.

A change seems to have come over Cartier during his years of inaction, and from the cautious, methodical, matter-of-fact navigator of the earlier voyages, he took on the character of a volatile and irresponsible gold-seeker. His colony was duly established at Cap Rouge, about nine miles beyond Quebec, but he soon left it to reconnoitre around Hochelaga, even going as far afield as the mouth of the Ottawa. The first winter at Cap Rouge was an uneasy one; Cartier had returned, but the attitude of the Indians was menacing, and they inquired angrily about their friends and relations who had been taken to France in 1536. All these unfortunates were long since dead, but Cartier sought to placate the natives by telling them that Donnacona and his colleagues were living off the fat of the land. By the following spring Cartier was irresponsibly and unaccountably on his way back to France, carrying among his luggage a dozen barrels of iron pyrites, which he fancied to be gold ore. Loaded with this rubbish, Cartier met Roberval on the southeastern coast of Newfoundland in June, as the latter was on his way to Canada after some months of piracy in the English Channel. Cartier proceeded home and Roberval went on to Cap Rouge to take charge of the colony. Roberval wintered at Cap Rouge, where the colonists withstood their second cold season, and in the spring of 1543 he ascended the St. Lawrence to the Ottawa, in a final bid to discover the Kingdom of Saguenay. Like Cartier, Roberval seems to have been easily discouraged, for he soon turned back, and abandoning the Cap Rouge project to the Indians, sailed for France with the survivors.

With Roberval's return home in the autumn of 1543, the first project of French colonization in Canada came to an end, not to be renewed until the coming of Champlain sixty years later. It may have been a premature attempt, and it certainly suffered from lack of perseverance: what may be said on the credit side is that it revealed a considerable area of the hinterland of a hitherto unknown corner of North America, and it focused France's attention on a region which was destined to become her proudest colonial possession.

10

MAGELLAN AND HIS SUCCESSORS

Christopher Columbus' magnificent plan of reaching the East Indies by sailing westward across the Atlantic was not realized in his lifetime, although to the end of his days he probably was convinced that he had set foot on the Asiatic mainland. It remained for his successor, the great Magellan, to carry his work to its logical conclusion by sailing to the Orient through a westward passage. Magellan, in short, is the true heir of Columbus, not merely in his purpose but in the manner of its achievement; he took up where Columbus had left off and carried to a successful though barren termination what Columbus had from boyhood striven to do. Columbus got half way; Magellan got the whole way, in a voyage that was the rational successor of the venture of 1492. With da Gama's expedition to complete the trilogy, we may have no hesitancy in proclaiming these three voyages the most important in human annals, and Magellan's outstrips the other two as a triumph over terrible difficulties.

Ferdinand Magellan — or Fernão de Magalhães, to give him his Portuguese name — was born of an aristocratic family in North Portugal about 1480, and was destined for an adventurous career in the East long before he entered the Spanish service. He had gone to India with Almeida in 1505, had served with great distinction at the siege of Malacca, and then had probably taken part in Abreu's exploratory voyage to the Spice Islands. After seven very active years in the East, he returned to Portugal, where he might well have retired on his laurels; but he is next heard of fighting the Moors in North Africa. At the conclusion of this campaign, Magellan found himself unemployed and passed over; he saw no future for his vigorous talents in his native land. In these circumstances it is not surprising that he came under the spell of his brilliant fellow countryman, the cosmographer Ruy Faleiro, who persuaded him to cast his lot with Spain. So, goaded on as well by the consciousness that he was in disfavor with the court at Lisbon, Magellan made his way to the sister kingdom, only to have his name bracketed by the Portuguese with that of Faleiro as a monster, a traitor, and a barbarian. It may appear difficult to offer an apology for Magellan's action, yet he was a man full of ideas and vitality, who felt himself thwarted at home, while as a great discoverer he in a sense belonged to no country but was justified to give his talents to that country which could best use them. And that country was Spain. Magellan's whole nature vindicates any suggestion of baseness in his denationalization; his was a noble character, undoubtedly the noblest of all the early explorers.

Under the revised papal donation of Alexander VI, the meridian of 46 degrees west had been made the dividing line of Spanish and Portuguese spheres of colonial enterprise. This line, if continued through the Poles, would pass across the opposite surface of the globe as the meridian of 134 degrees east. It was the hope of the Spaniards that some at least of the Spice Islands lay within their sphere, and as the Pacific section of the Line of Demarcation had never been determined, it seemed sensible to send out an expedition to establish the line, in the hope that Spain could lay a legitimate claim to the Moluccas. To express the problem cartographically: Portugal was granted all the New Lands *eastward* from the bulge of Brazil to the East Indies, while Spain was allotted all the region from the bulge of Brazil *westward* to the East Indies. No commission had yet determined the position of the East Indies, but the Spaniards, having got a strong footing in America, felt that here was the chance to extend their influence to the wealthy lands of the Orient. As it fell out (and as a glance at the map will show), they were wrong, for the 134th meridian, while placing most of Japan and New Guinea and half of Australia in their sphere, passes far to the east of the Spice Islands. But Magellan and his new employers did not know this in 1519.

There is no doubt that the idea of reaching the Orient by a passage around South America, and thereby establishing Spanish claims to the East Indies, was Magellan's; it was just as much his brain-child as the mighty scheme of 1492 had been Columbus'. With devoted Faleiro as an accessory, Magellan in the winter of 1518 visited the Imperial Court at Valladolid and persuaded Charles V and his counselors to authorize the undertaking. His task was easier than that of Columbus, but then Magellan had the discoveries of the previous quarter century to back up his arguments. Armed with the all-important royal commission, Magellan thereupon repaired to Seville, where he spent over a year in equipping his fleet.

Yet for all the royal acquiescence, the tools given to Magellan were hardly of the quality necessary for an undertaking of such magnitude; he was granted five ships, but they were very old and very patched-up, and one observer said that he would be afraid to sail even to the Canaries in them. Their names and burdens were: the *San Antonio*, 120 tons; the *Trinidad*, 110 tons; the *Concepcion*, 90 tons; the *Victoria*, 85 tons; and the *Santiago*, 75 tons. Of these only the next to smallest was destined to complete the voyage, and her appearance is appropriately (if inaccurately) commemorated on the front cover of every volume published by the Hakluyt Society.

It would appear that Magellan had difficulty in enlisting crews, with the result that his men were made up of the offscouring of the waterside and included sailors from all over Europe, besides Levantines and Negroes. One Englishman was enrolled, Master Andrew of Bristol, who served as master gunner on the *Trinidad*. For the post of second-in-command the logical choice was Faleiro, but an attack of insanity disqualified him, and the vacuum thus created was filled with disaffected captains. Considering the scope of the expedition, surprisingly few of its participants achieved the favorable recognition of history. One might mention Sebastian del Cano, who sailed the *Victoria* back to Spain; Duarte Barbosa, Magellan's brother-in-law, who had traveled widely in the Portuguese Indies; Antonio Pigafetta, an Italian gentleman from Vicenza, who became the official historian of the voyage; and the Portuguese João Serrão, captain of the *Santiago*, whose knowledge of Eastern waters and loyalty to his commander made him an important member of the undertaking. But more reputations were marred than made on the voyage, and of three of Magellan's captains, the less said the better.

On September 20, 1519, the fleet sailed from San Lucar at the mouth of the Guadalquivir, with Magellan flying his pennant from the masthead of the *Trinidad*, the best vessel of the fleet. A run of rather more than two months took them to the easternmost part of Brazil, and from there they held close in to the coast of South America, being always on the lookout for the straits which would take them to the South Sea. In this wise they explored the Bay of Rio de Janeiro and the Plate Estuary, ever hopeful, but constantly frustrated. As the year was getting late, Magellan decided to go into winter quarters, and the fleet anchored in the Bay of Port St. Julian in southern Patagonia (49° S). In this dreary region the expedition passed five months, from the end of March to the end of August 1520; they were by no means uneventful months, however. At Easter-tide a mutiny of the most serious nature broke out, with many of Magellan's captains and higher officers involved. Magellan kept the *Trinidad* loyal, as did Serrão the *Santiago*, but the other three vessels were seized by the mutineers. It looked like the end of the expedition then and there, but Magellan, in addition to his other admirable qualities, possessed an iron determination. With the *Trinidad* and the *Santiago* cleared for action, Magellan sent a boarding party under the redoubtable Barbosa to recapture the *Victoria*. This was done with a rush over the gunwales, and, realizing that they were outmaneuvered and outnumbered, all the mutineers gave in. They were dealt with according to their deserts, and of the ring-leaders one was stabbed, one was hanged, and some were marooned. Magellan dared not mete out capital punishment to the rank and file of the mutineers; he needed every man he had to work his ships, nor did he want to jeopardize his popularity further by unnecessary harshness. This policy had its rewards, for (except for the desertion of the *San Antonio*) there were no serious signs of unrest during the remainder of the voyage.

Trouble still lay ahead of Magellan at St. Julian, nevertheless, for the little *Santiago*, while on a coastal reconnaissance, went to pieces on a reef about seventy miles to the southward. Only one man was lost, but the crew had great difficulty in traveling overland to the base, and finally Magellan had to send out a relief party to bring them in. The loss of the *Santiago* was serious. For the rest of their stay at St. Julian events were happily few, although the Spaniards had some traffic with the giant natives of Patagonia, who, averaging more than six feet in height, towered above the short Mediterranean mariners.

By the end of August 1520 Magellan was on his way again, and after spending some time at the mouth of the Santa Cruz River, he discovered and entered the straits that bear his name on October 21. Thirty-eight days were spent in traversing the 320 miles between the oceans. This was a slow passage, since much time was taken in exploring the various ramifications and cul-de-sacs, as well as in looking for the recalcitrant *San Antonio*, which under the command of Estevan Gomez had deserted during the passage and sailed back to Spain. At length on November 28, 1520, seven years after Balboa had first sighted the South Sea, Magellan, with a fleet now reduced to three ships, entered the broad waters of the Pacific, thereby solving the riddle of the westward passage. In performing this great exploit, Magellan constantly showed his consummate skill as a navigator, although it is only fair to add that he met with better weather than is usual in those regions.

Now followed the most tedious period of the whole voyage, a terrible endurance contest of great intensity and great length — the crossing of the Pacific. On leaving the straits, Magellan steered north for a thousand miles or more along the coast of Chile, a procedure which had both advantages and disadvantages. It took him up to the belt of the favorable trade winds, which made his ocean crossing the speedier, but it resulted in his course being to the northward of the Pacific archipelagoes, which would have provided much-needed refreshment for his scurvy-ridden crews. In consequence of this course, the crossing must have been a saga of monotony, hardship, and disease. In ninety-eight days only two islands were seen; "St. Paul's," probably Puka Puka in the Tuamotu Group, on January 24, 1521; and ten days later, "Shark Island," possibly Flint Island at the south end of the Line Islands. Day after day the ships sailed onward; they crossed the Equator, and fearful that the Moluccas did not offer many opportunities for revictualizing, they shaped their course farther to the north, in the hope, perhaps, of attaining some part of China. Not until

March 6 did the ships drop anchor, when they reached Guam in the Ladrones. There Master Andrew of Bristol died of his exertions. Magellan's stay at Guam was short, for the thievery of the natives (commemorated for all time in the name of the archipelago) caused him to push on. Ten days later he reached the Philippines, his landfall being the southern point of Samar. Cebu was reached on April 7, and there he contracted an unfortunate alliance with the local ruler, who thereupon sought to make Magellan fight his battles. It was thus that Magellan found himself taking part in a futile expedition against the small island of Mactan, to the east of Cebu, where the heroic leader met his death in action on April 27, 1521.

After the tragedy of Magellan's death, the completion of the voyage tended to become an anti-climax. Yet Magellan's work was done, and men had sailed westward to the Orient. Probably in Magellan's own case, he had traveled farther east under Abreu in 1511–12, going beyond, though south of, the Philippines, so that it is perfectly true to say that he in person had been around the world. Though his tragic fortune denied him the privilege of sailing his ship from Spain back to Spain, he for all that showed a way to reach the Spice Islands, thereby succeeding where Columbus had failed. As a sailor, as a geographer, and as an explorer Magellan was an epic figure, greater perhaps than either Columbus or da Gama; possibly even the greatest of ancient and modern navigators.

The loyal Serrão took command after his leader's death, only to be slain treacherously by the natives a few days later, along with the brave and much-traveled Duarte Barbosa. The expedition had now reached a sorry pass; the crews so reduced that the *Concepcion* was burned and her men allotted to the *Trinidad* and the *Victoria*. Command now devolved on the *Victoria*'s captain, Sebastian del Cano, an able Basque navigator, whose reputation, however, had been stained by his participation in the mutiny of St. Julian. With a resilience commendable in men who had endured so much, the survivors decided to take on a load of cargo before attempting the return journey, and so they left the sinister island of Cebu and proceeded to Borneo, where they traded at the city of Brunei. They then returned to the Philippines and at Mindanao received instructions how to reach the Moluccas. Accordingly they shaped their course for the island of Tidore, where a visit of six weeks was made (November-December 1521), which turned out to be the only pleasant interlude of the entire voyage. The natives were friendly; presents were exchanged, and a good cargo of cloves was taken aboard. At this island it was decided that the vessels should separate; the condition of the *Trinidad* was so serious that her captain dared not hazard the voyage to Spain — the best he could hope to do was to struggle back across the Pacific to Panama.

It remained for the little *Victoria* to complete the circumnavigation alone. She steered south through the Spice Islands to Timor, and then set her course across the Indian Ocean for South Africa. In early May 1522 the crew sighted the high land east of the Cape of Good Hope, but the rounding of the Cape was so stormy that they had to stop for repairs further up the coast. On June 8 they crossed the Line, but the last lap of the voyage must have been terrible, for scurvy and starvation had reduced the crew to the greatest misery and distress. At length on July 9 they struggled into Santiago in the Cape Verdes. Even then their troubles were not over, for the Portuguese seized and imprisoned almost half of del Cano's pitiable remnant of a crew. With but eighteen Europeans and four Malays left — scarcely enough to work the ship — they sailed for Spain, and on September 8, 1522, three years less twelve days from their departure, they cast anchor near the mole of Seville. Soon afterwards the thirteen men left at Santiago were released, and the united crew were received by the Emperor Charles V at court. There has been a tendency to gloss over del Cano's accomplishment in bringing the *Victoria* from Tidore to Spain, but to sail a rotting ship half around the world with a skeleton crew would seem in itself a magnificent achievement. In any case, the first voyage of circumnavigation had been performed, and one can only regret that the great leader of the voyage had not the good fortune of completing it along with the heroic survivors.

It remains to consider the fate of the *Trinidad*, which set out from Tidore in April 1522 for Panama. In a desperate attempt to cross the Pacific, the ship beat her way against head winds far out into the ocean, possibly reaching a point well to the northwest of the Hawaiian Islands. But conditions were too much for her; it was the old story of scurvy and starvation again, plus constant head winds from the east. In despair Captain Espinosa gave over the attempt and returned to the Moluccas, where he and his men were made prisoners by the Portuguese. After three further years of many vicissitudes in the East Indies, four men, the only ones left of the *Trinidad*'s crew, reached Spain, raising to thirty-five the number of those who out of the initial complement of 280 "stayed the course." The voyage of the *Trinidad* may seem barren of results; yet paradoxically by not discovering anything, her men did in fact discover something. The voyage proved the existence of a wide ocean in latitudes much higher than those reached by Magellan.

THE MOLUCCAS AND PHILIPPINES

Magellan's voyage had indeed shown that the East Indies could be reached by a Pacific crossing, but it had also revealed the immense difficulties in the way. First of all, there was the length of the passage, with the attendant horrors of starvation and scurvy, which made every venture of the sort a terrible endurance test. In the second place, there was the phe-

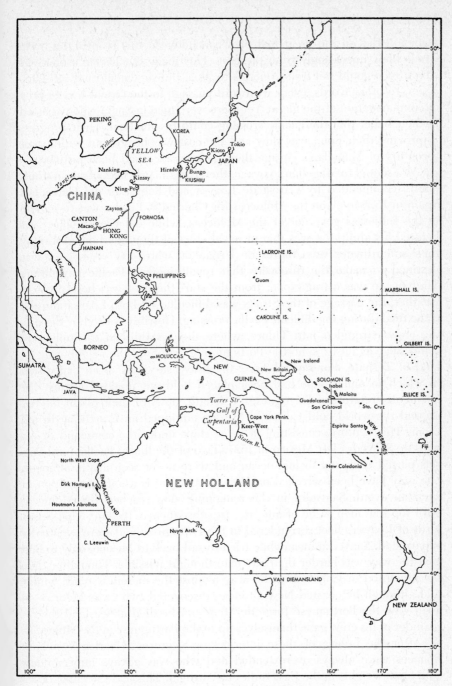

EASTERN ASIA AND AUSTRALIA

nomenon that in the great belt of ocean between the Tropics the trade winds blew unceasingly from the east. This made the Pacific a one-way street; men could sail from America to Asia, but they could not sail back again. In other words, every westward passage to the Orient had to be a circumnavigation of the globe. Yet there were men in Spain who persisted in their belief that the Pacific crossing could be practical. Their progress in proving their point was slow and the cost was heavy, but within half a century of Magellan's voyage their perseverance had been justified.

As a sequel to Magellan's voyage, therefore, a large fleet of seven ships, jointly commanded by Garcia de Loaysa and Sebastian del Cano, left Spain in 1525 to claim the Moluccas for Charles V. Loaysa was to remain in the Indies as governor of the Moluccas, while del Cano's office — as befitted his abilities — was that of naval chief of the undertaking. Among their subordinates was Andres de Urdaneta, who forty years later was destined to make the discovery that revolutionized Pacific navigation. The voyage was a tragic one; from the start the fleet was beset by bad weather, the passage of the Straits was difficult, and both Loaysa and del Cano died during the difficult Pacific crossing. Horribly wasted by disease, the crews struggled into Tidore, where they established themselves to stand siege against the hostile Portuguese garrison on the neighboring island of Ternate. For several years the brave survivors of an expedition in which so much hope had been placed held out unaided against the frequently reinforced Portuguese. At length, news of their plight filtered around the world, and Cortes in Mexico equipped an expedition to aid them. This venture, consisting of three ships under the command of Alvaro de Saavedra left Mexico in 1527. Two of the flimsy Pacific-built vessels parted company in mid-ocean and were never seen again, although one may have been wrecked on Hawaii, as there is a native tradition of such an event. Saavedra in the remaining ship reached the Moluccas with too few men to be of any use. In consequence, the surviving Spaniards of Loaysa's fleet surrendered to the Portuguese and were eventually repatriated. Saavedra meanwhile tried to sail back to Mexico, only to find that the way was harder than any man thought possible. Time after time he attempted in vain to beat his way against the merciless trade winds, and although he coasted New Guinea (discovered two years before — in 1526 — by the Portuguese Jorge de Meneses) he died at sea, and the remainder of his crew gave themselves up to the Portuguese in the Moluccas.

After the failure of these interlocking ventures, Charles V, whose finances were always overextended and who was always impecunious, sold Spain's rights in the East Indies to Portugal. This had the effect of reducing Spanish activity in the Pacific without stopping it completely, since voyages continued to be made in spite of the now official Portuguese monopoly. In 1537, for instance, Cortes sent two vessels from Mexico to search the equatorial ocean for islands believed to abound in gold. This voyage, headed by Fernando Grijalva and Alvarado, met with disaster, and emphasized again the terrible hazards of Pacific exploration. The Gilbert Islands were discovered, but the crew mutinied, slew Grijalva, and were finally wrecked off New Guinea. Seven survivors eventually reached the Moluccas. Another venture from Mexico was that of Ruy Lopez de Villalobos, who set out in 1542 to form a settlement in the Philippines, but reached the Moluccas instead. From Tidore he dispatched one of his captains, a man named Retes, to Mexico. Retes sailed along the whole north coast of New Guinea (which he christened), but could not make headway eastward across the Pacific, and returned to the Spice Islands. Thereupon Lopez de Villalobos surrendered to the Portuguese, and died at Amboyna in 1545. A far more shadowy Mexican venture was that of Juan Gaetano in 1555, which may have resulted in the discovery of the Hawaiian Islands, although this voyage is viewed with skepticism.

Yet the Spanish ill luck could not go on forever, and in 1565 it reached the turning point. In that year two auspicious things happened: the Philippines were successfully colonized, and a voyage was for the first time performed from the East Indies to America. Honors for these joint accomplishments go to Miguel Lopez de Legaspi and Andres de Urdaneta. Lopez de Legaspi took a fleet westward across the Pacific without a hitch, and in founding the city of Cebu on the island of that name, he established the first Spanish settlement in the Orient. Of course, this was in direct contravention of the treaty by which Spain had sold her rights in the East Indies to Portugal, but the Portuguese in the Orient were too few in number to undertake to evict the interlopers. Possession was in this case nine-tenths of the law, although Spain tried to rationalize her action on the ground that the Philippines were not involved in the surrender of her rights.

Spanish attempts at colonizing the Philippines, however, would have been doomed from the start, had not the return passage back to America been discovered; without the latter, the former was impossible. This noteworthy accomplishment was performed by Andres de Urdaneta, a veteran of del Cano's expedition, who had spent many years in Mexico as a monk, where he had gained a reputation as a geographer. After Lopez de Legaspi had planted his colony, Urdaneta volunteered to discover the route back to Mexico, and accomplished the feat by sailing boldly into a high latitude and crossing the Pacific in a wide northern arc, which took him at least to the forty-second parallel. He thus avoided the forbidding belt of trade winds, and although twice the time was occupied in sailing eastward as westward, Urdaneta proved that the voyage could be done. This route was followed regularly after his voyage, and became known as Urdaneta's Passage. It was used by the Acapulco galleon — the annual ship between Manila and Mexico — until the end of the eighteenth century.

THE SOUTH SEA ISLANDS

For the first four decades of Pacific navigation men had missed the bulk of the Polynesian archipelagoes. In general, the Pacific crossings had been too far north, although in some instances ships had sailed just out of sight of the islands, as Magellan's fleet had done when it passed between the Marquesas and the Low Archipelago. Save for the Ladrones and the Gilberts (and possibly Hawaii), no discoveries of note had been made, but the belief in the existence of a vast Southern Continent, based to a large extent on Peruvian myths, provided a new incentive for Pacific voyaging and inspired several Spanish voyages from South America. From Magellan to Lopez de Legaspi, expeditions either aimed at the Moluccas or the Philippines. Now there was a myth like that of the lost Atlantis to solve, a myth which was destined to have its devotees and enthusiasts just as much as the myths of Prester John and El Dorado. First to be inspired by the possibilities of a Southern Continent was Pedro Sarmiento de Gamboa, a man of great ability and energy, whose colorful career included studies in Inca tradition and history, and involved him in the pursuit of Drake through the Straits of Magellan, eventually taking him as a prisoner to London, where he excited Raleigh with tales of the wealth of Guiana. Sarmiento must have been a picturesque and engaging Renaissance figure, whose free-thought had him as often as not in hot water with the Inquisition, and whose belief in the mysterious Southern Continent provided the initial driving force for the subsequent voyages. Nevertheless, he was not fated to lead the first expedition. That office was given to Alvaro de Mendaña de Neyra, the young nephew of the recently appointed viceroy of Peru, who was commissioned "to convert all infidels to Christianity" — in other words, conquest.

With two Pacific-built ships, provisioned only for six hundred leagues, Mendaña sailed from Callao, Peru, late in 1567, accompanied by Sarmiento as one of his captains. Following close in Magellan's track, the fleet passed between the Marquesas and the Low Archipelago without sighting land, and then bearing due west had its first landfall in the Ellice Islands. Conditions made a landing impossible, so with tainted water and supplies running out, the ships sailed on; and finally in February 1568, eighty days after leaving Callao, they sighted the high land of Isabel in the Solomon Islands. Hope that this sizable land mass was the fabled Southern Continent gave way to disillusionment as Isabel and the other islands, one by one, turned out to be insular; as each island was discovered, it was regarded as continental until the contrary was proved, but that proof was soon obvious to all. Yet in the expectation of reaching their quest, Mendaña and Sarmiento spent six months in the Solomons, naming the group, quite inappropriately, in anticipation of the islands' natural riches. They made their first landing on Isabel, where they built a brigantine for convenience in exploring. After circling Isabel in this craft, ships and brigantine alike proceeded to Guadalcanal, where the ships made another stop, while the brigantine sailed on down the coast and over to Malaita and San Cristoval. A final call of the fleet was at San Cristoval, where the brigantine made its third cruise. But the islands, though large, were still islands, and mineral wealth, if it existed at all, was not easily available, although some of the men felt that there were sufficient signs of gold to warrant a permanent stay. However, relations with the natives were far from satisfactory; the exorbitant demands of the Spaniards for food sorely taxed the good nature of the aborigines, and at Guadalcanal a landing party was massacred, to be avenged by a wholesale burning of native villages by Sarmiento. After thoroughly overhauling their ships at San Cristoval, the Spaniards therefore sailed for Peru in August 1568. A stormy and hunger-ridden voyage of more than a year took them through Urdaneta's Passage to Callao, where the great undertaking ended. Great as it was, however, its results were far in the future, for the Solomon Islands were literally lost as soon as they were found. Never again could the Spaniards locate them, and it remained for Captain Cook to rediscover them two centuries later.

Mendaña, who had a good deal of the knight-errant in his make-up, never abandoned his vision. If the archipelago was not actually a continent, it was certainly the outpost of one; and Medaña in consequence dedicated himself to the foundation of a great colony in that quarter of the globe. Nearly a generation was to elapse before the perservering Mendaña was given a chance to realize his life's work, during which Spanish enterprise in the Pacific was to be sorely distracted by the incursion of English heretics into waters previously navigated solely by subjects of the Most Christian King. Drake in 1579, Cavendish in 1586, and Richard Hawkins in 1593 took men's minds from the enterprise of Pacific exploration, while for the Spaniards to colonize was merely to provide future havens for the advantage of the enemy.

Still, Mendaña hammered away at his favorite project until at last in 1595 his perseverance was rewarded. In April of that year he sailed from Callao at the head of a well-outfitted fleet bound for the Solomon Islands. Mendaña had made his first voyage as a chivalrous youth; he was now a rather weak and callous man in middle life, married to a woman who bore a striking resemblance to Lady Macbeth. This unscrupulous woman not only attached herself to the expedition, but brought along her brothers — making thereby a family party which effectively destroyed what little harmony might have existed among the fleet. To make matters still worse, the Peruvian authorities acted as they did in the case of Ursua's ill-fated expedition to El Dorado: they sent along every undesirable character they could find. Standing out from the ruffians that composed the crews was the Portuguese pilot, Pedro Fernandez de Quiros, whose courage and ability alone salvaged the wrecks of the undertaking.

Yet the voyage started auspiciously enough, with marriages taking place almost daily between members of the crew and the women who had come along. Three months out a mountainous island was sighted; this was Magdalena in the Marquesas. A week was spent in the southern part of this archipelago, which Mendaña named in honor of his friend the Marqués de Cañete, viceroy of Peru. Mendaña's men distinguished themselves by shooting the friendly natives as if they were sitting ducks, an act of brutality all the more terrible as it was absolutely useless. After this atrocious behavior, the fleet held its course for the Solomons, passing the Humphrey Islands, until in early September high land loomed up ahead. Mendaña was sanguine that this was his goal, for his navigation had been good. Actually, it was Santa Cruz Island, about two hundred and fifty miles short of San Cristoval, but in the same latitude (11° S). From that time on, the expedition went quickly to pieces. Two and a half dreadful months were spent at Santa Cruz, during which time the natives were slaughtered by the hundreds, while the Spanish losses were almost as great from diseases and homicide. In the murder of the natives and in the total disruption of the expedition, Doña Isabel Mendaña was the evil genius; it was perhaps a blessing for her husband when he perished of a tropical fever. By mid-November affairs had become so desperate that the only possible course was to attempt the passage to the Philippines, and in this crisis Quiros came to the fore. Under his guidance the survivors sailed the now rotten ships through uncharted seas, and after a voyage of almost three months they struggled into the harbor of Manila. Quiros' task had been rendered doubly difficult by the intransigence and selfishness of Doña Isabel. That lady, however, showed no concern; on reaching Manila she allowed herself to be entertained lavishly by the governor, and immediately thereafter she took unto herself a second husband.

Quiros, the hero of the expedition, made his way back to Mexico by Urdaneta's Passage, and proceeded from there to Spain, and eventually to Rome. The terrible trials he had passed through served only to increase the enthusiasm of this enigmatic character. In addition to his superb gifts as a navigator, Quiros possessed an intense religious mysticism, which however admirable in itself, was certainly more suited to the cloister than to the quarter-deck. As time went on, he became more and more a man with a vision — a vision of a New Jerusalem on the great Southern Continent, where the converted natives would live in Christian brotherhood with the Spaniards, in a manner worthy of the finest Utopias. With the fervor of a crusader, he hammered away at his altruistic project, for his heart yearned over the innumerable multitude of heathen, inhabiting lands yet undiscovered, who should be brought by him within the Church. Many Spanish and Portuguese explorers had a good deal of the missionary in them, it is true, but in Quiros' case the intensity of passion was extreme — it was that of an early Christian martyr.

Backed by the pope and the Spanish government, Quiros returned to Peru to carry out his project, and late in 1605 he sailed from Callao with three ships, on what was indeed the last great Spanish voyage before the fading of the heroic age. For the most part, the Pacific crossing was uneventful; Quiros was ill much of the time (one might suspect that he was somewhat psychopathic), and he issued voluminous orders in which reflections on piety and morality were strangely blended with hints on navigation and advice on diet. His course lay west-southwest from South America, almost to Pitcairn Island; then he turned north, to thread the Low Archipelago, and finally followed his old track with Mendaña to Santa Cruz. Bearing sharply to the south, he eventually reached — and discovered — the New Hebrides, which he was convinced was the continent of his hopes. Quiros put in at the great bay on the northern coast of Espiritu Santo and began to carry into effect his plans for the New Jerusalem.

At this stage, with Utopia within his grasp, the idealist completely overcame the navigator in Quiros, and his subsequent actions are so puzzling as to be almost inexplicable. He does seem to have antagonized his crews to the point of mutiny by his puritanical regulations, and his attempts to plant a town on the banks of the Jordan (for so he called the main river of the island) were thwarted by native hostility. In any case, after a visit of only three weeks, Quiros put to sea in his own ship and sailed back to America, leaving his second-in-command, Luis Vaez de Torres, dumbfounded in the harbor of Espiritu Santo. Quiros subsequently stated that his ship was blown from her anchorage by a sudden squall and could not regain the harbor; but it is perhaps significant that the squall had no effect whatever on Torres' vessel, and that officer, not without at least some justification, always regarded Quiros' action as plain, undisguised desertion. Possibly a more charitable explanation may be that Quiros' crew had become mutinous because of their captain's eccentricities, and that they forced him to sail back across the Pacific.

In any case, Torres no longer had any interest in the high-minded schemes of his chief, so after waiting some time in vain for Quiros' return, he quitted the New Hebrides and set his course to the Philippines. His voyage from a geographical standpoint was destined to be the most important part of Quiros' whole undertaking. After sailing southwest across the end of the New Caledonia, he bore northwest to the Louisiade Archipelago, and fell in with the eastern tip of New Guinea. From there he steered along the whole southern coast of the great island, passing through the Torres Straits, and possibly sighting the Cape York Peninsula of the Australian mainland. His voyage therefore proved the insular character of New Guinea, and vied (though somewhat apocryphally) with the cruise of the *Duyfken* in the discovery of the Southern Continent, which Mendaña and Quiros had sought. Torres continued to the Moluccas and Manila, but unfortunately the results of his voyage were lost, and it was not until his narrative fell into the hands of the English at the capture of Manila in 1762 that full justice was done to his merits and his name applied to the straits he discovered. As for the visionary Quiros, he returned to Spain, to urge on the government the desirability of further efforts for the discovery of the southern lands. His efforts were unsuccessful, and setting out in 1614 to make a last attempt, independent of government aid, he died without proceeding beyond Panama. His death was the swan song of Spanish voyaging; with his passing the great days of the Conquistadores were gone forever.

11

THE SEARCH FOR THE NORTHERN

PASSAGES

Until the middle of the sixteenth century, discovery and exploration had been almost altogether a Portuguese-Spanish monopoly. Then the hour at last struck when England, a remote island realm which the Renaissance reached late, came suddenly to the fore — to embark on a career of overseas expansion destined to surpass, and ultimately to eclipse, the accomplishments of the Iberian kingdoms. It is true that before the reign of Edward VI the men of Bristol and other West Country ports had done some voyaging, barely enough to constitute a false dawn and to give the seafaring population some little experience in sailing into the unknown. But these ventures were slight at best, slighter even than those of France, so that the real upsurge of English maritime expansion after 1550 must rank as one of the most significant phenomena in world history. Before that date there were the Cabot cycle of voyages, a brace of half-hearted American ventures in Henry VIII's reign, and William Hawkins' shadowy expeditions to Guinea and Brazil — these at a time when the Spaniards and Portuguese were carrying their flags from Panama to Malacca. After mid-century voyaging caught on in England with all the intensity and fervor that it had in the Portugal of Prince Henry's time, or in the Spain of Ferdinand and Isabella. One can point to the West African voyages of the 1550's as the first expression of the new spirit; they were successful, they were numerous, and they set the pace for what was to follow. Viewed in this light, Wyndham's Barbary voyage of 1551 sparked the flame for the intense activity during the reigns of Elizabeth and James which was to result in the establishment of the British Empire.

To account for this national upsurge, there were at least two factors besides the abstract contagion of the spirit of the times. One cannot overrate as an element the creation of the Royal Navy by Henry VIII, an act which bore some of its finest fruits in the days of Drake and Hawkins. Without the backing of a national fighting machine, English voyaging would have been impossible. Throughout the period the fighting service and the merchant service were so closely interlocked that they may be considered virtually one and the same.

Another element of great importance was the spread of propaganda for voyaging, especially among the more influential circles. Ironically, and yet appropriately, much of the impetus for England's outburst of overseas adventure was inspired by Spain's example, and it may be traced more specifically to the little colony of English residents living in Seville in the earlier part of the sixteenth century. Chief among these men were Robert Thorne, Sebastian Cabot (who may justifiably be called English, since he so considered himself), Roger Barlow, Henry Latimer, and Emanuel Lucar; and most of the group were Bristol merchants who had witnessed the first gropings of British exploration under the Cabots. As we have seen, Cabot, Barlow, and Latimer undertook an expedition up the River Plate in 1526, and since Seville was the center of Spain's trade with America, all members of the group were constantly in touch with voyages to the Indies. Thorne wrote in 1527 the letters that make up *The Book of Robert Thorne*, a propagandist work of geographical information, which was circulated in manuscript for many years and must have had quite an influence in court and mercantile circles alike, even though it was not printed until Hakluyt included it in his *Divers Voyages* (1582). This essay comprised the earliest statement of an overseas policy to be written by an Englishman and is all the more memorable since it contained the words: "There is no sea innavigable, no land unhabitable." Roger Barlow, too, helped spread the gospel; his translation of Enciso's *Suma de Geographia* was circulated in manuscript in much the same manner as Thorne's work. Lucar, a Bridgwater man, had been Thorne's apprentice and inherited his master's papers, which were used years later by John Dee and Richard Hakluyt. As for Cabot, he was the most experienced traveler and the most learned geographer of them all; we may be sure that he did his share of propaganda after he returned to England in 1547. These men started what might be called the Apostolic Succession of early English travel literature — literature which was designed to inspire Englishmen to overseas enterprise. After Thorne, Cabot, and Barlow came Richard Eden, John Dee, the two Hakluyts, and finally Samuel Purchas, producing together a century of geographical writing that played its part to the fullest in the early development of a greater Britain.

This mass of pleading — for so it may be called — had its initial objective in the quest of Eastern trade; in short, the same attraction which had started Portugal and Spain on their respective careers. As Elizabeth's reign wore on, other elements obtrude in England's policy, including warfare with the Spaniards in American waters, as well as the gradual development of thought favorable to the creation of plantations of Englishmen in North America. But these things lay in the future, and for many years following 1550 the quest of Eastern trade was the sole aim of British propagandists and theorists. Four routes lay open (in theory, at least) by which the Orient could be reached by ship from England. Each of these routes was attempted in turn; the first three proved either impossible or impracticable, and the fourth was not tried until the later years of the queen's reign, then remained undeveloped until the following century. The first route to be advocated and tried was the Northeast Passage, around Russia; the second route was the Northwest Passage, around North America; the third route was the Southwest Passage, through the Straits of Magellan; and the fourth (and successful) route was around the Cape of Good Hope.

THE NORTHEAST PASSAGE

In John Dudley, Duke of Northumberland, English voyaging for the first time had an enthusiastic patron who occupied the highest positions of state. To most students of history, he was a man with many black marks against him, yet his support of England's early colonial ventures goes far to redress the balance. With his friendship and backing, the impetus for voyaging to China around the north of Asia was further supplied by Sebastian Cabot and John Dee, the latter a young Welshman of brilliant erudition, whose dealings with the occult gave rise to the suspicion that he was in league with the Powers of Darkness. Cabot was by tradition and experience a "Northerner"; he had voyaged to Newfoundland as a boy, and had reached Hudson Straits as a young man, and his experiences in the Plate Valley had disillusioned him about the feasibility of a southern passage. As for Dee, he was wholly under the spell of the Arab geographers of the Middle Ages, whose theory it was that the Eurasian land mass sloped continuously southeast from the North Cape to China, so that the bulk of the voyage would take place in temperate waters. An even more cogent reason for adopting the northeastern route was economic, for England's chief article of export in those days was woolen cloth, and while it was realized that there was little sale for this commodity in the tropical regions of southern Asia, it was hoped that in the cooler lands along the way there would be populations of a sufficiently high cultural level to provide "a good vent for cloth." Men early perceived that such a condition would not obtain in the case of the aborigines along the Northwest Passage, but they reasoned that in the case of the Northeast Passage there might be people of Chinese stock and culture dwelling between the North Cape and Cathay, with whom trade could be carried on.

Under the preaching of Cabot and Dee, and with the blessing of the all-powerful Duke of Northumberland, a joint-stock company of Merchant Adventurers was formed, with the very influential backing of the leading citizens of London. Cabot, as governor of the company, organized an ex-

pedition of three ships, which sailed in May 1553 under the command of
Sir Hugh Willoughby. Failure and success lay before the venture; failure
in that the attempt to reach China was completely unsuccessful, and success in that Russia was reached instead, albeit unexpectedly. A storm off
Norway separated the ships, and Willoughby, after passing the North
Cape, sailed on to discover Novaya Zemlya. It was then August, and the
short Arctic summer was getting late, so the commander returned to Lap-
land to go into winter quarters — only to perish with all his men in the
terrible Arctic climate. Meanwhile Richard Chancellor, the second-in-command, had redressed the fortunes of the undertaking. After failing to encounter his chief at the rendezvous of Vardö (the "Wardhouse" of the
early narratives), he proceeded into the White Sea and dropped anchor
at the Russian village of Archangel. From there he journeyed southward
to Moscow, where he was well received by Ivan the Terrible. In truth, his
arrival at Ivan's barbaric court was a lucky thing, for at that time Russia
had no coastline on either the Baltic or the Black Sea, and its only contact with Europe was by the Moscow-Novgorod-Riga road, which was
under the rigid monopoly of the Hanseatic League. Chancellor was therefore able to gain extensive trading privileges for his countrymen, to the
mutual benefit of England and Russia, and to turn the flank of the Hanse
position in the bargain.

Chancellor was back in England by the summer of 1554, not indeed
having reached Cathay, but having performed a very substantial accomplishment nevertheless. In 1555 he sailed again to Russia, where he
learned of Willoughby's fate and also recovered his papers. His negotiations with the tsar led to the organization of Anglo-Russian trade, and an
ambassador from Ivan was sent to England with Chancellor in the autumn
of 1556. Chancellor's ship was wrecked in a storm on the Scottish coast,
and that stout Bristol seaman, who had proven such a good diplomat,
was drowned. His Russian colleague was saved and eventually reached
London — the first official representative of the Russian state to be seen
there.

Even as Chancellor was preparing to leave Russia on his ill-fated
return journey, another expedition was sailing from England to solve the
riddle of the Northeast Passage. This was headed by Stephen Borough,
a veteran of Chancellor's first voyage, who attempted this impossible
feat in the small pinnace *Searchthrift*, accompanied only by his young
brother William and a crew of eight — a daring undertaking indeed!
We are left a charming picture of old Sebastian Cabot, who went
down to Gravesend to wish the party god-speed; the "good old gentleman" inspected the vessel, dined with the crew at the Christopher Inn,
and then took part in the dance which followed. Borough made a valiant
attempt, which showed that he possessed the real Tudor touch of sea-

The Emperor Jahangir, by Bichitr (Mogul School, early 17th century). The bearded figure on the left is the poet, Sheikh Hasan Shisti, seen handing the monarch a panegyric; below him is a figure apparently representing the Sultan of Turkey; below again is an Englishman, thought possibly to be Sir Thomas Roe, but more likely King James I. The bottom figure may be Bichitr, the artist.

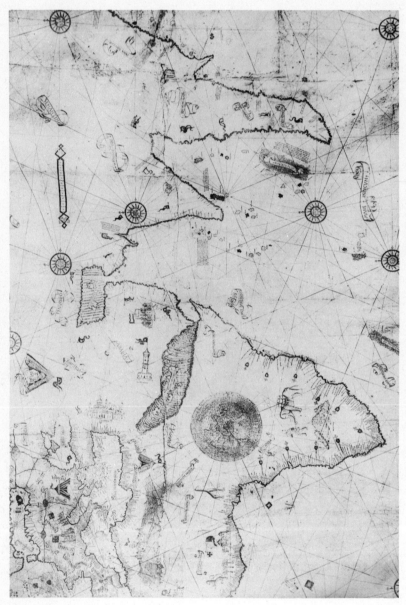

The eastern section of the Canerio Map, circa 1502–1504. This very important chart portrays Africa with considerable exactitude; India appears in its correct peninsula shape; there is a single, if distorted, Malay Peninsula; Arabia and the Persian Gulf are still Ptolemaic; Madagascar is out of place, but Ceylon and Sumatra are nearly correct.

manship. He reached Vaigatz Island between Novaya Zemlya and the Russian mainland, and in passing through the Kara Straits actually penetrated into the Kara Sea before being turned back by ice and weather. After wintering at Kolmogro near the mouth of the Dwina, he returned to England (1557), and with his failure attempts to reach China around Russia flagged for many years. The loss of enthusiasm was not due to this voyage alone; more important was the unexpected success of the trade with Russia. Cabot's Merchant Adventurers now became more appropriately known as the Muscovy Company, and voyages between London and Archangel grew to be a commonplace. More important in the pages of geographical history were the journeys of Englishmen across Russia to Persia and Central Asia, a direct result of the new Anglo-Russian trade, and an element of great importance in the subsequent growth of English knowledge of the Orient. These journeys will be described in a later chapter, but it might be pointed out, in justice to the memory of the enthusiasts of the Northeast Passage, that Englishmen did get far into Asia by the North Cape route. Meanwhile, the grand old figure of early English voyaging had passed on: Sebastian Cabot, whose sixty years of activity linked the days of Columbus with those of Elizabeth, died in 1557.

Not until 1580 was there another attempt to pass around the north of Asia. In that year Arthur Pet and Charles Jackman sailed, largely at the instigation of John Dee, who after Cabot's death had been an active advocate of the Northeast and Northwest Passages alike. In spite of the ill success of Borough's attempt, Pet and Jackman still hoped to pass by Vaigatz Island and through Kara Sea, but their story was only too similar to that of Borough. They passed Vaigatz and fought their way into Kara Sea, to be so beset by ice and fog that they were reluctantly constrained to set their course homeward. Even then further dangers were encountered, such as ice in the straits and shoals off Kolguev Island. Jackman's vessel vanished without a trace off Norway, and Pet with great difficulty reached the Thames.

Theirs was an isolated attempt; although there is evidence that English servants of the Muscovy Company, sailing from Archangel about the year 1584, crossed the Kara Sea and reached the mouth of the Ob River in northern Siberia. Yet the mythical Cape Tabin remained to be rounded; the cape beyond which, according to Dee, the sailing was easy, for the coast ran southeast down to China. Dee's pleadings fell on deaf ears, nevertheless, for no more expeditions were made from England during the rest of the century.

If the ardor of the English had cooled, this was not true of the Dutch, who had established a regular trade with the White Sea as early as 1577. They had an enthusiastic exponent in the person of Oliver Brunel, who had gone overland from Russia, through the Samoyed territory, to Siberia and had made a coasting voyage as far as the mouth of the Ob, while in 1584 he made an unsuccessful attempt to take an expedition past Vaigatz. Brunel's travels led to the fitting out of a fleet in 1594, headed by Willem Barents, who ranks in history as one of the greatest Arctic navigators. With Barents went Jan Huyghen van Linschoten, the celebrated traveler to the East. Their first venture took the Dutch the whole length of Novaya Zemlya, to its northern tip, after which Barents retraced his course to Vaigatz, and passed through the Kara Sea as far as the latitude of the Ob.

The relative success of this voyage led to another the following year (1595), like the first commanded by Barents with Linschoten as super-cargo. The high hopes placed in this undertaking were not realized, for the ships could not fight their way through the straits between Vaigatz and the mainland, and were obliged to return to Holland, victims of the unusual severity of a season which had kept the straits packed with ice throughout the summer.

Barents' third and last voyage was his greatest, ranking among the hardiest achievements of all Polar exploration. Sailing in 1596, he set his course neither by the Northeast nor the Northwest Passage, but boldly across the Pole. In this wise, he reached (and discovered) Spitsbergen, but as he could not penetrate the pack-ice beyond, he abandoned his original idea, and steered once more for Novaya Zemlya. After passing the farthest point of his 1594 voyage, Barents rounded the northern tip of the island, where his ship was crushed in the ice and he and his men were forced to spend the winter in great misery. The following spring the survivors set out in two open boats and after incredible difficulties reached Russian territory. Barents perished during the passage, and with him the driving force of Dutch exploration in this quarter, but his indomitable spirit had enabled a party of men for the first time to winter far within the Arctic Circle, suffering from all the hardships inseparable from such a first experience.

Only one later figure deserves mention in the search for the Northeast Passage: Henry Hudson, who sought a way between Greenland and Spitsbergen in 1607; the next year, after trying in vain to the east of Spitsbergen, he reached Novaya Zemlya, and strove like his predecessors to make the passage by Vaigatz, with the same inevitable result. With him the saga of the Northeast Passage ends — at least until its successful accomplishment by Baron Nordenskiöld in 1879.

THE NORTHWEST PASSAGE

England's initial burst of expansion had been in two directions: northeast in an attempt to solve the passage to China, which had soon turned to the more practical business of trade with Russia; and south-west to Guinea, and ultimately to Spanish America. Early enthusiasm gave way to a period of transition in the 1560's, after several of the leading spirits had died; Northumberland, whose patronage had been so valuable, perished on the scaffold at Mary's accession, and Sebastian Cabot died five years later in 1557. Hakluyt was yet to come, and of the original group of enthusiasts only Dee remained — Dee the necromancer, who had an encyclopaedic intellect and who trafficked in black magic. Yet Dee still clung to his vision of the route to Cathay, and as the North Cape way had been disappointing, and as the southern courses did not appeal to him, he turned to the Northwest Passage. His pleadings were eloquent, and it is significant that in these years he coined the term "the British Empire." Doubtless "English Empire" would have been more logical, but possibly distasteful to one of Cambrian ancestry. In this advocacy Dee found an unexpected ally in a Devonshire squire, the half-brother of Sir Walter Raleigh, Sir Humphrey Gilbert, who had composed an enthusiastic treatise on the Northwest Passage. This tract, entitled *A Discourse of a Discoverie for a New Passage to Cataia*, was written about 1566, circulated in manuscript for a decade, and finally printed in 1576. Gilbert's little book had great influence; more than anything else it is said to have prompted Frobisher's first voyage. In brief, the theory of the Northwest Passage was that once around Labrador, there was open water running southwest through the Straits of Anian. In his earlier days Sebastian Cabot had a theory that the land to the north of the straits was a northeastward extension of Asia, a theory long held in some quarters, although Dee believed that the straits were wide and in a low latitude. Anian itself was one of those migratory regions common in the cosmography of the day: originally conceived as that part of Asia above China, it moved to become a detached American land mass north of the straits, and finally (in Ortelius' Map) settled on the North American mainland north of California. In any event one can visualize the Renaissance conception of the waterway as a longer, wider, and far more southeasterly version of Bering Straits.

Dee and Gilbert between them built up a convincing case for the Passage, so convincing in fact, that large financial assistance for the scheme was forthcoming, chiefly from the Lok family, who earlier had been active in the West African trade. An experienced captain for the enterprise was found in Martin Frobisher, who in his early days had sailed on the Guinea voyages and who later had occupied his time in the most unblushing acts of piracy in home waters. After a farewell interview with Queen Elizabeth, Frobisher sailed in June 1576 with three small vessels and made for the southern tip of Greenland. One of his ships foundered and another deserted, but in the *Gabriel* of twenty-five tons Frobisher pushed on as far as the coast of Baffin Land. Here he found what he was looking for — or so he thought; a strait with Asia to starboard and America to port. Actually Frobisher's Straits (or Lumley's Inlet) was simply a cul-de-sac. But Frobisher was unable to carry his exploration further; Eskimos captured five of his men and the *Gabriel's* longboat, and he had only thirteen of the crew left. So with an exhibition of his colossal physical strength, Frobisher lifted an Eskimo and his kayak, as the unfortunate was paddling by, on to the deck of the *Gabriel*, and sailed for England with this "Asiatic" as a souvenir. Other souvenirs were brought home, too: samples of rocks said to contain gold, which had the effect of deflecting the entire purpose of the enterprise.

In spite of Frobisher's inability to follow the passage to the Pacific, the backers of the venture remained highly sanguine, and Michael Lok founded the Company of Cathay, with no less a personage than the queen as a subscriber. Probably the report of a gold mine in the straits had a good deal to do with it. Frobisher, now invested with his title of Admiral of the Company, sailed on his second venture in 1577, with a two-fold purpose: to lade one vessel with gold-bearing ore in the straits and to push on to the Pacific with the other two. As for the latter commission, Frobisher scarcely made a show of complying with it. Instead, he loaded all three ships in the straits and came immediately back to England. Indeed, the quest for the Northwest Passage had quickly degenerated into a bucket-shop mining venture; a commentary on the naive immaturity of the Elizabethans in commercial matters. Upon Frobisher's return, the ore was assayed with varying opinions — probably none of them disinterested, although Lok and Frobisher both had great confidence in the discovery.

It was at least with the virtue of frankness, therefore, that Frobisher set out on his third expedition (1578) with the sole purpose of loading ore, although it is only fair to add that this voyage did in fact achieve an advance in exploration. Thick weather prevented him from getting his latitude accurately, and he found himself in Hudson Straits, which he followed for two hundred miles before turning back to the ore deposits. Rightly he concluded that this would be a better passage to China than his previous discovery, which was simply a channel among "broken lands" and not a thoroughfare along the northern side of the American continent. From this reconnaissance, too, the old conception of the projecting Asiatic horn was abandoned, to be replaced by the idea of islands and open water between Labrador and the Pole. For the rest, however, Frobisher's last voyage was a failure. The season was a severe one, with very troublesome ice, which sank the ship that carried most of the expedition's equipment. Everyone was ill-tempered and anxious to get home, and as soon as possible Frobisher sailed for England — to find on his return that the bubble had burst. The company was bankrupt, and Lok was bankrupt and in a debtors' prison. Thus ended ignominiously the first round in the quest for the Northwest Passage.

Frobisher's failure quite naturally dampened the enthusiasm of the "Northwesterners," and several years elapsed before interest could be aroused in another attempt to find a way to Asia around North America. During these years Frobisher's backers passed from the scene, to be replaced by new men. Lok was in penury; Gilbert had been drowned while taking part in England's first colonization scheme in the New World (1583); as for Dee, the Welsh wizard had decided that the Continent was more suitable ground for his necromancy and had departed to Bohemia (1582) with several fellow charlatans. Into their places stepped William Sanderson, a wealthy citizen of London; Sir Walter Raleigh, Gilbert's half-brother; and Sir Francis Walsingham, whose spirit had not been deterred by his heavy losses in the Frobisher undertaking. This patronage resulted in the three voyages of John Davis, of Dartmouth in Devonshire, a sailor of both practical and theoretical skill, whose remarkable career on the seven seas places him in the forefront of Tudor mariners.

Davis' aim was to seek a passage through the sea which separates Greenland from the North American archipelago, which meant a more northerly course than Frobisher's. His voyages were closely associated with the little port of Dartmouth, and made up the ruling interest of the local population for several years. On his first voyage (1585) Davis made his landfall at southern Greenland, and worked his way up the west coast to Gilbert Sound (the present site of Godthaab), which he named in memory of Sir Humphrey. From this point he crossed over Davis Straits to Baffin Land and discovered Cumberland Sound, the waterway to the north of Frobisher's Straits or Bay, which gave Davis great hopes of passage to the Pacific. Bad weather, however, prevented this discovery from being exploited, and Davis felt compelled to sail for Dartmouth. In the spring of 1586 Davis was off on his second voyage, taking a rather similar route; he coasted Greenland to Gilbert Sound, crossed over to Cumberland Sound, which he explored, and then sailed southwards past the entrance of Hudson Straits and along the Labrador coast. By autumn he was back in England.

That Davis had made no startling discoveries was apparent, and his Devonshire backers began to lose heart. But Davis was made of different stuff than Frobisher; the latter, gallant though he was, was ever an opportunist, ready to throw over the search for a passage for the immediate return of an imaginary gold mine. Davis, on the other hand, grew more hopeful with each succeeding failure and pegged away at the passage with a determination that must command whole-hearted admiration.

To Davis the Passage was always "just around the corner"; his bulldog spirit was never sidetracked by secondary objectives, and he probably would have kept on with his search for the rest of his life had not the crisis of war with Spain put a halt to exploration. As it was, he was vouchsafed to make a third attempt, for he still retained the support of Raleigh, Sanderson, and Walsingham. Sailing from Dartmouth in the spring of 1587, he proceeded to Greenland, and passed along the west coast to the very high latitude of 72 degrees north. A mountainous head-land at the farthest point north yet revealed in these waters was appro-priately christened Sanderson's Hope, for indeed Davis had pointed the way to the true Northwest Passage, although he had not actually found it. All attempts to progress beyond this landmark were frustrated by ice, and Davis was compelled to steer across the straits for Baffin Land, as he had done on his earlier voyages. His route from there lay along the Labrador coast and so home, which he reached in September 1587 with his hope and enthusiasm not the least dampened. However, the Invin-cible Armada was in the making, and Davis' talents were needed the fol-lowing year for sterner duties. Never again did he have the chance to realize his dreams, although he was destined to go through the Straits of Magellan, to reach the Indies thrice around the Cape of Good Hope, and finally to meet a sailor's death in Malayan waters.

By all rules of logic, Davis' failure should have put an end to the search for the Northwest Passage, for the years following the Armada witnessed overland penetration of Southern Asia by Englishmen; Lan-caster's arrival in the East Indies by the Cape route; and the formation of the Honourable East India Company, which immediately organized annual voyages by the Cape. Clearly in the face of this successful solu-tion to the problem, it was foolish to waste time and energy in further attempts to reach Asia through the Arctic, and yet during the first third of the seventeenth century expedition after expedition left England to look for this will o' the wisp. Even the East India Company shared in these delusions, for in 1602, while Lancaster was trading in Sumatra on the company's first voyage, the directors sent out an expedition to the northwest under George Waymouth, which penetrated Hudson Straits before being turned back by mutiny. This satisfied the company that the Cape route was the only practical one, for they made no further attempts to reach China across the Pole, but others after Waymouth continued to search for the Straits of Anian, in what was indeed the heroic cycle of Arctic exploration, albeit of little practical result.

Of these old Polar voyages, the most celebrated was that in 1610 of Henry Hudson in the *Discovery*. Determined to look for the Straits of Anian to the south, Hudson sailed through Hudson Straits, and found himself at the entrance of a great bay, having come far beyond Frobisher's farthest point west. Here he bore to port, and generally keeping along the eastern side of the bay that bears his name, proceeded until his advance was barred by the extremity of James Bay. After beating up and down the latter body of water in a vain attempt to find a way through to the Pacific, the ship was frozen in, and the expedition spent the winter in great hardship. Inevitably mutiny broke out; with the coming of spring Hudson was set adrift in an open boat, and the mutineers struggled back to England.

Hudson's old backers were still sanguine about the passage, and having secured a charter, in 1612 they sent out Sir Thomas Button, charged with the dual commission of finding out Hudson's fate and of discovering the Passage. Button, in the *Discovery*, followed his predecessor's route through Hudson Straits and into the bay, where he bore across to the western side. Having sailed along the shore as far as the mouth of the Nelson River, he was compelled to winter in the same inhospitable environment that Hudson and his men had endured. Despite terrible ravages of scurvy, Button maintained sufficient control over his men, and the following spring was able to sail north, to seek a passage west of Southampton Island. Button reached his highest latitude in 65 degrees north; he named the position Roe's Welcome after Sir Thomas Roe, and sailed away to England, having found neither Hudson nor the passage.

Two years later (1615), the adventurers sent out the *Discovery* again, under the command of Robert Bylot, who had been on Hudson's fateful expedition, and with William Baffin as pilot. In this voyage, Hudson Straits were again the line of approach, but Bylot and Baffin decided to try their luck to the north of Hudson Bay, and to this end they held their course north of Southampton Island, which lies across the mouth of the Bay. They traversed uncharted waters to the mainland beyond, but concluding that they were in an enclosed bay and in danger of shoals, they were glad to return home. In 1616 the same mariners sailed in the stout old *Discovery* again, this time determined to try Davis' route between Greenland and Baffin Land. Their exploration of the waters between Greenland and the Canadian archipelago was a thorough piece of work, and a great geographical achievement. Proceeding along the west coast of Greenland, they passed far beyond Sanderson's Hope and reached the very high latitude of 78 degrees north, before their way was blocked by pack-ice. Crossing Baffin Bay, they coasted various islands north of Baffin Land, and then surveyed Baffin Land itself before returning to England, having in this wise made a complete circumnavigation of the waters between Greenland and the Canadian Arctic. Bylot and Baffin, by discovering Smith Sound (named for Sir Thomas Smith or Smythe, the first Governor of the East India Company) and Lancaster Sound (named for Sir James Lancaster), pointed to the two routes along which the discoverers of the nineteenth century made their way into the Polar seas, but it is doubtful if Bylot and Baffin realized their discoveries, for they were expecting to find a wide passage like Davis Straits.

Two expeditions, both sailing in 1631, signalized the final attempt to solve the Passage. These ventures, led by Luke Foxe and Thomas James respectively, resulted in the most thorough exploration of Hudson Bay thus far. Both men coasted the western side; James explored James Bay, and Foxe strove to find a passage (Foxe Channel) to the north of Hudson Bay, between Foxe Land and Southampton Island. These voyages did settle once and for all the question whether there was an outlet to the Pacific from Hudson or James bays, and both resulted in wonderfully graphic accounts of Arctic navigation. With the return of Foxe and James search for the Northwest Passage ended, and this whole phase of exploration was played out. For the money and energy expended, the early Polar mariners had little to show; perhaps one might limit the practical results to only two, for these voyages did give rise to the development of the whale fisheries around Spitsbergen, which flourished throughout the seventeenth century, and they also bore fruit when the Hudson's Bay Company was founded in the reign of Charles II.

12

THE AGE OF DRAKE

The attempt of the English to develop the southwest route to Asia was less premeditated and more gradual than were the enterprises for the two northern passages; there was no sudden campaign for it, such as heralded the voyages of Willoughby and Frobisher — rather was it the natural outcome of the voyages which led up to it. First came the Guinea ventures in the days of Northumberland and Queen Mary; then the slaving voyages to the Spanish Main; then the barely concealed warfare with the Spaniards around Panama, and finally Drake's circumnavigation. One phase led to another, naturally and organically.

England's original axis of expansion in the 1550's was northeast — for the Northeast Passage and Russia — and southwest — for Guinea and the West Indies. It has been described above how the ventures of Wyndham, Lok, Towerson, and others to West Africa were followed by the triangular slave trade — to Africa, then to Spanish America, and then home to England — a trade in which John Hawkins of Plymouth took a leading part. This trade, furthermore, was fully countenanced by the Spaniards in its early days, for although Spain and England were opposed on religious grounds, economically and politically the two countries were more friendly in the first decade of Elizabeth's reign than one would suppose. The turning point in their relations came quickly and (for the English, at least) unexpectedly, at San Juan de Ulúa on the Mexican coast in 1568. This event was the Pearl Harbor of Tudor England, and it brought to the foreground the personality of Francis Drake.

Drake was born at Tavistock in Devonshire about 1541, the son of a farmer of very advanced Protestant views. His father's protestantism was in fact so extreme that the elder Drake had to flee with his family into Kent, where he eked out a poor living as chaplain to the naval dockyard of Chatham. In this maritime and Protestant environment young Francis Drake grew up; it was in his blood and in his surroundings to be a violent anti-Catholic, an aggressively patriotic Englishman, and a man who was as much at home afloat as ashore. His education was at best sketchy: he learned to read and write, but precious little more. However, he was not cast in the reflective or studious mold. Rather was he a man of action, and in addition to his qualities of leadership, he possessed one gift to the ultimate degree — he could probably sail a boat better than any other man who has ever lived. When this is added to his characteristics of commanding men, of lightning opportunism rising at times to inspiration, of cheerfulness in misfortune and kindly charity in success, it is easy to see why he stands forth as one of the greatest seamen of all time.

It was through his distant relation, John Hawkins, that Drake got his start at sea, and in 1566 he sailed as purser on a slaving voyage commanded by John Lovell, one of Hawkins' captains. This voyage was not of great importance, and is chiefly noteworthy as being Drake's first experience at sea. Having sailed to West Africa, Lovell took on his cargo between Cape Verde and Sierra Leone; then crossing the Atlantic, he disposed of the slaves at Margarita, Curaçoa, and Rio de la Hacha. At the latter place, situated on the Spanish Main west of Maracaibo, Lovell was badly outwitted by the Spaniards, an experience which made a great impression on his young purser. After that, the fleet held its course for England, to arrive just as Hawkins was fitting out his third and most ambitious slaving voyage.

After hardly more than a few days at home, Drake sailed with Hawkins on this expedition; again he was in a subordinate capacity, but he had his own ship, the *Judith*, later in the voyage. Following the familiar course, the fleet assembled at the Canaries and then took on a cargo of slaves in the various estuaries and havens from Gambia southward. When the cargo was completed, Hawkins sailed across to the Caribbean, and sought to dispose of his slaves along the Spanish Main. But the attitude of the Spaniards toward the English trade had appreciably stiffened, and although Hawkins sold most of his slaves at Santa Marta, he had a nasty little skirmish at Rio de la Hacha, and met with armed hostility at Cartagena. Matters were indeed beginning to take on a menacing aspect.

By this time, according to Hawkins' account, the ships were in poor condition and needed repairs badly. Hawkins therefore put in at San Juan de Ulúa, a small harbor on the Mexican coast near Vera Cruz, from which the Mexican silver was shipped to Spain. It was his misfortune that the Spanish plate fleet sailed into port only two days later. Hawkins was in a tight place, but he was able to make an agreement with the Spanish commander, allowing him to refit and revictual upon proper payment. Nevertheless, the Spaniards treacherously attempted to seize the English ships. Fortunately Hawkins and Drake were on the alert, and were able to fight their two ships out of the harbor; but the largest vessel, the *Jesus*, was captured along with several others, and all the Englishmen who were ashore were either slain or made prisoner. The *Minion* under Hawkins and the *Judith* under Drake made their way back

across the Atlantic, both terribly crowded with such survivors of the
other vessels as had been rescued. There has always been a shadow on
Drake's name, for sailing away immediately after the attack, to leave the
Minion to shift for herself. This has never been satisfactorily explained,
and there may be factors involved of which posterity is ignorant; in any
case, however, both vessels had tragic passages home, suffering dread-
fully from overcrowding and shortage of food. They reached Plymouth
Sound separately in January 1569 to spread the tale of Spanish infamy.

In its political results, Hawkins's "third troublesome voyage" was
most far-reaching; it ended all hope of a recognized English trade in the
Caribbean, and it terminated the long period of Anglo-Spanish friendship and commercial intercourse, which had lasted since the days of
Henry VII. It was indeed a turning point; the treachery of San Juan de
Ulúa was never forgiven by the subjects of Elizabeth, and henceforth
there was "no peace beyond the Line." The first step along the path to
the Invincible Armada had been taken.

For Drake this event was the signal for a jehad; with the spirit of a
crusader he determined to carry fire and sword to the idolatrous Spaniards whether his country was officially at war with Spain or not. Other
Englishmen felt as Drake did and followed his example, but Drake was
ever in the fore in these unofficial hostilities. In 1571 he cruised in the
Caribbean with one small ship and made for the Isthmus of Panama, the
strategic region through which all treasure from South America had to
pass. This venture was primarily a reconnaissance; Drake learned of the
topography and defenses of the district, of the mule trains which conveyed the bullion across the Isthmus, and of the Cimaroons, tribes of
escaped Negroes and Indian women who lived in the fastnesses of the
Isthmus in defiance of Spanish attempts to exterminate them. His activities were by no means limited to the collection of intelligence; he captured much Spanish shipping along the coast, and took his prizes to a
secret harbor two hundred miles down the coast from Nombre de Dios,
which he called Port Pheasant. When he sailed for England, he had
already equipped this landlocked inlet as a base and had matured his
plans for an attack on the main stream of Peruvian treasure as it crossed
the Isthmus, an undertaking in which he fully realized the value of the
Cimaroons as allies.

With two vessels and crews numbering seventy-three in all, Drake
left Plymouth in May 1572, intending with his small force to sack Nombre de Dios, and then get away before the Spaniards could retaliate. He
sailed straight to Port Pheasant, where he constructed pinnaces, which
had been brought in sections from England. When all was ready, he
made his way along the coast as stealthily as possible and launched a
brilliant surprise attack on Nombre de Dios, driving out the defenders

and capturing the town. But the treasure, in the form of great bars of silver, was too heavy to move, a tropical cloudburst wet the English gunpowder, and a Spanish counterattack drove the English out. Drake was wounded, his brilliant planning and the equally brilliant execution of his plans were alike undone, and the English made a sorrowful escape back to Port Pheasant. After this failure, Drake decided on the alternate plan of attacking the Peruvian treasure train as it crossed the Isthmus, and to this end he entered into communication with the Cimaroons, whose coöperation in the plan was essential. Through them he learned that no treasure would be moved until the close of the rainy season, several months off. In the meantime, he was forced to remain in an unhealthy region, living as much on the sly as possible. Some of his men did succumb to tropical fevers, but he was able to keep his force occupied by capturing several small Spanish vessels, until word should come from the Cimaroons that the passage of the treasure train was imminent.

At the end of the rainy season the glad tidings arrived and with a picked body of men, Drake set out for Panama. From a tall tree along the trail he had his celebrated view of the Pacific, the first of his nation to see that ocean. By a fluke of ill luck, he missed a large convoy of treasure on the trans-isthmian road, but his tenacity was rewarded soon after when he made the rich capture of a second convoy, taken so close to Nombre de Dios that the hammering of shipwrights could be heard, at work on the vessels of the plate fleet. In this successful venture Drake received valuable assistance from a French Huguenot privateer, with whom he gratefully divided the spoil. His return to England was therefore a happy one, although Elizabeth's councilors, fearing international complications, made Drake keep under cover for two or three years.

Drake did not spend this period in idleness, for his active mind was hatching a scheme more ambitious than any he had so far undertaken. This was nothing less than a cruising voyage around the world. In the development of this project he received the coöperation of Sir Francis Walsingham, the Earl of Leicester, and Sir Christopher Hatton; in its earlier stages at least the scheme seemed to envisage a search for the mysterious Southern Continent, which the Spaniards had been looking for in the South Pacific. Word of Mendaña's voyage to the Solomon Islands had reached England, and the irrepressible John Dee (who at this time was still in London) was fired with enthusiasm for Terra Australis. Hatton, an intimate of Dee's, pushed the scheme in high circles (always however being careful to keep Burghley in ignorance), with the result that Drake's commission, while somewhat ambiguous, left little doubt that he was to look for new lands in the southern ocean. Drake thought otherwise, nevertheless, and with the sole connivance of Walsingham and the queen, he laid his plans for a cruising voyage along the

South American coast. In other words, the planning for the expedition was deceitful several times over: Burghley knew nothing about it at all; the crew shipped for a voyage to the Mediterranean; the backers at court expected a search for the Southern Continent; and only the queen, Walsingham, and Drake himself knew the real plans.

Drake's resolve to carry the undeclared war against Spain into the Pacific is said to have stemmed from the sight of the ocean from the tall tree near Panama. It had certainly determined the actions of his companion John Oxenham, who had served Drake valiantly in the Panama raid. For when Oxenham had reached England, he fitted out his own expedition, which included several pinnaces in sections, to be assembled on the Isthmus of Panama, and launched in the South Sea. At first this enterprise went successfully. Oxenham sailed to the Isthmus in 1576, assembled his pinnaces on the shores of the Pacific, and captured several valuable prizes among the Pearl Islands south of Panama. But with a humanity which in his case was suicidal, Oxenham released his prisoners, who straightway told the Spanish authorities of the presence of Lutheran marauders in the Pacific. A general alarm was sounded, and Oxenham was brought to bay with his Cimaroon allies in the fastnesses of the Isthmus. His end was tragic, but inevitable, and his execution at Lima was the price he paid for disregarding the pirates' precept that "dead men tell no tales." Drake knew of the inception of Oxenham's expedition, but not its tragic ending, and in his own planning there is little doubt but that he hoped to join forces with his colleague somewhere in the Pacific.

Against this background of theoretical peace but actual war in the Spanish colonies, of Oxenham's adventure in the South Sea, and of the plans for the discovery of the Southern Continent, Drake's voyage of circumnavigation took place. It was the climax of a career studded with high points; it was the second circumnavigation of the world and the first by an Englishman; and it was Drake's only voyage of actual discovery. In the autumn of 1577 Drake left Plymouth on his great venture with five vessels: the flagship *Pelican* (later renamed the *Golden Hind*), the *Elizabeth*, the *Marigold*, a pinnace, and a storeship. His combined companies amounted to about one hundred and sixty men, including his brother and nephew, as well as William Hawkins, nephew of John. John Winter captained the *Elizabeth*, while assigned to each ship were various well-born landsmen, classed as "gentlemen," of whom the ill-starred Thomas Doughty was the most conspicuous. Drake soon wished that he had never seen these ineffectual troublemakers; he was however spared the tedious loquacity of John Dee, who had hoped to make the voyage, but who changed his mind at the last minute.

Drake steered a course down the African coast to the Cape Verde Islands, and thence across the Atlantic to the Plate estuary. His passage was slow, and it was not until June 1578 that the fleet found itself at Port St. Julian on the coast of Patagonia, where Magellan had endured mutiny and hardship sixty years earlier. Here another tragedy was des- tined to be enacted, because of the strange and alarming behavior of the courtier Thomas Doughty. While the counts are even yet by no means clear, it would seem that Doughty had been spreading unrest among the crews; in particular, he had been inciting the men on the *Pelican* to mutiny and desertion. Believing himself to be possessed of occult powers, Doughty further had been practicing witchcraft in order to hinder the voyage. This last charge may seem frivolous to us today, but sailors have traditionally been a superstitious class, and moreover even the intelli- gensia of Elizabeth's time took their witchcraft seriously. In a larger sense the issue was whether the sailors or the gentlemen were to run the voyage. On this issue one may be sure that Drake himself had no doubts whatever, and he determined to put his foot down. Doughty was arrested, tried on the grounds of inciting mutiny and conjuring, condemned, and beheaded.

A few days later (it being Sunday), Drake called his company together and preached them a sermon, in which he uttered the classic words, "For I must have the gentleman to haul and draw with the mariner, and the mariner with the gentleman." Then he discharged all the officers from their posts, leaving them totally crestfallen while he continued his appeal. At the end, having won all to his will, he reinstated his officers, as servants of the queen under her General Francis Drake, to sail at his sole command against the Spaniard. By this act Drake established his authority once and for all, and established likewise a new tradition of naval discipline.

Having thus reconstituted his leadership, Drake sailed for the straits, through which he made a speedy passage. As he entered the broad waters of the Pacific a gale of terrifying intensity struck his fleet; the *Marigold* parted company with the fleet and was never seen again; Winter in the *Elizabeth* was blown back into the straits, and after wait- ing a month in vain for the sight of his chief, sailed home to England. Drake himself in the erstwhile *Pelican*, now rechristened *Golden Hind*, was blown south of the straits and around Tierra del Fuego, possibly to the longitude of the Horn — a course which had its effect on subsequent English cartography, as evidenced in the Wright-Molineaux Map of 1600, in that the continental land mass previously shown as the Southern Continent below the straits gave way to smallish islands with open water to the south.

A fortunate break in the weather enabled Drake to regain his course, and the now-solitary *Golden Hand* made her way along the coasts of Chile and Peru, raiding the shipping at Valparaiso and Callao and taking various prizes in the South Sea. No hostile craft had heretofore been seen in these waters, nor was there any alarm of Drake's coming, while the Spanish vessels were as lightly armed as they were unsuspecting. It was as if a fox had broken into a poultry farm. With the capture of the great galleon *Cacafuego* and her fabulous cargo of Peruvian silver, the voyage was "made" many times over. Drake ere this had heard of Oxenham's capture, and tried in vain to save him from his fate by releasing Spanish prisoners as emissaries to the viceroy of Peru, but since this attempt was hopeless, he steered north. Several captures were made off Nicaragua and Mexico; one of these prizes contained Don Francisco de Zarate, a Spaniard of rank, whose subsequent report embodies much information about Drake and the *Golden Hind*.

By this time replete with booty, Drake held his course northward, sailing farther up the North American coast than any man had done before him, possibly reaching the latitude of Vancouver Island. The purpose of this maneuver was to find the Pacific outlet of the Straits of Anian; it was Drake's contribution to the search for the Northwest Passage and is of interest in that it was made in reverse, from the Pacific instead of from the Atlantic. Having satisfied himself that no passage existed in these latitudes at least, Drake turned southward and put in at San Francisco Bay, where the *Golden Hind* was careened and overhauled. After a thorough rest and refit, Drake set out across the Pacific. His passage was a northern one, so that little in the way of discovery was accomplished; an island in the Pellew Group and the southern Philippines were seen and the *Golden Hind* continued her way to Ternate in the Moluccas. Drake's arrival there was opportune, for he found a state of war existing between Ternate and the neighboring Portuguese-controlled Tidore. A cordial treaty of alliance between the English and the sultan of Ternate resulted — doubtless an agreement more convenient than sincere. The sultan wanted to use the English as a stick to chastise the Portuguese; Drake needed something to show his colonial backers, who might well be disgusted with him otherwise for throwing overboard the search for the Southern Continent. It might also give the English a foothold in the East Indies which would be of use at some future date.

Having taken on a good cargo of cloves, Drake again pursued his way. In the treacherous seas between the Moluccas and Java the *Golden Hind* nearly came to grief on a submerged rock, with shoal water to leeward and no bottom to anchor on to windward. For a night and a day it looked as if all was over, but the stoutness of English oak and the providential easing of the wind turned the scale; the *Golden Hind* slid off the rock and continued her voyage in waters never before furrowed by an English keel. Drake's seamanship never appeared to better advantage than in this dangerous part of the voyage. Having careened his ship again on the south coast of Java, where he established friendly relations with the natives, Drake steered across the Indian Ocean for the Cape of Good Hope. By June 1580 he had rounded the Cape; and his final port of call was Sierra Leone, familiar ground, no doubt, as it was the scene of the slaving voyages of his youth. His trials and dangers were now over, and the course from Guinea to England Drake could steer blindfolded. Plymouth was reached without further incident on September 26, 1580, two years and ten months after the fleet had set out; as the *Golden Hind* entered the harbor Drake's first question to passing fishermen was whether the queen was alive and well.

Drake's circumnavigation fired the imagination of Englishmen as no other naval exploit had so far done, and stimulated the zeal of his fellows as nothing else could. Comparison with Magellan's voyage is interesting; both expeditions started with five ships, both finished with one; both witnessed mutiny and tragedy at the same desolate spot on the Patagonian coast; in both cases an important vessel of the fleet parted company in the straits and sailed homeward; and both passages took almost the same amount of time. On the other hand, while del Cano and the pitiful remnant of the first circumnavigation had little to show for their great performance, Drake's voyage was a brilliant financial success, for he had brought back treasure beyond the fondest dreams of avarice.

With such truly wonderful success as an inspiration, it is not surprising that plans for another expedition were soon under way. But in contrast with its predecessor, this voyage, under the command of Edward Fenton, who had served with Frobisher in the Arctic, was a complete failure, and is important in the history of navigation sheerly because it was the first English voyage planned to reach the Indies around Africa. Between planning and execution, unfortunately, there can be many a slip and although when Fenton sailed with four vessels in May 1582, he had the best intentions of reaching the Moluccas by the Cape of Good Hope, the direction of events passed out of his hands by the time he was off the Guinea coast. His crews, anxious to reap the harvest of Spanish shipping as Drake had done, showed mutinous unrest at the prospect of rounding Africa; for them it was to be the South American waters of the Pacific or nothing. Fenton therefore reluctantly altered his course for the Straits of Magellan. A successful attack on St. Vincent in Brazil followed, but Fenton had by this time lost hope of accomplishing his mission, and he was openly quarreling with his second-in-command, the younger William Hawkins. After the Brazilian raid, therefore, the expedition quickly went to pieces. Fenton sorrowfully sailed back to England, carrying Hawkins in irons, while one of his ships under John Drake, Sir Francis' nephew, deserted and sailed for the straits, only to be captured by the Spaniards off the River Plate.

As has been so often the case before and since, failure bred discouragement, and Fenton's tale of woe set back the search for a southern
Passage to the Indies by years. Elizabeth's sailors found the old familiar
triangle of England–West Africa–West Indies far more alluring, with its
relatively short voyages and large returns. Cruises in these waters became
annual commonplaces in the last two decades of the century, with Drake
and the Hawkinses ever to the fore. In 1582 the elder William Hawkins,
his brother John, and John's son Richard made a highly successful cruise,
raiding the Cape Verde Islands, Puerto Rico, and the pearl fisheries of
Margarita. Three years later Drake was back with fire and sword; in his
large expedition of 1585–86 he stormed Santo Domingo, Cartagena, and
St. Augustine, and then called at the Virginian coast to take home the
survivors of Raleigh's Roanoke colony. In 1587 he carried out the celebrated operation of "singeing the King of Spain's beard," when in spite
of the horrified remonstrances of William Borough, who fought strictly
according to book, he sailed boldly into Cadiz harbor and destroyed all
the shipping that lay within his reach. More symbolic, perhaps, was the
capture of the promontory of Sagres, where Henry the Navigator had
had his observatory a century and a half before. Portugal had indeed
fallen on evil days; as an integral part of Spain she did not even have a
fiction of independence, although England strove unsuccessfully to back
a revolt headed by the Pretender Dom Antonio.

With open warfare now existing between England and Spain, affairs
were fast reaching a crisis, and Philip's crowning attempt to conquer
England was made in the sailing of the Spanish Armada. It is too familiar a story to retell here, nor does it concern the history of exploration,
save that it was a central event in the reign of Elizabeth and many of
the participants on the English side — such as Drake, John and Richard
Hawkins, Frobisher, Fenton, Davis, Winter, Raymond, and Lancaster —
were great voyagers. But it did mark the passing of the sceptre of the
seas from Spain to England and pointed to the countless results that the
change was to bring.

Even as the wrecks of the Armada were struggling back to Spain,
an English voyage of circumnavigation was triumphantly entering Plymouth. This venture, under Thomas Cavendish or Candish, had sailed in
July 1586 and had been the speediest and least eventful circumnavigation thus far. Cavendish followed closely in Drake's track and made his
Atlantic crossing from Sierra Leone to Brazil. In the Straits of Magellan
he met a handful of the survivors of the force stationed there years
before by Sarmiento, for the purpose of intercepting Drake on his return.
After entering the Pacific in February 1587, he cruised along the coasts
of Chile and Peru, but he had the drawback of being the second privateer in those waters, and he therefore found the Spaniards better pre-

pared to meet him. Not unnaturally, his coastal raids were costly in human life, and his captures at sea for the most part were trifling. Off the west coast of Mexico, however, his luck turned, and he captured a homeward-bound Manila galleon, richly laden with precious metals, silks, and other valuable China goods. This stroke enabled the voyage to show a handsome profit, so Cavendish decided to steer for England. One of his ships was lost in the Pacific, but he sailed on in the *Desire*, and after touching at the Ladrones and the Philippines, passed through the narrow straits between Bali and Java. Cavendish refitted near the western end of Java, then made a prosperous voyage across the Indian Ocean and around the Cape of Good Hope. A call was made at St. Helena, and Cavendish, the first Briton ever to touch there, quickly realized its possibilities as a place of refreshment. England was finally reached in early September of 1588, hardly more than two years after the voyage began.

Emboldened by the success of this enterprise, Cavendish determined to tempt Providence a second time — and found to his sorrow that the elements are not always as kind. In 1591 he left Plymouth on another voyage of circumnavigation, with five vessels and John Davis as his second-in-command. From the first luck was against Cavendish and his men. His ships were ill found and so badly provisioned that food ran short during the Atlantic crossing. It was therefore necessary to capture Santos in Brazil to get provisions, and the resulting delay brought the fleet to the straits in a season of bad weather. From then on it was battledore and shuttlecock; they sailed into the straits only to be blown out again. Cavendish's ship, the *Leicester*, received such a buffeting that her commander steered for Brazil for a refit, while Davis, in the *Desire*, had another attempt at the straits. This time Davis reached the Pacific — but was blown back where he came from. He tried a third time and actually got clear of the land into the South Sea; but the gale was unceasing, and he had to put back into the Atlantic, with his ship like a sieve and his sails blown to ribbons. Davis' return home was painful to a degree; with sixteen survivors of the original company of seventy-six, of whom only Davis and the cabin boy were in health, the *Desire* struggled back to Berehaven in Ireland. Cavendish's fate was even worse. He had reached Brazil only to lose most of his men in fights with the Portuguese; he then tried to make port at St. Helena but was blown away when in sight of the island; so he then sailed north, to die at sea. Mystery surrounds the fate of his ship and the survivors, but the fact that Cavendish's farewell letter reached England, suggests that the *Leicester* managed to struggle home.

One more English voyage to the Pacific deserves to be chronicled; the expedition of Richard Hawkins, only son of Sir John. The purpose of this venture, even more than in the case of Drake's circumnavigation, was discovery with a view of empire-building. The voyage was intended "for the

Islands of Japan, for the Philippines and Moluccas, the Kingdom of China
and the East Indies, by way of the Straits of Magellan and the South Sea."
In other words, it was the frankest attempt the English had thus far made
to find the passage to the Indies by the southwest. Hawkins hoped to pay
his expenses by raiding the South American coast as Drake and Cavendish had done; his voyage resembled those of his predecessors, while he
suffered the penalty for being the third Englishman to cruise in the South
Sea.

Hawkins and his expedition left Plymouth in June 1593 in the fine
galleon *Dainty*, and made for the Straits of Magellan by the usual passage.
After sighting the Falkland Islands (discovered by Davis during Cavendish's fateful voyage), they passed into the Pacific and made their way
along the Chilean coast. Temptation to plunder was too strong for the
crew; they clamored to try their luck at Valparaiso, and the resulting raid,
though successful, revealed their presence to the Spanish authorities. A
fleet of six ships put out from Callao to head off the *Dainty* and brought
her to bay near Atacames, Ecuador. For three whole days a struggle of
epic heroism ensued; only when the *Dainty* was ready to sink did she
strike her colors. Sixty of her seventy-five men were killed and wounded,
and the gallant Hawkins was lying helpless with six wounds. Of such stuff
were the Elizabethans made. Hawkins eventually recovered, and after
years of imprisonment in Spain lived to return to his native Devonshire,
and later to serve against the Algerian pirates. But his dream of developing the southwestern route to the Indies ended with his capture, and the
Straits of Magellan were not again used by English mariners for many
years.

Rather was the Caribbean the scene of activity in the 1590's, and
English privateers cruised there during the final decade of the century
with annual frequency. During these years West Indian and South Atlantic waters were literally infested with English corsairs. In 1594–95 Sir
Robert Dudley (Leicester's natural son and the self-styled Duke of Northumberland) made a piratical cruise to the West Indies, ranging from Trinidad to Puerto Rico. In 1595 also, Sir James Lancaster, but lately returned
from his first voyage to the East Indies, sacked Pernambuco in Brazil.
Drake and Sir John Hawkins made their last voyage to the West Indies
in 1595. Hawkins died in mid-November as the squadron lay off Puerto
Rico, and Drake died on board the *Defiance*, off Portobello, at the end of
January, leaving the fleet to be brought back by Sir Thomas Baskerville.
This same year witnessed Raleigh's first venture in South America, in search
of El Dorado, and in 1596 his captain, Lawrence Keymis, continued the
search by surveying the rivers along the Guiana littoral. Jamaica, the
largest island thus far to be captured by the English, fell to the picturesque adventurer Sir Anthony Sherley in 1597, but he did not consolidate

his possession and relinquished his conquest directly he sailed for home. Most active of all the English in this period was the Earl of Cumberland, who either himself led or else sent out no less than ten piratical expeditions, which cruised all the way from West Africa and the Azores to the Caribbean (on one occasion even sacking Puerto Rico). Indeed, the forty years from the first timid ventures of Englishmen to the Guinea coast had witnessed a tremendous maritime florescence on a national scale, quite rightly associated with the man who was ever its most aggressive proponent and who will always remain its personification, Sir Francis Drake.

13

THE ENGLISH AND DUTCH REACH

THE ORIENT

JENKINSON AND THE PERSIAN TRADE

Sebastian Cabot was vindicated in a minor way for his advocacy of
the Northeast Passage to the Orient, for it was by the North Cape route
that Englishmen first penetrated into Asia. Chancellor had opened up
Russia to his countrymen; it remained for a sturdy and ambitious traveler
to cross the tsar's dominions to the lands of reputed wealth that lay beyond. This engaging figure was Anthony Jenkinson, a servant of the Muscovy Company, who in his earlier days had traveled in the Levant and
had written an account of the entry of Suleiman the Magnificent into
Aleppo. More than this, he even had an interview with the sultan, from
whom he obtained privileges of trade. Doubtless this experience opened
his eyes to the possibilities of Central Asia and the realms even further
eastward.

With these potentialities before him, Jenkinson sailed to Russia in
1557, to be well received in Moscow by Ivan the Terrible, who gave him
letters of recommendation for his journey. By the following spring
he was on his way down the Volga, accompanied by Richard and
Robert Johnson and a Tatar interpreter. At Astrakhan the party pur-
chased a boat and sailed boldly into the Caspian — the first Britons ever
to navigate that great inland sea and to display thereon the red-cross
flag of St. George. Their course took them to the Mangishlak peninsula
on the eastern shore, and having disembarked, they joined a large caravan
of a thousand camels bound for Turkestan. After a lengthy halt at Urgenj
on the Oxus, and a nasty skirmish with Turcoman tribesmen, the caravan
reached Bokhara in December. There Jenkinson was cordially received
by the khan, and the trio of Englishmen settled at this remote Central
Asian capital for the winter. Although the khan showed great interest in
Jenkinson's firearms and plied him with questions about Russia and England, little was accomplished. Jenkinson's intention had been to push on

to China in the footsteps of Marco Polo, but the lands to the east were in
a state of turmoil at this period, and trade with Cathay had practically
ceased. Even under the best of conditions, he was told, the journey from
Bokhara to Peking took nine months, and as he had taken almost that
time to come from Moscow, he was quite rightly appalled by the difficulties of overland trade between China and England. Nor was the prospect
of trade with India more hopeful, for in that hot climate English woolens
would be of no use; as for Bokhara itself, there were no industries of importance, and the inhabitants were too poor to buy English commodities.

Discouraged by such meager prospects of trade, Jenkinson and his
companions left Bokhara in March 1559 — and luckily in time to avoid a
hostile army that laid siege to the city exactly a week later. The return
journey was similar to the outward one; Jenkinson reached Moscow in
the autumn poorer than when he left, but with a vast fund of information;
he had moreover traversed ground which his countrymen were not to see
again for another three centuries.

With China and India out of the picture, Jenkinson turned his attention to Persia and went back to England to obtain a sanction from his employers for a trading venture thither. In 1561 he sailed on his second mission, and after spending the winter in Moscow, he descended the Volga
and crossed the Caspian Sea to Derbend. This region was at that time in
Persian hands and was administered by a surprisingly friendly governor
named Abdullah Khan, who was to remain steadfast in his attachment to
the English until his death several years later. Escorted by a guard of
Abdullah's soldiers, Jenkinson proceeded overland to Kazvin, where the
reigning monarch, Shah Tahmasp, had his capital. Jenkinson's reception
by the Sophy was by no means favorable; his letters from Queen Elizabeth were in Latin, Italian, and Hebrew, languages which not one of the
shah's subjects understood. Furthermore, Tahmasp showed great bitter-
ness because Jenkinson was a Christian. After he was dismissed from
court with contumely, Jenkinson's face was at length saved by the friendly
intervention of Abdullah Khan and the shah gradually became more
genial, even to the extent of sending the Englishman a present. Jenkinson
failed to obtain any privileges in Kazvin, however, though he did interview some Indian merchants, who gave him good hopes of establishing a
spice trade through Persia. More concrete results awaited him on his return journey, for he visited Abdullah Khan at Javat in the Caucasus, and
got from that almost autonomous autocrat a really valuable grant of trading privileges, involving the exchange of English woolens for Persian
silk. Jenkinson was back in England in 1564, and although he made at
least two more voyages to Russia, he never returned to Asia again. None
the less, he was a true pioneer, as well as one of the greatest of English
travelers and the first of his race to visit Central Asia. His ability as a

geographer is shown in his celebrated map of Russia (1562, included in the Ortelius Atlas of 1570), which in addition to Muscovy portrays the adjacent Moslem lands of his travels.

Jenkinson's timely deal with Abdullah Khan bore speedy results, for in 1564 a second British mission set out from Russia to Persia. This was composed of Thomas Alcock, a kinsman of the founder of Jesus College, Cambridge, and Richard Cheney, both employees of the Muscovy Company. They proceeded by way of the Volga and the Caspian to Shemakha, Abdullah's capital in the Caucasus, south of Derbend. Here Cheney remained, while Alcock pushed on to the Court of Shah Tahmasp at Kazvin. Alcock was duly received by that monarch, but had the misfortune to be murdered on his return journey. Cheney on his part had a highly successful mission, and got back to Russia with a valuable stock of goods and with a very favorable view of the Persian trade.

So encouraged were the promoters of this commerce that in 1565 another mission was sent out, composed of Richard Johnson, Jenkinson's old colleague of the Bokhara trip, and Arthur Edwards. They made their way to Abdullah Khan at Shemakha, only to have their hopes dashed by the sudden death of this friendly Moslem governor, whose passing was a great blow to the budding English trade. In spite of this tragedy, Edwards journeyed to Kazvin, where he found the changeable Tahmasp so affable that he came home in quite a hopeful mood.

As Edwards had been away at least two years, it was not until 1568 that he set out on his second mission to the Sophy. In company with Lawrence Chapman, he visited Shemakha and Tabriz, the latter city at this time a highly important market and caravan center. From there Edwards went on to Kazvin, where to his humiliation he found that the shah had forgotten all about him. However, Tahmasp eventually granted some trading privileges, in consequence of which Chapman went on a tour of exploration through the province of Ghilan, on the southern shores of the Caspian.

Yet the true difficulties of this highly involved trade were not revealed until the fifth mission to Persia, which set out in 1569 under Thomas Banister and Geoffrey Ducket. Even during their descent of the Volga the expedition had a bitter fight with marauding Tatars, in which Banister was wounded, and they reached Astrakhan to find it besieged by the Turks. After these troubles, they went on to Shemakha, where they saw little commercial activity. Thereupon Banister traveled to Kazvin, where he spent six months at the court of the shah. Returning to the Caucasus for the purchase of silk, the Englishmen found the plague raging, and Banister with several of his colleagues perished. Ducket now took charge of the remainder of the party; he was forced to make the tedious journey back to Kazvin to obtain the shah's order for the release of English merchandise. After securing this, he traveled far southeast into central Persia, reaching Kashan, where he bought silks, spices, and precious stones. This profitable transaction was wholly undone by the capture of the English vessel by Cossack pirates, after a desperate fight in the Caspian. The surviving English, all of them wounded, struggled back to Astrakhan in an open boat, and after being further discomfited by ice-jams in the Volga, finally reached their native land in 1574.

It is not surprising that after this woeful experience the Anglo-Persian trade languished so completely that only one subsequent attempt was made to revive it. In 1574 Arthur Edwards set out with a large party, which included Christopher Borough, the son of Chancellor's old companion Stephen Borough. Edwards himself went no further than Astrakhan, but Borough and several others crossed the Caspian to Baku, only to find that the Turks had conquered the whole region of the eastern Caucasus, while Shemakha was in ruins and much of the land desolated. Some little trade was done with the Turks, but the outlook was far from promising. The return voyage across the Caspian made difficult by pack-ice and short rations, dampened the Britons' enthusiasm completely. Thus ended the last English venture for the Persian trade across Russia: the distances were too great, the hardships were too extreme, the shah was too fickle, and the Turkish peril was too menacing to warrant any further attempts. As Lawrence Chapman realistically wrote after his mission to Persia: "Better it is in my opinion to continue a beggar in England during life than to remain a rich merchant seven years in this country." Perhaps if Abdullah Khan had lived and if the Turks had not extended their conquests to the Caspian, the story might have been different. As it was the English had little to show for their efforts except a vastly increased knowledge of Asia. At the same time, one cannot withhold one's admiration for these hardy and enterprising men, who constantly kept before their eyes the desirability of tapping the spice trade before it entered Turkish territory, and who were eager always to seize any opportunity of exploring to the eastward.

PENETRATION THROUGH THE LEVANT

In addition to the four main routes to India and China with which the Elizabethans experimented (the two northern and the two southern passages), there existed a fifth route: namely the route from the eastern Mediterranean to the Persian Gulf. It was by all odds the shortest, and was that which had been used by caravans since time immemorial. But it was highly dangerous, and it involved three methods of transport: merchant ship through the Mediterranean, which had to run the gauntlet of the Spanish fleet and Moslem corsairs; caravan across the Syrian Desert and down the Euphrates Valley, a hazardous undertaking at best; and finally native craft from Basra to India, which involved a degree of "roughing it" discouraging to even the hardiest of men. Insofar as it was a suitable route at all, it was useful only for individual travel; for large-scale enterprise under English control it was even less adapted than the trans-Caspian trade with Persia, which had proved so disappointing.

This overland route was a development of the Levant trade, upon which England embarked with much enthusiasm in the middle years of Elizabeth's reign. Trade between England and Turkey was nothing new; Hakluyt states that from 1511 on, for at least a quarter of a century, ships from London, Bristol, and Southampton had trafficked with the Greek Islands of the eastern Mediterranean, and had sometimes touched at Syrian ports as well. Jenkinson's visit to Aleppo has already been referred to, and it is recorded that in 1550 Richard Chancellor and Roger Bodenham, destined to go to Russia and Mexico respectively, had cruised to the Aegean islands. Prospects of a two-way trade were indeed good; the Levant produced commodities in demand in England; goods from the farther Orient could be transshipped from caravan; and, most important of all, there was a good vent for English cloth. At that period, the sultan of Turkey was Murad III, a miserly and lecherous monarch, whose ruling interests were money and women. The English could not supply the latter, but by organizing trade they could help fill the Sultan's coffers. It was doubtless a blessing for Christendom that Murad had these tastes, for he preferred to spend his time wandering around his harem rather than leading an active military campaign against the European states, as his grandfather Sulieman had done. Likewise, he was well disposed toward strangers, even infidels, who would bring trade to his dominions.

It was perhaps more than a chance happening that the rise of the Levantine trade coincided with the decline of the trans-Russian trade with Persia, for hardly had the wrecks of the Banister-Ducket expedition returned to England when Sir Edward Osborne and Richard Staper, influential aldermen of London, sent out representatives overland to Constantinople on an exploratory mission (John Wright and Joseph Clements, 1575). These men were followed three years later by William Harborne, who procured a very favorable grant of privileges from Murad. Harborne's residence at the Sublime Porte was a most fortunate one. He was received with much Oriental splendor, and in turn presented the sultan on behalf of the newly formed company with a number of presents, among them a mechanical clock with sundry devices thereon, worthy of the inventiveness of Heath Robinson.

With so favorable a start, Harborne (created ambassador in 1583) soon obtained a strong position at the Turkish Court, contributing very materially to the extension of English trade throughout Murad's dominions, and in the year of the Armada he even caused embarrassment to the

Spaniards by his efforts to induce the Turks to attack them. It was not long before factories of the Levant Company sprang up in Constantinople, Alexandria, Aleppo, and other commercial centres of the Ottoman Empire. A brisk trade ensued; the English sending woolens, rabbit skins (in demand as fur trimmings), tin, mercury, and amber, and receiving in return from the Turks spices, pepper, dyes, silks, and cotton goods. This trade prospered for many years, and although in the reign of James I the Levant Company came to be overshadowed by its offspring, the East India Company, to the end it ranked high among the joint-stock enterprises. One ironical note deserves emphasis: by 1614 the Levant Company was actually sending from England to Turkey pepper and spices brought from Sumatra and Java in East Indiamen. This is a far cry from the days when Oriental luxuries reached Europe through Suez and Venice!

However, it is not so much the progress of the Levant Company's trade that concerns Renaissance travel, as it is the creation of English outposts in the Levant, which pointed the way to Southern Asia. Of these outposts, that at Aleppo was by all odds the most significant geographically, since from its hospitable portals many Britons for the next half-century set forth into the obscure regions of the Middle East and the lands beyond — a goodly company of some of England's most distinguished wanderers. Aleppo is indeed most strategically placed for the Eastern traveler, standing as it does within easy reach of half a dozen good harbors in the Mediterranean and commanding the gateway to the Euphrates Valley; it is therefore on the natural line for Baghdad, the Persian Gulf, and India. Enterprising merchants, even before the coming of the English factory, had made use of it as a departure and arrival point, to and from remoter Asia. Thus in 1563 Cesare Federici, Merchant of Venice, as he styled himself, passed through the city on his eighteen years' wanderings in Southern Asia; wanderings which took him to Goa, Negapatam, Bengal, and Pegu, and which resulted in a very useful travel book, which, published in English in 1588, had its share of influence in the foundation of the East India Company. Another Venetian, Gasparo Balbi, had an adventurous journey over much the same route in 1579–1583, going like Federici as far afield as Pegu, the Burmese city which in those days was a place of fabulous wealth and magnificence. Both Federici and Balbi were keenly observant of the economic possibilities and productions of the lands through which they passed; their books were of far greater use to the mercantile community than mere records of adventure would have been.

John Newbery, an adventurous Elizabethan, set out from Aleppo down the Euphrates Valley in March 1581, on what was the first journey by an Englishman along this road. Dressed as a Moslem trader, Newbery proceeded via Baghdad and Basra to Ormuz, which he found filled with

Venetian traders, who caused him much trouble. After a stay of some time in Ormuz, he set out northward across Persia to Isfahan and Tabriz, and continuing with considerable speed, he traversed Asia Minor to Constantinople, which he reached a year after leaving Aleppo. Newbery did not cover new ground for a European, but he did for an Englishman. It is a pity that his journey was performed at such a pace: he spent nine days in Baghdad, three in the royal city of Isfahan, and only a week in the highly important commercial center of Tabriz. But his journey pointed the way for later travels in the Middle East, and his progress as far as Ormuz brings us almost within sight of the creation of the Honourable East India Company.

As far as private trading went, Newbery's journey must have been a prosperous one, for on his return to London he had no difficulty in finding five adventurers who put up a considerable amount of capital so that they might accompany him on his next enterprise. His plans this time were more ambitious. Nothing short of India and the lands beyond were his aim, and to this end he sought the counsel of no less an authority than the ineffable Dr. John Dee, as well as that of Richard Hakluyt the younger, who showed him a letter from the Jesuit Thomas Stevens, the first Englishman in India. Furthermore, he had the wholehearted backing of the Levant Company, including Osborne and Staper. With five companions, John Eldred, William Shales, William Leeds, James Story, and Ralph Fitch, Newbery sailed for Aleppo (or Tripoli, to be exact) on the *Tiger* in February 1583. (Had the First Witch in *Macbeth* read her Hakluyt?) By Late April they had reached Syria; a month later they were on their way down the Euphrates; in June they had arrived at Baghdad. Basra was reached in August, and two of the party, Eldred and Shales, remained behind to trade. Newbery and his three remaining companions sailed to Ormuz, where they encountered bitter hostility from the Venetian merchants, who, fearful of English competition, secured the arrest of the entire party. The English were sent to Goa for trial, arriving there in November 1583. It is more than passing strange that the first party of Englishmen ever to reach India should have come as prisoners. Luck was on their side, however, for Stevens, the English Jesuit who had already been in Goa for four years, procured their release on bail. Story obtained complete freedom by undertaking to paint a church and by marrying a half-caste, while the other three wanderers, fearing that Goa might well be too hot for them, jumped their bail, and made for the interior — just in time, as it happened. They traveled eastward to Bijapur, the capital of a native kingdom of that name, where they were well beyond the clutches of the Portuguese. Thence they went to the colorful city of Golconda, famed for its diamond mines, where Leeds, a jeweler by trade, brought his expert knowledge into effect. Turning north, they entered the Mogul's dominions

at Burhanpur, and eventually reached the court of the mighty Emperor
Akbar at Fatehpur Sikri, near Agra. After obtaining an audience with that
sovereign, in order to present the letter from Queen Elizabeth, the trio
of Englishmen broke up. Leeds accepted a post as jeweler at Akbar's
Court; Newbery started overland for England; Fitch set out eastward
down the Jumna and the Ganges. Newbery, as leader of the expedition,
had given much thought to Indian trade since he left Aleppo; he had seen
how the Portuguese controlled the Persian Gulf and the western approaches to India, and he had seen how vulnerable the Mediterranean
could be while a state of war existed between England and Spain. His conclusion was that the only practicable Anglo-Indian trade must be by the
Cape route, direct to Bengal and Burma. When he left Agra, therefore,
it was with the intention of returning to India by sea, and meeting Fitch
somewhere in the Ganges Delta. But Newbery was not destined to realize
his plans; on the way back across Asia he met a lonely death, unknown
how or where.

Fitch on his part proceeded down the Jumna to its junction with the
Ganges at Allahabad, and after inspecting the famous ghats at Benares
and examining the technique of gold-washing at Patna, he set out overland to Kuch Bihar, at the very foot of the Himalayas. He was probably
attracted there by reports of the trade which crossed the mountains from
Tibet. From Kuch Bihar he proceeded to the Ganges Delta, in a futile
attempt to keep his tryst with Newbery. This involved a wait, which the
resourceful Englishman put to profitable use by trading with the native
and Portuguese communities alike. In this way Fitch was able to live as
he went, apparently greatly assisted in his trading by his fluency in languages and his adaptability to his surroundings.

Two years had now elapsed since Newbery and Fitch parted, and the
latter, rightly concluding that his partner had come to grief, gave up waiting and sailed across to Pegu. For more than a year Fitch remained in
Burma, where he made a hazardous excursion two hundred miles up country into the Siamese Shan States in order to study the Chinese trade. Of
the brilliant city of Pegu and its royal court Fitch gives a long description,
enlarging on the king's harem and his white elephants, the stately palm
trees in the streets, the gilded pagodas, and also the methods of capturing wild elephants. All the while, he was keenly observant of the natural
products of the country and its commerce with India. In January 1588 he
sailed in a Portuguese trading craft to Malacca, where he remained many
weeks, gleaning all the information he could about its trade with the
Spice Islands and Southern China. Malacca was his farthest point; from
there he returned to Pegu, where he again stopped for several months,
thence to Bengal and Ceylon. He intended to sail back to Portugal from
Cochin, but he arrived at the India port to find that he had just missed

the last ship of the season. He was therefore obliged to proceed to Goa, where he escaped detection because of disguise. Then he made his way to Ormuz and Basra, and in this manner was able to return to Aleppo and England by the way he came. His arrival in England in April 1591 must have been a happy but disconcerting one, for his relatives had given him up as dead and had divided his estate. Nevertheless his return had an important effect on England's Eastern planning, since Fitch was carefully interviewed by the great — Lord Burghley and Richard Hakluyt among them.

England was not to be alone in her attempt to wrest the position of Mistress of the Eastern Seas from Portugal, for just as Fitch — and Newbery before his death — had emphasized to Englishmen the possibilities of Oriental trade, so had the Dutchman Linschoten extolled the trade to the Hollanders, who, having lately overthrown the rule of Spain, were ready for overseas enterprise. The career of Jan Huyghen van Linschoten (1563–1611) was not as spectacular as that of Ralph Fitch, but his writings were even more useful and famous. As a young man he had gone out from Lisbon to Goa in 1583 — one of the first of his nation to do so, and for six years he lived (though apparently a Protestant) as a dependent of the Archbishop of Goa. During this time he never went far from the Portuguese capital, but his avaricious thirst for knowledge enabled him to get detailed information of land and sea as far afield as the Spice Islands and China, while his keen insight made him realize the growing rottenness of Portugal's power. It was natural, therefore, that when Linschoten returned to Holland he devoted himself to persuading his countrymen to send expeditions to the East; and his book, the famous *Itinerario*, was translated into English, German, Latin, and French, and became the navigators' vade mecum for Eastern seas.

LANCASTER AND HIS SUCCESSORS

With the defeat of the Armada, and the failure of the Northern Passages, the trading community in England began to regard the Cape route to India with favor, and as early as 1589 promoters were active with plans for a voyage to the East around Africa. These plans came to fruition in 1591: in April an expedition of three ships sailed from Plymouth under the command of George Raymond, a distinguished veteran of the Armada fight. One of his captains was another Armada warrior, James Lancaster, who in addition to his skill as a seaman had lived in Portugal for several years and was thoroughly familiar with the people and the language. There appears to have been little cargo carried; the purpose of the voyage was primarily reconnaissance rather than trade.

The fleet made a fast passage to the Cape — barely over three months — but the crews suffered so severely from scurvy that it was necessary to spend a month at Table Bay and to send one of the ships back to England with a skeleton crew. After giving the men an opportunity to recover, Raymond took the two remaining ships around the Cape and along the South African coast, but a terrific storm struck them in the Mozambique Channel and Raymond's ship, the *Penelope*, went down with all hands. Lancaster sailed the battered and lonely *Edward Bonaventure* to the Comoro Islands, only to have several of his men massacred by the natives. Zanzibar offered better refuge; here Lancaster spent three months, effecting repairs and beating off a Portuguese attack. Contrary winds kept him south of the Indian mainland, so he made his crossing by way of Ceylon and the Nicobars. Failing to get a pilot for Achin, a wealthy port on the northern tip of Sumatra, he passed above the island and finally dropped anchor at Penang, off the west coast of the Malay Peninsula, in June 1592. Three months were spent here, but the place was so unhealthy that Lancaster had only thirty-four men left when he set sail again in September. With this pitiful remnant, Lancaster cruised in the Straits of Malacca, plundering every vessel that he came across, native and Portuguese alike. Eventually, fear of retaliation caused him to retreat to Junkseylon, farther up the Malay Peninsula, whence he started homeward in November. The ship touched at Ceylon, which the indefatigable commander hoped to use as a base for attacks on Portuguese shipping, but the crew, who by this time had gone through quite enough, were so mutinous that Lancaster was compelled to steer for England. With barely enough men left to work the ship, the *Edward* made very heavy weather of it rounding the Cape, touched at St. Helena, had a miserable time in the Doldrums, and finally struggled to the Island of Mona in the West Indies, near Puerto Rico. Some refreshment was obtained here, and a start was made on the homeward lap. A bad storm off Bermuda, however, drove the *Edward* back to Mona, which the crew reached in the last stages of destitution. Some mutinous sailors at this point cut the cables of the *Edward* and drifted away in her, leaving Lancaster and nineteen other men to shift for themselves. How these starving mariners endured another month's hardship we may wonder; but they did, and Lancaster and twelve companions were rescued by a Dieppe ship and eventually reached their native land.

An English ship had thus for the first time rounded the Cape and reached the East Indies; this much cannot be contradicted. On every other score the venture was a failure: the ships were lost; the cargoes were lost; most of the men were lost. It was enough to discourage even the bravest adventurers. Yet the Elizabethans would not admit defeat; in a few years they had founded the East India Company and in a short while thereafter had built up a highly profitable traffic. One might ask how the Portuguese had been able to voyage for a century to India with clockwork regularity and how by contrast the English had lost everything on their first attempt. There are several explanations, of which the following may be mentioned. The English had to sail about fifteen hundred miles further each way: this meant more wear and tear on the ships and more of a provision problem. The Portuguese had a chain of fortified posts all along the East African coast, which provided refuges for refreshment and refitting; the English had no place to stop without considerable risk. Moreover, Lancaster's voyage was unduly prolonged, as his ship, not being double-sheathed, deteriorated rapidly in tropical waters. She was also short of stores and provisions, and at first was overcrowded. These defects all added up to produce the tragic ending of the voyage. Of course the great menace of a voyage to India was scurvy, far more so than was the case in a crossing of the Atlantic, and there are all too many instances in this period of ships drifting helplessly at sea, nine-tenths of their crews dead and the survivors too weak to work the craft.

Most of these defects were remediable, but the Tudors like most other people had to learn by experience, and experience took time. Thus the second expedition to the East Indies was even more disastrous than the first (if it were possible to be so). This venture, led by Captain Benjamin Wood, is known mostly from Portuguese sources, and the details of the voyage are so shadowy that we will never know the whole story, or anything like it. Wood's expedition was sent out by Sir Robert Dudley, who had maritime interests and who (as has been already noticed) had led a privateering cruise to the West Indies. Wood himself was a sailor of experience; he had served under both Raleigh and Cumberland, and therefore had something of the pirate in his makeup. With three ships he set out from England late in 1596; one vessel was lost off the Cape, but two were observed by the Portuguese as they passed Mozambique the following year. Wood's fleet touched at the Indian coast below Goa, being thus the first English vessels to reach the mainland of the peninsula. From there they rounded Ceylon, plundering as they went, and made for the Straits of Malacca, where they had a week-long running fight with the Portuguese. Wood's crews must by this time have been sadly depleted by scurvy, for the fleet had to retire to Old Kedah, on the Malay Peninsula near Penang, to recuperate. As there were now only enough survivors to work one vessel, Wood burned the other and proceeded up the coast to Martaban near Pegu, where the *Bear*, the remaining ship, was wrecked. Seven survivors eventually reached Mauritius by canoe, it is said; and one man lived to be taken off by a Dutch vessel in 1601.

The complete failure of Wood's expedition must have been so discouraging that it is perhaps fortunate another competitor had entered the Indies trade with considerably better results. Inspired by Linschoten's pleading, the Dutch, who hitherto had done no voyaging off the usual European and Mediterranean sea routes, equipped an expedition of four ships, which, under Captain Cornelius Houtman, sailed from the Texel in the spring of 1595. Like the English, Houtman's men suffered so severely from scurvy that they had to put in at the Cape of Good Hope and at Antongil Bay in Madagascar to recuperate. But they then sailed straight across the Indian Ocean to the Straits of Sunda and dropped anchor at Bantam in Java without the loss of a ship. At this port, the center of the Javanese pepper trade, a long time was spent. Both natives and Portuguese showed considerable hostility, and Houtman and some of his men were imprisoned. However, the Dutch succeeded in making a commercial treaty and departed with a good cargo. They proceeded eastward to Bali, and then returned along the south coast of Java, thereby acquiring a more correct impression of the width of the island than had prevailed and laid the ghost of Java's being the northern part of the Southern Continent. Houtman's voyage home was uneventful, yet he reached Holland with but three of his ships and one third of his men. In spite of the high mortality, the Dutch skipper had enough to show for his venture to inspire the merchants of Amsterdam with a determination to exploit the trade.

In 1598, therefore, two fleets sailed from Holland for the East by the Cape route, and two more (Mahu's and van Noort's, which will be described later) by way of the Straits of Magellan. Of the Cape fleets, the first to sail was composed of two ships, with Houtman in command and John Davis, the great navigator of the Arctic, who was now temporarily in Dutch service, as chief pilot. This expedition proved disastrous. After touching at Cochin on the Indian mainland, the fleet sailed to Achin in Sumatra, where Davis was surprised to learn that the fame of Queen Elizabeth had penetrated to the East Indies and was gratified to discover that the local rajah was anxious to hear about the English nation. But the Dutch were not as acceptable as the English, and during the visit a treacherous attack was made on them, in which one ship was lost and Houtman was killed. Davis' presence of mind and courage saved the other ship, which was then taken up the Malay coast. After a vain attempt to reach the port of Tennasserim, Davis steered for Holland; he reached Middelburg in July 1600 and forthwith returned to England to place his services at the disposal of the East India Company.

Better luck awaited the second Cape fleet, a large armada of eight ships under Jacob van Neck and William van Warwijk. Part of the fleet touched at the island of Mauritius, which was given its name after Maurice of Nassau, Prince of Orange. Bantam was next reached, where much trade was done and a factory established. Sending four vessels directly back to Holland (1599), Neck sailed eastward with the remain-

The capture of the great Portuguese carrack São Antonio in the Strait of Malacca by the joint squadrons of Lancaster and Spilbergen, 1602. This is the only picture of the first fleet of the English East India Company: at the upper left is the Red Dragon of Captain Lancaster; at the upper right the Hector of Captain John Middleton; upper left-center the Ascension. In the lower foreground are two Dutch ships and a galley.

The Return of Sir Edward Michelborne's Expedition from the East Indies, by Adam Willaerts (1577–1660). This interloping venture, composed of the ship Tiger and the pinnace Tiger's Whelp, reached Milford Haven June 27, 1606, and Portsmouth July 9; it is difficult to say which harbor is represented here. The large ship is the Tiger; the small craft in the right foreground may be the pinnace. This is the earliest painting of an English Indiaman.

der to Madura, Celebes, and Amboyna. At Amboyna the fleet again divided: two ships went to the Banda Islands and the other two to Ternate in the Moluccas. Both groups returned to Holland independently in 1600, having done much to establish Dutch supremacy in the Archipelago. This voyage led to the formation of the Dutch East India Company (1602) and the concentration of Dutch colonial effort on Java and the Spice Islands to the east. Perhaps the very completeness of this concentration tends to lessen the interest of subsequent Dutch voyages — they ran so true to form. Therefore, after the expeditions of Houtman and Neck, the chief geographical importance of the Dutch ventures is that they paved the way for the discovery of Australia.

In spite of the failures of the first two English voyages, there was still enthusiasm in London for the formation of an organization trading to the East, and feeling was further provoked by the result of the new Dutch monopoly in doubling and even tripling the price of pepper. Accordingly in 1599 a group of influential merchants, under the leadership of Sir Thomas Smythe, formed a joint-stock company, which on December 31, 1600, the last day of that very remarkable century, received its charter as the Honourable East India Company. An expedition was not long in the making, and in April 1601 four tall ships sailed from Tor Bay on the company's first voyage. Lancaster flew his flag as commander in the *Red Dragon*, the most famous of the old Indiamen, and John Davis, as befitted his abilities, was along as chief pilot. They reached the Cape in September; the personnel of three of the ships had suffered severely from scurvy, but Lancaster had dosed the crew of the *Dragon* with lemon juice, with very beneficial results. A stop was made at Table Bay during which the depleted crews were brought up to strength by the reinforcement of healthy men from the flagship. Another long call was made at Antongil Bay in Madagascar, so it was not until June 1602 that the fleet cast anchor at Achin in Sumatra. Lancaster and his sea-beaten mariners received a highly enthusiastic welcome from the local ruler, who was even more pleased with his guests a little later, when the English with the help of the Dutch captain Spilbergen captured a large Portuguese vessel in the Straits of Malacca. Sending one fully laden ship direct to England, Lancaster proceeded with the other three to Priaman, half way down the west coast of Sumatra, and from here went on to Bantam in Java. Two months were spent in Bantam; a number of Britons stayed behind to form the first English post in the Far East, and Lancaster sailed for home in February 1603. A terrible storm was encountered off the African coast; the *Dragon* lost her rudder and was driven southward into the hail and snow of the South Atlantic. But by luck, courage, and good seamanship she attained St. Helena, and the rest of the voyage was uneventful. With all his ships and half his crews,

Lancaster anchored in the Downs in September 1603, two and a half years after setting out. Lancaster deservedly received the accolade of knighthood for his leadership of the expedition, but thereafter he rested on his laurels and never again sailed to the East.

Profitable and encouraging as Lancaster's voyage had been, it was still a little too late, for the Dutch had got into the East Indies first and by their energetic and monopolistic methods had obtained a powerful lead which they never surrendered. In consequence, the second voyage of the English East India Company ran head on into determined Dutch competition. This expedition was headed by Captain Henry Middleton and was composed of the same four ships that had sailed with Lancaster; the *Red Dragon* being again the flagship. The fleet sailed in March 1604, and after an unscheduled stop at the Cape to repair the ravages of scurvy, reached Bantam toward the end of the year. The English factors left there by Lancaster had a sorry tale to tell of bitter opposition and violence from Dutch, Portuguese, and Javanese alike. Middleton's arrival changed all this; he made a good loading of pepper and sent two ships back to England. With the other two ships the commander proceeded to the Moluccas in search of cloves and nutmegs, to be dogged throughout his course by Dutch opposition. At Amboyna, Middleton had just established friendly relations with the Portuguese governor, only to have all hope of trade removed by the arrival of a large Dutch fleet under van der Hagen and the surrender of the Portuguese fort. Much the same thing happened in the Moluccas proper, where the arrival of the same Dutch fleet, followed by the destruction of the Portuguese fort at Tidore, put many difficulties in the way of Middleton, who was an unwilling spectator of these events from the quarterdeck of the *Dragon*. Still, an English craft had penetrated to the nethermost part of the Indies, and had been received at Ternate, where Drake had made a treaty with the local ruler a quarter of a century earlier. After this, the *Dragon* returned to Bantam, to join her consort which had been in the Banda Islands. A detachment of men was left to continue the Bantam factory, and the ships departed for England. Off the Cape, the *Hector*, one of the two ships sent home earlier, was found drifting helplessly with a scurvy-ridden crew, the companion vessel having vanished without a trace. Sailors were transferred to the *Hector* from the other ships, and the fleet proceeded to England, arriving in May 1606. In spite of the loss of one vessel and the heavy mortality of the crews, Middleton's voyage was regarded as a success, and like Lancaster he was knighted. Yet the shadow of Dutch monopoly must have seemed ominous to the directors of the company.

Not only were the activities of the Dutch a source of worry to the promoters, but so too was the duplicity of their own sovereign. With flagrant disregard of the company's charter, which had conferred a monopoly of Eastern trade on that body, James I gave a licence for a voyage to an adventurous courtier named Sir Edward Michelborne, who had had a somewhat sordid career as a soldier of fortune. Sailing late in 1604 with a small fleet piloted by the indefatigable John Davis, Michelborne proceeded to Sumatra. Being unsuccessful there, he sailed on to Bantam, pilfering and plundering along the way and generally making the English name hated in those waters. From Java, Michelborne made his way up the east coast of the Malay Peninsula toward Siam, but off Patani the English had a furious battle with Japanese pirates, in which Davis was killed. Disheartened, the fleet turned homeward and reached Portsmouth in the summer of 1606, having done the English cause in the East far more harm than good. Another mark had been scored for Dutch supremacy in Java and the islands.

Doubtless because of this unfavorable turn of events in the archipelago, the directors of the East India Company determined to explore other fields; and to this end they dispatched the third voyage to the Indian mainland. This venture, led by William Keeling, who had been captain of the unfortunate *Hector* in Middleton's fleet, was a highly significant one. Keeling left Plymouth in April 1607 with the *Dragon* and the *Hector*, a third ship having sailed alone a few days earlier. After his unfortunate experience with scurvy on the second voyage, Keeling followed Lancaster's and dosed his men with lemon juice, with the happy result that the health of his crews seems to have been well above average. Keeling had an eye, too, for his men's happiness; he set them to learning Shakespeare in their spare time, and when the fleet cast anchor off Sierra Leone the crew gave performances of *Hamlet* and *Richard II* on the *Dragon's* deck, before a host of enthusiastic natives. As E. I. Fripp, in *Shakespeare, Man and Artist*, graphically puts it: "What a picture the entry [in the *Dragon's* log] calls up! — the little English *Dragon* anchored with her sister-ships in the bay of Sierra Leone, not ten degrees north of the equator, and her crew, encouraged by the captain, entertain the chief's able interpreter and his fellow darkies with a performance in Elizabethan costume of 'The Prince of Denmark.' This was a means of promoting trade and friendship hardly within the calculation of modern advertising, but entirely in the spirit of the Romantic Queen."

Calls were made at the Cape and Madagascar, and at Socotra the vessels separated. Keeling in the *Dragon* went to Bantam, and the *Hector*, under William Hawkins (possibly a scion of the great seafaring family), sailed to Surat in the Gulf of Cambay. Except for Wood's unfortunate voyage, the *Hector* was the first English ship to reach the Indian peninsula. Hawkins proceeded overland to Agra, where he was well received by the Mogul Emperor Jahangir, so that his mission indeed laid the foundation of later British power in India, although at the time he was unable to obtain any definite trading privileges. Meanwhile the *Hector* had sailed on to Java and had been taken by Keeling eastward to the Banda Islands — just in time to see the Dutch take over that highly important archipelago.

After Keeling's voyage, therefore, the policy of the East India Company was directed more and more toward the exploitation of the possibilities on the Asiatic mainland. This is not to say that the islands were abandoned by them; far from it, for the English held on tenaciously in the East Indies Archipelago until their eventual liquidation at the Amboyna Massacre in 1623. This high-handed outrage of the Dutch finally drove the English from Java and the Spice Islands and resulted in undisputed Dutch hegemony throughout that area.

Subsequent voyages may be described more briefly. The company's fourth voyage (1609) called at Aden and Mocha on the Arabian coast and ended disastrously in a shipwreck off Surat, after which some of the men under Captain Robert Coverte made their way across Asia to Aleppo. The fifth voyage, under David Middleton, traded in the Banda Islands, in spite of Dutch opposition. The sixth voyage, under Sir Henry Middleton, went to Arabia, only to have its commander imprisoned at Mocha. Upon his release, Middleton proceeded to Surat and then to Bantam, where his flagship, the *Trade's Increase*, the largest merchant vessel of her day, was destroyed, and poor Middleton died of a broken heart (1613). On the seventh voyage, Captains Hippon and Floris reached Siam (1611–1613), and on the eighth voyage (1611–1613) Captain John Saris reached Japan, being the first English skipper to do so. Saris' experience was noteworthy: he landed at Hirado (north of Nagasaki) where he was greeted by William Adams, an English sailor who had come across the Pacific to Japan in a Dutch vessel many years previously. Adams had become a highly esteemed figure in Japan, and he took Saris all the way to Tokyo to call on the emperor. Saris bestowed on the mikado the presents sent by the East India Company and was allowed in return to establish a factory at Hirado. His factor, Richard Cocks, remained there for ten years, but the efforts of the merchants met with slight success and the post was abandoned in 1623.

Only one other voyage of the company in this period deserves special mention. That was the expedition of Captain Thomas Best, which sailed from England in 1612, and which, by a brilliant victory gained over a much larger Portuguese squadron off Surat, really opened Western India to British enterprise and paved the way for the mission of Sir Thomas Roe to the court of the Great Mogul in 1615–1618.

THE SOUTHERN CONTINENT

Belief in the existence of a mysterious southern land mass dated from the Middle Ages: Marco Polo wrote of the southern region of "Locach"; other geographers referred to the Golden Province of Beach, and the conception had continued through the portolan charts of the Dieppe school of cartography and the voyages of Mendaña and Quiros. As coast after coast of the hitherto unknown world was revealed by the Renaissance explorers, the search for an austral continent was forced into ever narrower limits, so that after 1600 the voyagers were able to approach the problem with a reasonably scientific spirit. It followed logically, therefore, that the first half of the seventeenth century should witness the solution of the riddle which had exercised geographers for three hundred years or more. Credit for the discovery and early exploration of Australia should go entirely to the Dutch, who not only found the new continent but put definite limits to it as well; this indeed is the outstanding contribution of the Netherlands to the cause of discovery, a contribution recognized in the early name of the land — New Holland. Even before the Dutch voyages there was in the Low Countries a substantial tradition for the theory of a southern continent, for the planispheres of Ortelius and Mercator show a great antarctic land mass running right around the globe, separated from South America by the Straits of Magellan and approaching Java in the East Indies. Certainly when the Dutch established themselves in Java, they must have felt that Terra Australis was not far distant.

Until the last decade of the sixteenth century the Dutch did no extensive ocean voyaging. In that decade they not only reached the East Indies by the Cape route and sent out three successive voyages to the Northeast Passage, but they also dispatched two fleets to sail around the world. These ventures were the first experiences the Dutch had of Pacific navigation; though they had no direct bearing on the discovery of Australia, they provided the background for it. The first of these two enterprises was a fleet of five ships under the command of Jacob Mahu, which sailed from Rotterdam in June 1598 — having aboard an English pilot, William Adams. From the outset the expedition was unfortunate: Mahu died; the crews were decimated by scurvy; and the ships were scattered after passing through the Straits of Magellan into the Pacific. One ship returned home through the straits, one struggled across to the Moluccas, and one wound up in Peru. Adams's vessel, having steered along the coast of Chile, took a northern crossing and with great difficulty reached Japan — the crew being by then in extremity. Adams and the other survivors landed at Bungo (the modern Oita, on the southern island of Kiushiu); they were imprisoned for a time and were never

allowed to leave. But the Englishman afterwards rose high in the emper-
or's favor and was thereby largely instrumental in procuring commercial
privileges for the Dutch. As related earlier, Adams took Captain Saris to
see the emperor in 1613, and he was likewise a great help to Richard
Cocks, left by Saris as the East India Company's agent. Adams lived on,
highly respected in his adopted country, until about 1620.

In contrast with Mahu's expedition, that of Olivier van Noort was
successful and uneventful. Leaving Goree with four ships in September
1598, he passed the Straits and crossed the Pacific virtually in Magellan's
track. Stops were made at the Philippines and Borneo, and after putting
in at the Dutch post on Java, van Noort returned home (August, 1601)
around the Cape. It was the fourth circumnavigation and the first Dutch
one. No discoveries were made, but van Noort brought back much information about the countries of the East.

Meanwhile, as the Dutch pushed further from Java throughout the
Spice Islands, they became more and more aware of a mysterious void
on the map, to the south and southeast of the East Indies. Certainly New
Guinea appeared a shadowy and little-known land with great possibilities, and it seemed worth while to investigate the southern coast of that
island. For this purpose a pinnace named the *Duyfken*, under the command of William Janszoon, was dispatched from Java in November 1605.
This little craft coasted southern New Guinea for nearly a thousand
miles, from the Vogelkop to Torres Straits, and then, unaware that the
latter was in fact a strait, turned southward and sighted the low desert
coast of the Cape York peninsula. Australia was thus discovered,
although no one on the *Duyfken* realized it at the time. To those aboard
the sterile land on the horizon was but a southern extension of New
Guinea, a belief which their course as far as Cape Keer-Weer (Turn
Again), in the latitude of fourteen degrees south, did nothing to shake.
Their return to Bantam in June 1606 was therefore hardly a cause for
jubilation; Torres' passage of the straits two months later was unknown
to geographers for a century and a half, and the belief that Cape York
(and ultimately the whole of Australia) was attached to New Guinea
lingered on far into the eighteenth century.

Since therefore, no one realized that Janszoon's voyage revealed the
Southern Continent, men were still hopeful of finding that land in the
Pacific. A Dutch circumnavigation by Joris van Spilbergen, begun in
1614, brought no advance in geographical knowledge; it passed through
the Straits of Magellan, and after sailing up the South American coast
as far as Mexico, crossed the Pacific to the Philippines. However, an
expedition of two ships which set out in 1615 led to quite important —
if negative — discoveries. Under the leadership of Jacob Le Maire and
Willem Corneliszoon Schouten this fleet sailed boldly around the south-

ern tip of South America — named by Schouten in honor of his native place of Horn in North Holland. No land was seen to the southward, and it was therefore evident that the Southern Continent, contrary to the maps of Ortelius and Mercator, did not extend to the Straits of Magellan. After the passage of the Pacific the chronicle of the fleet becomes ironic. One ship was burned, and on reaching Java the other vessel was confiscated by the Dutch authorities on the grounds that the trading monopoly had been infringed. The survivors were shipped back to Holland in Spilbergen's fleet, and during the voyage Jacob Le Maire died of a fit of anger — as well he might. Schouten lived on to spread the news of the passage around Cape Horn and the absence of an austral continent in that area.

While the Dutch were sweeping the seas below South America, they were also exploring the southern waters of the Indian Ocean. Their skippers found that sailing conditions were more favorable well to the south of the tropics, and Dutch merchantmen soon followed a course east from the Cape, and then a great-circle course to Java. In pursuing these directions the ship *Eendracht*, commanded by Dirk Hartogszoon, got too far off her bearings to the southeast, and in October 1616 fell in with an unknown coast in 26 degrees south. This turned out to be West Australia; Hartogszoon steered north and followed the coast for three hundred miles as far as Northwest Cape before bearing away for Java. This coast was at once regarded as being part of the long-sought continent, and it soon received the name of Eendrachtsland; Australia was at last becoming a reality, and Dirk Hartog's Island has ever since remained a monument to that navigator's landfall.

Further voyages in the two succeeding years (Haevick Claeszoon's in 1617 and Lenaert Jacobszoon's in 1618) reached the coast in the neighborhood of Northwest Cape, and in 1619 Frederik Houtman touched the west coast at the present site of Perth and sailed north for four hundred miles, almost to Dirk Hartog's Island. During this passage the rocks subsequently known as Houtman's Abrolhos ("obstacles," in Portuguese) were discovered, while those aboard concluded that the coast formed part of the continental land mass seen by Hartogszoon. A further idea of the shape of that mass was gained as a result of the voyage of the *Leeuwin* (1622), which reached Cape Leeuwin, the southwestern tip of the island-continent. There was as yet no clear relationship between the west coast and the Cape York peninsula, and exploration of the two regions continued, uncoördinated and independently. In 1623 Jan Carstenszoon coasted New Guinea and penetrated into the Gulf of Carpentaria as far as the Staten River; but like Janszoon in the *Duyfken* he failed to pass through Torres Straits, and thereby missed the solution of the riddle about the connection between Australia and

New Guinea. A vast extension of knowledge, however, resulted from the voyage of François Thijszoon in the *Gulden Zeepard* (1627); from Cape Leeuwin he surveyed the southern coast as far as the Nuyts Archipelago in 133 degrees east, a distance of nearly eight hundred miles, which took the Dutch just above half way across the whole southern face of Australia.

Within twenty-one years of its discovery, then, half of the south coast, all of the west coast, and the western side of the Cape York peninsula had been revealed by the pertinacity of the Dutch mariners. It remained for Abel Tasman to prove the insular character of Australia by sailing round it to northern New Guinea without sighting it (1642), although he discovered both Tasmania and New Zealand in the process. Two years later he sailed into the Gulf of Carpentaria, and continued along the north coast as far as Northwest Cape, thus linking the discoveries of Janszoon and Hartogszoon and establishing the connection between the Cape York peninsula and West Australia. Nevertheless, what could be seen of the land itself was uninviting and disappointing; doubtless because of this, exploration languished after Tasman for more than a century. Then finally in 1770 Captain Cook on his first voyage discovered and surveyed the whole eastern side of the continent, and passed through Torres Straits to establish forever the true shape of Terra Australis.

14

TOURISTS IN THE EAST

The outstanding event in continental India in the sixteenth century was the foundation of the Mogul Empire. From a land of petty states, constantly bickering and fighting with each other, India was transformed for the most part into an enlightened Oriental despotism ruled by a powerful prince, whose policy was generally one of tolerance toward Europeans, and whose cultured court came to be an essential place of resort for Christian travelers. This extraordinarily distinguished Oriental dynasty was founded by Baber, a Moslem chieftain from Turkestan, who was a direct descendant of Tamerlaine in the fifth generation. For many years he had had a successful career as a conqueror in his native Turkestan, and in Afghanistan as well, when a chance opportunity gave him the occasion to try his fortunes in India. In the third decade of the century an unpleasant tyrant named Ibrahim was ruling the Kingdom of Delhi, and his harsh methods so angered his Afghan subjects that they called in Baber to redress their grievances. Baber thereupon invaded India with a small but well-equipped army, and at the Battle of Panipat, fought in April 1526, he routed the vast army of Ibrahim and left that tyrant dead on the field. Baber thus gained possession of Delhi and Agra, but he had to fight to retain his prizes, and in the great Battle of Kanwaha (March, 1527), he overthrew a powerful coalition, led by the Rana of Mewar. This gave Baber control of the Punjab and Rajputana and enabled him to establish his capital at Agra, where he died three years later. Baber was succeeded by his son Humayun, whose reign was trying, to say the least, for he lost all his father's conquests before regaining them. His claim to the Kingdom of Delhi was disputed by Sher Shah, who ruled Bengal, and after ten years of warfare Humayun was driven out of India completely, and was compelled to seek exile in Persia. Years later Sher Shah was fortuitously killed in a campaign in Central India, and Humayun was able to return and to overthrow the remainder of the enemy's forces (1555). Like that of his father Baber, Humayun's triumph was of short duration; after ruling but a year he was killed by falling off the parapet of his palace, and his reconquered realm passed to his young son, destined, under the name of Akbar, to be the greatest of his line, if not the greatest of all Oriental monarchs.

Succeeding to a very shaky throne at the age of fourteen, Akbar soon displayed the talents of a born ruler; talents that enabled him to have one of the most brilliantly successful reigns in history. In 1560, when eighteen years of age, Akbar discharged the regent, Bairam Khan, and by the time he was thirty he had securely established his position as the undisputed ruler of a larger portion of India than had ever before acknowledged the sway of one man. This was accomplished by a highly successful series of campaigns which carried his conquests from Afghanistan to the Bay of Bengal. In 1572 he conquered Gujarat, which gave his domains access to the sea, with a coast line of several hundred miles along the Gulf of Cambay and the Arabian Sea on either side of Diu. It was by the title derived from this region that Queen Elizabeth addressed him in the letter borne by John Newbery: Zelabdim Echebar (Jellaladin Akbar), King of Cambaya. It was not long, however, before he was simply known as the Great Mogul, or its curious derivative, the Great Magor.

Akbar's policy toward his subject territories was just as sage as his conduct in his wars had been. His abilities as a civil administrator and as a lawgiver were of the highest type, while his realm prospered so greatly that he received more revenue from it than the British did from the same area three centuries later. With a keen consciousness of the pomp which goes with so great power, he created a new capital city, Fatehpur Sikri (1569), situated near Agra and replete with mosques and palaces. It was later abandoned because of its poor water supply, but even today its ruins testify to the great magnificence of Akbar's Court.

Although Akbar was one of the greatest conquerors in the East, yet his territorial interests did not run counter to the Portuguese. He was essentially a landsman, the descendant of Central Asian chieftains; not until the conquest of Gujarat did his domains reach the Arabian Sea, but even then his heart was in the Punjab and Rajputana. For the traditional Moslem commercial system in the Indian Ocean which Almeida and Albuquerque had overthrown, Akbar had apparent indifference; if he heard of it at all, he certainly never lifted a finger to restore it. Rather did he look with favor on Portuguese trade as being of economic advantage to all concerned.

It may have been that Akbar's tolerance of the Portuguese was also due in part to his religious views. Akbar had been born and brought up a Mohammedan, but he early developed into a free-thinking philosopher which led him to seek the true religion in an eclectic system. He therefore encouraged the visits of Portuguese missionaries to his court, and he sought by every means to obtain information on all other religions. As a result of these enlightened inquiries he formulated his own religion: a creed of pure deism with a ritual based upon the system of Zoroaster. This religion, having no vital force, never extended its influence beyond the palace and died with Akbar himself, but the consequent spirit of toleration, so alien to the militant austerity of Islam, extended through the reigns of Akbar's son Jahangir and his grandson Shah Jehan.

It seems appropriate, therefore, to touch on the character of the Moguls and their court, inasmuch as between the years 1580 and (let us say) 1650 these potentates were visited by distinguished travelers of many nations; and far more than their fellow rulers — the Grand Signor, the Sophy of Persia, and the Emperor of China — were the Moguls friendly toward Europeans. To them and their court, then, was due much influence for early travel in Southern Asia.

We hear nothing of Portuguese travel within the hinterland of north central India until late in the sixteenth century: military expeditions stayed near the coast and traders seldom went beyond the port towns. With the rise of Akbar's brilliant court the situation swiftly changed, and from the arrival of the first Jesuit mission in 1580 the presence of cultivated Westerners in Fatehpur Sikri, Agra, Delhi, and Lahore was the rule rather than the exception. In that year Akbar sent a request to Goa for information about Christianity, as a result of which Rudolfo Aquaviva and two other Jesuits were dispatched to Fatehpur Sikri. Akbar received them well, and listened to them with intelligent attention. However, his suggested test of the truth of the two conflicting religions by ordeal by fire (a Moslem holding the Koran and a Jesuit bearing the Bible were to enter the fire together) was politely declined by both parties. None the less, the influence of Western civilization made its way at the Mogul's capital: a later Jesuit, Jerome Xavier, translated the four Gospels into Persian for Akbar, and the introduction of illuminated Books of Hours had a distinct effect on the brilliant Mogul school of painting. No doubt the Protestant case was explained by the three Englishmen, Newbery, Fitch, and Leeds, during their visit to Agra and Fatehpur Sikri in 1585; Leeds, a jeweler, remained behind in that capacity at the emperor's court and apparently died there. A later English visitor to Akbar was the enigmatic John Mildenhall, who was attendant upon the court from 1603 until the Mogul's death in 1605.

Generally speaking, the Jesuit missions to China did not have nearly so easy a time as those to the Great Mogul. One priest, nevertheless, did so strongly ingratiate himself with the Chinese that he became the best remembered of all Europeans in the Celestial Empire for centuries afterwards. An urbane and highly civilized cleric, Matteo Ricci was in his own right a mathematician, an astronomer, a man of letters, and a citizen of the world, whose polished and mellow sophistication made a lasting impression on the Chinese. But access to China, and especially to the capital city of Peking, was not easy; and Ricci's mission was one of delay and frustration, lasting not merely for years, but even for decades. Ricci went to China about 1582, and although he hoped to make his way to the capital, it was only after various disappointments that he was able to establish his mission on the West River near Canton. His clocks, his globes, and his mathematical instruments soon excited the curiosity of the more intelligent Chinese, although it is said that he aroused their antagonism by showing them a world map with China placed insignificantly off on one side, instead of being in the center of the world, like a gem in a ring. Ricci strove to correct this mistake by drawing a hemispherical map in which China filled the whole central area; his map was engraved and enjoyed wide popularity.

After seven years, troubles at Canton caused Ricci and his followers to seek a new home, and the mission was moved to the foot of the mountains a hundred and fifty miles to the north — near the well-known Meiling Pass. Ricci had by this time become completely acclimatized: he wore Chinese dress and attained such fluency of the language that he was able to compose a number of devotional works in the vernacular. His hopes, however, of speedily reaching Peking were constantly disappointed, although he took every opportunity to move his mission northward. In 1595 he migrated from the Meiling district to Nanchang, the capital of Kiangsi Province, situated midway between Canton and Nanking. Three years later he was able to proceed to Nanking itself, and even to penetrate to Peking, which had all along been his goal. But he was not allowed to remain, and with his mission was compelled to retrace his steps to Nanking. However, news of the presents which Ricci carried reached the Imperial Court, and finally in 1600 the Jesuits were summoned to Peking by the emperor himself. Ricci was well received by the emperor, the presents were greatly admired, and the mission was allowed to settle in the capital. Until his death in 1610 Ricci's reputation among the Chinese was constantly increasing, as was also the amount of his labors. His work in the Peking period was the foundation of the subsequent success of the Catholic Church in China. In consequence of his great personal popularity and his having composed a number of important treatises in Chinese, Ricci (under the Chinese form of *Li-ma-teu*, from *Ri*-cci *Mat-teo*) has perhaps remained the best known European name in China.

In spite of the fact that the Jesuits had thus established themselves in the Celestial Empire, current ideas of Central and East Asia geography were still so vague that it was far from generally recognized that Cathay and China were but different names of the same land. The Jesuits therefore decided to attempt an overland journey from India to China in search of the mysterious Empire of Cathay. The travels of medieval missioners had taken place upwards of three centuries earlier, and the last European to penetrate Central Asia had been Anthony Jenkinson, who in 1558 had only got as far as Bokhara. The fastnesses of Turkestan and Mongolia were therefore *terrae incognitae*, where prosperous realms might well flourish unknown to the Western world.

For this perilous journey the choice fell to Benedict Goes, an Azorean, who as a lay member of the Jesuit order had previously served as a soldier in India. Leaving Agra late in 1602 with the blessing of the Mogul Akbar, Goes and his two companions chose the circuitous route used by merchants around the western extremity of the Himalayas and through the cities of Eastern Turkestan. This route took him first to Lahore, then by way of Peshawar and the Khyber Pass to Kabul. From the Afghan capital he crossed the Hindu Kush to the Oxus and proceeded up that river to its source. Such a passage meant that Goes had to cross some of the most rugged country in the world, passing through the heart of the Pamirs, with mountain peaks 25,000 feet high around him, and traversing the Wakhjir Pass (16,150 feet), where many of the caravan were frozen to death. After fighting their way for six days through snowfields, Goes and his companions got over the Roof of Asia, and made their way down to Yarkand in Chinese Turkestan.

It is curious that Goes should have selected so difficult a route. The famous Silk Road of classical and medieval times ran from Balkh to Kashgar via the Alai Trough, a broad and almost level valley, which though flanked by lofty mountains, had its watershed at a mere ten thousand feet. As this was situated only two hundred miles north of Goes's route, he could have taken it with little difficulty and far less risk, but possibly the caravan to which he had attached himself preferred the more arduous road.

For a full year Goes was detained in Yarkand, during which time he made an excursion to Khotan, two hundred miles to the southeast on the borders of Tibet. At length, in November 1604, he joined a caravan bound for China, and proceeded along the southern slopes of the Tian Shan mountains, passing through Turfan and Khamil. He eventually reached Suchow, twelve hundred miles in a direct line from Yarkand and about nine hundred from Peking. Goes at last was in China; and before this he had reached the conclusion that Cathay and China were one and the same: a conclusion which Ricci in Peking had by this time reached independently. Goes was again held up for a prolonged period, although he was able to communicate with Ricci in the capital. Ricci sent out a native convert to help Goes, but this man, arriving at Suchow in March 1607, found the missioner prostrated by illness. Goes died a few days later; a great traveler, who "seeking Cathay, found Heaven." It has been said that he was the first European of modern times to set foot on Chinese soil from the west, and thus to assign to that land its true place on the map of the world.

Another mountaineering Jesuit, memorable as the first European to cross the Himalayas from India, was Antonio de Andrade. In 1624 he left Agra, ascended the Ganges to its headwaters, and visited the sacred shrine of Badrinath, high in the mountains of Garhwal. From there he crossed the Mana Pass (18,000 feet) between Kamet and Nanda Devi, and reached the Sutlej River in a very remote mountain plateau known as Little Tibet. He returned by the same route — and was so full of enthusiasm that he repeated the journey the following year, and spent several years doing missionary work in this out-of-the-way district. In 1631 Andrade's colleague, Francisco de Azevedo, left the mission at Tsaparang on the Sutlej and proceeded three hundred miles northwest to the town of Leh on the upper Indus, which lies within that part of Kashmir known as Ladakh. His return thence to India took him through the extremely mountainous country of eastern Kashmir and across the Rotang Pass to Lahore. By this journey Azevedo opened up a vast stretch of country between the Pamirs which Goes had traversed and the Mana Pass which Andrade had crossed.

Five years earlier (1626) the eastern Himalayas were for the first time explored by Europeans, when the missionaries Estevão Cacela and João Cabral went north from Kuch Bihar, crossed the mountains by the Donkia Pass between Bhutan and Sikkim, and established their station at Shigatze in Tibet. This town, situated on the Brahmaputra about a hundred and forty miles west of Lhasa, has always been one of the greatest centers of Buddhism, containing as it does the huge Teshilumpo Monastery, with several thousand cenobites. Cabral returned by way of the valley of the Arun River into Nepal, a route which took him between the two loftiest mountain massifs in the world: Everest and Kangchenjunga. The Everest expeditions of our own day have by this token a respectable ancestry of more than three centuries of reconnaissance.

EARLY EUROPEAN VISITORS TO INDIA

The court of the Great Mogul at Agra, the brilliant if hybrid Portuguese capital of Goa, and the lavish Burmese metropolis of Pegu alike attained great fame in the Renaissance and beckoned the curious traveler ever eastward. Linschoten's residence in Goa, the visit of Newbery and Fitch to Abkar's court, and the sojourns of Federici and Balbi in India and Burma have already been described. There were, however, contemporaries and successors who deserve some attention: most of them French, one a Portuguese Jew, and one an Italian.

Certainly one of the first of his nation to reach southern Asia was Vin-

cent Leblanc, a sailor from Marseilles, who, having been shipwrecked off
Crete in 1568, used this misfortune as a cause of ten years' wanderings.
From Crete he visited Syria, Palestine, and Arabia, and then traversed
Persia to reach India, and eventually Burma. Like Federici, Balbi, and
Fitch he spent much time in Pegu, and like them he had much to say
about the barbaric lavishness of the Burmese capital. He apparently
visited Sumatra and Java, and he probably returned to Europe by the
Cape of Good Hope; at least he mentioned visiting both Madagascar and
Abyssinia, but then Leblanc never let geographical difficulties trouble
his narrative. In fact, it must be confessed that the great traveler from
Marseilles was rather a poor narrator, and it has been suggested that some
of his journeys at least were never made. By his own account, he returned
to France in 1578, but he was immediately sent on a mission to Morocco,
and was present at the battle of Alcazar-Kebir, where King Sebastian was
slain. A later journey, in 1592, took him down the West African coast to
Guinea. This seems to have been his last venture, although he lived until
about 1640. His celebrated book, *Voyages fameux du Sieur Vincent Leblanc Marseillois*, appeared in Paris in 1649 and was translated into English in 1660.

A more reputable traveler than Leblanc, of especial interest for having
been the first man to go around the world from west to east, was Pedro
Teixeira, an observant Portuguese of Jewish extraction. Teixeira's profession is uncertain; he may have been a soldier; he may have been a
physician; he may have been a speculator in narcotics and precious
stones — probably he was all three at one time or another. In any case he
was an early member of that class of travelers whose reason for journeying
about was mostly pure curiosity; India was to see many like him in the
next few decades. Having reached Goa in 1586, Teixeira sailed down the
East African coast the following year on a punitive expedition which reduced Lamu and Mombasa to obedience and called at Ormuz on the way
back. The following season saw Teixeira on another expedition, this time
to Ceylon, after which he appears to have settled in Cochin. A prolonged
residence followed, where he seems to have been a trader, in which capacity he crossed Persia on one occasion to the Caspian. In 1597 he sailed
to Malacca, where he lived two and a half years, before starting homeward. His return journey, begun in May 1600, took him to Borneo and
then to Manila. Here he shipped on the annual Acapulco galleon, which
crossed the Pacific to Mexico by Urdaneta's Passage. Having traversed
the land of New Spain, he joined the plate fleet, an dafter a call at Havana,
finally landed in Spain in October 1601.

It is doubtful if Teixeira saved much time by taking such a complicated
itinerary, but he did perform a novel journey, gaining the distinction of
having seen both Malacca and Mexico on the same voyage. Not many

travelers in those days visited both the East and the West Indies. For all his effort in getting back, however, Teixeira was off to India again in less than two years, evidently to collect some debts still owing him. His business in Goa was soon cleared up, and he proceeded home by another route, unusual for a Portuguese — the land route from Basra to Aleppo, which very few of his countrymen had taken since Tenreiro had first used it in 1528. Teixeira's account of this passage occupies the bulk of his account of his journeying, and his narrative is one of the fullest and most interesting that has been left us by an overland traveler in the Middle East.

While Teixeira was going around the world from west to east his path may have crossed that of Pierre Olivier Malherbe, a shadowy and elusive figure who has been hailed as the first Frenchman to make a circumnavigation. Yet even more than in the case of Leblanc, Malherbe's narrative is suspect. Everything was grist to his mill: Mexico, the silver mines of Potosi, Patagonia, the Philippines, China, and all of Southern Asia. By his own account he was the honored guest of Akbar in India and of Shah Abbas in Persia; he visited the Grand Lama of Tibet and went to Samarkand. In fact he went everywhere and met everybody with such abandon that our suspicions are perforce aroused — a feeling borne out by the fact that Malherbe receives no mention at all by his contemporary travelers! Perhaps he is best regarded as a link between Sir John Mandeville and Louis de Rougemont.

The unfortunate and isolated French voyage to the East Indies has enriched posterity with one highly valuable narrative of Eastern travel — that of François Pyrard of Laval. This venture, organized by the shipping interests of Normandy, sent out two vessels in 1601, but the voyage was doomed from the start by lack of discipline and the ravages of scurvy. Pyrard's ship was wrecked on one of the Maldives, a group of coral atolls southwest of India and the accompanying vessel, after trading in Sumatra, was abandoned in a sinking condition off the Azores. Pyrard and his shipmates were made prisoners and sent to the native capital of Malé. With laudable resourcefulness Pyrard set about learning the Maldive language, and before long had gained favor with the king, but was unable to leave the archipelago. His five years' residence there, however, gave him an intimate knowledge of that out-of-the-way part of the world such as few travelers have ever gained. At length a hostile expedition descended on the Maldives from Bengal and carried away Pyrard to Chittagong. Living among Lascar pirates, he made his way along the Malabar Coast to Calicut, and, having been taken prisoner by the Portuguese at Cochin, he eventually reached Goa. He was released through the good offices of a French Jesuit and joined the Portuguese forces and served in two campaigns. The first took him north, to Diu and Cambay; the second and longer venture carried him to Ceylon, Malacca, and the Eastern

Archipelago, and enabled him to describe fully the trade of southeastern Asia. But it is the vividness of his passages about Goa that makes his travel narrative memorable; his picture of its decadent grandeur, the corruption of the government, and the relaxing and sensual way of life is unforgettably graphic, while there are many personal touches that go far to make his book a living document.

At last in the winter of 1609–1610 Pyrard was sent back to Europe, together with various other foreigners whose presence had become embarrassing to the Portuguese authorities. His ship doubled the Cape and touched at St. Helena, but was wrecked on the Brazilian coast near Bahia. It was only after an unexpected sojourn in South America that Pyrard saw the shores of Europe again and finally reached his native Laval in 1611, after an absence of ten years.

An equally interesting and perhaps more learned traveler was Jean Mocquet, who held the office of apothecary to Henry IV of France. Having an irresistible desire to travel, he obtained Henry's consent on condition that he collect curiosities for the king's cabinet at the Tuileries, of which he was eventually appointed custodian. Mocquet made at least two voyages to Morocco, and in 1604 took an interesting trip to South America, exploring the coast from the Amazon to the Orinoco. On this voyage he gained a wide knowledge of the region later to become French Guiana, and returned with much information about the flora and anthropology of the district. His most extensive venture took place in 1608, when he sailed for India in a Portuguese vessel. The outward passage was not a happy one: Mocquet suffered severely from scurvy, and his ship was so badly handled in a storm off the Cape that she had to be laid up six months for repairs at Mozambique. This delay gave Mocquet a chance to recover his health and enabled him to explore the littoral of Southeast Africa; his treatment by the Portuguese, however, led to a lasting prejudice against that nation. Finally arrived at Goa, he became apothecary to the governor, Furtado de Mendoça, and also served in that capacity at the hospital, where he met Pyrard. His duties were not too onerous and he was able to spend much time in the neighboring countryside, collecting drugs, precious stones, and other rarities. His experiences in India, nevertheless, made him as violently anti-Hindu as he was anti-Portuguese, and his description of life in Goa is sordid and tragic. Mocquet returned to Europe in the same fleet as Pyrard, but his vessel escaped shipwreck, and his passage home appears to have been without incident.

Another Frenchman, whose path crossed those of Pyrard and Mocquet, was the somewhat mysterious Sieur de Feynes, Comte de Montfart, who made an overland journey to India of several years' duration. His way took him from Aleppo to Isfahan and Ormuz, and he reached Goa about the time that Pyrard and Mocquet were there. His wanderings appear to have carried him as far as Canton; in the account of his travels he tells us that he also visited Cochin China, Siam, and Pegu. Such is the scope of his itinerary that critics have viewed his account with suspicion, but the cut-and-dried style of the narrative, plus the fact that the author was mentioned by both Pyrard and Mocquet, indicate that Montfart's relation is essentially true. Strangely enough, his narrative was published in English before it appeared in France, having been put forth by a French resident in London in 1615.

Considering the number of Italian travelers who reached India in the fifteenth and sixteenth centuries, it seems strange that there was only one secular tourist of any distinction from Italy in the later Renaissance. Disappointed in love and filled with a desire to see the world, Pietro della Valle left Venice in 1614 on a pilgrimage to the Holy Land. After visiting Mount Sinai he proceeded to Damascus and Aleppo and then, following the well-worn caravan route, crossed Mesopotamia to Baghdad. By this time he was sufficiently cured of his broken heart to marry a beautiful Circassian, who accompanied him on his travels until her death. Della Valle spent several years wandering in Persia, during some of which time he was attendant at the court of Shah Abbas. But the hardships of the road were too much for his wife, who died near Persepolis about 1622. The sorrowing husband thereupon had the body embalmed and took it along with him as an extra piece of luggage, being accompanied also by his wife's young maidservant. By 1623 he had reached Surat. From there he made his way slowly and carefully down the west coast of India as far as Calicut. From Goa he sailed to Muscat; thence he traveled by way of Basra to Aleppo and finally reached Rome in 1626. His wife's remains were at last given a decent burial, and having become a papal chamberlain, della Valle married the Georgian maidservant, by whom he had fourteen sons. His book, published in the form of letters (1657–1663), is especially valuable for its thorough descriptions of Persia and Western India.

SOME WANDERING BRITONS

From the return of Fitch until the closing years of the sixteenth century it does not appear that any Englishman penetrated to Southern Asia by the overland route, but travel was too much in the air for Britons to forego the lure of the Orient indefinitely. Perhaps the first extensive Eastern journey undertaken after Fitch's time was that of the unscrupulous adventurer Sir Anthony Sherley, who was sent by the Earl of Essex to Persia, in the hope of persuading Shah Abbas to enter into an anti-Turkish alliance with the states of Europe. Sherley left Venice in the spring of 1598 with his young brother Robert and a large party of Englishmen and proceeded to the Middle East. His voyage was venturous: he and his party were put off the ship as troublemakers, and made their way with great difficulty to the Syrian coast in an open boat. From Aleppo they crossed to Baghdad, where a murderous plot against them was revealed in the nick of time; they escaped into Persia, and reached Kazvin, where they were received by the shah.

During the ensuing winter Sherley was able to persuade Abbas to join the alliance, and the Englishman was sent back to Europe to enlist the support of the Christian sovereigns. Sherley's return was just as full of incident. After an adventurous crossing of the Caspian, the party proceeded to Moscow, only to be imprisoned by the tsar, Boris Godunov. They obtained release the following spring (1600), sailed from Archangel around the North Cape to Germany, and made their way to the Imperial Court at Prague, where Sir Anthony was warmly greeted by the Emperor Rudolph II. Rome was the next objective, and after an inconclusive audience with the Pope, Sherley, who had quarreled with everyone along the line, threw over his commission, and retired to Venice, to practice as a charlatan. For the next quarter-century Sir Anthony figured as a dangerous and dishonest schemer in Venice, Prague, Morocco, and Madrid, finally dying in Spain in obscurity and poverty (as he deserved).

Meanwhile his younger brother Robert, along with several other Englishmen, had been left as hostage with the shah. Robert's record was considerably better than Anthony's. He served with distinction against the Turks, he was at one time Governor of a Persian province, and he married a Persian lady who was distantly related to the shah. At length Abbas became wholly exasperated with the failure of Sir Anthony's mission, and in 1608 he dispatched Robert to Europe as his ambassador. Wearing Persian dress and accompanied by his Persian wife, Robert crossed the Caspian, and having visited Moscow, went overland to Poland. Although he was everywhere well received, there was little enthusiasm for a Turkish war. Robert passed through Italy and Spain and finally reached England empty-handed. King James gave him a friendly hearing and arranged a return passage for him and his wife on an East Indiaman, but Robert's voyage back to Persia was destined to be a tedious one. A landing on the Persian coast was prevented by a plot against his life, and he was compelled to sail on to India. From the mouth of the Indus he made his way to Ajmere, where he was entertained by the Emperor Jahangir, then he followed a long and difficult passage overland to Persia. In the middle of the Afghan desert Sherley had the curious fortune to met Tom Coryate, who was "hot-footing it" on his walking trip to India.

When Robert reached Isfahan, he found that the shah's favor had cooled. Because of this, the Englishman was soon on his way home again. He obtained passage to Goa, only to be imprisoned there by the Portuguese for a whole year. At length he sailed to Lisbon on one of the Portuguese vessels, and made the round of the European capitals a second time — not on behalf of an anti-Turkish alliance, but to arrange commercial treaties with respect to the export of Persian silk. These negotiations kept him for years in England, and involved him, by no means amicably, with the East India Company, who played off a native Persian ambassador of their own against him. The issue became so complicated that Charles I appointed a third ambassador, Sir Dodmore Cotton, to determine their claims and sent all three out to Persia in 1627 by the Cape route. Arrived back in Persia, the native emissary committed suicide, and Robert found himself completely dropped by Shah Abbas, who was no doubt thoroughly exasperated by the total failure of a quarter century's dealings with Europeans. Shunned by the Court, Sherley reached Kazvin a sick man and died broken-hearted. Cotton perished at the same time, and the survivors of the expedition made their way painfully homeward, as chronicled in the very human account of Sir Thomas Herbert. So ended the wanderings of Robert Sherley, a figure who merited the claim of being "the greatest traveler of his time."

During Robert Sherley's initial residence of almost a decade in Persia, several Europeans passed through who left references to him in their writings. Chief among these travelers was an ill-assorted pair, consisting of a sight-seeing clergyman, John Cartwright, and a merchant to the Levant, John Mildenhall, who was on his way to the court of the Emperor Akbar as a self-appointed ambassador. Cartwright got no further than Persia, but as a very early archaeologist he appears to have been the first Englishman to have visited all four of the great sites of Oriental antiquity: Susa, Nineveh, Babylon, and Persepolis.

Mildenhall parted with Cartwright near Isfahan and went across country, via Kandahar and Lahore, to Agra, where Akbar was then holding his court. For two whole years (1603–1605), Mildenhall was closely attendant upon the Great Mogul, seeking all the while to obtain commercial privileges for England in India. In this he met with the bitter opposition of the Portuguese Jesuits, but he eventually succeeded in arranging a treaty with Akbar and departed overland to England with the precious document. He had, however, no authority whatsoever to act in the capacity he did, and when he returned to London in 1607, he was chagrined to learn that neither the crown nor the East India Company was the least interested in the fruit of his labors. After some years of futile negotiations with the company, Mildenhall departed for the East in 1611 on a private trading venture. This took him again to Persia, where he contravened the privileges of the company and had his goods confiscated by its agents. He then proceeded to India with one of the agents, Richard Steel. Falling sick at Lahore, he struggled on to Ajmere, where he died in 1614.

His tombstone, in the Christian cemetery at Agra, is the oldest English monument in India. Mildenhall remains a mysterious figure: was he a patriot or a charlatan?

A more official, if hardly more successful, mission was that of William Hawkins, who went to India as the East India Company's agent on the third voyage in 1607, the first of the company's ventures to touch the Indian mainland. Hawkins went ashore at Surat, and after more than a year of negotiation with Mukarrab Khan, a man of great local importance, he proceeded to Agra, where he was attendant upon the Emperor Jahangir for nearly three years. During his sojourn with the Great Mogul, Hawkins was well cared for; he was made captain of a squadron of cavalry, was married to a native girl of the emperor's choosing, and took his place among the grandees of the court, living and dressing in Mohammedan fashion. But he was unable to obtain a grant for the establishment of an English factory at Surat, and the company's trade had to be conducted unofficially, on a day-to-day basis. Trading privileges, and even then poor ones, were not officially granted until 1612.

Hawkins' position at Agra was not rendered easier by the unexpected arrival of some survivors of the fourth voyage, wrecked on the *Ascension* off the bar of Surat. It is to be feared that these sailors, more drunk than sober, did not create a good impression, though one of them, Captain Robert Coverte, performed quite a remarkable journey homeward, going by Ajmere, Kandahar, and Isfahan across Afghanistan and Persia. Another member of the same voyage, named William Nichols, struck eastward, and made his way across the peninsula to Masulipatam. Most important of these mariners, however, was John Jourdain. Before reaching India, the *Ascension* had touched at Aden, and a journey inland to Sana (whither Varthema had gone a century earlier) gave Jourdain the title of the first Englishman to visit Yemen. In India he visited Agra, Jodhpur, and Ahmadabad in Gujarat; he also discovered "Swally Hole," a harbor near Surat, afterwards used regularly as an anchorage by the ships of the East India Company. In 1612 he went to Sumatra to engage in the pepper trade, and then to the Spice Islands of Amboyna and Ceram to buy cloves. His residence in the East Indies (interspersed by a return to England) was a lengthy one, and he stoutly maintained the privileges of the English East India Company in the islands until his death in a sea-fight with the Dutch off Patani in 1619.

While Hawkins was negotiating with Jahangir in Agra, the charge of the English in Surat was given to William Finch, a good traveler, but a man evidently hard to get along with. In 1610 Hawkins summoned him to Agra, whence he was sent out to buy and sell indigo. In the following year he traveled by way of Delhi to Lahore, a colorful city, which as one of the chief cities of the Great Mogul was second only to Agra in importance.

By this time Finch had quarreled with Hawkins openly, and as he now regarded the prospects of English trade in India as hopeless, he threw over his duties, and joined a caravan for Persia. We know nothing more of his journey, save that he died in Baghdad, but his journal was brought home by his servant, Thomas Styles, and was utilized by Purchas. From this valuable document we have an excellent picture of Jahangir's India, as well as important descriptions of the routes from Lahore to Srinagar in Kashmir, from Lahore to Kabul, and from Kabul to China.

Like Finch, Hawkins died on his return journey, and like him also he left a very interesting account, printed by Purchas in the *Pilgrimes*. Sailing homeward with his Oriental bride in 1612, Hawkins found himself returning by the roundabout route of Aden and Java; during the long passage the ship became so unseaworthy and the crew so weakened by sickness that they were forced to put into a port on the Irish coast, where the picturesque traveler died. His experiences at Jahangir's court nevertheless enabled him to leave to posterity a vivid and lively picture of the colorful pageant that Agra must have been in the days of its enlightened despots.

Two more of the East India Company's servants deserve notice for their wanderings in India in this period: Nicholas Withington and William Methwold. In 1613 Withington was sent to Ahmadabad on a commercial venture, during which he saw much of interest in the Gujarat area to relate. While there he received word that the *Expedition*, with Robert Sherley on board, had reached the mouth of the Indus, and Withington was ordered to make his way overland to Tatta, a port on the river. This involved an adventurous journey through a part of India seldom traversed by Europeans. Traveling with a group of native merchants, he entered Sind, and almost reached Tatta, but a local chief arrested the whole party and hanged the merchants. Withington, as an Englishman, was spared but was kept a prisoner for some weeks in the hills lest he spread word of the crime. Only with great difficulty did he make his way back to Ahmadabad and Surat.

Withington's account of Western India is matched in interest by that of William Methwold on the other side of the peninsula. Methwold, perhaps the ablest of the company's agents in the early days, had a long and useful career in the East, and spent the years 1618–1622 as factor at Masulipatam on the Coromandel Coast. He put his spare time to good advantage by observing the peoples and the natural products of the region and in his journey to the fabulous diamond mines of Golconda he performed an interesting geographical service, which has warranted him the attention of posterity.

Although the *farman* issued in 1612 had granted the English company some few privileges, the basis of trade was still quite unsatisfactory, and

Portuguese agents at Jahangir's court were doing their utmost to rob the English of their precarious foothold in India. It was to remedy this state of affairs that King James in 1615 sent a full-fledged ambassador to his brother monarch, in the person of Sir Thomas Roe. Jahangir was at that time residing at Ajmere, a beautiful city set in well-wooded hills two hundred and fifty miles west of Agra. Roe made his way there soon after he landed at Surat. For nearly three years he remained resident at the court, striving manfully to extract a commercial treaty which would establish the company on a secure basis. In this attempt he met with Portuguese and native opposition, as well as heart-rending procrastination and the fickle *volte-face* of court officials, and he was forced to follow the emperor, first to Mandu, where an ineffectual campaign was in progress, and then to Ahmadabad in Gujarat. Roe soon found that the earthshaking conqueror was a hen-pecked husband, under the thumb of his favorite wife, Nur Mahal, but by gaining the favor of the young prince (later to become Shah Jehan) the Englishman was finally able to obtain a *farman* for favorable conditions of trade at Surat. In his wanderings through India with the court, the ambassador was accompanied by his chaplain, Edward Terry, whose account remains one of the principal sources of Roe's mission.

Not all the travel in India was done by men connected with the East India Company, however, for in the person of Thomas Coryate we have the first real English sight-seer to visit Hindustan: not an ambassador, or a chaplain, or a factor, but a traveler who came all the way to Southern Asia for no other purpose than to see what it was like. Coryate already enjoyed great fame as a wanderer, for he had made a much publicized walking trip across Europe to Venice, which resulted in his celebrated book, the *Crudities* (1611). On his second venture he sailed to Constantinople, and after visiting the Holy Land, set out from Aleppo in September 1614 on his long tramp across Asia. His way took him through Persia, where in Isfahan he waited two months in vain for an audience with Shah Abbas. Although he failed to see the Sophy, he did have the curious meeting (already referred to) with Robert Sherley and his wife in the midst of the Afghan desert. His first stop in India was at Multan, where he had a debate on religion with a Moslem; he then continued by way of Lahore and Agra to Jahangir's court at Ajmere. After a ten months' walk from Aleppo, Tom now found himself in luxury and consequently spent a whole year at Ajmere. He was on hand to welcome Sir Thomas Roe when the latter approached the city, and he remained close to the ambassador during the rest of his stay. This did not prevent him from having a very unofficial audience with Jahangir, evidently to that monarch's amusement. From Ajmere, Coryate made an interesting excursion to Hardwar, a famous Hindu shrine on the upper Ganges, and continued to Kangra in the

Himalayas, between Simla and Kashmir, being thereby perhaps the first Briton to penetrate the mountains. At length he rejoined Roe at Mandu, and later made his way to Surat, in the hope of getting passage for England. But his exertions, plus the hospitality of the English merchants, were too much for his long-suffering constitution, and he died late in 1617 from dysentery and overdrinking.

Coryate was but one of a well-defined group of British travelers, who like him were born sight-seers, although none of the others went as far afield as he. In this class one must include Fynes Moryson, who traveled throughout Europe and the Near East in the later days of Elizabeth — a traveler whose encyclopedic writings are indeed a mighty source for "Shakespeare's Europe." Then there was the truculent Scot, William Lithgow, always in trouble and always having hairbreadth escapes, who in the course of nineteen years' wanderings traversed over thirty thousand miles, but who, like Moryson, did not get east of Syria. Another notable tourist was the scholarly George Sandys, who after visiting Constantinople, the Holy Land, and Egypt, came out to Virginia and lived some years in Jamestown. All of these men wrote classics of travel in the days of Elizabeth and James, a good tradition kept up in the next reign by Sir Thomas Herbert, who accompanied and chronicled Robert Sherley's last voyage to Persia, and by Sir Henry Blount, who made an interesting tour of the Ottoman Empire in the 1630's. To this later generation belongs the astounding Cornishman, Peter Mundy, who covered whole continents in his peregrinations.

CHAPTER

15

THE EARLY COLONIZATION OF
NORTH AMERICA

UNSUCCESSFUL BEGINNINGS

France had bad luck with her colonial experiments in the sixteenth century: Cartier's attempt to found a settlement on the St. Lawrence was a complete failure, and Villegagnon's colony in Brazil came to an even more tragic end. But the French did not lose heart, and the Protestant movement in France provided a large minority of religious dissidents from whom likely volunteers could be secured for overseas plantation. This factor was the more significant since the Huguenots were especially numerous in the port towns, such as Le Havre, Dieppe, and La Rochelle. Yet the Huguenot emigration was not prompted solely by desire to escape the rigorous persecution of the Counter Reformation. These seaman of the Norman and Breton ports had engaged in large-scale privateering against the Spaniards for many years past, as had their forebears. Perhaps for this very reason Cartier's Canadian scheme and Coligny's Brazilian one had been poorly supported and had failed so utterly, for both Canada and Brazil lay far off the Spanish trade routes. But a settlement on the Florida coast, flanking the Florida Channel through which every Spanish plate fleet had to run, held enormous strategic possibilities. Not that any Frenchman was so uncritical as to expect the Spaniards to accept such a situation tamely, but it was certainly reasonable to look for huge financial returns, should a colony be successfully planted.

This idea of a French settlement on the southeastern coast of North America, predicated both on religious and strategic grounds, was the conception of Admiral Gaspard de Coligny, a staunch Protestant, who nevertheless was adviser to the queen, Catherine de Medici, and whose bitter anti-Spanish feeling made him the counterpart of the Duke of Alba, Philip II's cruel and bigoted adviser. In this sense the colonists were mere pawns on the chessboard of high politics, and their eventual fate must be regarded in the light of the international drama that was then being played with such intensity.

For the leader of what was intended to be a preliminary reconnaissance, Coligny selected Jean Ribaut, a sailor of great experience, a zealous Huguenot, and a loyal Frenchman. With two ships under his command, Ribaut sailed from Le Havre in the winter of 1562; two months later he dropped anchor off the Florida coast near the site of St. Augustine. Sailing on to the northward, Ribaut entered the St. John's River on May Day, naming it therefore the River of May. After this interlude the fleet continued along the Georgia coast, and by the time that Ribaut had reached South Carolina his enthusiasm had so far got the better of him that he decided to build a fort and start a settlement. A site was selected near the mouth of the Broad River below present-day Beaufort; Ribaut christened it Port Royal, and Port Royal it still remains. Here a stockade was erected, named Charlesfort, in honor of the boy-king, Charles IX, and volunteers from the ships' companies offered to remain behind as colonists. One is reminded of Columbus' initial settlement of Navidad, and doubtless the problems facing both colonies must have been very similar. Certainly extemporized and unplanned Charlesfort was painfully deficient of essentials, and Ribaut sailed back to France in June, promsing to return by the end of the year with a fleet of supplies.

But this was not to be: Ribaut reached home to find France in the throes of religious war, and after taking part in the futile defence of Dieppe, he fled to England. Loyal as he was, Ribaut did not forget his colony, for his book *The Whole and True Discovery of Terra Florida* was published in London in 1563, and he sought to interest Queen Elizabeth in planting an English settlement at Port Royal. In this scheme Ribaut had the misfortune to become involved with the notorious adventurer Thomas Stukeley (the father of Raleigh's betrayer), as a result of which the unlucky Frenchman found himself in prison. His colony at Charlesfort quite naturally languished. The men were able to subsist with the aid of friendly Indians, but the longer they waited for Ribaut's return, the more desperate their situation became. By the spring of 1563 the only hope for the colonists lay in abandoning the place and attempting to reach France. They constructed a pinnace, a most makeshift affair, with moss for caulking, sails made out of sheets, and cordage supplied by the Indians; and in this home-made craft they boldly set forth into the Atlantic. Their voyage must have been terrifying; they eventually had to descend to cannibalism when their food ran out. Nevertheless some of them did make the ocean crossing and were finally picked up by an English ship when in sight of land. They had indeed sailed opportunely, for a Spanish force came to Charlesfort after they had left and burned it to the ground.

Despite the complete failure of Port Royal, affairs in France were by no means unpropitious for the renewal of the attempt. The religious strife between Catholics and Protestants had been halted — temporarily, at least — by the Peace of Amboise in 1563, and the Huguenots, with Coligny at their head, were in a strong position. Ribaut, it is true, was still imprisoned in England, but his lieutenant on the 1562 voyage, René de Laudonnière, had proved his worth at Charlesfort, and was therefore the natural choice as leader of the second expedition. A fleet of three ships sailed from Le Havre in April 1564 under Laudonnière's command and with three hundred sailors and colonists aboard. Two months later the fleet entered the River of May and shortly thereafter laid out their settlement of Fort Caroline, near present-day Jacksonville. In contrast with extemporized Charlesfort, a deliberate beginning was made to plant a permanent colony, but from the start the settlement was plagued with trouble. There was mutiny and there was famine; Laudonnière's dealings with the Indians were tainted with duplicity, besides which the leader was constantly ill, and for a while was imprisoned by the mutineers. Some relief was provided by the fortuitous arrival of several English vessels under Sir John Hawkins in the summer of 1565, and a few days later the long-suffering colonists were overwhelmed with joy at the arrival of Ribaut himself with powerful reinforcements. It looked as if the colony had turned the corner.

Events now began to move quickly and the unlucky Frenchmen had only a few days of peace vouchsafed them in their fool's paradise. Philip of Spain had been informed through his ambassador at the French court of Ribaut's release from England and of the equipping and departure of his fleet; and the strategic implications of a French stronghold aflank Spain's life-line demanded instant action. A brave and skilful sailor, Pedro Menendez de Aviles, was sent out with a strong fleet to eliminate the threat: Ribaut had arrived in Florida on August 28; Menendez's ships were sighted a week later. In this crisis Ribaut, with more courage than wisdom, made a fatal mistake: he divided his forces. Menendez had no sooner reached Florida than he set about creating a base which he called St. Augustine, and on September 10 Ribaut sailed from Fort Caroline to crush the Spaniards there. A gale blew his ships out to sea, when within sight of the Spaniards, and Fort Caroline was left defenseless. Menendez was not slow to take advantage of the situation, and marching overland with five hundred men he stormed Fort Caroline and slew more than half the garrison. About a hundred fugitives, among them Laudonnière and Le Moyne the artist, escaped and managed to get back to Europe on one of the remaining French ships. Ribaut's fate was worse; his fleet was wrecked in the storm, and the Spaniards came upon the defenseless survivors wandering along the shore below St. Augustine. No prisoners were taken.

Such was the fate of the French colony in Florida, which is immortalized in de Bry's engravings (done after Le Moyne's drawings) in the second volume of the *Grands Voyages*. Retribution for the cold-blooded brutality of the Spaniards was swift, efficient, and merciless. Dominique de Gourgues, a French Catholic, but a friend of Ribaut's, determined on a private war of revenge. In the summer of 1567 he sailed to Florida with three ships and attacked the Spanish post at Fort Caroline. Surprise was complete; again, as in the massacre of Ribaut and his men, no prisoners were taken. After the liquidation of the Spanish garrison, de Gourgues sailed back to France. There is in all these acts an air of finality: the revenge was complete, but France never again attempted to renew the colony within the Spanish sphere of influence.

Unsuccessful though France's Florida colony had been, there were nevertheless men across the English Channel who hopefully projected a plantation of Englishmen in eastern North America. Dee and Sir Humphrey Gilbert were the most active of the group. Whereas the French had selected Florida for its strategic threat to Spanish shipping, the English inclined toward Newfoundland and Nova Scotia as having the advantage of a short ocean crossing and a latitude similar to the British Isles. By the meteorological ideas of the time, places in the same latitude were believed to have the same climate, a conception which the Canadian winter soon rudely shattered. Nevertheless Gilbert, with some show of reason, was sanguine about Newfoundland being the American equivalent of Great Britain. He was supported in this by one Anthony Parkhurst, an amateur enthusiast who had made Newfoundland his hobby and had shipped on several voyages there with the annual fishing fleets. Sir Humphrey also used the information of David Ingram, one of the sailors in Hawkins' third voyage (1567), who had been put ashore in Florida and who had made his way along the coast to Nova Scotia. Even in his work written in advocacy of the Northwest Passage (*A Discourse of a Discoverie for a New Passage to Cataia*) Gilbert had spoken for the settlement of America by Englishmen, as a source of wealth and as a means of disposing of criminals and other undesirables. After the failure of the Frobisher voyages, Gilbert must have transferred his interests in the Northwest Passage to the possibilities of colonizing northeastern America. In June 1578, therefore, when Frobisher's star was setting on his third voyage, Gilbert obtained a six-year patent from Queen Elizabeth "to inhabit and possess at his choice all remote and heathen lands not in actual possession of any Christian Prince," a document which was truly the foundation of Empire.

Armed with this patent, Gilbert sent out a voyage of reconnaissance in 1580 which, under a Portuguese pilot named Simon Fernandes, evidently coasted parts of Nova Scotia and Maine. In spite of Fernandes' apparently favorable report, Gilbert must have had his troubles in getting the colonization scheme started; it was not until June 1583 that the first fleet of British colonists for the New World left England. From the very start the venture seemed undisciplined and half-hearted; the largest vessel deserted and returned to Plymouth, and another ship embarked on a career of piracy. With the remainder Gilbert proceeded to Newfoundland, and reached the harbor of St. John, where he found the crews of the polyglot fishing fleet — Spanish, Portuguese, French, and English — engaged in drying their catch on shore. In the presence of this quite remarkable international community, Gilbert took possession of the harbor and the land within two hundred leagues of it, in the queen's name. But the men were ill and mutinous, and after a mere fortnight in his colony Gilbert gave orders to set sail for England. One ship was wrecked on either Cape Breton or Sable Island, and Gilbert with the two remaining vessels steered southward, in the hope of paying expenses for his failure by waylaying a well-laden Spanish merchantman. Bad luck dogged him to the last, and he went to the bottom when a squall engulfed his craft off the Azores. One ship alone reached England, to tell of the frustration of the enterprise.

Schemes for colonizing the New World were not dropped because of this setback: a projected Catholic colony under Sir George Peckham at least reached the planning stage, and when Gilbert's six-year patent ran out in 1584 it was renewed by his half-brother, Sir Walter Raleigh. In the same year Richard Hakluyt penned his powerful plea for American colonization in his *Discourse of Western Planting*; in the same year, too, we first hear the name Virginia applied to that part of eastern America between Florida and Norumbega. Raleigh must have had drive and enthusiasm, for that very spring (1584) his captains, Arthur Barlow and Philip Amadas, set out on a coastal reconnaissance of the land named in honor of (and in fact by) Elizabeth herself. Reaching the North Carolina coast near Cape Lookout, they passed through one of the inlets into the waters beyond and set about exploring Pamlico and Albemarle Sounds. In this wise they discovered Roanoke Island, which seemed an excellent location for a colony.

Raleigh was quick to follow up such an encouraging report as his captains brought him, and the following year (1585) he sent out his first colonizing fleet, under the command of Sir Richard Grenville. With this celebrated Elizabethan seaman, later to gain immortality in the fight of the *Revenge*, sailed Ralph Lane, the chief political figure among the colonizers, who filled the post of deputy governor of the colony. Also among the group were Captain Amadas; Thomas Cavendish (whose fame as a circumnavigator was still in the future); Thomas Hariot, a brilliant mathematician and freethinker, to whose pen we owe the history of the colony; and John White, whose fine water-color drawings of Virginia (now in the British Museum) are among the most precious documents of our American heritage. No women were taken.

Having settled his colony on Roanoke Island, Lane turned his attention to exploration and investigated the inland waterways of North Carolina in a far more thorough fashion than Amadas and Barlow had done in 1584. These journeyings took him not only up the Roanoke and Neuse Rivers, but on one occasion led him northward to reach the shores of Chesapeake Bay, near the site of Norfolk. It would seem that these excursions were made as much in the hope of finding gold as in the cause of geographical research. Certainly the colonists were not above reproach in this as in other respects: their relations with the Indians were unfriendly, and they neglected the agricultural possibilities of their surroundings. Consequently, in considerably less than a year Lane and his men found themselves in a hostile land with precious little to eat. In this crisis a deliverer appeared in the person of Sir Francis Drake, homeward bound from his great raid on the West Indies. His invitation to take the colony home was only too gratefully accepted, and in June 1586 Lane and his men sailed away from Virginia. A second group of colonists arrived under Grenville a few days later. Finding Roanoke Island abandoned, Grenville landed fifteen volunteers as a token colony and then sailed for England.

Raleigh had lost a fortune in this venture, and was forced to make over his interests to a company of merchants, although he remained within the picture as an enthusiast and an adviser. Under his impetus a second colonizing venture was sent out to Virginia: in April 1587 a fleet of colonists, including women, sailed under the governorship of John White, and Roanoke Island was reached in July. No sign of Grenville's fifteen men was found. However, we have some record of the first summer at Roanoke, inasmuch as White returned to England in the early autumn for supplies and reinforcements. After that there is only silence. War with Spain, and especially the battle of the Armada, cut the communications with Virginia, and it was not until 1590 that things were sufficiently normal for White to equip another fleet. That was the final act of the tragedy; White reached Roanoke amid the perils of a Hatteras tempest, which rendered a thorough search impossible, and found no colonists; nor any sign of them, save for the word "Croatoan" carved on a tree. Such was the fate, and such the mystery, of Raleigh's "Lost Colony."

THE FOUNDATION OF CANADA

The first generation of French Canada centers around the name of Samuel de Champlain; to a far greater extent was he the single creator of

France's American empire than was any single Englishman the creator of Virginia or New England. It was his drive, his vision, his persistence, his life-long devotion to a single cause that made him one of the greatest of all colonial figures and resulted in the establishment of France's proudest colony. Where Cartier, Villegagnon, and Ribaut had failed, Champlain, through a long life of singleness of purpose, started in New France a settlement which bid to eclipse the rival enterprises of England and even Spain.

Champlain was born in the small seaport of Brouage, south of La Rochelle, about 1567, his ancestors having been fishermen and sailors. His family may have had Huguenot connections; certainly the district around La Rochelle was a Huguenot stronghold, while the Old Testament name of Samuel savors strongly of Protestantism. Champlain, however, was always a nominal Catholic and latterly a devout one; but perhaps because of his family environment he possessed a broad tolerance, which enabled him to give his best for a Huguenot master like de Monts.

The founder of Canada first appears as a young army officer, serving under Henry IV against the Catholic League (a reactionary, Spanish-backed coalition) in Brittany. At the end of the campaign (1598) he was demobilized, and filled with desire to see the New World, he made his way to Spain, as the easiest channel for reaching the West Indies. Luck was with him, and he obtained passage on a fleet which left San Lucar in February, 1599. Thus he was able to have a thorough tour of the Spanish Indies: a month in Puerto Rico; another month in Mexico City; a trip to Portobello and Panama, which inspired him to make a proposal for an interoceanic canal; a visit to Cartagena; and finally several months in Havana. He returned having seen most that was worth while in the Caribbean basin; he returned, furthermore, convinced of the abuses and inefficiency of the Spanish colonial system, and with a vision that he could plant a French empire overseas that would be free of the cankers that beset New Spain and Panama.

On Champlain's return to France he discovered that his military service in Brittany had stood him in good stead, for he found an old army friend in the governor of Dieppe, who gained him an audience with Henry IV. Through the governor, too, he secured a berth on an expedition sailing to Canada, led by a rollicking Rabelaisian named François du Pontgravé. This was not Pontgravé's first voyage to the St. Lawrence, for he and others like him had developed a fur trade in the last decade of the old century, which had led to the establishment of a rendezvous at the mouth of the Saguenay. Little is known of these ventures, but it is clear that before Champlain's arrival in Canada a number of voyages had taken place, in the track of Cartier and Roberval. In fact in 1600 Pierre Chauvin, who held the fur-trading monopoly, set out with Pontgravé and the Sieur de Monts to start a colony at Tadoussac, but the Canadian winter did its worst, and the survivors returned to France the following spring.

Champlain's voyage with Pontgravé was one of reconnaissance, but it boded much for the future. He was in Canada about three months in the summer of 1603; he landed first at the trading post of Tadoussac, where he and Pontgravé made an alliance with the Algonquin Indians which was destined to last a century and a half and to be of decisive importance in the future of French Canada. From the Saguenay, Champlain and his companions proceeded up the St. Lawrence in a pinnace, passing the sites of Quebec and Montreal and reaching the head of navigation at Lachine Rapids. The passage beyond was barred to any craft except a canoe, so they were forced to return, but Champlain learned from the natives of the land to the westward, of the Great Lakes, and of Niagara Falls. He returned to France convinced that the land was particularly suitable for colonization and that the Canadian waterways offered easy access to the Pacific. His charming little book, *Des sauvages, ou voyage de Samuel Champlain de Brouage, fait en la France nouvelle* (Paris, 1603), was the literary result of this venture.

In spite of Champlain's enthusiasm for the St. Lawrence Valley, his first colonizing experience lay in quite another direction. With the publication of his book, Champlain found himself an accepted expert on North America; he therefore had no difficulty in gaining a place in Sieur de Monts' Huguenot venture of 1604. De Monts was a wealthy and public-spirited country gentleman from the same part of France as Champlain, and he planned a colony founded on the principles of religious toleration and hard work; but contrary to Champlain's advice, he selected the Bay of Fundy as the site, instead of a location along the St. Lawrence. Along with de Monts and Champlain went Pontgravé and an old soldier, the Seigneur de Poutrincourt, determined to establish for himself a mighty lordship in the wilds. The expedition sailed in March 1604 and two months later reached Nova Scotia. A thorough exploration of the Bay of Fundy was then made to determine a suitable location for the settlement, and Sainte Croix Island at the head of Passamaquoddy Bay was selected. Champlain was busy all summer working on the colony, but when September came he departed on a cruise down the Maine coast, a navigation which took him around Mount Desert Island, up the Penobscot to the site of Bangor, and along the Boothbay region to the mouth of the Kennebec. Let us hope that he enjoyed his cruise along that picturesque coast as much as many of his successors have.

Champlain returned to Sainte Croix to face a severe winter, during which half the colonists perished of cold and scurvy. Total discouragement resulted, and the colony was saved from abandonment only by the

A large portion of the map of Jorge Reinel, circa 1519. A considerable advance over the Canerio Map is evident: Arabia and the Persian Gulf reflect recent Portuguese discoveries, India has nearly its proper width and shape, the Malay peninsula is accurate, there is a realization of the bulge of Indo-China, and the islands of the East Indies begin to appear. Brazil, too, is shown with almost exaggerated accuracy.

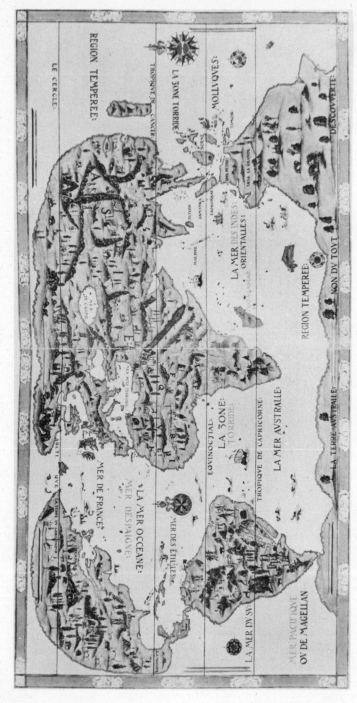

The "Dauphin" map of the world, made in 1546 by Pierre Desceliers of Dieppe for the prince who became Henri II. Note the cartographic development of the St. Lawrence; the wedge-shaped inlet on the New England coast, which is the River of Norumbega; the Plate River system in South America; the semi-circular bulge of China; the conventional rendering of Japan; also the vast southern continent, coming up in a broad land-mass to Java.

timely arrival in the summer of 1605 of Poutrincourt from France with reinforcements. Poutrincourt moved the settlement across the Bay of Fundy to the Nova Scotia side, and started his new post at Port Royal (now Annapolis). Things turned out better there, although the establishment was by no means permanent, for the suspicions of the English were aroused, and in 1613 Governor Argall of Virginia sent up a fleet from Jamestown, which destroyed the colony. Argall was more humane than Menendez at Fort Caroline, for he allowed the Frenchmen to be taken back to their native country, but French settlement of what came to be known as Acadia was put back for a generation. Champlain was far away at the time of Argall's raid, and had his concerns in the St. Lawrence valley then. However, for the first two years of the Port Royal colony (1605–1607) he was an active participant, and during two successive summers he repeated his initial cruise along the New England coast. In 1605 he explored the shore-line from the mouth of the Kennebec to Massachusetts Bay and Cape Cod; in 1606 he rounded Cape Cod and possibly reached Buzzard's Bay.

Upon his return to France in 1607 he found that de Monts had reached an agreement with the king, by which he gained a fur-trading monopoly in exchange for a promise of a permanent colony. De Monts selected Champlain to head the colony while he himself elected to remain in France, to manage the affair at home. In the spring of 1608 Champlain sailed for the St. Lawrence with his old comrade Pontgravé, and on July 3 of that year he founded the city of Quebec. In the first year of its history, the story of so many French colonies was repeated: a terrible winter, a high mortality from scurvy, and a relief expedition the following spring. By that summer matters were sufficiently under control for Champlain to indulge his passion for exploration, and in July he was off with a war-party of Algonquins for a campaign against the hated Iroquois. This venture took him up the Richelieu River and through Lake Champlain to the site of Ticonderoga, where the enemy was encountered. European firearms turned the trick, and the Iroquois were heavily defeated, but the lasting hatred of the Five Nations was gained in a few minutes — an event fraught with destiny for the French in Canada.

For several years thereafter, Champlain was hard at work on the infant colony, going across the Atlantic to France every winter and laboring in the summer at Quebec and along the St. Lawrence. In 1613, however, he was able to renew his explorations, and in the summer of that year he traveled up the Ottawa River far past the site of Ottawa, to present-day Pembroke, a full two hundred miles' journey from the St. Lawrence. Two years later he made his greatest and most famous expedition. After ascending the St. Lawrence and the Ottawa, he passed his farthest point of 1613, and having crossed Lake Nipissing and descended the French River, he reached the Great Lakes in the northern part of Georgian Bay. He then voyaged southward along this arm of Lake Huron and traversed the very involved system of waterways between Lake Simcoe and the eastern end of Lake Ontario. Crossing this water above the Thousand Islands, he appears to have penetrated into New York state as far as the site of Syracuse. In this region his Huron companions were badly beaten in a battle with the Iroquois, and he was forced to return with his disconsolate allies to Canada. After a winter with the Indians, Champlain returned to Quebec as he had come — by the round-about passage of Georgian Bay and the Ottawa River. This turned out to be Champlain's last great journey of discovery, and although he labored in Canada two decades more, it is doubtful if he left the now-familiar haunts of the St. Lawrence Valley. Yet the impulse that he started grew and flourished, especially in the activities of the *coureurs de bois,* who for two centuries carried French influence down the Mississippi to the Gulf of Mexico, and from Hudson Bay to the Rocky Mountains.

Perhaps the first, and certainly one of the greatest, of these obscure frontiersmen was a young friend of Champlain's named Etienne Brûlé, who lived among the Huron Indians until he in effect became one of them — which, however, did not prevent them from eventually cooking and eating him. It is regarded that Brûlé had visited Lake Huron as early as 1611 with a party of Indians, and four years later he took a remarkable journey which entitles him to the front rank among explorers. Having accompanied Champlain as far as Lake Simcoe, Brûlé left his chief and set off southward with a dozen Hurons. He reached Lake Ontario at the site of Toronto and navigated it to its western end. Then he crossed the neck of land west of Niagara and launched boldly into Lake Erie, being thereby the discoverer of three of the five Great Lakes (for he must have reached Ontario before Champlain, who had a far more tortuous course from Lake Simcoe). Now followed the most remarkable part of Brûlé's journey. Having crossed the lake to a landing above Buffalo, he proceeded through western New York to the head-waters of the Susquehanna and floated downstream to Chesapeake Bay. French Canada and English Virginia had at last made an overland contact, while the present state of Pennsylvania was for the first time traversed by a European.

No journey of even comparable importance was to be made until that of Jean Nicollet to Lake Michigan twenty years later; in fact these intervening years were given over to the successful consolidation of the Canadian colony, which was, in truth, Champlain's great masterpiece. Yet by the time that the Pilgrim Fathers landed at Plymouth, the French had explored the river systems of the St. Lawrence and the Ottawa, had discovered Lakes Huron, Ontario, and Erie, and had descended the Susquehanna to the Chesapeake. In contrast, the English colonists did not traverse such extensive areas of the interior until the eve of the Revolution.

VIRGINIA AND NEW ENGLAND

The failure of the Roanoke colony and the long years of the Spanish war set back English colonization for half a generation, but the urge for settlement remained and successful planting was merely delayed. Meanwhile voyages of exploration continued at irregular intervals, most of them gauged with an eye toward eventual colonization. Even in Gilbert's time (1580) a captain named John Walker had visited the coast of Maine and had explored "the River of Norumbega" — obviously Penobscot Bay — and in 1593 one Richard Strong made a little-known venture from Cape Breton southward. In 1602 Bartholomew Gosnold performed a far more celebrated voyage. Sailing under the orders of Shakespeare's patron, the Earl of Southampton, he made the crossing of the Atlantic from the Azores to Massachusetts Bay. After exploring that region he landed on Cape Cod, naming both it and Martha's Vineyard. On Cuttyhunk, which he called Elizabeth Island, he built a house and engaged in profitable trade with the natives, later returning to England with a fine cargo of furs, sassafras, and other commodities. More than any earlier venture, Gosnold's voyage served to put the future New England "on the map," and the stimulus thus created gave rise to a series of annual voyages. The following year (1603) Martin Pring, backed by the merchants of Bristol, and urged on by Richard Hakluyt, reached the coast of Maine and proceeded southward to Martha's Vineyard; in 1605 George Waymouth had his landfall at Nantucket, and turning north, explored the Kennebec and Penobscot regions. In the next year Pring was back again on the same coast, and in 1607 a colony was attempted by George Popham and Sir Ferdinando Gorges at the mouth of the Kennebec. It was abandoned the following spring; the Maine winter had treated the English as badly as the Canadian winter had treated the French.

More important by far than all these sporadic voyages and forlorn attempts was the successful settling of Virginia in 1607 — the first permanent English colony in the New World, and hence the direct progenitor of the United States. The initial expedition of the *Sarah Constant* and two other ships, under the command of Captain Christopher Newport, indeed marks the beginning of a new age and was perhaps as significant for the future as was Columbus' First Voyage. For the most part, the early history of Jamestown and its surroundings was one of colonization rather than of exploration, yet the surprisingly thorough survey of Captain John Smith, who reconnoitred the Chesapeake Bay region in an open boat in the summer of 1608, must command our admiration. His

Map of Virginia (Oxford, 1612) displays how he ascended the principal rivers, such as the Susquehanna, the Potomac, the Rappahannock, the York, and the James, to the "fall line," if not beyond. This was the most important geographical work done in Virginia for over half a century, and shows that the whole Chesapeake area, from southern Pennsylvania to northern North Carolina, and inland to the Piedmont, was well explored. Smith's map remained the standard until the Herrman Map of 1673.

Smith left the colony for which he had done so much the year following his exploration (1609), never to return; but if he had given his best for Virginia, he was destined to give his best likewise for the region known loosely as "the North Part of Virginia" or Norumbega. In two voyages (1614 and 1615) he surveyed the coast as Gosnold and Pring had done and returned to England sanguine for the possibilities of the land as a region for colonization. Indeed his was the best coastal survey of the shores from Cape Cod to Maine done thus far; Smith's observation of the natural features was detailed and at least three of the names he gave — Plymouth, the Charles River, and Cape Anne — survive to this day. His *Description of New England* (London, 1616), with its fine map, therefore had great influence on subsequent settlement, while the title of the book is additionally significant as fixing on that region the name by which it has been known ever since. In consequence it was not surprising that his pleading soon had its effect; in December 1620 the *Mayflower* landed the Pilgrim Fathers on Plymouth Rock, to begin the long and distinguished history of Massachusetts. Just two centuries had elapsed from the settlement of Prince Henry the Navigator on another rock at Sagres, and in that period the modern world had been born.

THE CARTOGRAPHY AND NAVIGATION OF THE RENAISSANCE

THE MANUSCRIPT TRADITION

A proper understanding of the manuscript cartography of the days of the great discoveries, requires a glance backward to the portolan charts of the Middle Ages, for these practical mariners' maps, so different from the world-delineation of Ptolemy or of the Medieval *mappae-mundi*, formed the base on which the map making of the great voyages grew. These meticulous productions were made by seamen for seamen, and in consequence of their influence and method the epic discoveries of the Portuguese and Spaniards were recorded more quickly and more accurately in manuscript maps than they were in early printed maps, which were still bound by Ptolemaic conventions, as well as even by those of the unrealistic *mappaemundi*.

Portolan charts have their origins in remote antiquity: the oldest surviving specimens date from about 1300, but these are so highly finished and so conventionalized that they could not possibly have sprung full-blown into existence; the famous Carte Pisane (in the Bibliothèque Nationale, Paris) probably has an unbroken line of descent, through many generations of Mediterranean mariners, from Marinus of Tyre. From the time of the Carte Pisane for three centuries or more a steady stream of these very conservative, stylized, and conventional charts emanated from the ateliers of Italy, Majorca, and other centers on the Mediterranean littoral; so standardized in character that they are generically known as "normal portolans." Drawn on vellum in colored inks, and distinguished by compass lines and windroses, these highly accurate and beautiful maps portray the coast lines of the Mediterranean, the Black Sea, and the Atlantic shores of Western Europe and North Africa — in other words, the old Greek *oikoumene*, a feature which may perchance hint at their origin. Little or no detail of the continental interiors appears in normal portolans besides decoration, but the coast lines are usually drawn with a studied meticulousness, and the names of sea-ports and headlands show a consistent continuity that is very striking. There are, of course, differences between one chart and another, just as there are between the productions of one chart-house and another, but generally speaking the cartographic detail is so standardized that the description of a typical normal portolan does for all the rest. For this very reason, the normal portolan was a wonderfully satisfactory sea captain's chart. Quite logically the cartographers of the early Renaissance were not slow to apply portolan principles to the coast lines revealed by the great discoverers, so that from the mid-fifteenth century for, say, a hundred or a hundred and fifty years we have a series of charts in the portolan tradition, but displaying the progressive stages of discovery from Cape Bojador to China, and from Labrador to the Straits of Magellan. It is accordingly to these charts rather than to the normal portolans that emphasis will be given in this chapter, still we must not lose sight of the fact that the technique and inspiration of the great cartographic landmarks came from the normal portolans of the fourteenth and fifteenth centuries.

The emancipation of the portolan from the Greek *oikoumene*, and the extension of its principles to the area of the newly discovered lands, dates from the middle of the fifteenth century, and the chart of Andrea Bianco, dated 1448 and preserved in the Ambrosian Library, Milan, is the earliest surviving map to record the voyages of Henry the Navigator. A normal portolan of the Atlantic seaboard from England southward, this map shows the African coast from Cape Bojador (the standard limit for normal portolans) to Cape Roxo in Guinea, south of the Gambia River; portraying thereby the Senegal and Cape Verde, and incorporating the findings of Nuno Tristão's voyage of 1446. This chart is of further interest as being perhaps the earliest portolan map made in England: the legend states that it was drawn in London. Furthermore, it shows a large island to the southwest of Cape Verde, which some experts have held to be Brazil. If this be so, then the Bianco Map indicates the discovery of America by an unknown Portuguese expedition half a century before Columbus. This theory has by no means met with universal acceptance.

There must have been many portolan charts executed in the following years which displayed the Portuguese discoveries, but they have long since disappeared and not for another two decades do we find a chart showing a further extension of knowledge. In an atlas from the establishment of the prolific Venetian cartographer Gratiosus Benincasa, dated 1468 and preserved in the British Museum (Add. MS. 6390), there is a very important map which reveals a knowledge of the voyages of Cadamosto and de Sintra. The coast line is extended past Sherbro Island in

Sierra Leone to Cape Mesurado in Liberia — the farthest point reached before the Gomes venture of 1469. Compared with this and the later Benincasa maps, the celebrated Planisphere of Fra Mauro (1459, in the Marcian Library, Venice) marks no advance; it shows the coast as far as Cape Roxo, but the shores of Africa beyond are portrayed with medieval fantasy. It is only fair to admit, however, that the Fra Mauro map is surprisingly good for the interior of Abyssinia (the result of information received from the Ethiopic mission to Florence in 1441); the Asiatic portion of the map derives from Marco Polo.

A little-known Portuguese chart of the early 1470's (Bib. Estense, Modena) carries the Guinea coast to Lagos in Nigeria, revealing the discoveries of Santarem and Escolar in 1471.

Not until 1489 is there a surviving record of another cartographic advance. In that year four charts were done in Venice by Cristoforo Soligo, showing with great accuracy the discoveries of the Portuguese in the Gulf of Guinea and the voyages of Diogo Cão down to lower Angola. These highly significant charts, sometimes called "Ginea Portogalexe" from an inscription on the first map, are included in an atlas in the British Museum (Egerton 73), composed of a collection of thirty-five charts by the leading Italian cartographers of the day. It would appear that the Soligo maps are copies of lost Portuguese originals made immediately after Cão's return from his first voyage in 1484.

Dias' voyage around the Cape of Good Hope is recorded in the rather crude world map of Henricus Martellus Germanus, a German who made it in Italy *circa* 1489–1492 (British Museum, Add. MS. 15760). In this representation, the west coast of Africa trends much too far to the southeast, but the Cape is shown, as well as the shore discovered by Dias beyond the Cape. Asia is wholly Ptolemaic, with a truncated India and two Malay peninsulas separated by the Sinus Magnus (the eastern peninsula being the survival of Ptolemy's land bridge, which enclosed the Indian Ocean and ran from southeastern Africa to southeastern Asia). Still cruder is the representation of Africa on the famous Behaim Globe, which may have been copied from the Martellus Map, or else from some common prototype. As the earliest known globe (1492, preserved in the Germanic Museum, Nürnberg), the Behaim "Erdapfel" is one of the most celebrated geographical relics in existence, although it ranks with the Catalan Atlas and the Fra Mauro Planisphere in preserving archaic and medieval cartography. Its creator was Martin Behaim, the famous Nürnberg traveler referred to in an earlier chapter, who had lived for years in Portugal and the Azores, consorting with all the voyagers and geographers who came his way. In making this globe, which he outlined by hand in color on a vellum surface, Behaim sought to summarize the geographical knowledge of the day. By a contemporary statement (in Schedel's *Nürnberg Chronicle* he would have us believe that he accompanied Cão to the Congo: probably he never got south of the Gulf of Guinea. Yet Behaim was the first great German geographer, and as the maker of the oldest surviving globe he is forever entitled to respect.

Another well-known cartographic treasure is the controversial Columbus Map in the Bibliothèque Nationale in Paris (AA 562). Considered at one time to be the work of Columbus himself, or of his brother Bartholomew, it is now regarded as of Portuguese origin and dates *circa* 1499–1500. It portrays Europe and Africa as far as the Congo and is especially noteworthy because of its wealth of nomenclature down the African coast. A smaller world map is set in its own circle at the left end of the main chart; this small map is of importance as it displays South and East Africa much more accurately than the Martellus Germanus Map or the Behaim Globe. This would indicate that the map was done shortly after the return of da Gama in 1499: the Asiatic portion, however, gives no hint at all of da Gama's voyage, which is first recorded in the La Cosa Map of 1500. Yet this small inset map may well bridge the gap between Behaim's Globe and the great maps of the first years of the new century.

With the turn of the century and the earliest Portuguese voyages to India, the cartographic horizon was greatly widened, and a number of very important maps record the discoveries along the coasts of East Africa and southern Asia. This small and exclusive group includes the La Cosa Map, the Hamy-Huntington Map, the Cantino Map, the Canerio Map, the Egerton Atlas, the Wolfenbüttel Chart, the Pesaro Map, and the maps known respectively as Kunstmann 2 and Kunstmann 3.

The great world map of Juan de la Cosa, Columbus's erstwhile pilot, remains the key document of Renaissance cartography. This chart, dated 1500 and preserved in the Madrid Naval Museum, is the oldest existing map to portray the Columbian discoveries; it is also the oldest existing map to record da Gama's voyage to India. The African coast from Guinea to the Cape of Good Hope is excellently set out; the east coast displays some knowledge, but is rather crudely drawn in a convex arc, stretching from Natal to the Red Sea. Southern Asia is still wholly Ptolemaic, but there is a legend on the truncated base of India to the effect that this land was discovered by the Portuguese.

An advance is exhibited in the chart usually regarded as being next in date, the King-Hamy or Hamy-Huntington world map (Italian, *circa* 1501–1502; Huntington Library, MS. HM. 45). In this planisphere East Africa is much more accurate, and Somaliland and Cape Guardafui are shown, probably in accordance with information resulting from Diogo Dias' voyage up the coast after he separated from Cabral in 1500. Southern Asia is still Ptolemaic, but the western nipple of India is elongated into a moderate peninsula, on which the city of Calicut is indicated.

There are the two conventionalized Malay peninsulas, separated by the Sinus Magnus, but Malacca is named on the western one.

A far greater development is evident in the next map, the wonderful Cantino Planisphere, a Portuguese chart of 1502, preserved in the Biblioteca Estense at Modena. This fine map was acquired in Lisbon the very year that it was made by Alberto Cantino, the agent of Hercules d'Este, Duke of Ferrara, and it embodied the very latest intelligence. For the first time the whole of Africa is portrayed with almost uncanny accuracy; India, for the first time since the Catalan Atlas, is given its true peninsula shape, albeit too tapered toward the tip; there is a single Malay peninsula, although it is too wide and extends too far south. Ceylon, Sumatra, and Madagascar are outlined with fair accuracy, though the two latter are placed rather too far south. Notwithstanding these perfectly reasonable errors, the Cantino Map was far and away the best world map made up to that time.

A certain retrogression is evident in the next map, to which the dates 1502–1504 have been assigned. This world map, generally similar though slightly inferior to the Cantino Map, is the work of Nicholas de Canerio, a Genoese probably living in Portugal; it is the property of the French Ministry of Marine and is at present on deposit in the Bibliothèque Nationale, Paris. Compared with the Cantino Map, the Canerio Map portrays Africa as being wider and has less accurate details, but India is done with more precision, as the peninsula is blunter and a little more true to form. Like the Cantino, the Canerio Map has a single wide and elongated Malay peninsula. The great significance of the Canerio Map, however, derives from the fact that it is regarded as the original from which the African, Asian, and American maps in the 1513 *Ptolemy* — the first modern printed atlas — were engraved. In fact the influence of this map appears to have been so extensive that cartographic scholars speak of the "Canerio type" as a generic term for maps of this class.

If the 1513 *Ptolemy* is the first printed atlas in the modern sense, the earliest manuscript atlas to outline the new discoveries of Asia and America is the highly interesting and inportant Egerton Atlas in the British Museum (Egerton 2803). This exquisite volume includes a world map and nineteen regional maps, comprising between them the then-known world. It is of Italian origin, and may be from the chart-house of Vesconte de Maiollo or Maggiolo of Genoa; the date 1508 has been assigned to it, in accordance with a leaf of astronomical tables. Of its various charts, the world map is doubtless the most interesting. This appears to derive from the Canerio Map, or from a common ancestor; certainly the delineation of the Malay peninsula is very close to that of the Canerio, but India is appreciably better. Madagascar is for the first time placed correctly and drawn with accuracy; Ceylon is in place but inaccurate;

Sumatra is so named for the first time; and there is perhaps a slight suggestion of Indo-China and even of China itself.

Mention might also be made of the fine Portuguese chart of the Indian Ocean of 1509 at Wolfenbüttel, which is the oldest surviving *original* Portuguese chart of that area (the Cantino and Canerio Maps being presumably copies of lost originals). This chart is of the Canerio type, though India is truer and Madagascar is correct, and the Malay Peninsula is shortened considerably.

In this highly select fraternity of world maps done in the first decade of the sixteenth century must be included the Canerio-type charts known as Kunstmann 2 and Kunstmann 3, preserved in the Wehrkreisbücherei in Munich. Kunstmann 2 includes America, Africa, and southern Asia to the Bay of Bengal; Kunstmann 3 includes America and Africa only. For the eastern hemisphere they show little or no improvement on the Cantino and Canerio Maps, which in their Old World portions they resemble, but the fact that they were done about 1503–1506 makes it impossible to omit them.

By the time of Albuquerque, therefore, cartography had reached a very considerable state of accuracy for the whole outline of Africa and for most of southern Asia as far as the Bay of Bengal (Arabia and the Persian Gulf being still a bit sketchy); to the east of the Ganges Delta, however, mapping was still haphazard and nebulous. Abreu's voyage in 1512 was the first to reveal the lower part of the Malay Peninsula and the East Indies as far as Ceram. Abreu had along with him one Francisco Rodrigues, whose *Book*, written about 1514, contains several maps of the islands from Sumatra eastward; the original manuscript is in the Library of the Chamber of Deputies, Paris. Rodrigues in this work also included charts of China, probably based on information gathered from some Oriental pilot. Such cartographic intelligence as Rodrigues (and doubtless others like him) brought home was soon incorporated in portolan charts themselves, and the three charts of 1517–1519 by Pedro and Jorge Reinel (two in the Wehrkreisbücherie in Munich, and one in the British Museum, Add. MS. 9812) display an increasing knowledge of Malaysia. In particular, the later Munich map, known as Kunstmann 4, outlines Sumatra and the Malay peninsula with great precision; Java and the islands to the east are portrayed with less accuracy; Indo-China has begun to assume its hemispherical bulge; and the coast is indicated as far as southeastern China. Notice should also be taken of the so-called Miller Atlas in the Bibliothèque Nationale (DD 683). This important Portuguese atlas, probably the work of Lopo Homem in 1519, displays the East Indies in considerable detail, besides showing a more accurate outline of southern Arabia and the Persian Gulf than had been done previously. The map of the Spaniard Garcia de Torreno (1522, Royal

Library, Turin), shows the Philippines for the first time, and is doubtless based on information received from survivors of the Magellan circumnavigation. With the accurate mapping of the coasts from Europe to China and the Philippines within a quarter century of da Gama's voyage, the main cartographic problems of the Eastern Hemisphere may be considered to have been solved.

In the case of the Western Hemisphere, cartography springs fullblown into being with the Juan de la Cosa Map of 1500. La Cosa knew the West Indies as well as any man of his time, Columbus possibly excepted. He had sailed as a pilot on the Second Voyage, and in 1494 he had accompanied the admiral on the *Niña's* cruise to Cuba and Jamaica. In 1499 he had ranged the South American coast with Ojeda and Vespucci; he later participated in Bastidas' voyage (1501) and finally went with Ojeda to found a colony on the Spanish Main (1509), only to meet his death in a fight with the Indians. Significant as are the African and Asiatic parts of his chart, the American portion is even more important. The West Indies — both the Greater and Lesser Antilles — are portrayed excellently from first-hand knowledge. La Cosa drew Cuba as an island; an act which, it is said, gained him the undying enmity of Columbus. South America from Trinidad to Maracaibo is well done, being based on La Cosa's own voyage of the previous year; east of Trinidad the trend of the coast is too southerly, but there are many names in this portion, and an inscription near Cape São Roque to the effect that V. Y. Pinzon had discovered it in 1499. North America is more conjectural, but the Cabot voyages are indicated: on the eastern tip of the land mass is an inscription "Cavo de Ynglaterra," and half-way down the coast (which runs almost due east and west) is the legend, "Mar descubierta por Yngleses." As the oldest surviving cartographic record of the voyages of Columbus and Cabot, and of da Gama's passage to India, it is not too much to call the La Cosa Map the most important in existence.

Further important discoveries were recorded on the Hamy-Huntington Map. The South American coast is here laid down on more strictly portolan lines, and the eastern littoral of Brazil is so well done as to display a knowledge of Cabral's voyage and (if we may date the map 1502) also of Vespucci's voyage for Portugal in 1501. Newfoundland and Labrador are crudely shown for the first time, revealing a knowledge of the voyages of Gaspar Corte Real and Fernandez: their discoveries, "Terra Cortereal" and "Terra Laboratoris," appear as large islands in the north Atlantic. Little advance is noticeable in the Cantino and Canerio Maps, although there is a realization of the position of Greenland and the existence of Florida is suggested, while the Canerio is rich in place names along the Brazilian coast. The Atlantic chart of Pedro Reinel, *circa* 1502 (known as Kunstmann 1 and preserved in the Wehrkreisbücherei, Munich) shows the Corte Real discoveries in more detail and with considerable nomenclature, but as the land is placed at the extreme upper left-hand corner of the map, it is impossible to say whether or not the cartographer conceived it to be part of the American land mass. The world map known as Kunstmann 2, done perhaps a little later than the above, is in its American position strikingly similar to the Hamy-Huntington Map, although it is far richer than its prototype in place names, both in the Corte Real discoveries and in Brazil.

A distinct progression in cartography of the newly discovered northern lands is evident in the chart formerly attributed to the Majorcan Salvat de Pilestrina, but now considered Portuguese, and dated about 1503–1504; it is usually known as Kunstmann 3, and has already been referred to. In this chart Greenland, Davis Straits, Labrador, and Newfoundland are all excellently portrayed: the latter island, however, is represented as part of the continental land mass. The Pesaro Map of 1505–1508 (Oliverian Library, Pesaro), is another early and important map with some unusual features. In its delineation of Africa and Asia it is a conventionalized Canerio-type chart, but its New World portions have something in common with both the La Cosa and Hamy-Huntington Maps. South America is suggestive of the latter, but the Plate estuary is shown more emphatically in the Pesaro example, the mouths of the Amazon appear quite exaggerated, and the coast is carried past the Gulf of Uraba and along the Central American littoral to Honduras, ending in a blunt peninsula which may indicate Yucatan. North America, with three large and almost continuous land masses, harks back to the La Cosa Chart, with its long east-and-west coast line: indeed the Pesaro Map suggests the influence of La Cosa, Vespucci, and Bastidas to a greater degree than any of its fellows. Its Central American portion is better than that of any other map for a decade or more to come. The world map in the Egerton Atlas of 1508 alone approaches it in this respect, but this is smaller and may have been reworked at a later date, as witnessed by the indication of the Pacific coast and the Isthmus of Panama. Like the Pesaro Map, the Egerton Atlas contains a regional map of South America with the mouth of the Amazon in even more exaggerated form, but the portrayal of a large island of John the Baptist off the Brazilian coast somewhat undermines one's confidence in the cartographer's integrity. The Egerton Atlas, none the less, is good in its representation of Newfoundland (still conceived as a peninsula); it shows Cabot Straits as a bay, with Nova Scotia to the west, and Davis Straits, also as a bay, with Greenland to the north and east.

Notice should also be taken of the two Glareanus hemispherical maps, done on polar projection about 1510–1520 and preserved in the John Carter Brown Library in Providence. The Northern Hemisphere is derived closely from the great Waldseemüller printed map of 1507, while the Southern Hemisphere displays a noteworthy advance in the conception of the oceans. The sea lying between South America and the Malay Peninsula broadens and joins itself at east and west with the Atlantic and Indian Oceans, so that in this map for the first time we have the Pacific virtually as we know it.

We must now consider several cartographic curiosities. There is, for example, the Lenox Globe (made perhaps about 1507; now preserved in the New York Public Library). On this engraved copper ball of excellent workmanship South America appears for the first time as an island-continent. There is a southeastern, hornlike cape below Brazil, and the Pacific coast is outlined conjecturally, trending northwest from this cape; doubtless pure guesswork, but not too far removed from the truth. The prime importance of the Lenox Globe, however, arises from the fact that it is the oldest surviving post-Columbian globe. Another oddity is the sketch-map in the Bibliotheca Nazionale in Florence; it is dated 1506 and is usually attributed to Bartholomew Columbus. This portrays a Ptolemaic Asia with two Malay peninsulas separated by the Sinus Magnus, and a continental South America connected with the eastern Malay peninsula by the Isthmus of Panama. If the attribution to Bartholomew is correct, this may explain his brother's theories about the manner in which the new lands were actually part of Asia. A third curiosity is the globe made by Johann Schöner of Nürnberg in 1515 (Archducal Library, Weimar). South America here assumes its cone-shaped southern tip, and is separated from a large southern continent by a strait. It is impossible to say whether this anticipation of Magellan's voyage was pure guesswork, whether the nature of the Plate estuary had been mistaken and regarded as a strait by a shadowy Portuguese voyage of 1514, or whether some unchronicled expedition had in fact revealed the existence of a strait. In any case, here is a representation of the Straits of Magellan done several years before that navigator traversed them: an element which may have conceivably have influenced him in his navigation.

Returning to more legitimate cartography, we find an advance in the tracing of Central America in the chart of Jorge Reinel, *circa* 1519 (Kunstmann 4). Here Balboa's discovery of the Pacific appears, and the Isthmus is outlined from Colombia to Costa Rica; Yucatan and Honduras also are shown for the first time. A northern development is evident in the sketch-map of Alsonso de Pineda, *circa* 1520 (Indian Archives, Seville), which portrays Florida in its true peninsula shape, and traces the Gulf coast to Yucatan and beyond. Further acquaintance with the west coast is apparent in the world map of Vesconte de Maiollo, 1527 (destroyed by enemy action in 1944, while in the Ambrosian Library, Milan). South America on this map was wholly outlined (albeit conjecturally); except that Yucatan is shown as an island and a strait to the Pacific appears to the south, Central America and the Gulf region are excellently done. However, beyond western Mexico the Pacific coast curves in a very sharp arc, to bring the coastline within a hairbreadth of the Atlantic, somewhere near Hatteras. After that the coast runs north, to make an hourglass bulge of northeastern North America. This phenomenon was obviously the result of the mythical Sea of Verrazano, a feature repeated in Verrazano's own map (in the Vatican) made two years later. None the less, these two maps display a more proper realization of the Atlantic coast of North America than any that had gone before.

The culminating point of this early colonial period of portolan cartography may be said to have been reached in the works of the great Portuguese map maker, Diogo Ribeiro; after him there were additions and corrections of detail, but in the main his continental outlines, both of the Eastern and Western Hemispheres, are so accurate that his maps might have been done two centuries later. Like many of his countrymen, Ribeiro spent most of his life in the service of Spain: he held the position of Cosmographer Royal for many years, and in that capacity it was his function to keep up to date the *Padron Real*, or master map of the world, which hung in the Casa de Contratación in Seville. An intimate friend of Ferdinand Columbus, Sebastian Cabot, and Ferdinand Magellan, he prepared charts for the circumnavigator before the great venture of 1519. It is more the pity, therefore, that only three maps are definitely attributed to him: two world maps (1527 and 1529) in the Grand Ducal Library at Weimar, and a third (1529) in the Vatican. Of the three, the Vatican example is perhaps the finest. This outlines the coast of Europe, Africa, and southern Asia well beyond Hong Kong with great detail and remarkable accuracy; the East Indies are indicated with moderate thoroughness; the east coast of the Americas from Newfoundland to the Straits of Magellan is admirably portrayed, and the west coast is excellently delineated from Mexico to Peru. There remained much to be done, it is true, such as the mapping of the Pacific coasts of Asia and North America, and also Australia; but generally speaking, Ribeiro's charts were not surpassed in continental outline until the days of d'Anville.

Ribeiro was by no means the only great Portuguese cartographer of the period. There were the Reinels, Pedro and Jorge, father and son, who made the charts in Munich (Kunstmann 1 and 4, and the 1517 map) and in the British Museum, already referred to. Like Ribeiro the Reinels worked in Spain and helped in the preparation of the Magellan expedition. Then there were the Homems, Lopo the father, and Diogo the son. Lopo prepared the wonderfully pictorial and decorative Miller Atlas in Paris and the fine planisphere of 1519 (sold at Sotheby's in London in 1930); Diogo made many atlases and charts after the mid-century, now preserved in Paris, Venice, Vienna, and elsewhere. Perhaps Diogo's most attractive work is the magnificent atlas made for Philip II of Spain and Mary of England in 1558, now one of the outstanding cartographic treasures of the British Museum (Add. MS. 5415). But the figure who is often considered the greatest of the Portuguese cartographers is Fernão Vaz Dourado. Born in Goa about 1520, Vaz Dourado served in the siege of Diu in 1546, and apparently lived in India the greater part of his life. He may have come to Portugal about 1570; certainly he regarded King Sebastian as his patron and most of his productions date from the reign of that stubborn visionary. It is said that his charts of the Indian Ocean and the East Indies were used by Linschoten, along with those of another fine chartmaker named Bartolomeu Lasso; if so, this would go far toward accounting for the Dutchman's knowledge and accuracy. Seven or eight of Vaz Dourado's atlases have survived, the finest perhaps being the atlas of 1568 in the Biblioteca Nacional in Lisbon, the atlas of 1571 in the Torre de Tombo, Lisbon, and the atlas of 1573 in the British Museum (Add. MS. 31317).

Portugal, then, produced the most distinguished group of portolan chart makers of the sixteenth century. Compared with her sister kingdom, Spain had little to show. La Cosa and Garcia de Torreno have of course left us their maps, and in mid-century the skilled cartographer Alonzo de Santa Cruz did some distinguished work; but generally speaking, when the Spaniards wanted a map, they got a Portuguese to make one. In one part of Spanish territory, however, the old portolan tradition was still vigorous, and in the charts of the Olives family of Majorca (three of whom worked between 1530 and 1590) we have a series of maps and atlases characterized by the technical excellence which always marked the Catalan-Balearic school.

Other old portolan centers of the Mediterranean basin continued to maintain active cartographic establishments. At Ancona was the office of Conte Freducci (active 1497–1556); at Genoa was the well-known house of Maiollo or Maggiolo (active 1504–1586). Messina had several firms at least, chief among them being those of Jacobus Russus (active 1520–1588) and Juan Martines (active 1564–86). Crete produced Georgio Calapoda (active 1537–1565), and Turkey the picturesque navigator Piri Reis, who made a world map in 1513, the West Indian portions of which are said to have been derived from Columbian sources. Most prolific of all was the Venetian cartographer Battista Agnese (active 1527–1564). Over seventy of his atlases have survived, and are represented in every important library in Europe and America. These dainty productions of Agnese's are usually small in scale; unlike most portolan charts they are of slight practical use, but are invariably objects of great decorative charm. As such they have always had a considerable attraction for connoisseurs.

Yet one feels, not only about the Agnese maps but also about the other charts produced within the Mediterranean basin, that they are rather second-hand — their cartography was at best the copy of a Portuguese original, and more often than not, a copy of a copy. Nevertheless, the very amount produced must drive home the fact that there was a keen demand for portolan charts among sea captains throughout the century; the portolan chart was the practical navigators' chart of the Renaissance and was not displaced in this role by the printed map until the end of the period.

Both decorative beauty and first-hand knowledge were combined in the remarkable but short-lived Dieppe school of cartography. This enterprising French seaport sent forth expeditions, piratical and otherwise, to West Africa and Brazil quite early in the sixteenth century. Jacques Cartier sailed from nearby St. Malo, and a Dieppe fleet under one Parmentier is reputed to have gone to Sumatra in 1529. Dieppe's sailors and cartographers, therefore, were among the most experienced in continental Europe, and the charts of this school, most of them dating from the 1540's and 1550's, are the first to display a realization of the St. Lawrence and the configuration of eastern Canada. Of the Dieppe chart makers, the most distinguished was Pierre Desceliers, whose masterpiece is the highly decorative but meticulously exact Dauphin Map of 1546, a planisphere done for the prince who became King Henry II (now preserved in the John Rylands Library, Manchester). To Desceliers, too, is assigned the lovely Harleian Mappemonde in the British Museum (Add. MS. 5413) and a fine planisphere of 1550 in the same library (Add. MS. 24065). Desceliers's maps, like the other productions of the Dieppe school, are noteworthy for the portrayal of a great southern continent, which, as "Java la Grande," comes up in a broad antarctic peninsula right to the East Indies. Other figures from the Norman port are Nicolas Desliens, maker of a fine world map of 1541 in the Dresden Library and another, dated 1566, in the Bibliothèque Nationale, Paris (D 7895); and Nicolas Vallard, maker of a very beautiful atlas of 1547 in the Huntington Library (MS. HM. 29). One Dieppe cartographer, Jean Rotz, made his way to England, where he became Cosmographer Royal to Henry VIII; it has even been suggested that this man was a Scot named John Ross. His wonderfully pictorial atlas, called the Boke of Ydrography and dedicated to his royal patron, is perhaps the greatest glory of the Dieppe school (British Museum, Royal MS. 20 E ix). The maps of America in this atlas are the oldest surviving maps of the Western Hemisphere done in England.

This summary description of the Portuguese school, the various Mediterranean schools, and the Dieppe school, terminates our survey of the portolan tradition. England, whose maritime glory was late in coming, produced no native chart makers before the days of Elizabeth, and then her maps (such as those of John Dee and William Borough) were relatively slight and sketchy. Holland, so soon to lead the world in printed cartography, produced no portolan charts of the sixteenth century known to the present writer; nor did Germany, even then so active in geographical theory. The palm must therefore go to the practical navigators and chart makers of Portugal and Normandy.

Before taking leave of the subject, a reference might be made to the matter of map projection in the sixteenth century portolan charts. Inasmuch as any formalized projection was deliberately used, that favored was the cylindrical equidistant projection. In this projection, which may be pictured as Mercator's pressed down at the poles, the meridians of longitude are all vertical straight lines, the parallels of latitude are all horizontal straight lines of equal length and at equal distance, and the poles are as long as the equator. For the Tropics this projection is quite accurate, but its distortion increases as the poles are approached. Fortunately for the sixteenth century chart maker, most of the Renaissance discoveries were within the Tropics. North America, on the other hand, suffered greatly from lateral distortion, which may explain why it appeared such a huge land mass, even in printed maps done on other projections in the following century.

Note: Good photographic reproductions of most of the charts mentioned above may be found in the following works of reference, noted in full in the Bibliography. The charts marked with an asterisk are reproduced in this book.

Carte Pisane	Jomard, *Les Monuments de la géographie*, p. 28; *Imago Mundi*, Part I (1935), p. 16.
Normal Portolans	Nordenskiöld, *Periplus, passim*.
Catalan Atlas	*Choix de documents géographiques, conservés à la Bibliothèque nationale* (Paris, 1883); Nordenskiöld, *Periplus*, pls. 11–14.
Bianco Map (1448)	Azurara, *Chronicle* (Hakluyt Society, 1899), Vol. II.
Fra Mauro Map	Santarem, *Atlas*, Supplement (1854), full-size reproduction; La Roncière, *Découverte de l'Afrique*, pl. 36 (Africa only).
Benincasa Map (1468)	Cadamosto, *Voyages* (Hakluyt Society, 1937), p. 84.
Modena Portuguese Chart	Peres, *Descobrimentos Portugueses*, p. 148.
Soligo Charts	La Roncière, *Afrique*, pls. 25, 27, 29, 30.
Martellus Germanus Map	La Roncière, *Afrique*, pl. 32 (Africa only); Nordenskiöld, *Periplus*, p. 123 (inferior); Greenlee, *Cabral* (Hakluyt Society, 1938).
Behaim Globe	Ravenstein, *Behaim*; Kammerer, *La Mer Rouge* (hereafter referred to as *MR*), Vol. II, pl. 141.

Columbus Map

La Roncière, *Afrique*, pl. 30 bis (large map); Kammerer, *MR*, II, pl. 140 (inset map); La Roncière, *La Carte de Christophe Colomb* (1924).

* La Cosa Map

Vascano, *La Cosa* (full size); Nunn, *Mappemonde* (3 plates); Santarem, *Atlas*, pl. 144; Jomard, *Monuments*, pls. 10–12; Nordenskiöld, *Periplus*, pls. 43, 44; Kretschmer, *Entdeckung*, pl. 7 (America only); Kammerer, *MR*, II, pl. 144 (Africa only); Williamson, *Voyages of the Cabots* (small-scale, but clear).

Hamy-Huntington Map

Nordenskiöld, *Periplus*, pl. 45; Kammerer, *MR*, II, pl. 145.

Cantino Map

Stevenson, *Maps*, no. 1 (full size); Cortesão, *Cartografia*, pl. 2; Harrisse, *North America*, pl. 6 (America), pl. 8 (Asia); Ravenstein, *Da Gama*, (redaction of South Africa).

* Canerio Map

Stevenson, *Canerio* (full size); Kretschmer, *Entdeckung*, pl. 8 (America only); Kammerer, *MR*, II, pl. 151 (Asia and Africa); Ravenstein, *Da Gama* (redaction of Asia and Africa).

Egerton Atlas

Stevenson, *Atlas*; Williamson, *Voyages of the Cabots*, p. 196 (world map); Pacheco Pereira, *Esmeraldo* (Hakluyt Society, 1937), African maps.

Wolfenbüttel Chart

Imago Mundi, Part III (1939), p. 8.

Pesaro Map

Imago Mundi, Part VII (1951), p. 82.

Kunstmann 1

Kunstmann, *Atlas*, pl. 1; Kretschmer, *Entdeckung*, pl. 9 (North America); Cortesão, *Cartografia*, pl. 3.

Kunstmann 2

Kunstmann, *Atlas*, pl. 2 (America only); Stevenson, *Maps*, no. 2 (full size); Kretschmer, *Entdeckung*, pl. 8 (America only); Kammerer, *MR*, II, pl. 153 (Asia and Africa).

Kunstmann 3

Kunstmann, *Atlas*, pl. 3 (Atlantic section); Stevenson, *Maps*, no. 3 (full size); Kretschmer, pl. 9 (North America); Williamson, *Voyages of the Cabots*, p. 220 (Atlantic section).

* Kunstmann 4

Kunstmann, *Atlas*, pl. 4 (America only); Stevenson, *Maps*, no. 5 (full size); Kretschmer, *Entdeckung*, pl. 12 (America); Kammerer, *MR*, II, pl. 163 (Asia and Africa); Cortesão, *Catrografia*, pl. 5.

Rodrigues Maps

Santarem, *Atlas*, pls. 66–71; *Suma . . . of Tome Pires and Book of F. Rodrigues* (Hakluyt Society, 1944), 21 maps.

Reinel Map (1517)

Cortesão, *Cartografia*, pl. 8; Kammerer, *MR*, II, pl. 161.

Reinel (British Museum)

Geographical Journal, June 1936, pp. 522–523.

Miller Atlas

Kammerer, *MR*, II, pls. 1, 23, 40, 45, 102, 119.

Garcia de Torreno

Stevenson, *Maps*, no. 6 (full size); Kammerer, *MR*, II, pl. 164 (South Asia and East Indies).

Glareanus Hemispheres

Wroth, *Early Cartography of Pacific*, pls. 5, 6.

Lenox Globe | Kretschmer, *Entdeckung*, pl. 11; Fite and Freeman, *Old Maps*, no. 7; Stevenson, *Globes*, p. 72.

B. Columbus Map | Fite and Freeman, *Old Maps*, no. 5.

Schöner Globe | Kretschmer, pl. 11; Stevenson, *Globes*, p. 84.

Pineda Sketch-map | Nordenskiöld, *Periplus*, p. 179; Kretschmer, *Entdeckung*, pl. 14.

Maiollo Map (1527) | Stevenson, *Maps*, no. 10 (full size); Harrisse, *North America*, pl. 10; Fite and Freeman, *Old Maps*, no. 12.

Verrazano Map | Stevenson, *Maps*, no. 12 (full size); Almagia, *Monumenta*, pls. 24–26.

Ribeiro Maps | Stevenson, *Maps*, nos. 9, 11 (full size); Santarem, *Atlas*, pls. 64, 65. Almaiga, *Monumenta*, pls. 21–23; Cortesão, *Cartografia*, pls. 17, 20, 21; Nordenskiöld, *Periplus*, pls. 48, 49; Kretschmer, *Entdeckung*, pl. 15 (America); Kammerer, *MR*, II, pl. 168 (Asia and Africa).

Homem Map (1519) | Kammerer, *MR*, II, pl. 162.

Homem Atlas (1558) | Cortesão, *Cartografia*, pls. 18, 19.

Vaz Dourado Atlases | Kunstmann, *Atlas*, pls. 8–12; Cortesão, *Cartografia*, pls. 25–51; Lagoa, *Atlas*.

Lasso-Linschoten Map | Cortesão, *Cartografia*, pl. 52; Kammerer, *MR*, III, pl. 94.

Santa Cruz Gores | Nordenskiöld, *Periplus*, pl. 50.

Piri Reis Map (1513) | Akçura, *Piri Reis*; P. Kahle, *Verschollene Columbus-Karte in einer Türkischen Weltkarte* (Berlin, 1933).

* Desceliers, Dauphin Map | Jomard, *Monuments*, pls. 13–18; Nordenskiöld, *Periplus*, pls. 51–53.

Vallard Atlas | *Histoire de la Marine* (Paris: L'Illustration, 1934), p. 105 (Canada).

Dee Map of America | Hakluyt, *Principal Navigations* (Hakluyt Society, 1904), end of Vol. VIII.

Jean Rotz's Atlas still awaits adequate treatment.

PRINTED MAPS OF THE RENAISSANCE

Printed maps of the late fifteenth century and a large part of the sixteenth as well (under which heading I include maps engraved on copperplates and also woodcut maps) were all under the dominance of Ptolemy's *Geography*. Editions of Ptolemy were published at frequent intervals, and from the Bologna edition of the *Atlas* (misdated 1462, but probably printed about 1477) to the appearance of Ortelius' *Atlas* in 1570, most of the cartographical publications of importance were editions of the *Geography*. Printed cartography was far longer under Ptolemaic influence than portolan cartography, even though Renaissance editors strove to keep their editions up to date by supplementing the classical maps with maps based on modern information. Generally speaking, printed cartography before 1570 falls into two classifications: first, editions of Ptolemy; second, single maps, either issued by themselves or included in books of a geographical nature. In either case, one is struck by the lack of continuous development so conspicuous in manuscript maps. In the latter, every chart usually shows some improvement on the one that has preceded it, but in printed maps one must not be surprised to find such a retrogression as the very excellent "Ramusio" Map of the Americas in the 1534 edition of Peter Martyr being followed by the 1540 Basel Ptolemy, which has a map of the Western Hemisphere that looks like the scribble of a child.

In studying early printed maps, therefore, one must keep in mind the constant backslidings and bizarre anachronisms from which manuscript portolans were free: a truncated India and the double Malay Peninsulas separated by the Sinus Magnus, for example, survived at least down to the 1540's, and as late as 1556 Girava's *Cosmographia* contained a world map which for amateurishness and crudity of outline is not paralleled in manuscript maps since the days of Martellus Germanus. The latter, of course, is an extreme case, and the good existed along with the bad; but not until the rise of the Dutch school did printed cartography assume a constant rate of progress. In two departments, however, printed maps developed far ahead of manuscript maps: in regional topography (particularly of Europe) and in map projection.

While the earliest printed editions of Ptolemy (Bologna, *circa* 1477, and Rome, 1478) contained only Ptolemaic maps, the archaic nature of classical cartography was so evident that in the next two editions (Berlinghieri's metrical version, Florence, *circa* 1482, and the Ulm edition, 1482), were added four maps along portolan lines of France, Spain, Italy, and Palestine. The Ulm Ptolemy furthermore contains a world map on which Greenland is displayed as an additional peninsula of Scandinavia.

The earliest printed map to portray any of the Renaissance discoveries is the Contarini Map of 1506 (known from a unique copy in the British Museum), a copperplate engraving done on a double cordiform projection. It bears some similarity, especially as regards the Old World, to the Hamy-Huntington Map. Africa is generally correct, outlined much as in the latter chart; southern Asia is still Ptolemaic, except for an elongated western nipple of India. America descends from an unknown prototype. The Antilles and South America resemble their portrayal on the Cantino Map, but the discoveries of the Cabots and the Corte Reals appear as a northeastern promontory of Asia, which inclines southwest to China. Japan in consequence is located west of Cuba, and south of what would be New England. An inscription on the map states that Columbus reached the Asiatic mainland west of Japan. Greenland is drawn as an additional peninsula of Scandinavia.

To 1507 is assigned the very large woodcut world map of Martin Waldseemüller, known from a unique copy in Schloss Wolfegg, Württemberg.

In this map Africa is well set out, but Asia is Ptolemaic, with Polian influence. As the commemorative map of the voyages of Vespucci, its interest is wholly American. It is the first map of any sort to bear the name "America," and shows North and South America as island continents, separated by a strait. A small and very secondary map at the top of the main chart nevertheless portrays the two continents joined by the Isthmus of Panama. In this respect the Waldseemüller Map is well in advance of any surviving manuscript portolan of similar date. South America, though angular, is portrayed with some premonition of the truth; North America is hopelessly narrow.

Both advance and retrogression are evident in the double coniform world map of the same year, made by Johann Ruysch, and long regarded as the earliest printed map of America. This map, which was bound in copies of the 1507–1508 editions of Ptolemy printed in Rome, was the work of a German geographer who had sailed on a Bristol voyage (either Cabot's or a later one) to northeastern America. It is a beautiful map, engraved on copper; Africa is true to form, India appears in its real peninsula shape, and the Malay Peninsula and Sumatra are shown very much as in the Cantino Map. America is suggestive of the Contarini Map: Newfoundland and near-by coasts are a northeastern projection of Asia, and there is a broad open sea between Cuba and Java. South America is delineated from Colombia to Brazil, but Ruysch dodged the issue of the west coast by putting there instead a large decorative scroll bearing a legend of excuse.

These three maps, the Contarini, the Waldseemüller, and the Ruysch, are our most precious examples of cartographic incunabula, at least as far as America is concerned, and in the years immediately following nothing as pretentious is recorded. There is a very fair woodcut map of Africa in the Latin version of the *Paesi* (Milan, 1508), and there is an excellent and highly interesting map of the West Indies and the Spanish Main (even displaying a suggestion of Yucatan) in the 1511 Seville edition of Martyr's *Decades*. The Sylvanus world map in the Venice Ptolemy (1511) shows no advance in knowledge, although it is justly celebrated for its decorative qualities, while maps in Johannes de Stobnicza's *Introductio in Ptholomei Cosmographiam* (Cracow, 1512) are mere copies of the two small inset maps at the top of the 1507 Waldseemüller Map.

In 1513 a great step was made in printed cartography. In that year there appeared in Strassburg a vitally important edition of Ptolemy, begun by Waldseemüller years before, and carried to completion with the addition of no less than twenty modern maps to supplement the traditional Ptolemaic ones. Five of the new maps record the discoveries of the Portuguese and Spaniards and appear to have been copied from the Canerio Map (or a common prototype). Besides two large-scale maps of Africa and one of southern Asia, there is a handsome world map and a chart of the Atlantic from the West Indies to Guinea, ofter referred to, out of respect to Columbus, as the Admiral's Map. In truth, the 1513 Ptolemy is well called the first modern atlas. For years to come, it remained the standard atlas of Europe and went through a number of editions. In the 1522 edition there are two interesting additions: a none-too-accurate map of the East Indies and a map of China and Japan.

Despite the fact that the Strassburg Ptolemy held the field against all comers for more than a quarter of a century, a number of individual maps of importance were done between 1513 and 1540. In 1516 Waldseemüller made a second huge woodcut planisphere, closely copied from the Canerio Map and now known from a unique example at Schloss Wolfegg. It is fine in its Asiatic details and shows some knowledge of Java and the East Indies. This improvement on Waldseemüller's first map could not have had great circulation, however, for the 1520 Vienna edition of Solinus contains a reduced but exact copy of the 1507 map, done with magnificent disregard of all the exploration of the previous thirteen years. This Solinus map, nevertheless, has always been a collector's item, inasmuch as it is the earliest map, contained in a book, bearing the name America. A map of far more consequence appeared in 1531: the double cordiform map of Oronce Finé, which came out in the Grynaeus-Huttich *Novus Orbis* (Paris, 1532). On this chart Africa and Asia are drawn in accordance with current information, but North America follows the conception of Columbus as being a mere continuation of Asia, which is connected with South "America" by a narrow neck of land. The latter continent is excellently represented and is shown to be separated from a large south polar land mass by the Straits of Magellan. That part of the Pacific outside the straits is called "Mare Magellanicum," which is the first time the discoverer's name appears on a printed map.

For the most accurate representation of both the Americas printed in this period, one must turn to the so-called "Ramusio" Map, which appeared in the 1534 Venice edition of Peter Martyr (known from copies in the John Carter Brown and New York Public Libraries). This exquisitely executed production, notable alike for its delicacy and accuracy, is almost identical cartographically with the manuscript planispheres of Diogo Ribeiro, and it may well have been copied from one of them. All the coasts, from Newfoundland to the Straits of Magellan, and the West Indies as well, are admirably laid down; the west coast is shown from Mexico to Peru, and again in southern Chile. Nothing even approaching it in excellence was to be printed until the Cabot Map ten years later.

Notwithstanding the chaste simplicity of the "Ramusio" Map in its cylindrical equidistant projection, experiments in the solution of the problem of projecting a sphere on a plane surface continued. In 1538 a double cordiform map was printed by a youthful enthusiast who was destined to leave the most famous name in the long and involved history of map projections: Gerard Mercator. This, his first effort, was closely patterned on the work of Oronce Finé, differing chiefly from the latter's map in that it portrays North America as a continent, separated from Asia by a strait. At this formative stage in his career, Mercator nevertheless revealed a curious belief in fantasies, such as the double Malay peninsula and various mythical Atlantic islands. However, "North America" and "South America" were here named for the first time. Only two copies are known of Mercator's map: one in the New York Public Library and one in the possession of the American Geographical Society.

Notice should be taken, too, of the very fine and very large world map attributed to Sebastian Cabot and probably published in Antwerp in 1544. This elliptical map, printed from several copperplates, and known from a unique copy in the Bibliothèque Nationale, Paris, is truthful and accurate. No myths appear, but the recent explorations of the French in Canada and the Spanish in the Gulf of California are alike recorded and display a great advance in the cartography of North America, while the portrayal of the complete course of the Amazon reveals knowledge of Orellana's voyage. Naturally, in view of Cabot's own explorations, the Plate valley is well done, while the west coast of America is complete from California to the Straits of Magellan. Tierra del Fuego is indicated, but no southern continent; Asia is excellent and is charted well into China; the East Indies are carefully set down as known at the time; only Japan appears as a traditionally conventionalized island. Perhaps the chief interest in the map is the important bearing on the Cabot voyage of 1497; a legend so placed as to refer most nearly to Cape Breton Island states that this land was discovered by John Cabot and Sebastian his son on June 24, 1494 (sic). A second edition of the map, dated London 1549, has vanished completely, albeit Hakluyt recalled seeing a copy in "her Maiesties privy gallerie at Westminister."

Meanwhile Ptolemy had taken a new lease on life, under the aegis of Sebastian Münster, and four editions were published by that scholar in Basel between 1540 and 1552. While Münster betrayed some consciousness of the new discoveries, his maps are archaically crude and unattractive. He was distinguished rather as a descriptive geographer than as a map maker, and it would perhaps be unkind to pass judgment on his cartography. Far more attractive are the small but elegant Italian editions of Ptolemy which appeared in Venice between 1548 and 1574. These contained very delicate copperplate maps, designed by the skilled cartographer Giacomo Gastaldi; the 1548 edition is of importance as including for the first time a whole series of plates of the New World. The later editions (1561 *et seq.*) were brought up to date by Gastaldi's follower, Girolamo Ruscelli.

These Venetian editions of Ptolemy underline the fact that in the middle decades of the sixteenth century Italy had become the main map-producing center of Europe, as well as the principla area for their distribution. Venice and Rome were the leading cities of cartographic activity, and a vast number of individual maps, engraved on copper, were issued. An enterprising Roman publisher, Antonio Lafreri, set about assembling series of these maps, binding them, and selling them as rather haphazard collections. For this undertaking he engraved about 1570 a handsome title-page, showing Atlas supporting the world — a motif here first used and one which gave rise to our term "atlas" for a bound volume of maps. Other publishers, such as one Duchetti, had a hand in the venture, while the maps themselves were the work of many cartographers, of whom Giacomo Gastaldi is by far the most prominent. The unsystematic manner in which the Lafreri Atlas was gathered together makes collation very difficult, but as many as 661 different maps have been identified in the various extant copies, the greatest number in any one copy being 161 (in the British Museum). In date there is almost as much variety; most of the maps were published originally between 1556 and 1572. As for subject, the majority are regional maps of Europe or town plans, but there are a number of highly interesting maps of America and of the new discoveries in Asia and Africa. Many of the maps are beautiful examples of cartographic engraving.

The Lafreri Atlas marks the high point of Italian cartography, for the primacy in map making shortly passed to the Netherlands, where it was to remain for a century or more. Holland had long nourished a fine school of engraving; she had given birth to several geographers of great eminence (Ortelius and Linschoten, for example); and she was shortly to embark on a great period of naval and colonial expansion. Time and place were therefore ripe for the Low Countries to become the undisputed center of the map trade.

Lafreri's Atlas was, as we have seen, a haphazard collection of single maps already published, and all the earlier atlases, of Strassburg, Basel, Venice, and elsewhere, had been firmly rooted on a Ptolemaic foundation — that is to say, they invariably had a set of Ptolemy's maps and a supplement of modern ones. But by the third quarter of the century the time had come for Ptolemy to be dropped overboard. This revolution in the history of map publishing was accomplished by Abraham Ortelius. Born in Antwerp of German parents in 1527, Ortelius began his career by working as a colorist of maps; later he became a map dealer, thereby acquiring an extensive knowledge of existing maps and map literature. His critical

genius soon made him aware of the shortcomings of the atlases of his day
and determined him to produce an atlas free from the limitations and defects of those circulating in mid-century. The result was his epoch-making
Theatrum Orbis Terrarum, which, first appearing in Antwerp in 1570, went
through upwards of forty editions by 1624, appearing in Latin, Dutch,
German, French, Spanish, and English; and all the while the editions were
being constantly added to. It was the Atlas of the Renaissance par excellence, embodying and expressing as it did the spirit of free inquiry that
characterized the age. The first edition contained fifty-three maps; the
last 166; hardly one has any trace whatsoever of the age-long influence of
Ptolemy's *Geography*. Here at long last was a completely modern atlas;
the period of cartographic incunabula, characterized by a slavish following of old doctrines and strongly influenced by Ptolemy, was closed — to
be succeeded by a new period, distinguished by an effort to found the
knowledge of the earth not on the writings of the ancients but on first-
hand information and scientific investigation. Manuscript cartography
had, as we have seen, freed itself long before, but it was Ortelius' great
accomplishment that brought about the emancipation of the printed atlas.

Several features of Ortelius' maps deserve comment. His delineation
of Scandinavia, Greenland, and the Arctic regions was better than anything done previously, and he displayed a fine knowledge of the East
Indies. On the other hand he bestowed a great southwestern wedge on
Chile, which resulted in South America's becoming almost rectangular,
and he put in a vast southern continent. North America is conjecturally
portrayed as separated from northeastern Asia by the Straits of Anian.
His interiors, especially his regional maps of Europe, are admirably full
of detail; where knowledge was lacking he inserted highly decorative animals, while his oceans are crowded with shipping and sea monsters. Perhaps the most remarkable feature of the *Theatrum* was its bibliographical
check list of every cartographer of whom Ortelius could find in any record;
he was able to name no less than eighty-seven geographers and cartographers.

Ortelius' reputation, none the less, has been outshone by that of his
friendly rival and neighbor, Belgian-born Gerard Mercator, whose name
will always be in the forefront in the history of cartography and map
projection. Mercator had a long and unspectacular career of usefulness,
punctuated by a few very spectacular productions. As a young man he
made the fine cordiform world map of 1538. For years thereafter he was
active in the instrument trade and as a globe maker, at the same time preparing regional surveys and topographical maps, and getting himself into
trouble during the Reformation as an extreme Protestant. But for all his
activity, it was not until 1569 that he produced another milestone in the
progress of cartography. In that year he published his famous world map

on the projection that bears his name. This map (known only from the copies in the Bibliothèque Nationale, Paris, and the Stadtbibliothek, Breslau) is in detail similar to the Ortelius Map of 1570, but its great importance attaches to its novel type of projection, which was designed with the practical objectives of enabling mariners to sail to their destinations by following a fixed rule. All the compass directions, in other words, are straight lines: Mercator's chart therefore made "straight" sailing on a uniform compass course, especially for short distances, a practical matter. The great circle, however, is represented by a curved line on Mercator's projection, and great circle courses must therefore be calculated and laid down by a standardized formula. In essence the projection resembles the old cylindrical equidistant projection of the portolan makers in that the parallels and meridians are straight lines intersecting at right angles, and the poles are lines as long as the equator. But whereas the old charts had lateral distortion only, and no vertical distortion, Mercator's projection involved both lateral and vertical distortion at a definite mathematical ratio. This resulted in the parallels of latitude being pulled farther and farther apart as the poles were approached, and gave Greenland the same size as South America. It was, in brief, scientific distortion for practical ends. Yet, epoch-making though the map was, it remained little known and little used for thirty years — doubtless because Mercator did not explain the mathematics of his projection. Its universal adoption, therefore, dates from 1599, when Edward Wright published a set of rules and tables for its construction.

In view of the revolution in cartography, which the map of 1569 embodied, it is quite curious to hear of Mercator's preparing an edition of Ptolemy, which appeared in 1578. As Ptolemy, nothing need be said, save that it seems sadly out of date for that period, but the maps were fine examples of copperplate engraving, which added greatly to Mercator's reputation as a craftsman.

Mercator must have felt more in his element in the preparation of his great Atlas, a work which he did not live to see completed. In 1585 the first part came out, comprising France, the Low Countries, and Germany; the second part, including Italy, the Balkans, and Greece, followed in 1590; in 1594 the great cartographer died, as he was putting the finishing touches to the third part, which included Britain, Scandinavia, Asia, Africa, and America. His son, Rumbold, published the completed work in 1595 and dedicated it to Queen Elizabeth. Some years later, the copperplates of Mercator's maps fell into the hands of an enterprising cartographer named Jodocus Hondius, who exploited them as a vested interest for himself and his heirs. The first Hondius-Mercator edition appeared in 1606; during the next seventy-five years as many as fifty editions were published by the Hondius family. In popularity and dissemination, therefore, it rivaled the *Theatrum* of Ortelius.

Mercator and Ortelius, then, set the pace for the great school of Dutch cartography, which was to have almost a monopoly of map making for upwards of a century. Atlases and single maps of great distinction issued from contemporary and later chart houses of Antwerp and more particularly of Amsterdam. A few of these productions, dating from the latter part of the sixteenth century, may be noticed. A beautiful atlas entitled *Speculum Orbis Terrae* was published in Antwerp in 1593, by Gerard and Cornelius de Jode, whose name recalls the great Jewish cartographers of Majorca and Portugal. Of more practical importance was Luke Wagenaer's *Spieghel der Zeevaerdt* (Leyden, 1584), translated as *The Mariners Mirrour* (London, 1588). This book was a detailed coast pilot of the Atlantic and Baltic coasts from North Africa to Scandinavia; so useful did it prove that the word "waggoner" became naturalized in seafaring English, meaning any volume of sea charts or even of sailing directions. Linschoten's *Itinerario* (Amsterdam, 1596) also contained a series of very distinguished maps, especially of Africa, southern Asia, and the East Indies. These were based on the Portuguese portolan charts of Vaz Dourado and Bartolomeu Lasso, and therefore — in the case of the East Indies and Malaysia particularly — were ahead of any printed maps done previously. What Linschoten did for the Orient was done for the New World by Cornelius Wytfliet, whose *Descriptionis Ptolemaicae Augmentum* (Louvain, 1597) was the first atlas devoted solely to America. Editions of Wytfliet, like those of Mercator and Ortelius, were published well into the seventeenth century, linking the earlier figures of the school with the great names of the Baroque period: the Blaeu family, Jan Jansson, and Peter Goos.

In the period 1575–1625 the rest of continental Europe produced few maps of importance and no atlases, so active and so concentrated was the Dutch trade. In Germany the Dutchman de Bry made pictorial and attractive maps for his *Grandes* and *Petites Voyages*; in Italy two accurate maps of Africa appeared in Lopes' *Congo* (Rome, 1591), and in France a delicate and accurate map of the Western Hemisphere was published with Hakluyt's edition of Martyr's *Decades* (Paris, 1587). This latter map is thought to be the work of Francisco Gualle, a Spanish navigator who claimed to have found the Northwest Passage.

In England things were more active, largely because of Dutch influence. Christopher Saxton published a splendid atlas of English county maps (1574–1579) and in 1598 the English edition of Linschoten appeared with maps engraved by English cartographers. They were copied from the Dutch originals, to which they were inferior. A good native school of cartography was in the making, however. A clever craftsman named Emery Molineux had made a magnificent pair of globes in 1592, the first to be manufactured in England (still preserved in the Middle Temple, London). Hakluyt, who for lack of native talent was forced to use the Ortelius world map in his 1589 edition of *Principal Navigations*, was keen to stimulate English map making; and in Edward Wright, who solved the riddle of Mercator's projection, England had the best theoretical cosmographer in Europe since Mercator's death. The result of Hakluyt's urging and Wright's elucidation was the celebrated and excellent Wright-Molineux Map, made probably by Wright himself after Molineux's terrestrial globe on Mercator's projection. Appearing in some (but by no means all) of the copies of the 1598–1600 Hakluyt, this map was the best representation of the earth's surface to be printed up to that time. It was referred to by Shakespeare, and it must have been a familiar object to the captains of the early East Indiamen and Virginia-bound vessels. The Wright-Molineux Map may therefore be regarded as the high-water mark of Renaissance map making, and as such furnishes a fitting climax to this study.

Note: Reproductions of most of the printed maps mentioned above may be found in Baron A. E. Nordenskiöld's *Fac-Simile Atlas* (Stockholm, 1889); in E. D. Fite and A. Freeman's *A Book of Old Maps* (Cambridge, Massachusetts, 1926); and in Arthur L. Humphreys' *Old Decorative Maps and Charts* (London, 1926). The only adequate reproduction of the Cabot Map thus far published is in Jomard's *Monuments de la géographie* (plates 36–39).

THE SCIENCE OF NAVIGATION

The chief aids to navigation at the command of sixteenth-century seamen (besides the portolan chart) were the compass and the astrolabe. Until the latter part of the century too little was known about electronics to warrant a literature on the compass, but the importance of the astrolabe in position-finding at sea was so great that the navigational manual became a fundamental part of Renaissance scientific writing.

To get a pinpoint bearing at sea it is necessary to determine accurately both latitude and longitude. The determination of the latter was beyond the technical ingenuity of Renaissance man, who was perforce content to reach approximations by dead reckoning (the use of the log-line, plus guesswork about the vessel's speed). Latitude, on the other hand, could be found with fair accuracy by the astrolabe, and with still greater accuracy by the cross-staff, provided the observer was equipped with a table of the sun's declination throughout the year. In this way the observer could take the sun's altitude above the horizon at noon, and by making compensation for the date, could determine the latitude which he happened to be in. This method of determining position from the sun's angle was a very ancient one, and tables of declination appear to have been computed in the East by the Arabs. As early as 1252 such tables had been introduced into Christian Europe by Alfonso the Wise, king of Castile. These so-called Alfonsine Tables were doubtless based on tables prepared in Moorish Spain under the Omayyad Caliphate. Later in the thirteenth century one Robert Angeles of Montpellier made similar tables, which were probably used by medieval sailors and cartographers.

Two centuries later a Spanish Jew, Abraham Zacuto, and a German, Johann Müller of Königsberg (therefore called Regiomontanus) independently constructed tables far more accurate than any that had gone before. Regiomontanus' work quickly went through a number of printed editions (the first *Tabula Directionum*, Nürnberg, *circa* 1475; Hain 13799), but it is questionable to what extent a work emanating from inland Europe got into the hands of practical navigators. Zacuto's *Almanach Perpetuum*, on the other hand, circulated widely in manuscript among those very men who needed it most. We have seen how close Zacuto was to the maritime interests after he came to Portugal, and it is known that the tables he supplied for Vasco da Gama were largely responsible for the successful passage to India. Although but one printed edition of his tables is known (Leiria, 1496; Hain 16267), his influence in the days of the great voyages was indeed considerable.

Tables of the sun's declination however, comprised but one element of nautical knowledge; a comprehension of astronomy made up another element, and the first bona fide navigational manual resulted solely from the unification — one might almost say the marriage — of these two elements. As mentioned earlier, the standard medieval textbook on astronomy was Sacrobosco's *Sphaera Mundi*, which in turn was an intelligible recension of Ptolemy's *Almagest*. Zacuto and Sacrobosco were brought together in the earliest of all known navigational manuals: the anonymous Portuguese *Regimento do estrolabio y do quadrante*. It is very possibly the work of Zacuto's colleague, Joseph Vizinho; the earliest surviving edition appeared in Lisbon about 1509, but there were in all probability earlier ones now lost. So fundamental is this excessively scarce little volume that all later treatises on navigation, even to the present day, may simply be regarded as revised and enlarged editions of the original *Regimento*. In the matter of latitude alone, it shows great advance over the simple tables of the sun's declination; it has calculations for the finding of latitude at night by means of the polestar, tables of latitudes of known places, besides a section on dead reckoning. Altogether it was the model for all following manuals.

If Portugal was the first nation in overseas expansion, Spain was the second; and the *Regimento* was followed in 1519 by the *Suma de Geog-*

raphia, witten by Balboa's old enemy, Fernandez de Enciso, and printed in Seville. This book gives a highly abridged version of Sacrobosco, a table of the sun's declination, and a gazetteer of the then-known world, with latitudes of the places mentioned. Enciso's work was followed by a book in Spanish, written by one of the Portuguese *émigrés* who did so much for geography in the service of the sister kingdom. The author was Francisco Faleiro; he was a brother of Ruy Faleiro, who was Magellan's close confidant: the three, and also Diogo Ribeiro the cartographer, had all come to Seville from Portugal about the same time. Faleiro's *Tratado del esphera y del arte del marear* (Seville, 1535), bears a close resemblance to the *Regimento*, in that it was a recension of Sacrobosco and Zacuto, enlarged and brought up to date. Faleiro's own contribution, however, was not a happy one. Ambitious of solving the problem of longitude, he advanced the theory of its determination by variation of the compass, based upon calculations of his brother Ruy. As was inevitable, this method was so involved as to be wholly without practical value, in addition to which it showed an ignorance of secular variation, and resulted merely in keeping men's minds fixed on wrong considerations.

Fortunately, however, Faleiro's work was not definitive; two years after its appearance the greatest and most comprehensive of the early manuals came out. This was the celebrated *Tratado da sphera* (Lisbon, 1537), by Pedro Nunes, a brilliant Portuguese of Jewish extraction, who served as chief cosmographer at the court of John III of Portugal, and was also professor of mathematics at the University of Coimbra; he was as well a correspondent of John Dee's. Nunes remarkable book included a Portuguese translation of Sacrobosco; a section on the sun and moon by George Peuerbach, Regiomontanus' teacher; the first book of Ptolemy's *Geographia*; various problems of navigation; and an elaborate discussion of the nautical chart. Curiously enough, Nunes discarded Zacuto's tables for the sun's declination in favor of those of Regiomontanus — a hint at Nunes' insight, for the German's calculations were slightly more accurate. Likewise he displayed more advanced and more critical intelligence in the matter of cartographic theory, describing for the first time, as he did, the loxodromic curve, and showing ideas on map projection which made him the connecting link between the early Renaissance cartographers and Mercator. On the practical side, he described the method of great-circle sailing. So complete and so modern is his book that writers on navigation come back to it again and again as a point of departure.

Nunes' work was so good that with the scientific knowledge of the time it could not be improved upon; all that successive writers could do was to follow it. Two Spaniards put out manuals in the mid-century years, closely patterned on Nunes, which became deservedly popular throughout Europe. The first of these was the *Arte de navegar* (Vallado-lid, 1545) by Pedro de Medina, who is said to have been one of Cortes' captains and who was entrusted by the crown with the examination of the pilots for the West Indies. His book was an especial favorite in France, where it went through five editions, and it also appeared in Ital-ian and in English (two editions). More comprehensive in scope was the *Breve compendio de la spera y de la arte de navegar* (Seville, 1551), by Martin Cortes. Stephan Borough came across the book while on a visit to Spain, and realizing its worth, brought home a copy to England, where Richard Eden translated it (1561). Cortes' handbook proved even more popular in England than Medina's did in France, for it was published in no less than eight editions. It deserved its use, for it rivaled Nunes' man-ual as the most complete statement of navigational science that had thus far appeared; it contained splendid practical descriptions of the con-struction and use of both cross-staff and astrolabe, and it also advanced the suggestion that the magnetic pole and the true pole of the earth were not the same.

As in so many other respects, England came into the field after Spain and Portugal to make a strong third, and from the publication of Wil-liam Cuningham's *The Cosmographical Glasse* in 1559 a galaxy of Eng-lish mathematicians added to the growing literature of navigation. Such names as Leonard Digges, William Bourne, John Davis the navigator, and Thomas Blundeville may be mentioned, but the greatest British genius in the field was Edward Wright, whose cartographic work has already been referred to. His book *Certaine Errors in Navigation . . . Detected and Corrected* (London, 1599), by explaining the construction of Mer-cator's projection, revolutionized the making of charts, and by instructing in the use of compass and cross-staff brought about a general improve-ment in navigation.

England during this period was also the source of much writing on the compass and magnetism. It is said the Columbus in 1492 observed for the first time that the pointing of the needle to true north was rather the exception than the rule, and that therefore a declination must exist, varying from place to place. For almost a century sailors were baffled by this phenomenon, until in 1581 William Borough, the navigator and cartographer of the Arctic, brought out his *Discourse on the Variation of the Compas or Magneticall Needle*. In the same year as instrument maker named Robert Norman wrote a work called *The Newe Attractive*, in which he described his discovery of the needle's inclination or dip away from the horizontal when magnetized. Norman devised a dip-circle, and found quite accurately the value for the inclination in London. The principles enunciated by both Borough and Norman were put before the public in practical language by William Barlow, archdeacon of Salisbury and later chaplain to Henry, Prince of Wales, in *The Navigators Supply*, (1597). This ingenious ecclesiastic is reputed to have been the inventor of the compass-box, a detailed engraving of which adorns the title-page of his book.

Barlow's work, however, as well as the writings of Borough and Norman, was eclipsed by William Gilbert's masterpiece, *De Magnete, Magneticisque Corporibus* (1600), a book which more than any other laid the foundations of the modern sciences of magnetism and electricity. Gilbert, the most distinguished man of science in Elizabethan England, advanced in his book his great conception that the earth is nothing but a large magnet, a factor which explains not only the direction of the magnetic needle north and south, but also the variation and dipping of the needle. He was also the first advocate of Copernican views in England, besides being a chemist and a physician of great accomplishments.

With the almost simultaneous appearance of Gilbert's *De Magnete*, Wright's *Certaine Errors*, the Wright-Molineux Map, and the great three-volume Hakluyt, Renaissance navigational science may be said to have reached its height. The problems of latitude, cartography, and the compass were all solved: only the problem of longitude remained, to be struggled with by the hit-or-miss method of dead reckoning for another century and a half. Impractical methods of determining longitude were indeed suggested in the Renaissance, such as lunar distances and compass variation, while old Sebastian Cabot on his death-bed told Richard Eden that he had received knowledge of the secret by divine revelation. But the solution of finding one's east and west distance from another given place had to wait on the invention of the chronometer by "Longitude" Harrison in the eighteenth century.

SHIP DESIGN IN THE DAYS OF GREAT DISCOVERIES

The fifteenth century witnessed several innovations destined to have a tremendous influence — the invention of printing, the widespread introduction of gunpowder, and the advent of the three-masted ship, without which the great discoveries in all probability could never have been made. Before the year 1400 ship design had changed but little since classical times: there was the oared galley and there was the sailing ship with one mast and one large sail. Such development as had taken place since the days of Actium was the work of the Arabs on the southern littoral of the Mediterranean. Instead of the clumsy square sail, the Arabs had evolved the lateen sail, a triangular sail set fore and aft to the mast, which became as characteristic of Islam as the Crescent itself. From the primitive spritsail which the Romans occasionally used on their *artemon* or rudimentary bowsprit, the Arabs developed a small foremast, which they called the "mizzen," meaning a balance or adjustment, since this

A model of an English full-rigged ship, circa 1485, probably the best portrayal of a fifteenth-century ship we have. Scale dimensions: 500 tons; length between perpendiculars, 106 ft.; length of keel, 76 ft.; beam, 38 ft.; depth of hold, 19 ft. The naus used by the early Spaniards and Portuguese were of similar hull-design, but had topsails and smaller mainsails.

A model of an Elizabethan galleon of 700 tons, viewed from the port bow. Note sail-plan, with topsails, topgallant sails, spritsail, and bonaventure mizzen. Scale dimensions: length between perpendiculars, 142 ft.; length of keel, 100 ft.; beam, 38 ft.; depth of hold, 18 ft. Lancaster's Red Dragon *was approximately this size.*

rig was an aid to steering rather than an additional means of speed (the term "mizzen" was only later applied to the after mast, since it was the only mast on a *nau* or ship that carried a mizzen or lateen sail). These innovations were adopted by the Christian seamen of the Mediterranean during the Middle Ages to some extent, but they do not seem to have affected Northern Europe, and it is questionable how much they were used by the Peninsula peoples of the Atlantic seaboard, at least in the earlier Middle Ages; certainly most of the Atlantic mariners clung to the single mast and the square sail until the time of Henry the Navigator. It is all the more remarkable, therefore, that within a short period in the early fifteenth century the three-masted ship, which was to have so marked an influence on the progress of discovery and of civilization, should have been suddenly introduced. To what skillful shipwright posterity owes this wonderful invention, no one can tell, but it was probably the result of the increasing size of ships, first noticeable about 1400.

Another innovation, of almost equal importance and roughly contemporary in date (though perhaps somewhat earlier), was the development of the rudder. Originally ships had been controlled by steering oars, lashed to the quarter and worked the way in which one would steer a canoe. It is not difficult to realize what an awkward and unwieldy arrangement this was, especially with a big ship in rough weather. However, in the later Middle Ages the rudder came to be hung on the stern post by pintles and gudgeons, and was worked by a tiller. This had the further effect of differentiating the bow and stern of the ship, which had previously been constructed on similar lines. By the time of the Tudors this difference had developed into the rakish bow and the transom stern, which were henceforth to remain characteristic of the sailing ship.

In this evolution it is reasonable to think that Henry the Navigator played an important part: certainly the types of vessels that he used showed that he was very much alive to the progress of ship design. His earlier captains appear to have sailed in a small craft called a *barca*, a boat of twenty-five tons or more, only partially covered in, and carrying a crew of fifteen or so. The *barca* had one big mast with a square sail and a smaller or mizzen mast, which was rigged occasionally when circumstances demanded. On such a vessel Gil Eannes rounded Cape Bojador, but his companion on the next voyage, Baldaya, sailed in a *barinel*, a larger ship, similarly rigged, which could be rowed as well. Both types of craft were slow and unwieldy, while the *barinel* needed a crew of oarsmen besides.

By 1440 the revolution in ship design was in full swing, for Azurara states that at that time caravels were used by Henry's captains. The caravel has all the earmarks, therefore, of being the invention of the Prince's shipbuilders: it was certainly a Portuguese development, and as Sagres was the fountainhead of maritime activity, it is a logical conclusion that the caravel should have originated there. This craft was intrinsically a revolutionary vessel, with respect both to rigging and hull design. She was three-masted and usually lateen-rigged, with the mainmast forward and two smaller masts aft, in which case she was known as a *caravela latina*. She might on occasion, however, be square-rigged as the *Niña* and the *Pinta* were; in this, the *caravela redonda*, the mainmast was stepped amidships, but in both lateen and square-rigged types the hull design was the same — long and narrow. In size the caravel was of medium tonnage by the standards of the day, say anything between fifty and two hundred tons.

What was striking besides the masting were the dimensions of the vessels. Earlier ships had been broad, tubby affairs, whose beam usually equalled half the length — a one to two ratio. By contrast, a caravel of a hundred feet over-all would have a beam of only twenty-five or thirty feet — a ratio of one to three or even one to four. The relatively rakish appearance of the caravel was further accentuated by the great reduction in size of the forecastle, otherwise the traditional top-heavy superstructure would have been in the way of the lateen sail on the mainmast. It was thus the combination of hull, size, and rig that made the caravel far and away the most efficient sailing vessel built up to that time. Excellent in windward work, these ships could sail anywhere but into the "eye of the wind," while their daily runs in favorable weather sometimes rivaled the logs of the famous clipper ships of a later day. No wonder that Cadamosto, who was certainly in a position to know, said that Henry's caravels were the best ships that sailed the seas.

For more than half a century the caravels held a monopoly in the ocean voyages: Cão used them, Dias used them, and two of Columbus' three vessels on the First Voyage were square-rigged caravels. But the storms that Dias met off the Cape and that Columbus met off the Azores showed that caravels were rather too frail and too low in the water for very heavy seas, while for the long voyage to the Indies they were too small for a satisfactory "pay load." The next development was therefore the *nau* or ship (Spanish *nao*), a big three-master of four hundred tons and upwards, with a high poop and forecastle, and with a sail-plan of square sails on the fore- and mainmasts, and a lateen sail on the mizzen. First heard of about 1450, such vessels were used by da Gama, as well as by Columbus in the Grand Fleet on the Second Voyage, and with their various derivative types were destined to do the work of overseas voyaging for many a long year. Perhaps the best known variant of the *nau* was the galleon, conspicuous alike in the Spanish plate fleets and in Elizabeth's navy; it is considered to have been larger than the *nau*, but the technical differences are still in dispute. Then there was the huge carrack, sometimes of seven or eight decks and a thousand tons or more and capable of carrying a thousand people on board.

The problems of marine archaeology of the fifteenth and sixteenth centuries are greatly accentuated by the almost complete lack of accurate contemporary evidence, either documentary or pictorial. Iconography derived from the seals, engravings, and paintings of the time is seldom reassuring; while for lack of positive evidence the numerous modern models — for example, of Columbus's *Santa Maria* — run the gamut of nearly every type of three-master of the Renaissance. Nor are the contemporary models themselves much of a help; they are mostly of the "votive" type, built to be hung in churches, and consequently they bear little resemblance to the ships themselves.

To this general observation there are happily several exceptions, which enable us to form at least some small part of an accurate picture of the ships that were used in the days of the great discoveries. For instance, in the interesting manuscript entitled "The Pageants of Richard Beauchamp, Earl of Warwick" (British Museum, Cotton MS; Julius E.iv) there are several sketches of ships of the period 1485–1490 which are so convincing that they have been used as the basis of the construction of a fine modern model of an English ship of the early Tudor period. This model, in the Science Museum in London, has the following scale dimensions: tonnage, about 500; length from stem to stern, 106 feet; length of keel, 76 feet; breadth, 38 feet. The model is accepted as the best representation of a large ocean-going ship of the time, and although English, is probably not too far removed in hull design from the ships used by the Spanish and Portuguese from Columbus' day through the first quarter of the sixteenth century. The Portuguese and Spanish ships, however, usually had spritsails and topsails as well as the three sails shown in the model.

For the design of the caravels that did the work of discovery in the fifteenth century, we have even scantier evidence; but in the graceful model of the *Santa Maria* (in this instance conceived as a caravel rather than a *nau*) made by Captain Julio F. Guillen for the Naval Museum in Madrid there exists a very convincing representation of a caravel hull. This same design was also used in the full-size *Santa Maria III*, built for the Seville exhibition of 1929 and now appropriately at Huelva near Palos. Samuel Eliot Morison thinks that, as a reproduction of the original, the *Santa Maria III* is not entirely accurate, as the vessel of 1492 was a small ship rather than a caravel and probably had a high forecastle; also the stern assembly of the *Santa Maria III* was copied from a woodcut in Breydenbach's *Travels*, which was printed in Mainz in 1486. None the less, as a square-rigged caravel, *Santa Maria III* has all the earmarks of being a very truthful rendering of her fifteenth-century prototypes; and it is more than likely that the vessels used by Prince Henry's captains, by Cão, and by Dias were very similar in appearance to this model, although in all probability they were lateen-rigged and had no bowsprit. The dimensions of *Santa Maria III* are: tonnage, 120; length of hull, 84 feet; length of keel, 61 feet; beam, 25 feet; total height of mainmast, 92 feet.

While the fundamentals of *nau* and galleon remained reasonably constant throughout the sixteenth century, yet there were various modifications, especially in hull design and sail-plan, which all added up to make the big ship of Drake's day far different in appearance from the craft that Columbus knew. In the late fifteenth-century ships, as seen in the Earl of Warwick model, there was a bluff, high, almost perpendicular bow, and a high, rounded stern; the lines amidships were almost straight, and the wales were parallel to the waterline, so that the general effect was that of a high, chunky vessel. As the Renaissance wore on, ships began to take on more and more of a modern look. Early in the sixteenth century the flat transom stern was introduced; then the high bow gradually developed into a long, low rake forward, with a more conspicuous bowsprit. Instead of the awkward straight lines of the hull, vessels came to be built with sheer, or the fore-and-aft upward curvature of the decks, while the introduction of gun ports (about 1515) and the formalizing of the gundeck led to the development of the tumble home, or inward curvature of the hull as the gunwales are approached: a feature designed to strengthen the hull for the weight of the artillery, and one which often assumed exaggerated proportions. The sail-plan of da Gama's *naus* — spritsail, square sails and topsails on the fore- and mainmasts, and lateen sail on the mizzenmast, — was developed into nine sails, with the addition of topgallant sails on the fore- and mainmasts, and the addition of a small fourth mast, called the bonaventure mizzen, abaft the main mizzen. This picturesquely named rig was of assistance in whip-staff steering (the whipstaff being a verticle handle attached to the tiller and worked from the deck above).

We can form an absolutely accurate picture of an Elizabethan galleon from the remarkable series of shipwright's drafts done about 1586, and preserved in the Pepysian Library, Magdalene College, Cambridge. The plans are contained in a manuscript acquired by Samuel Pepys and called "Fragments of Ancient English Shipwrightry"; they are probably the work of the master-shipwright Matthew Baker, and the specifications appear to correspond to the known dimensions of the *Elizabeth Jonas*, a celebrated vessel rebuilt in 1597–98. These unique drawings depict a craft of almost seven hundred tons burden, with a length of keel of 100 feet; rake forward, 36 feet; rake aft, 6 feet; length between perpendiculars,

142 feet; breadth, 38 feet; and depth of hold, 18 feet. The modern model, as beautiful as it is accurate, made from these plans for the Science Museum in London is therefore the best representation of a sixteenth-century ship that we have. Its rakish lines and singularly modern rigging put it at least midway between the *naus* of Vasco da Gama's time and the seventy-fours of Nelson's day.

THE GEOGRAPHICAL LITERATURE
OF THE RENAISSANCE

THE LITERATURE OF THE PORTUGUESE
DISCOVERIES AND CONQUESTS

The great strength of Portuguese geographical literature lies in the remarkable series of historical chronicles, which, beginning with that of Azurara in the later days of Henry the Navigator, reached their zenith in the mid-sixteenth century with the almost simultaneous composition of the works of Barros, Correa, Castanheda, and Braz Albuquerque. This method of historico-geographical narrative lasted well into the seventeenth century and enriched Portuguese literature with a collection of geographical chronicles not even approached in the literature of any other nation. Neither the literatures of England, France, nor Holland had any works of a comparable nature (although England excelled in her own specialty, the collections of voyages); perhaps the nearest approach to the great Portuguese chronicles would be found in Spain, where Oviedo y Valdes wrote a chronicle of the same stately grandeur as that of Barros. But for a continuous series of these works, most of them on a high level and extending over the better part of two centuries, Portugal stands unexcelled. There alone did the prose chronicle vie with the epic in glorifying the nation's maritime and colonial career.

Portugal's first chronicler, the early fifteenth-century Fernão Lopes, does not concern us, but his mantle was passed on to his pupil, Gomes Eannes de Azurara (died 1474), who became famous as the first European to leave an account of tropical Africa. Azurara was a court official of the learned type; he served at various times as royal librarian, keeper of the archives, and royal chronicler. Although he did not begin his historical writing until middle life, he was nevertheless the author of several chronicles, of which the *Chronicle of the Discovery and Conquest of Guinea* is most pertinent to the subject. This work was his masterpiece and is the most important source for the Henrician voyages.

It begins the narrative with the capture of Ceuta, takes the story through the days of Gil Eannes and the rounding of Cape Bojador, and after treating the later voyages in detail, breaks off with the expedition of Vallarte the Dane in 1448. Madeira and the Azores are likewise described, albeit rather briefly. For the first half of the fifteenth century, the chronicle is a veritable mine of information.

Azurara was well qualified to write a masterpiece of this kind, for he had access to the national archives and he was a scholarly classicist imbued with the spirit of the early Renaissance; he was also able to use the notes of Afonso Cerveira, a very shadowy personage who may have written a long-lost account of the early voyages. As a historian Azurara was laborious, accurate, and conscientious — being often suggestive of Livy. He had great respect for authority and was possessed of an almost blind admiration for Prince Henry the Navigator. Without doubt, the *Discovery and Conquest of Guinea* circulated extensively in manuscript, but it is none the less striking that a book of this importance should have existed so long unprinted. Not until 1841 did the first edition appear in Paris, almost exactly four centuries after the painstaking Azurara had sought to exalt his Prince and the deeds of his countrymen.

The story of the Portuguese in Guinea was continued by Ruy de Pina (1440-1521), a diplomat who was ordered by John II to write a chronicle of his reign. Pina was not as good a chronicler as Azurara; his book tends to be dry, but it is nevertheless written with frankness by an experienced contemporary of the events and is especially valuable in describing the Portuguese in Elmina and Benin in the 1480's and 1490's. Pina's chronicle of John II, like the work of Azurara, remained long in manuscript, having been written about 1500 but not printed until 1792. It was used extensively in its manuscript form by both Resende and Barros; in fact the former plagiarized it quite brazenly, to an extent not fully realized until Pina's book finally appeared in print.

Quite a similar career to Pina's was that of Garcia de Resende (1470-1536), who saw many years of service at court and on foreign missions and who also wrote a chronicle of the reign of John the Perfect. Resende depended almost entirely upon Pina's work, so that his book contains little that is original, but he incorporated a wealth of anecdote and gossip and cast the glamor of poetry over Pina's prosaic record. Resende was in fact a poet of note: his most celebrated verse is found in his *Miscellanea*, a rhymed commentary on the most notable events of his time, which includes much doggerel, in the manner of Skelton rather than of Camoens, about the Portuguese conquests in India. This poetry was included with the second edition of his chronicle, which was published in Evora in 1554. The first edition appeared in Lisbon in 1545.

Compared with the chronicles, there are very few first-hand narra-

tives of voyaging that have come down to us, probably owing to the
Portuguese "conspiracy of silence," by which detailed information about
the new discoveries, especially information dealing with matters of navigation, was kept "top secret" by the Portuguese authorities. In consequence, the only Henrician accounts that have survived are the excellent
and very readable logs of Cadamosto's voyages (to which is added the
expedition of his friend, de Sintra); there is also the story of Diogo
Gomes' venture, told briefly and not very satisfactorily in his old age to
Martin Behaim. For da Gama's first voyage, there survives one of the
great accounts of an epic voyage that has come down to us — the *Roteiro*.
Written by an unidentified member of the fleet (possibly one Alvaro
Velho), this graphic logbook of day-to-day events is a plain, unadorned
narrative; yet its pure simplicity and earnestness makes it a powerful
description of a mighty undertaking. In its scope as a human document,
the *Roteiro* is rivaled only by Columbus' *Journal*.

Just as the discovery of America was heralded by the news-letters of
Columbus and Vespucci, so were the Portuguese conquests in the Orient
initially made known to Europe by a spate of this type of ephemeral literature. The earliest notice of these conquests to appear in print seems
to have been the Latin oration delivered by Diogo Pacheco, King Manuel's representative at the Vatican, to Pope Julius II. This little tract,
published in Rome in 1505 under the pretentious title, *Obedientia Poten-
tissimi Emanuelis Lusitaniae Regis per Dieghum Pacettum Oratorem ad
Julius II, Pont. Max.*, was the first official report of the activities of the
Portuguese in southern Asia. It was followed by a pamphlet, printed in
Rome the same year, entitled *Copia de una littera del Re de Portagallo
mandata al Re de Castella, del viaggio et successo de India*, which pur-
ported to be a letter from Manuel to his brother monarch, Ferdinand of
Aragon, and which dwelt chiefly on Cabral's voyage and da Gama's
second expedition. A German tract appeared in Nürnberg, probably in
1505 too, with the title *Den Rechtenweg ausz zu faren von Liszbona gen
Kallakuth*; this is symptomatic of the avid interests in the new discoveries, even in landlocked central Europe. In 1506–1507 was published the
*Gesta proxime per Portugalenses in India, Ethiopia, & aliis Orientalibus
Terris*, in Latin editions in Rome (1506) and Cologne (1507), and in
both Latin and German editions in Nürnberg (1507); this relates chiefly
to the campaigns of Almeida along the coasts of East Africa and Malabar. Almeida's naval victories off Quilon and Cananor were the theme of
a printed letter from Manuel to Pope Julius II: *Epistola . . . de Victoria
contra Infideles*, probably printed in Rome in 1507. More strictly geographical was the king's letter to Julius, printed in Rome the following
year by Stephan Plannck of the Columbus *Letter* fame: *Epistola de Pro-
vinciis, Civitatibus, Terris, et Locis Orientalis Partis*. King Manuel's

colorful embassy to Rome in 1512, following the fall of Malacca, kept alive public interest in the mysterious East and in conquests — both made all the more vivid to the credulous Europeans by the arrival in Rome of Tristão da Cunha, one of the foremost voyagers, accompanied by a huge performing elephant and a richly caparisoned cavalcade of Persians in national costume. Pacheco again made the oration on this occasion (printed in Rome in 1514), while the letter from Manuel to Pope Leo X was presented by da Cunha. The letter was published under the title, *Epistola . . . de Victoriis habitis in India et Malacha*, in both Rome and Vienna in 1513, and a German edition came out in Augsburg the same year. Another *Epistola* of 1513 relates to Portuguese victories in Morocco, while the last of these early pamphlets, and the only one of purely American interest, is the *Copia der Newen Zeytung aus Presillg Landt* (Nürnberg, 1514), a news-letter dealing with an early Portuguese voyage to Brazil.

Before going on to the great chroniclers of the mid-sixteenth century, mention should be made of one of the earliest printed collections of voyages — and incidentally one of the most influential books ever published — the celebrated *Paesi novamente retrovati*, compiled by the Italian Fracan da Montalboddo and first printed in Vicenza in 1507. This collection is largely composed of Americana, but it also includes Cadamosto's account of his voyages to Guinea, besides the voyage of de Sintra. Furthermore, it printed two letters of Girolamo Sernigi, an Italian merchant in Lisbon, describing da Gama's voyage, and it included a very full narrative of Cabral's expedition, written by a participant and translated from Portuguese into Italian. When added to the accounts of Columbus, Vespucci, and Pinzon, these formed a volume whose importance can neither be overrated nor overemphasized. The *Paesi* had six Italian editions, six French, and two German ones (to be followed by the numerous editions, based on the *Paesi*, of the Swabian mathematician Simon Grynaeus), and it was in consequence the book par excellence by which the news of the great voyages and the great discoveries — east and west — was disseminated throughout Renaissance Europe. For news value as regards both the Orient and America, no other book printed in the sixteenth century could hold a candle to it.

The chronicle as a vehicle for historico-geographical narrative reached its peak in the writings of Barros, Castanheda, and Correa, who all lived at the height of Portuguese wealth and power. It is difficult and perhaps unfair to say which of the three men is the best: where one is deficient, the others make up, so that all three should be taken together. Barros was (and still is) the most celebrated; he was the most learned, the best stylist of classical Portuguese prose, and he made brilliant use of his documentary material. But there is no substitute for first-hand knowledge: Barros had never been to India, while Castanheda and Correa had both spent many years there. Castanheda was neither the scholar nor the stylist that Barros was, but he wrote an impartial book of outspoken sincerity which was the fruit of years of residence in the East. Correa was even closer to events, for he had been the great Albuquerque's secretary; and he may well be Portugal's greatest writer on the East, if only because the events in India are presented so vividly by an eye-witness.

João de Barros (1496–1570), called the Portuguese Livy, was born out of wedlock of noble parentage at Vizeu in North Portugal, educated at the Palace, and began his career of literature as a boy. After some service in West Africa, he entered India House in Lisbon in 1528, where he was destined to serve, first as treasurer and later as factor, for forty years. His position there gave him complete access to all the archives and documents connected with the Portuguese discoveries and conquests. He had genius enough to perceive fully the possibilities of the material at his disposal, and about 1540 he set to work to write the story of his country's overseas empire. His work was thorough and therefore slow; the first *Decade* did not appear in print until 1552, the second followed in 1553, the third came out in 1563 (all three printed in Lisbon), and the fourth and last, prepared for the press by João Lavanha, Cosmographer Royal of Philip III of Spain, was not published until 1615 in Madrid, many years after Barros' death. This massive four-volume work bears the simple title *Asia*; it is more often referred to, however, as the *Decades*. Its scope may be seen from the following summary of its contents:

Decade I (1420–1505), includes the African voyages, the development of Guinea, the discovery of the Cape of Good Hope, the voyages of da Gama, Cabral, and affairs in India until the coming of Almeida.

Decade II (1506–1515), includes the viceroyalty of Almeida and the governorship of Albuquerque.

Decade III (1516–1525), includes much information about Portuguese exploitation of the East Indies, and deals with southern and eastern Asia generally. It comprises the governorships of Lopo Soares, Lopes de Sequeira, and the two Menezeses, as well as the final mission of Vasco da Gama.

Decade IV (1526–1538), carries the history of Portuguese India down through the first siege of Diu, and covers the hotly disputed governorship of Vaz de Sampaio, and the very successful rule of his successor, Nuno da Cunha.

Barros' qualifications for writing the *Decades* were fully equal to his theme. On all counts he was a great historian, and his text is distinguished by its impartiality, its balance, its clearness of exposition and orderly arrangement. As a stylist Barros is equally distinguished; the simple grandeur of his language is admirably suited to the somber majesty of his subject. In every respect Barros' *Decades* are magnificent; it is an incomprehensible misfortune that so far they have never (except for short passages) been translated into English.

Students of Portuguese literature have been for so long disposed to glorify Barros that his contemporary, Fernão Lopes de Castanheda (*circa* 1500–1559), has fallen into relative oblivion. Yet Castanheda in his own right was a very able historian, and in his lifetime at least his works enjoyed a European reputation. The natural son of a man of aristocratic family, Castanheda was born at Santarem at the beginning of the century; he received a good education and went out to India in 1528 — a period when the memory of Albuquerque's conquests was still fresh in men's minds. Castanheda spent many years in the East (authorities differ between ten and twenty years) and traveled at least as far as Malacca, and possibly even to the Moluccas. He early conceived the plan of writing a worthy history of Portuguese India. For twenty years, so it is said, he labored on this work, which under the title *Historia do descobrimento e conquista da India pelos Portuguezes*, came out in eight books at Coimbra between 1551 and 1561. Castanheda did not bother about the African voyages; he told the story from Vasco da Gama to João de Castro, and as a result of his diligent researches on the spot and his conscientious sincerity and earnestness, he turned out a work which ranks beside those of Barros and Correa. His *Historia*, volume by volume, appeared just before Barros' *Decades*; there seems little doubt that the latter made use of Castanheda's book, and since it was the first in the field, the *Historia* initially enjoyed a superior prestige. In consequence, it was, at least in part, translated into Spanish, Italian, French, and English — the latter edition done in 1582 by one Nicholas Lichefield (who was probably the well-known Tudor translator, Thomas Nicholas, in a thin disguise) and dedicated to Sir Francis Drake. One interesting source that Castanheda had utilized was the *Roteiro* of da Gama's first voyage. It is said that Castanheda returned to Portugal in penury; but he was warden of the University of Coimbra, and he spent his later years (quite pleasantly, we hope) in academic circles.

In contrast with the writings of Barros and Castanheda, the great historical chronicle of Gaspar Correa (*circa* 1490–1565) was not printed for three centuries after its composition; the *Lendas da India*, which the author with supreme understatement called "a brief summary," was finally published in eight volumes in Lisbon in 1858–1866. Correa had a more colorful career than his brother historians. When he went out to

India as a well-connected youth in 1512, it was natural that a good position should be awaiting him, and it is not surprising that he quickly became one of Albuquerque's principal secretaries and accompanied the governor on the campaign to Aden and the Red Sea. After Albuquerque's death, Correa served for years in various responsible positions; he was for a while inspector of the works at Goa, then as official architect he went all over India building churches. Later he was head of the factory at Cochin, and he took part in the capture of Diu by the Portuguese in 1531. In addition to his other versatile qualities, he possessed an artistic turn of mind, and at the instigation of João de Castro he painted portraits of the viceroys and governors from Almeida's day onward, for the Palace at Goa. But Correa was not without his grievances, and he resented the tedious and dishonest officialdom and the abuses committed by those in power; he particularly disliked the da Gama family and their followers. He was brutally murdered in Malacca about 1565, probably by assassins of the da Gama faction. In view of his lifetime's experience in the East, Correa was able to write his *Lendas* with a vividness and picturesqueness which can come only through participation in events and acquaintance with the principal actors. In this respect his work stands even above Castanheda's, as well as above that of those less-favored historians who never had first-hand knowledge. It is only fair to add, however, that Correa's accuracy has sometimes been called into question.

But as has been stressed, if one of the great Portuguese historians excels in some respects, other writers may exceed him in yet other respects. If there is no substitute for first-hand knowledge, there is also no substitute for consanguinity. The *Commentarios of Afonso de Albuquerque*, written by his illegitimate son Braz (1500–1580), have therefore a value of their own, especially as Braz came into possession of all his father's papers. Since Braz was only three when his father began his career in India, his memory of his parent could not have been too vivid, but he lived in the family surroundings, he had the source material, and he was determined to leave a fitting literary memorial to his father.

Braz's own career was hardly an exciting one. His only colonial experience was when as a young man he served as governor of Elmina in Guinea, a post in which he failed to distinguish himself. Following this, he held various positions at court, immersed himself in his studies, and lived his later years on his estate. His book appeared in Lisbon in 1557; there is an excellent English translation published by the Hakluyt Society (1875–1884) in four volumes. It is an extremely interesting and valuable biography, and although Braz's prejudices were strongly with his father, yet he betrayed a surprising amount of dispassionate restraint, coupled with fairness toward the Governor's enemies.

Emphasis must be given at this point to the wonderful series of letters (*Cartas*) written by the great Albuquerque himself to his sovereign, Manuel the Fortunate. These incomparable reports, in the forceful and direct prose of a highly intelligent general, sometimes rise to a Biblical grandeur and eloquence and present a vivid picture of the conquest of India, such as we can get from no other source. They were not printed in the conqueror's lifetime, but have been included under the title *Cartas seguidas de documentos que as elucidam,* in the comprehensive edition of Albuquerque material published by the Lisbon Academy of Sciences (7 volumes, 1884–1935).

Two works of implicational rather than direct value are the chronicles of Damião de Goes (1502–1574), the brilliant diplomat, humanist, and free-thinker, whose portrait was painted by Dürer and whose scholarly circle of friends included Luther and Erasmus. Goes wrote a chronicle of John II (Lisbon, 1567) and one of Manuel the Fortunate (4 parts; Lisbon, 1566–67). These books deal with Portuguese history in general, but they also include a vast amount about Portugal's discoveries and conquests, taken from Barros and Castanheda, as well as from various documentary sources; and they were written with a true critical spirit. They therefore have a genuine value which places them beside the chronicles that are purely colonial in subject. Goes' chronicle of Manuel was slavishly followed by Bishop Jeronymo Osorio da Fonseca, whose *De Rebus Emmanuelis* (Lisbon, 1571), is little more than a Latin translation of the earlier work. Osorio demands a word in his own right, however; he was such a stylist in Latin that he became known as the Portuguese Cicero. His well-stocked library at Faro was carried off to England by the Earl of Essex following the 1596 raid and was presented to the Bodleian Library at Oxford.

A volume of a different type, but none the less of prime importance, is the *Livro dos descobrimentos das Antilhas e India* (Lisbon, 1563) by Antonio Galvão (1503–57). This volume is a chronological epitome of all discoveries and travels worthy of note, ancient and modern, undertaken up to the year 1555. Galvão had gone out to India in 1527, and had had a long and distinguished career as governor of the Moluccas, even being offered the native throne of the island of Ternate. He returned to Portugal about 1540, was coldly received, and found his services slighted. His later years are obscure, and he died in poverty, but not before he had composed this famous treatise of unique historical value. In his surprising knowledge of the Spanish discoveries in America, and even in the exploits of the French and English, Galvão showed great resourcefulness in assembling material and a real instinct for going to the right sources. His book is therefore wonderfully complete and very accurate; it is no surprise that Richard Hakluyt realized its worth, when in 1601 he translated it (or caused it to be translated) under the title of *The Discoveries of the World.*

This remarkable succession of historians is followed by lesser men. Yet there were three histories, one written before and two after the turn of the century, which merit notice. The *Historiarum Indicarum Libri* XVI (Venice, 1588–89), by the Jesuit J. P. Maffei, was based on Barros and also includes a fine set of Jesuit accounts written from the East and a life of Loyola. The *Historia general de la India Oriental* (Valladolid, 1603) by the Spanish Benedictine Antonio de San Roman is also written from an ecclesiastical slant and is notable as being the largest original treatise on the Portuguese Indies written in Spanish. The third book meriting attention is the uncritical but informatory *Chronica do João III* (Lisbon, 1613), by Francisco de Andrade, which covers the period 1521–1557 and devotes much attention to affairs in India during that time.

One great writer of the classic chronicler-historian type lingered on, to have his works appear in the seventeenth century. This was Diogo do Couto (1542–1616), the literary heir of Barros. Couto went to India as a soldier in 1559 and saw ten years' campaigning throughout the Indian Ocean area. Upon the expiration of his service, he returned to Portugal, possibly on the same vessel with Camoens. Later he went out to India a second time and remained there until his death, serving as keeper of the archives at Goa and spending his later years in bringing Barros' *Decades* up to date. Not knowing that Barros' Fourth Decade existed in manuscript, Couto wrote a Fourth Decade of his own, which was printed in Lisbon in 1602; then João Baptista Lavanha brought out the real Barros version in 1615, and Couto himself added seven more decades. Three of these (the Fifth, Sixth, and Seventh) were published in 1612, 1614, and 1616 in Lisbon, Madrid, and Lisbon respectively; some of the remaining books were later printed from faulty copies, the canon of the whole work was finally given a proper edition with the publication of a full-blown Barros-Couto edition in twenty-four volumes in Lisbon, 1778–1788. This comprised eleven complete decades and two versions of the Fourth. Couto left an incompleted fragment of the Twelfth Decade, and his successor at the Goa archives, Antonio Bocarro, wrote a Thirteenth Decade, beginning at the year 1612. This was published in 1876. Such, in brief, is the knotty bibliographical history of Portugal's greatest chronicle. Couto was a more critical writer than Barros and like him a clear and correct stylist; he did much to perpetuate the grand manner of geographico-historical literature in Portugal. With his superior intelligence Couto realized that he was living at the close of the heroic era of Portuguese India, and in his *Dialogo do soldado pratico portugues*, a dialogue between a soldier, an ex-governor, and a judge, he analyzed the decline of the colonial empire of his homeland. This frank and revealing work was first printed in 1790, with the title *Observaçoes sobre as principaes causas da decadencia dos Portuguezas an Asia*.

The last writer to attempt a chronicle of the Portuguese Empire in the grand manner was Manuel Faria e Sousa (1590–1649). This historian and poet, known for his commentary on the *Lusiads*, wrote an exhaustive *Asia Portugueza* (3 volumes; Lisbon, 1666–1675) and a lesser *Africa Portugueza* (Lisbon, 1681), but his work is hardly up to the Barros-Couto standard. Writing before his country had freed herself from the Spanish crown, Faria e Sousa tends to be pro-Spanish: the Portuguese have always been inclined to regard his works as Spanish literature, while the Spanish themselves have never been particularly interested in him. Faria e Sousa is therefore a sad example of falling between two stools.

Sixteenth-century Africa had sufficient history apart from India to deserve some literary treatment of its own, and there are four or five books of prime importance dealing with the Dark Continent in that period. Only one work, however, concerns Guinea, though this was Portugal's oldest colony. This treatise is an excellent coast pilot entitled the *Esmeraldo de Situ Orbis*, written by Duarte Pacheco Pereira, the vanquisher of the Samuri of Calicut. When this doughty warrior returned from India about 1505, he set to work compiling this highly useful manual of West African navigation. Like so many Portuguese works it remained long in manuscript, not being printed until 1892, but it must unquestionably have seen wide use as a seaman's manual in the Renaissance.

The Kingdom of Congo and adjacent Angola engendered one very celebrated volume: the *Relatione del Reame di Congo* (Rome, 1591), written by the papal chamberlain, Filippo Pigafetta, from the verbal account of Duarte Lopes, a settler in the Congo, who had been sent to Rome on a mission. Pigafetta expanded Lopes' narrative to include most of Africa, and the book is the best account of the equatorial regions produced in the century. As noticed earlier, it was translated into English under Hakluyt's direction in 1597 as *A Report of the Kingdome of Congo*. Two lesser works bring the story of the colony well into the seventeenth century. The earlier of these, *Da Mina ao Cabo Negro*, was by Garcia Mendes Castellobranco, a soldier who had served with Paolo Dias and who was living in Angola as late as 1620; the later work, *Terras e minas Africanas*, was by another soldier, Rebello de Aragão, who spent the years 1593–1631 in the colony. Both treatises were published for the first time in *Memorias do ultramar*, edited by Luciano Cordeira (Lisbon, 1881).

The Mozambique region likewise produced a classic, the *Ethiopia Oriental* (Evora, 1609) by João dos Santos. This narrative gives a highly interesting relation of the region in the troublous years toward the end of the sixteenth century, describing the topography, population, flora, and fauna of a land from which Portugal expected great possibilities. Unfortunately it is a book of the very greatest rarity, but quite a satisfactory abridged translation appeared in Purchas' collection.

Abyssinia gave rise to no less than three works of the first order in the sixteenth century, as well as several more in the ensuing period. Of these, the most important is *Ho Preste Joam das Indias* (Lisbon, 1540) by Francisco Alvares, the priest who accompanied Lima's mission to Ethiopia in the years 1520–1527. Although disliked by both Barros and Correa, Alvares was an excellent observer, and his book forms a very important description of the customs, manners, and history of the country. It proved popular throughout Europe and went through a large number of editions in various languages, being presented in English in the vast collection of Purchas (who curiously accords Alvares the accolade of knighthood). Both the other works are concerned with the campaigns between the Abyssinians and the Moslems, in which the Portuguese contingent under Cristovão da Gama took part. One account, entitled *Historia das cousas que o muy esforcado Capitao Dom Christovao da Gama fez nos Reynos do Preste João* (Lisbon, 1564), was by Miguel de Castanhoso, a soldier who participated in the struggle, and whose narrative has therefore that peculiar vividness that comes from an actual performer in an heroic episode. The other book, the *Breve relaçao da embaixada do Patriarcha do João Bermudez trouxe do Emperado da Ethiopia* (Lisbon, 1565), was by the much traveled and highly experienced cleric João Bermudez and covers the same field as Castanhoso's work. It too was put before the English reader by Purchas.

Two very important Jesuit accounts of the following century strengthen still further the literature concerning Abyssinia. The earlier work is the *Historia de Ethiopia* by Pedro Paez (1564–1622), a missionary who after years of imprisonment and slavery in southern Arabia resided in Abyssinia from 1603 until his death many years later, during which time he visited the source of the Blue Nile. His work remained in manuscript until 1905. Better known to English readers is Jeronimo Lobo (1593–1678), who traveled in East Africa and Abyssinia for ten years after 1624 and whose account, in Telles' *Historia de Ethiopia* (Coimbra, 1660), was translated by Samuel Johnson and became thereby the original inspiration of *Rasselas*.

Several Portuguese writings on Brazil deserve to be chronicled. There is first of all the foundation document of the land: the letter of Pedro Vaz de Caminha to King Manuel, a long communication written from Porto Seguro while Cabral's fleet was there in 1500. It is surely one of the most important documents concerning the discovery of the New World, and has been admirably put before the English reader in W. B. Greenlee, *The Voyage of Cabral* (London: Hakluyt Society, 1938). Not for many years, however, was Brazil of sufficient importance to have a regular historian; only in 1576 did the celebrated *Historia da Provincia Sãcta Cruz* by Pedro de Magelhães Gandavo appear in Lisbon, a valuable and indispensable source for the early history of the colony. Eleven years later Gabriel Soares de Sousa wrote his *Tratado descriptivo do Brazil* (edited by Varnhagen; Rio de Janeiro, 1865), which in its description of the coast, the hinterland, and the native tribes is probably the best of all the early narratives. In the next century, the Jesuit Fernão Cardim journeyed through Brazil, residing in Bahia in 1609, and visiting the southern Indians some years later. His *Narrative epistolar* is quite an outstanding tale of his experiences (edited by Varnhagen, Lisbon, 1847). The three important non-Portuguese writers on Brazil, Hans Stade of Hesse, Andre Thevet, and Jean de Lery, will be considered under their respective national literatures later.

Like Africa and Brazil, China was treated in a small but distinctive literature, some of it from non-Portuguese sources. If we except the very interesting description of Mendes Pinto (to be noticed shortly), the earliest books on China by Renaissance travelers date from the 1560's. Best known is the *Tractado das cousas da China e de Ormuz* (Evora, 1569–70), by Gaspar da Cruz, a missionary who went to China in 1556. A great deal of his material came from one Galeotto Pereira, who had been a prisoner in China for some years, and who wrote a book of his own — *Alcune cose del paese della China* (Venice, circa 1561). This account was translated into English and included in Willes' *Historye of Travaile* (1577), being thereby the first work on China to be put before the Elizabethans. Da Cruz's book was translated by Purchas.

The activities of the Spanish missionaries reaching China by way of Mexico and the Philippines from 1575 onward were responsible for the next two books. The first, by a Spanish cleric named Bernardino de Escalante who never went to China, was a compilation of fact, hearsay, and conjecture, based on Barros, da Cruz, and other writers, and evidently was written to encourage Spanish colonial effort in the Far East. Considering the second-hand manner in which it was compiled, it is by no means without value. It was printed in Seville in 1577 as *Discurso de la navigación que los Portugueses hazen a los reinos y provinvias del Oriente*, and was translated by John Frampton, to appear in London in 1579. A longer, more celebrated, and more authoritative book was the *Historia de las cosas mas notables, ritos, y costumbres del gran Reyno de la China*, by Juan Gonzalez de Mendoza (Rome, 1585), who like Escalante had never been to China, but who nevertheless was an expert compiler. Mendoza's work gave an exhaustive description of the country and its people, together with accounts of travel of Spanish missionaries across the Pacific to China; it also included Antonio de Espejo's relation of New Mexico. For upwards of a century Mendoza's treatise remained the standard Western classic on the Celestial Empire, and as such it had a well-deserved popularity. It was translated widely, and appeared in English in 1588, being rendered by Robert Parke at Hakluyt's suggestion and dedicated to Thomas Cavendish, the circumnavigator.

Of the Portuguese writers on the topography of the Indian Ocean's periphery, two were first represented in the collection of Ramusio (*Delle navigazioni e viaggi*, Volume I; Venice, 1550). Of these the earliest was Thomé Lopes, who went to India on da Gama's second voyage and who wrote a good account of the Malabar Coast and the activities at Calicut. A fuller description, covering the coasts from East Africa to the Malay Peninsula and even including the Spice Islands, was that of Duarte Barbosa, Magellan's brother-in-law and shipmate. Barbosa has great value as a descriptive writer and anthropologist; he has left us a fine account of the ports of East Africa and much interesting information about Aden and Ormuz. Obviously he knew the west coast of India well, and he evidently had first-hand knowledge of Pegu and Sumatra; further east his information came from other sources. His description of Malacca is the earliest recorded by any Portuguese writer, and his passages on Malabar are of paramount interest, because of his long residence there and his knowledge of the language. Barbosa has received his due at the hands of the Hakluyt Society, which has published a competently edited text of his *Book* in two volumes (1918–1921).

A work very similar in scope, and recently rescued from oblivion by the Hakluyt Society, is the *Suma Oriental of Tomé Pires* (2 volumes, 1944). Pires, who was sent on the first Portuguese embassy to China in 1517, had a wide acquaintance with the East and had resided for some time in both Malacca and Java. His work treats of the lands from the Red Sea to the Spice Islands and contains an interesting section about China, written, however, before Pires has visited it. Pires wrote more amply about the lands beyond Malacca than did Barbosa, while like his elder he was a good ethnographer.

Not many Portuguese in those days penetrated the hinterland of the Indian peninsula. We are all the more fortunate, therefore, in being left with the impressive accounts of two Portuguese travelers who visited the great city of Vijayanagar in south central India at the height of its power. This metropolis was the capital of a mighty kingdom, which at its widest extent stretched across the peninsula from sea to sea, and which every Hindu ruler to the south acknowledged as supreme. It was at length destroyed by a confederacy of Moslem sultans (of Bijapur, Ahmednagar, and Golconda) in 1565, but when visited by Domingos Paes about 1520 and Fernão Nuniz some fifteen years later, the place must have provided a fine spectacle of Oriental magnificence. The interesting narratives of these two men have been published in English in Robert Sewell's *A Forgotten Empire* (London, 1900).

Strictly navigational, in contrast, are the three *Roteiros* of João de Castro, who was perhaps the greatest figure in Portuguese India after the death of Albuquerque, distinguished equally as a warrior, an administrator, a man of letters, and a geographer. His career has been sketched earlier in the book: suffice it to say that his works are among the most interesting that ever emanated from the Portuguese Empire. These comprise three outstanding contributions to navigational literature; the first is a "rutter" from Lisbon to Goa; the second is a coast pilot of western India from Goa to Diu; the third, dealing with the coasts and navigation of the Red Sea, was the fruit of de Castro's hazardous voyage to Suez. All three *Roteiros* were published in Lisbon in 1940.

Since de Castro's *Roteiros* were scientific in scope, it is perhaps fitting to mention at this place another technical work, although of quite a different nature. This is the *Coloquios dos simples e drogas he cousas medeçinais da India* by Garcia da Orta. This volume, published in Goa in 1563, was the third book printed in India, and the first scientific work; it is also noteworthy as containing an ode by Camoens. Its author was the leading medical practitioner in Goa and a distinguished botanist on the side; he had a famous garden of exotic plants, in which Camoens and other men of learning were wont to gather. Garcia da Orta's book thus grew out of his medical profession and his botanical hobby and is the foremost example of *materia medica* produced in any Portuguese territory in that period. It is approached, however, by the work of another Portuguese colonial, Christoval Acosta's *Tractado de las drogas y medicinas de las Indias Orientales* (Burgos, 1578). This writer, not to be confused with the Spanish-American scientific author of the same name, was born in Mozambique and like Orta practiced medicine for many years in India. Evidently he found time to travel far and wide in the Orient in the pursuit of his study of natural history, in the course of which he suffered shipwreck, captivity, and other hardships. Acosta's *Tractado*, written after he had come to Europe and settled in Spain, is of additional interest since it contains many woodcuts of Eastern plants previously unknown in Europe.

Considering the duration and extent of the Portuguese colonial effort, there are surprisingly few narratives of personal travel in sixteenth-century Asia that have come down to us. One might include among the literature of the Lusitanian Empire the *Itinerario* of Ludovico di Varthema (Rome, 1510), if only because that remarkable sightseer visited India in the very early days of the Portuguese conquest. More appropriate as being strictly Portuguese literature is the *Itinerario* of Antonio Tenreiro (Coimbra, 1560). Tenreiro, a picturesque character with long experience in the

East, traveled through Persia to Tabriz on an official mission, and in 1528 made a very adventurous journey across the Mesopotamian Desert from Basra to Aleppo. Even with all the coming and going in the Portugal of those days, after his return Tenreiro appears to have enjoyed a nation-wide fame as a traveler and raconteur. Another interesting trans-Persian journey was that of Mestre Afonso, whose *Itinerario* appeared in Lisbon in 1565; there is also the clear and erudite *Itinerario da India por terra* by Gaspar de S. Bernardino (Lisbon, 1611). Still more famous was Mendes Pinto, whose fantastically adventurous travels, long suspected as being mere fiction, appeared as the *Peregrinaçam* (Lisbon, 1614). Pinto's friend and colleague, Francis Xavier, was the subject of two popular biographies written toward the end of the Renaissance, both of them uncritical and eulogistic works by fellow-Jesuits: *De Vita Francisca Xavierii* (Antwerp, 1596) by Horatio Torsellino; and *Historia da vida do Padre Francisco de Xavier* (Lisbon, 1600) by João Lucena. Both books en-joyed great popularity and were much translated. Still another side of life in the Portuguese Indies appears in Francisco Rodrigues Silveira's *Mem-orias de um soldado de India*. This interesting narrative is that of a soldier in the ranks, who served in the East from 1585 to 1598, and as such bears comparison to Bernal Diaz's vigorous account of his Mexican campaigns. Although written in 1608, Silveira's book was not published until 1877; the original manuscript is preserved in the British Museum.

The last of the famous free-lance Portuguese travelers was Pedro Teixeira, who made two voyages to India. After spending the last fourteen years of the century in the East, he returned across the Pacific to Mexico, and thence to Portugal; being, it is said, the first man to go around the world from west to east. In 1604 he was back in Goa, shortly to return overland from Basra to Aleppo. His *Relaciones . . . de un viage hecho por el mismo autor dende la India Oriental hasta Italia por tierra* (Ant-werp, 1610) concerns for the most part the Basra-Aleppo journey. Teixeira's work, which is written in Spanish, also treats of the Persian monarchy.

Two series of events concerned with Portuguese India appeared to inspire belles-lettres as no other happenings did. These were the sieges of Diu in 1538 and 1546, and the various shipwrecks of homeward-bound Indiamen on the East African coast. The first siege of Diu was commem-orated in prose by a participant, Lopo de Sousa Coutinho, who wrote *Do cerco de Diu* (Coimbra, 1556); and in the epic poem of Francisco de Andrade, the chronicler, *Primeiro cerco de Diu* (Coimbra, 1580). The second and more spectacular siege drew forth the *Commentarius de Rebus in India apud Dium gestis* (Coimbra, 1548), by Diogo de Teive, a noted Portuguese humanist; also the *Historia do segundo cerco de Diu*, by Leonardo Nuñes, who fought at Diu beside his hero, João de Castro.

The same event also inspired the stirring epic poem by the Azorean lyricist Jeronymo Corte-Real, the *Sucesso do segundo cerco de Diu* (Lisbon, 1574); a work of real merit, containing vigorous and well-colored descriptive passages.

Under the general heading of siege literature may be included Antonio Castilho's *Cerco de Goa e Chaul* (Lisbon, 1573), which commemorated Luis de Ataide's heroic defence of the Portuguese capital; also Jorge de Lemos' *Cercos de Malaca* (Lisbon, 1585), which described some of the attacks by the Moslem King of Achin on the Portuguese stronghold. One of Portugal's few conquests in this later period is related in Abreu Mousinho's *Conquista del Reyno de Pegu* (Lisbon, 1617), which narrates the capture of the Burmese metropolis. Jeronymo Corte-Real also wrote a famous classical epic on the wreck of the *São João* on the Natal coast in 1552 — *Naufragio de Sepulveda* (Lisbon, 1594), a poem still considered by some Portuguese critics as second only to the *Lusiads*. Since Corte-Real was a close relation of the brothers who perished off Newfoundland in 1500–1501 he probably felt in his element in writing this heroic verse of a terrible marine disaster. Following closely on the tragedy of the *São João* was the disaster of the *São Bento*, also wrecked on the Natal coast (1554). Manuel de Mesquita Perestrelo, the hero of the ordeal and the man who later made an excellent survey of the African coast, wrote a powerful account entitled *Naufragio da Nao Sam Bento* (Coimbra, 1564). This contains passages of real beauty — the terrors of the storm, the shipwreck itself, and the tribulations of the survivors on land are told with inspiring power. The great prose epic on the subject of shipwrecks, however, is the collection of first-hand accounts made by Bernardo Gomes de Brito under the title *História trágico-marítima* (2 volumes; Lisbon, 1735), a group of twelve narratives of notable wrecks that befell Portuguese ships between 1552 and 1602, and which is a moving tribute to a great race of seamen.

Distinguished as the foregoing accounts in prose and verse, of Portuguese heroism at Diu and at sea, may be, they are all eclipsed by the great masterpiece of Luis de Camoens. The *Lusiads* is indeed the national poem par excellence and the supreme epic of Portugal's conquests in the East. Critics have remarked that Camoens is an entire literature in himself, and an adequate discussion of the *Lusiads* is obviously beyond the scope of this essay. For the purposes of geographical literature, it may be observed that the voyage of Vasco da Gama occasioned its composition and formed the skeleton around which it grew, and the magnificent Tenth Canto relates the deeds of the Portuguese in India up to the days of Camoens himself. In its stately grandeur, the *Lusiads* is to Portuguese poetry what Barros' *Decades* are to Portuguese prose. Their national literature never again reached such heights, nor has the literature of any other country writings to surpass these two masterpieces in their special fields.

Spanish geographical literature has its own distinctive character. Spain, it is true, produced no Barros or no Camoens, but thanks to the energy and intelligence of eye-witnesses, posterity has been left with a series of stirring accounts of the Columbian voyages and of the conquests of Mexico and Peru. Though some were written by men of other nationalities than Spanish, yet in the geographical sense, the texts may be considered Spanish; and all these relations, when taken together, constitute an epic literature of the first century of Europeans in the New World.

First not only in priority but in importance is Columbus' *Journal* of the First Voyage, which Sir Clements Markham has dogmatically called the most important document in the whole range of the history of geographical discovery, because it is the record of the enterprise which radically changed the history of mankind. To our loss, the original draft of this remarkable account has long since vanished, but an early sixteenth-century transcript by Bishop Las Casas survives in the National Library in Madrid, and the text has often been reprinted. Compared with the full text of the *Journal*, the highly abridged account that appeared in the various printed editions of the *Columbus Letter* (printed in Barcelona, Rome, Basel, and Paris in 1493; in Basel in 1494; and in Strassburg in German in 1497) is but a shadow, albeit the printed version was of contemporary importance as the means of disseminating the knowledge of the great discovery. The *Journal* itself is a careful diary, which is truly the mirror of its author. Its full and copious entries show the workings of a vivid imagination, the appreciation of scenic beauty, and a power of observation which nothing seems to escape. As a record of history's most important voyage, it is as noble as it is complete.

If Columbus kept a similar journal on his Second Voyage, as his son Ferdinand implies, it has disappeared without a trace. There were, however, various diarists and chroniclers who made up for this deficiency. Dr. Diego Alvarez Chanca, the fleet's physician, wrote an excellent relation of the outward voyage and of affairs in Hispaniola up to the founding of Isabela. This narrative remained long in manuscript (still preserved in the Royal Academy of History, Madrid), and was not printed until 1825, when it was included in Navarrete's *Colección de los viajes*. For Columbus' cruise to Cuba and Jamaica there is the highly interesting compilation of Andres Bernaldez, a friend of the admiral's in his later days. Bernaldez got his story at first hand from Columbus and embodied it in his *Historia de los Reyes Católicos* (Granada, 1856). Like the First Voyage, the second brought forth a brief news-letter, composed by a

Milanese named Nicolo Syllacio or Scyllacio from correspondence received from an Aragonese sailor in the fleet. This little tract, of the very greatest rarity, was printed in Pavia late in 1494 under the title *De Insulis Nuper Inventis* (Church Catalogue, 9).

For the Third and Fourth Voyages the outstanding original sources are the two letters which Columbus wrote to Ferdinand and Isabella, known from transcripts made by Las Casas (preserved in the National Library, Madrid); in addition the naïvely delightful will of Diego Mendez describes that worthy's journey in a canoe from Jamaica to Hispaniola, to bring help to the marooned admiral. These three documents, along with the accounts of Dr. Chanca and Bernaldez for the Second Voyage and the printed *Columbus Letter* for the First Voyage, have appeared complete in English in *Select Documents Illustrating the Four Voyages of Columbus*, edited by Cecil Jane (Hakluyt Society, 1930–1933).

The foregoing narratives, whether by Columbus or his colleagues, were episodical accounts, voyage by voyage. By the time of Columbus' death, however, his accomplishments could be seen in sufficient perspective for the great historians of the Columbian period to get to work, and during the course of the sixteenth century four very able writers recounted the story of the admiral's career: Peter Martyr, Bartolomé de las Casas, Ferdinand Columbus, and Gonzalo Fernandez de Oviedo y Valdes.

Peter Martyr d'Anghiera (1457–1526) has the distinction of being the earliest historian of America. An urbane and sophisticated Italian, thoroughly imbued with Renaissance humanism, he entered the priesthood in order to enjoy ecclesiastical revenues and lived most of his life at the Spanish Court, where he tutored young nobles and filled various diplomatic appointments. Hardly had Columbus returned from his First Voyage when Martyr met him in Barcelona; and having gathered a wealth of first-hand intelligence, Martyr determined to write a history of the conquest of the New World (a term which Martyr himself coined). In 1505 Martyr was made Dean of Granada Cathedral; he spent his later years living like a caliph at Valladolid, but he must have seen Columbus when the admiral was at court between his other voyages, and in one way or another he assembled the material for his history. His writings appeared in installments. In 1504 was printed in Italian in Venice the small pirated pamphlet known as the *Libretto*, which described the first three voyages and constituted the First Decade of Martyr's main work. A Latin version appeared in Seville in 1511, three decades were issued in Alcala de Henares in 1516, and the complete series of eight decades was published as *De Orbe Novo* in Alcala in 1530. By the time Martyr had finished his *Decades* he had, of course, gone far beyond Columbus; but he kept up to the minute with his material, as he served for some time on the council of the Indies, during which period all communications that related to the colonies passed through his hands. The result was a historical survey of America through the conquest of Mexico, which included the post-Columbian voyages, the story of the Panama colony, and the campaigns of Cortes. Yet for all this later material, it is mainly because of his narrative of Columbus that Martyr deserves to be remembered.

Martyr was too intelligent a person to view Columbus uncritically, and he doubtless was more interested in the admiral's accomplishments than in the man himself. Therefore, for a thoroughgoing eulogy we must turn to the biography of Columbus by his illegitimate son Ferdinand (1488–1539). One is reminded of a similar biography written by Albuquerque's natural child, but Ferdinand had a great advantage over Braz, in that he knew his father well and had been his shipmate on the Fourth Voyage. Ferdinand was a pious, studious, and scholarly person, determined to leave a fitting literary memorial to his father. His inherited sinecures brought him considerable wealth, which enabled him to travel extensively throughout Europe, consorting with learned society and collecting books. In 1525 he settled down in Seville, where he planted a large garden with American trees and gathered together a great library, which survives today in fragmentary form as the Biblioteca Colombina. His life's work was his *Historie*, finished shortly before his death, but not printed until 1571 (in Venice). Like so many books written by sons of great men, it suffers from almost blind adulation, but it is of great value in dealing with the Fourth Voyage, and it remains the only source of information about many events in the life of Columbus. Ferdinand had been to America, he had full recollections of his father, and he had access to many of his father's papers; these three factors are enough to make the *Historie* a book of outstanding importance.

If Ferdinand Columbus and Peter Martyr were the only historians to know the admiral, one other man was sufficiently close to the events to write with almost as great — if not actually as great — a background of authority. Bartolomé de las Casas had come out to Hispaniola in 1502, a hopeful young emigrant fresh from the University of Salamanca. His humane nature was quickly revolted by the cruelties practised by his fellow countrymen on the native inhabitants, and he forthwith dedicated his life to ameliorating the lot of the Indians. In 1510 he took holy orders, being, it is said, the first priest to be consecrated in the New World. His activities thereafter took him throughout the Caribbean region; he was successively a missionary in Cuba, Governor of the Pearl Coast of Venezuela, and bishop of Chiapas in Mexico. All this while he labored manfully on behalf of the natives, gaining the title of the Apostle of the Indians, and wrote a series of propagandist polemics, which under the generic title of the "Las Casas Tracts," appeared in nine parts in Seville in 1552–53. What is even more to the purpose was his great historical work, which, like so many outstanding Spanish and Portuguese writings, was condemned to remain for centuries in manuscript. This treatise was the good bishop's *Historia de las Indias*, written by Las Casas as an old man, when he had returned to Spain about 1552. As it stands, the *Historia* (finally printed in 1875) is a masterly chronicle of American events from 1492 until 1520, based on Columbus' journals and a great mass of other Columbian material, as well as on Las Casas' own observations and experiences in the West Indies. Professor Morison has characterized this work "the one book on the discovery of America that I should wish to preserve if all others were destroyed."

Last of the four early Spanish historians was the most celebrated and probably the greatest, Fernandez de Oviedo y Valdes (1478–1557). His was a career of a man of action with literary tastes. After distinguishing himself as a soldier under Gonsalvo de Cordova in the Italian wars, he came to America in 1514 with the notorious Pedrarias and spent the next thirty-four years (barring half-a-dozen trips to Spain) in the Caribbean region. First serving as inspector of the gold works at Darien, he was later governor of the province of Cartagena, and then commander of the fortress at Santo Domingo. Oviedo had the knack of being at the right place at the right time; he was in Panama when Pizarro sailed to Peru; he was in Santo Domingo when Orellana passed through on his way from the Amazon to Spain; and he saw Quesada when the latter returned from Bogotá; while as regards Columbus, he was able to draw upon oral sources to which neither Martyr, Ferdinand, nor Las Casas had access. He must have very early determined to write his history, and on a visit to Spain in 1523 he was appointed historiographer of the Indies. Three years later (1526) his first work, *La natural historia de las Indias*, appeared in Toledo; this was a geographical summary containing much botanical and anthropological information that had hitherto been hard to come by in Europe.

On a subsequent visit to Spain nine years later Oviedo published the first part of his life's work: *La historia general de las Indias* (Seville, 1535), a volume which embodied a great deal of his previous book and gave a narrative of the discoveries and conquests of the Islands, including a good, though somewhat meager, account of Columbus' voyages. Little more that Oviedo wrote was printed in his own lifetime: a version of Xeres' account of the conquest of Peru (Salamanca, 1547), and a relation of Magellan's voyage (Valladolid, 1557) make up the fragment of a massive work which, if published when it was written, might have given its author the literary stature of Barros. Both the second and third parts of the *Historia*, dealing with the conquests of Mexico and Peru respectively and the exploration of the other regions of Latin America, remained three hundred years in manuscript and were finally published in four volumes by the Royal Academy of History in Madrid in 1851–1855. As Oviedo's work stands, it is a noble monument; in fact, it is the greatest classic of the early years of Spanish activity in the New World to be chronicled by a contemporary. Yet its author was a man of his time and his people, and in his efforts to glorify the Spanish conquerors, he displayed too little sympathy for the Indians to please Las Casas, who stigmatized Oviedo's *Historia general de las Indias* as containing as many lies as it did pages.

Oviedo's great work, by taking the story down to the mid-sixteenth century, has brought us far beyond the period of Columbus. Perhaps it is fitting at this point to return to the days before Cortes and to mention a few of the publications which played their part in bringing America before the reading public of Europe. Notice might be taken of the *Mundus Novus*, a spurious tract which ran through many editions between 1504 and 1508 in Paris, Rome, Vienna, and Augsburg; it was based on the letter which Vespucci had written to Lorenzo de Medici about his so-called third voyage (the enterprise of 1501 for Portugal). About 1505 another Vespucci account appeared in Florence; it covered all four of his supposed voyages and was based on a letter he had written to the Florentine Piero Soderini. Martin Waldseemüller published an edition of this *Quattuor navigationes* at St. Dié in Lorraine in 1507, in which he proposed that the New World should be called America. Apart from this interesting feature, the Vespucci tracts, while highly prized by the bibliophile, are of little value to the historian, inasmuch as the text is characterized throughout by the most extraordinary vagueness, and as the author's first and fourth voyages are now universally acknowledged to be apocryphal.

These relations of Vespucci, as well as the Columbus accounts from Martyr's pirated *Libretto*, were used by Fracan da Montalboddo in his collection of voyages, the *Paesi novamente retrovati*, a book which has already been referred to in connection with the early Portuguese voyages. This group of relations also included the expeditions of Niño, Pinzon, and the Corte Reals, and it became the direct ancestor of Ramusio's much larger collection. The outstanding importance of the *Paesi* as the principal means of spreading the news of the discoveries has previously been stressed.

Reference has also been made to the *Suma de Geographia* (Seville, 1519), by Martin Fernandez de Enciso, Balboa's old enemy. While largely of navigational interest, this work is also a descriptive geography of the then-known world, and its West Indian section is of great interest and importance as being the first American coast pilot. In fact, this part was translated separately by John Frampton and printed in London in 1578 as *A Briefe Description of the Portes, Creekes, Bayes, and Havens of the Weast India*; the whole work was previously translated about 1540 by Cabot's shipmate Roger Barlow — to remain in manuscript until our own day.

The conquest of Mexico gave rise to a remarkable series of official reports, as well as two stirring accounts of the campaign: Cortes' *Letters* to the Emperor Charles V and the histories of Lopez de Gomara and Bernal Diaz del Castillo. Cortes' *Letters* were five in number. The first, which presumably described the campaign up to the departure from Vera Cruz, has been completely lost, although it is believed to have been printed at the time. Its loss is more than compensated for by the survival of the others, particularly of the Second and Third Letters, whose dignified and forceful simplicity led Prescott to compare them to Caesar's *Commentaries*. As to their contents, the Second Letter takes the story through the initial occupation of Mexico City, the *Noche Triste* and the retreat to Tlaxcala; the Third describes the siege and capture of Mexico City; the Fourth deals with the pacification of the country; and the Fifth relates to the campaign into Honduras. Although the Fifth Letter remained in manuscript until the last century, the other three enjoyed a European reputation, and between 1522 and 1532 at least fourteen editions were printed, not only in Spain but in Italy, France, and Germany as well. There is no reason for doubting that these documents were not the composition of Cortes himself; as a youth he had studied at Salamanca, and the straightforward, energetic style suggests the writing of an educated man-of-action.

"The two pillars, on which the story of the Conquest mainly rests," wrote Prescott, "are the Chronicles of Gomara and of Bernal Diaz, two individuals having as little resemblance to each other as the courtly and cultivated churchman has to the unlettered soldier." Francisco Lopez de Gomara (1510–55) never visited the scene of his master's glory, but when Cortes returned to Spain in 1540, the young cleric became his private chaplain and secretary and for the next few years was veritably his "man Friday." Gomara's resulting *Historia de las Indias y conquista de Mexico* (Saragossa, 1552), is a eulogistic panegyric of his hero, which in consequence sorely galled the other participants of the conquest, while Gomara shares the distinction with Oviedo of incurring the withering scorn of Las Casas. Yet one cannot deny that, in spite of all its partiality, Gomara's history is a good history; he derived his information from the highest sources, and he wrote with an elegant brevity and a sense of arrangement that contrasted favorably with the rambling incoherencies of many of his contemporaries. Small wonder that it was a favorite book of the time and was much translated, even going through two editions in English by Thomas Nicholas (1578, 1596). Yet the unmeasured laudation of Cortes at the expense of his old companions-in-arms brought about such a reaction in Spain itself that there was great opposition to the reprinting of the book.

A valuable balance was supplied by the narrative of Bernal Diaz, who regarded Gomara as a meretricious sycophant and Las Casas as an unrealistic fanatic. Diaz wrote from the point of view of the man in the ranks; he had served as a junior officer throughout the campaign, from the landing at Vera Cruz to Cortes' march against Olid in Honduras. He had fought the Tlaxcalans, he had battled his way across the causeway on *Noche Triste*, he had been all through the seige of Mexico. In all, he tells us that he had taken part in one hundred and nineteen battles, and his body was covered with wounds. For this service his only rewards were an Aztec princess and a magistracy in Guatemala, but he had the satisfaction that comes alone from distinguished service, and his heroic robustness shows itself in every line of his book. There is nothing urbane or polished about Diaz' *Historia*. It is the unadorned, day-to-day account of one of Cortes' soldiers; its very simplicity and frankness give it a genuine flavor, which together with the great events it depicts, makes it one of the most powerful and stirring soldiers' narratives ever written. Diaz survived all the perils of the conquest and lived to a ripe old age, during which he composed his book. His work came out long after his death, appearing in Madrid in 1632 under the title *Historia verdadera de la conquista de la Nueva España*.

If Gomara extolled the heroism of Cortes, and if Diaz wrote of the bravery of the rest of the army, there is yet another contemporary account which treats of the Aztecs themselves. This is the *Historia universal de Nueva España*, by the Franciscan Bernardino de Sahagun, who came to Mexico as a missionary in 1529. Sahagun was too intelligent a man to view the native rites and beliefs with the blind hatred of his brother clerics. On the contrary, the Aztecs interested him so much that he made Mexican archaeology a lifelong hobby, even to the extent of living in a native town and learning the language with such fluency that (according to Prescott) he composed his book in it. Sahagun's *Historia*, while treating of the Conquest in its final pages, is predominantly concerned with the religion, the mythology, and the social institutions of Mexico. So much of the traditional native life had been destroyed during and immediately after the Conquest, that most records of it have come down to us largely through Sahagun's observations. With him may be mentioned the interesting Europeanized Aztec, Ixtlilxochitl, whose *Relaciones* parallel those of Sahagun. The works of both these men were published together in Mexico in 1829.

It is natural that an event as stirring as the conquest of Peru should bring forth a goodly body of contemporary literature (some of it hardly non-partisan), so that posterity is left with a useful heritage of record, generally similar in character to that which has just been surveyed in connexion with Mexico. Earliest in date of the writers on Peru was unquestionably Francisco de Xeres, Pizarro's secretary, who prepared his account of the Conquest on the spot, by order of his master. Xeres had come from Spain with Pizarro in 1530 and had taken part in the campaign across the Andes to Cajamarca, down to the time of Atahualpa's murder. Shortly thereafter he returned to Spain, along with the first shipment of Peruvian gold, and the first edition of his narrative, the *Verdadera relación de la conquista del Perú*, appeared in Seville in the same year (1534). Xeres' narrative is not of great length, but the author was an actor in the deeds he described, and there is consequently a freshness and a reality which is missing in the other accounts of the Conquest, save perhaps in that of Pedro Pizarro.

A longer and more detailed relation of the fall of the Inca Empire is that of Augustine de Zarate: *Historia del descubrimiento y conquista del Perú* (Antwerp, 1555). Zarate, "a highly respectable authority" as Prescott calls him, had been comptroller of accounts in Castile, and was sent to Peru in 1543 in the suite of Blasco Nuñez Vela, to bring some order to the financial affairs of the strife-ridden colony. One can imagine him as a prosaic civil servant fresh from Spain, finding himself in the midst of the rough-and-tumble of the Peruvian civil wars. In the course of the struggle he was captured by Gonzalo Pizarro, and was forced at the point of a gun to sign a decree appointing Gonzalo governor of Peru. It is understandable therefore why his history is by no means partial to the Pizarrists.

Zarate must have found that times were hardly propitious for the execution of such financial reforms as he contemplated; nevertheless, he happily conceived the idea of making his countrymen at home acquainted with the stirring events taking place in the colony. In this resolve he had but little coöperation from Pizarro's veterans, at least one of whom threatened to take dire vengeance on anyone so rash as to chronicle the exploits of the Conquistadores. Yet Zarate persevered, and prepared a thoroughly useful history, but such was his fear of retaliation from his countrymen, that his book was not printed until seven years after his return to Europe and was then published in the Low Countries. At length, when most of the principals had died, an edition appeared in Spain (Seville, 1577), and in 1581 an English translation by Thomas Nicholas was put before the Elizabethan public.

Perhaps even more important than either of the foregoing works is the *Relaciones del descubrimiento y conquista de los reynos del Perú* by Pedro Pizarro, a cousin of Francisco. This narrative is preëminently the tale of an eye-witness, for Pedro had come from Spain to join his more famous relative Francisco in 1529 and had served at that leader's side throughout the campaign; after Francisco's assassination, he embraced the royalist cause against his cousin Gonzalo; later he retired to Arequipa in southern Peru, where he served as an official for many years. Pedro was evidently a conquistador of the better type; he was primarily a soldier and a man of little education but considerable intelligence, and he strove to tell the story of the Conquest as he had seen it. As a result his work is a simple, straightforward account, written in the spirit of an honest partisan. He is in consequence comparable to Bernal Diaz, and like Bernal he has left us a narrative of the highest value. Although Pedro wrote his book in 1572, it was not printed until Navarrete included it in his *Colección* (1837): Pedro's labors may have waited long for recognition, but they now have the further reward of a scholarly edition in English (New York, Cortes Society, 1921).

For a full-dress chronicle of Peru, geographical and historical, we must go to the writings of Pedro de Cieza de Leon, a soldier who had served in the ranks in the campaigns in the Magdalena Valley in Colombia, and who had come to Peru with Gasca. Cieza de Leon therefore reached that land toward the end of the civil wars; but he lived there for sixteen years, during which time he wrote exhaustively on the ethnology of the Incas, as well as on the internecine strife of the Spaniards. Only the first part of his *Crónica del Perú* appeared in his own lifetime (Seville, 1553), namely the bulk of the geographical section, giving a minute topographical view of Peru and Colombia at the time of the Conquest, together with many interesting particulars of the existing population. The rest of Cieza de Leon's work remained in manuscript until the last century, but thanks to the Hakluyt Society we have in English his three volumes concerning the Peruvian civil wars, as well as the second part of the geographical section.

The civil wars gave rise to another vivid narrative, conspicuous for its copiousness of detail; the *Historia del Perú* (Seville, 1571), by Diego Fernandez. Like Cieza de Leon, Fernandez was one of Gasca's soldiers and his relation of the events in Peru between 1543 and 1556 was so outspoken that it was suppressed by the Council of the Indies shortly after its publication. Much the same ground is covered in the Florentine Nicolo de Albenino's *Verdadera relación* (Seville, 1549), which is the earliest report on Gonzalo Pizarro's rebellion against Nuñez Vela.

Far more than those of the Aztecs, the institutions and history of the Incas aroused the curiosity of the conquerers, and several memorable works have come down to us about the ancient empire of the Andes. That many-sided genius, Pedro Sarmiento de Gamboa, wrote a history of the Incas which chronicles the Inca dynasty from its inception to the days of Atahualpa. This treatise, which remained in manuscript until its publication in translation by the Hakluyt Society in 1907, is the work of an enlightened and intelligent man, free from bigotry and superstition, and not without a kindly measure of philanthropy for the unfortunate natives.

An even more authoritative writer on Peruvian archaeology, perhaps because it was "in the blood," was Garcilaso de la Vega, who called himself "the Inca," because he was the son of an Inca princess and a Spanish conquistador. Born in Cuzco about 1540, Garcilaso spent his formative years among his mother's people, absorbing their legends and their folklore in a way that an outsider could never do. At the age of twenty he left Peru for Spain, never to return. He served in the Spanish army for some years and then settled down in Cordova to write. His great work appeared in two parts; the first part, *Commentarios reales que tratan del origen de los Incas* (1609), gives the most complete picture of civilization under the Incas that has been written, though at times the author's desire to display the ancient glories of his people throws the book somewhat out of balance. The second part, *Historia general del Perú* (1617), is a history of the conquest. Garcilaso was also the author of a history of de Soto's journey, called *La Florida del Inca* (Lisbon, 1605).

Before taking leave of Peru, we might notice the work of a freelance Italian wanderer who spent fourteen years in America and who, upon his return, compiled a justly popular book. Girolamo Benzoni, a Milanese, came to the Caribbean region as a young man in 1541, and after visiting the Greater Antilles, the Spanish Main, and Central America, sailed from Panama to Peru, about which he gives a good though brief history. Benzoni therefore covered more ground than any other writer of the times, for with the exception of Mexico he had traveled with some thoroughness throughout Spanish America. His book, quaintly illustrated with woodcuts, proved deservedly popular: it first appeared in Venice in 1572 as *La Historia del Mondo Nuovo*, and went through many editions, the most celebrated of which formed Parts Four, Five, and Six of de Bry's *Grands Voyages*.

To our loss, the early history of the Orinoco Valley and the quest for El Dorado gave rise to surprisingly few works of literary stature. Federmann's expedition resulted in a good narrative by his clerk: *Indianische Historia: Ein . . . Historia Nicolaus Federmanns . . . erster Raise* (Hagenau, 1557). The early German ventures in Venezuela likewise received good accounts from the soldier-priest Juan de Castellanos, who also prepared the first published relation of the Ursua-Aguirre journey. Castellanos' *Elegias de illustres varones de Indias* were a series of eulogies (not elegies) in verse, the first part of which appeared in 1588, the second and third parts not being printed until 1847. Their author devotes several cantos to the bloody career of Aguirre and stands forth as the champion of Ursua's lady. A more sober story of this expedition is that of Fray Pedro Simon, who wrote his *Noticias historailes* early in the next century (Cuenca, 1627). For this material Simon depended largely on the unpublished journal of one Vasquez, a soldier who served throughout the journey; thus, while Simon's work was by no means contemporary with the events, his narrative is based on an impeccably authentic source. The sensational voyage of Orellana down the Amazon was recorded by Oviedo, Cieza de Leon, and Herrera, and the latter part of the search for the Gilded Man falls within the province of Tudor literature, inasmuch as it resulted in the writings of Sir Walter Raleigh and Captain Keymis.

If Spain failed to produce a Camoens, at least the early history of Chile gave rise to an epic poem of some celebrity. This is the *Araucana* (Madrid, 1578) by Alonso de Ercilla y Zuñiga, a soldier who had campaigned against the savage Araucanian Indians. Prescott describes the epic as "a military journal done into rhyme," and remarks, "surely never did the Muse venture on such a specification of details, not merely poetical, but political, geographical, and statistical." It seems a far cry from the *Lusiads*, although one may be reminded of the major general in *Pirates of Penzance*. Yet the poem does describe the entire conquest of the country and contains much spirited invective against the greed of the Spanish.

Although Brazil, as a Portuguese settlement, has already been referred to in the earlier section of this chapter, yet on geographical grounds one of the non-Portuguese books which proved very popular might be mentioned here along with the literature of the rest of South America. The much-read Renaissance classic of this region is the *Warhafftige Historia* by Hans Stade of Hesse (Marburg 1557, and many later editions). Stade had been a soldier in the Portuguese service stationed in southern Brazil; he had been captured by cannibalistic Indians and was therefore able to give a realistic, if gory, account of their practices. His book was much reprinted; the most elaborate of the later editions, embellished with many gruesome engravings of Brazilian cannibalism, forms Part Three of de Bry's *Grands Voyages*.

Another German, contemporary with Stade, is one of our chief informants about the early days of Europeans in the Plate Valley. Ulrich Schmidt or Schmidel went to Buenos Aires with Mendoza, and upon the colony's failure, he ascended the river to Paraguay, ultimately to make his way eastward across country to the Brazilian coast. His *Warhafftige Beschreibunge* was printed in Frankfort in 1567 and was subsequently included as Part Eight of de Bry's collection. Of equal importance is the *Commentarios* of Alvar Nuñez Cabeza de Vaca (Valladolid, 1555), relating the voyager's journey from the Atlantic across Brazil to Asuncion in Paraguay; it was written by one Pero Hernandez, Cabeza de Vaca's secretary, while his chief was incarcerated in Paraguay at the orders of his rival Irala.

Cabeza de Vaca's book was actually published in two parts, of which the *Commentarios* forms the second. The first section, known as the *Relación*, deals with his remarkable exploits along the northern coast of the Gulf of Mexico, when as a survivor of Narvaez's ill-fated Florida expedition, he wandered for years in southern Texas. Another remarkable narrative of what is now southern United States is the account of de Soto's journey, written by an anonymous participant calling himself "a gentleman of Elvas" and published as *Relaçam verdadeira . . . no descobriměto da provincia da Frolida* (Evora, 1557). This thrilling record was translated by Richard Hakluyt himself in 1609 as *Virginia Richly Valued* — obviously as an encouragement to the Jamestown colony. Garcilaso de la Vega's *La Florida del Inca* (Lisbon, 1605) is an authoritative work on de Soto's journey, written to do the explorer's memory justice and based on conversations with an officer who accompanied de Soto, as well as on written reports of two common soldiers. There are also accounts by Luis Fernandez de Biedma, factor of the expeditions, and Rodrigo Rangel, de Soto's secretary — published in 1841 and 1851 respectively. To round off the narratives of the South and Southwest is the splendid account of Coronado's expedition, rescued from oblivion in relatively recent years: Pedro Casteñeda's *Relación de la jornada de Cíbola* (Boston, 1896).

There were two celebrated sixteenth-century writers on the natural productions of the Western Hemisphere. The earlier Nicolas Monardes, was a physician from Seville, and his *Dos libros de todas las cosas de Indias Occidentales* (Seville, 1565), is a work on botany and therapeutics similar in scope to the book of Dr. Garcia da Orta of Goa. John Frampton translated it in 1577 as *Joyful Newes out of the Newe Founde Worlde*, which contains the first illustration of tobacco printed in England. Monardes' own name is perpetuated in the genus *Monarda*, and he had the further distinction of introducing the nasturtium into Europe. Another author with botanical interests was the Jesuit Joseph de Acosta, who resided in Peru from 1570 until about 1585, and then visited Mexico before returning to Spain. His *Historia natural y moral de las Indias* (Seville, 1590), is an authoritative production, divided into two parts. The natural history section is concerned with such matters as the geography, the flora, and the fauna of the New World; and the moral history treats of the archaeology of Mexico and Peru. It was translated into English in 1604.

Before taking leave of Spanish America, we must not forget a large general history, written at the end of the period of the discoveries; the *Historia general* of Antonio de Herrera, published in Madrid in eight volumes, 1601–1615. Had Herrera possessed the ability, he might have produced a work to rival the classics of the great Portuguese chroniclers.

As it stands the *Historia* is a vast store of facts, written as annals, with a chronological arrangement. In consequence it is extremely bewildering; there is no continuity of the narrative, and it is difficult to keep the thread of what Herrera is saying. For a researcher with patience and imagination, Herrera must always remain an immensely valuable source, but it is doubtful if his book ever recommended itself to the general reader. For his earlier material, Herrera drew largely upon Las Casas's unpublished history.

One other area of Spanish activity remains to be considered: the Pacific Ocean. Magellan's voyage is well covered by two narratives: that of Antonio Pigafetta is of the very highest value; that of Maximilian of Transylvania is derived second-hand but is nevertheless useful. Antonio Pigafetta, a gentleman of Vicenza, accompanied Magellan's fleet as a volunteer, and all through the tedious months of sailing he kept a journal, which was published on his return (the oldest surviving edition, *Le Voyage et navigation faict par les Espaignolz ès isles de Mollucques*, Paris, 1525). In this journal hearsay evidence is to a great extent mingled with the author's personal experiences, but on the whole it gives much the best and fullest account of the expedition. Such passages as those dealing with the discovery of the Straits, the dreadful crossing of the Pacific, and Magellan's death in the Philippines are told with vivid and graphic realism, while his tribute to his leader is strongly moving in its sincere simplicity. Indeed, as the first-hand narration of one of history's three greatest voyages, Pigafetta's book rivals Columbus' *Journal* and da Gama's *Roteiro*.

In contrast with Pigafetta, Maximilian was a mere historian of the event, but his intelligence and enthusiasm enabled him to turn out a carefully written account, based on the best sources that he could find, namely the participants. A son of the Catholic Archbishop of Salzburg, Maximilian was living in Spain as a pupil of Peter Martyr's when the *Victoria* returned from her great voyage, and he was able to interview the survivors at the time of their reception by the Emperor at Valladolid. This intelligence he embodied in a letter to his father, which is of such sound and well-balanced quality as to supplement admirably the relation of Pigafetta (*De Moluccis Insulis*, Rome and Cologne, 1523).

Under the heading of Spanish literature dealing with the western Pacific, we should certainly include the promotional compilations about China by Bernardino de Escalante and Gonzalez de Mendoza, although the works of these men have been previously noticed under the Portuguese section. Yet it was the Pacific Ocean which gave the Spaniards access to the Far East, enabling them to build up their important colony in the Philippines and to embark on extensive missionary work in Japan and China. Mendoza's book, in particular, was the standard reference book on China for a century or more, being printed in many editions in many languages throughout Europe; in its popularity and influence as as work of regional geography it can be compared only to Leo's *Africa*. It was followed by several other works of importance, concerned with the Far East and the Asiatic islands, especially the Philippines and Japan. Of these, one of the most important is the *Historia de las Islas del Archipiélago, y Reynos de la Gran China* (Barcelona, 1601) by Fray Marcelo Ribadeneyra, a Franciscan friar who had visited the Philippines, Japan, and Macao in the 1590's. The earlier part of the book is devoted to the discovery and early history of the Philippines, but the bulk of the volume concerns the missionary work and martyrdoms in Japan, and there is a section of information brought by missionaries from China and Siam. A better-known publication, dealing with the voyages of Magellan's successors and Spanish enterprise in the islands of the western Pacific is Antonio de Morga's *Sucesos de las Islas Filipinas* (Mexico, 1609), a historical work of fundamental importance for the Philippines, which treats of Legaspi's conquest, and includes an account by Quiros of Mendaña's second voyage. Spain's interest in the East Indies is emphasized by a valuable book published the same year: *Conquista de las Islas Molucas* (Madrid, 1609), by the well-known Spanish poet and historian, Cervantes' friend Bartolomé Leonardo de Argensola; a work written with unusual elegance and judgment, becoming a man of letters. In addition to the writings of Morga and Argensola, there are several good narratives of Mendaña's and Quiros' voyages which have lain for centuries in manuscript among the Spanish archives, to be rescued from oblivion by the Hakluyt Society.

It is perhaps appropriate at this point to mention with great emphasis the many volumes of Jesuit *Letters* which were published from the second half of the sixteenth century through the seventeenth. These letters form a highly significant subject by themselves; their authors were in many cases Spaniards who had crossed the Pacific from Mexico in the Acapulco galleon, and the letters are to a large extent concerned with missionary activity in Japan, China, the Philippines, Malaysia, and the East Indies, but perhaps Japan and China are treated most largely in these narratives. These letters are a rich mine of valuable and interesting information on the Far East such as had not, until then, penetrated Europe. The pleasant literary style of the writers and their shrewd observations on the facts and happenings which they describe make their writings a particularly interesting study of Oriental affairs in the Renaissance. In such a brief survey as the present one, it is the author's lasting regret that he cannot do full justice to this fascinating subject.

At the close of a survey of Spanish geographical literature, great emphasis must be laid on the earliest bibliography; Antonio de Leon

Pinelo's *Epitome de la biblioteca oriental y occidental, náutica y geográfica* (Madrid, 1629). This is an extremely important book, not only because of its own very considerable merits, but also because it is the precursor of all the subsequent great bibliographical works of Americana.

THE GEOGRAPHICAL LITERATURE OF THE
REMAINDER OF CONTINENTAL EUROPE

It must be admitted that during the Renaissance the geographical literature of the countries outside the Iberian peninsula (England possibly excepted) was inferior in both quality and quantity to that produced by Spain and Portugal. Of course, this is to be expected; Spain and Portugal contributed most of the explorers, and the literature of exploration followed in their wake, though this literature would not have attained the stature it did, had not these two countries possessed a series of writers of outstanding ability. Some of the writers were neither Spanish nor Portuguese — Columbus and Peter Martyr, for example — but their affiliations when they wrote were Spanish, and as such a case might be made that their works fall within the province of Spanish literature. While the other countries of Continental Europe produced few explorers, yet they did have a large and interested reading public, and many of the great geographical classics of Spain and Portugal found their way into translations, in Italy, France, and even Germany. Interest in the New World and in southern Asia was by no means confined to the Iberian peninsula; men throughout Europe were eager to learn of the new discoveries (hence the amazing popularity of the *Paesi*), and the propagation of this knowledge was by no means the monopoly of any one country. Yet as far as original works go, one feels a sense of anti-climax after crossing the Pyrenees.

Of non-Iberian Europe, Italy probably had the longest tradition of travel literature. The Renaissance originated in Italy; it was a land of cultured cities and had at that period the most cultivated and urbane population in Europe. It was therefore natural for the Italian public to be avidly interested in the new discoveries, even though (except for hard-hit Venice) these discoveries did not directly concern the Italians.

Even at the beginning of the Renaissance, as we have seen, Poggio had taken down Nicolo Conti's narrative, which was first printed as *India recognita* (Milan, 1492; Hain 13208), and of course the writings of Marco Polo were deservedly popular in fifteenth-century Italy. Contemporary publication was given to the Venetian missions to Persia in Ambrogio Contarini's *El viazo a Persia* (Venice, 1487; Hain 5673). This narrative was included, along with the travels of Barbaro, of one Aloigi di Giovanni to India in 1529, and of a Venetian who served with the Turks in the first seige of Diu, in *Viaggi alla Tana, in Persia, in India* (Venice, Aldine Press, 1543). This charming little book, forming an important collection of early travels, appears to be the only work of geographical interest that emerged from the house of Aldus. Varthema, of course, wrote the greatest work of free-lance travel in southern Asia in that period; his book is deservedly a classic memorial to one who was a world-famous traveler in a day of many famous travelers (Rome, 1510).

That great interest was shown in Italy over the discovery of America is obvious from the various editions of the Columbus *Letter* printed in Rome in 1493; from Peter Martyr's *Libretto* (Venice, 1504); and from the many editions of Montalboddo's *Paesi novamenta retrovati*, which included the relations of such Italians as Columbus, Cadamosto, and Vespucci. And if Asia had her Varthema, so did America have her Benzoni, an intelligent sight-seer untouched by Spanish patriotism, who wrote a popular book with a frankness that enraged the Spaniards. Likewise, had it not been for the pen of Pigafetta, knowledge of Magellan's circumnavigation would be far more limited; while for southern Asia in the later days of Portuguese power we owe much to Cesare Federici's *Viaggio nell India Orientale et oltra l'India* (Venice, 1587), and to Gasparo Balbi's *Viaggio dell' India Orientali*, 1579–1588 (Venice, 1590). The last of the classic Italian travelers of the Renaissance was Pietro della Valle, whose *Viaggi* (Rome, 1657–63), is rich in material about Persia and India.

A highly noteworthy traveler and writer on geography should be mentioned here, for although he defies classification as a European, yet his life's work was written in Italy. This quaint figure was Al Hassan Ibn Mohammed Al Wezaz Al Fasi, better known by his Christianized name Leo Africanus. Born in Granada some years before its capture by the Spaniards, Leo was taken to Morocco by his parents at an early age, and during his early manhood traveled throughout Moslem North Africa, even penetrating to Timbuctoo and the Niger valley. On one fateful occasion, while on a coastal voyage, he was captured by Christian pirates, and since he was a person of quite unusual intelligence, he was sent as a present to Pope Leo X (Giovanni de Medici). Pope Leo was so pleased to find that his slave was a man of learning that he freed him and gave him a pension; the Moor was soon converted to Christianity, and was baptized with the Pope's names as Giovanni Leone. Leo probably arrived in Rome about 1520; for the next twenty or thirty years he lived there and appears to have been a general favorite with the literati. All the while he was engaged in writing his fine work on Africa, making the first draft in Arabic and then translating it into Italian. This book, which proved to be a very popular and quite definitive work, first came out in Ramusio's collection (Venice, 1550); it was reprinted extensively throughout Europe and was translated into English by John Pory in 1600. It is to be feared that Leo never saw his book in print, however; for he returned to Tunis before mid-century and died there about 1552, apparently in the faith of his fathers.

The most celebrated figure in Italian geographical literature of the sixteenth century was Gian Battista Ramusio (1485–1557), a Venetian well born, well educated, and from youth imbued with a love of geography. It is said that he opened a school of geography in his house in Venice, and as early as 1523 he conceived the ambitious scheme of bringing together accounts of all the more important voyages and travels. To this end he labored for more than thirty years; he spared no pains in ransacking Italy, Spain, and Portugal for contributions, which he translated when necessary into the picturesque Italian idiom of his day. In 1550 the first volume of his *Delle Navigazioni e Viaggi* appeared in Venice, devoted for the most part to Africa and Southern Asia. Among its more important relations were included Leo's *Africa*; the accounts of Cadamosto, da Gama, Cabral, and Vespucci from the *Paesi*; Varthema's travels; Alvares' work on Abyssinia; the description of India and adjacent lands by Thomé Lopes, Duarte Barbosa, and Andrew Corsali; the journeys of Conti and Santo Stephano; and Pigafetta's journal of the Magellan voyage. The second volume, which did not appear until 1559, after Ramusio's death, is concerned with Central Asia, Russia, and the Northern Seas. Included in it are the travels of Marco Polo (in a curious composite recension of various texts, resembling most closely the recently discovered codex in Toledo Cathedral); Hayton of Armenia; the Venetian missions to Persia; Paolo Giovo's book on the Turks; and, in the second edition (1574), the journeys of Rubriquis and Odoric, Heberstein's travels in Russia, and the apocryphal voyages of the Zeni to Greenland. The third volume (Venice, 1556) is purely of American interest, including among its contents Peter Martyr's first three Decades; the entire 1535 edition of Oviedo y Valdes; Cortes' Second, Third, and Fourth Letters; Cabeza de Vaca's relation of his wanderings; Coronado's journey; the voyages of Ulloa and Alarcon along the Pacific Coast; Xeres' account of the conquest of Peru; Orellana's voyage down the Amazon; as well as the exploits of Verrazano and Jacques Cartier. Ramusio, who truly earned the sobriquet of the Italian Hakluyt, was preëminent as an editor; he handled his material with great skill and produced a collection of unique value.

French geographical literature of the Renaissance bears considerable resemblance to Italian. There were fewer French explorers and travelers, but there was a very intelligent reading public, whose curiosity about non-European lands was satisfied by numerous translations. Thus the

Columbus *Letter* had a French edition in 1493, and the *Paesi* proved quite popular with at least six printings, while the Pigafetta account of Magellan's circumnavigation was published in France possibly before it was in Italy. A Renaissance Frenchman interested in the New World could read in his own language Peter Martyr, Oviedo y Valdes, Lopez de Gomara, Benzoni, Las Casas, and Acosta; for the Portuguese Indies he had Castanheda, Alvares, and Maffei at his disposal; for North Africa he had Leo Africanus; and for China he had Gonzalez de Mendoza. But one looks in vain for original French geographical works of the first rank, and even good publications of a secondary nature are few and far between.

The few geographical works by Frenchmen that existed were for the most part concerned with the French attempts at colonization — in Canada, in Brazil, and in Florida. Thus we have the precious *Brief Récit de la navigation faicte ès isles de Canada* (Paris, 1545), by Jacques Cartier, and the excellent descriptions of the St. Lawrence by Jean Alfonce, Roberval's chief pilot (*Les Voyages avantureux*, Poitiers, 1559, and the *Cosmographie*, Paris, 1904). For Villegagnon's Huguenot colony at Rio de Janeiro there are two authorities: André Thevet and Jean de Lery. Thevet, a Franciscan friar who had traveled widely in the Levant, and who occupied the semi-official position of French geographer royal, took part in the expedition as an observer, and after a year with the colonists he returned to France to write his authoritative *Les Singularités de la France antarctique* (Paris, 1557). Impartial though Thevet was, as a Catholic priest he was strongly suspect by the Calvinists, and a fellow-colonist, Jean de Lery, wrote his *Histoire d'un voyage fait en la Terre du Bresil* (La Rochelle, 1578), to correct what he called the errors and falsehoods of the friar.

The Huguenot attempts at colonization in Florida had their chroniclers, too. In *The Whole and True Discoverye of Terra Florida* (London, 1563), Jean Ribaut gave the first detailed account of his voyage to the shores of North America. It will be recalled that Ribaut returned to France, but had to flee to England; his book was accordingly printed there and was not published in France until 1875! René de Laudonnière wrote three notable letters concerning the French in Florida, which were published as *L'Histoire notable de la Floride* (Paris, 1586), and were dedicated to Sir Walter Raleigh. An elderly carpenter of Dieppe, Nicholas Le Challeux, wrote a plain, straightforward account of the massacre of the French by the Spaniards in *Discours de l'histoire de la Floride* (Dieppe, 1566), and the vivid narrative of Jacques Le Moyne is included along with his magnificent pictures in the second part of de Bry's *Grands Voyages*. The tragic histories of both the futile colonial attempts of Brazil and Florida are related in Voisin de la Popellinière's

Les Trois Mondes (Paris, 1582), an important cosmographical book, which contains a great deal of information on early America.

Not until the first years of the seventeenth century was a French colonizing venture successful, when the establishment of a permanent settlement in the St. Lawrence Valley was accomplished by Samuel de Champlain. Fortunately Champlain was as good a writer as he was a colonizer, and in *Les Voyages du Sieur de Champlain Xaintongeois* (Paris, 1613), we have the great classic on the foundation of Canada. As an admirable complement to Champlain's book, there is the delightful *Histoire de la Nouvelle France* (Paris, 1609) by Marc Lescarbot, a lawyer with a taste for belles-lettres, who accompanied Champlain on his colonizing venture at Port Royal in Nova Scotia in 1606.

A few first-hand French narratives of travel in the East, particularly of travel in the latter part of the period, have come down to us. For the Levant there is the copiously illustrated *Navigations et pérégrinations orientales* (Lyons, 1567), by Nicholas de Nicolay, a work that merited an English translation in 1585 by Thomas Washington. Frenchmen began arriving in India about the same time as the English and Dutch; the voyage of François Pyrard of Laval (Paris, 1619) provides a superb description of Goa in the days of its magnificent decadence. There is also the interesting *Voyages en Afrique, Asie, Indes Orientales et Occidentales* (Paris, 1617), by Jean Mocquet, Henry IV's custodian of the museum at the Tuileries; and the relation (long suspected of being mere fiction) of Sieur de Feynes, Comte de Monfart, published in England (before it was in France) as *An Exact and Curious Survey of All the East Indies* (London, 1615). The unreliable and bewildering *Voyages fameux du Sieur Vincent Leblanc Marsiellois* (Paris, 1649), might also be mentioned, while the ill-fated voyage to the East Indies (1601) in which Pyrard took part is chronicled in François Martin's *Description du premier voyage faict aux Indes Orientales par les François* (Paris, 1604). A useful collection, including the rather dubious account of Pierre Malherbe, is found in Pierre Bergeron's *Traite de la navigation et des voyages de découvertes* (Paris, 1629).

German geographical literature of the Renaissance contains even fewer first-hand narrations of travel than the French. But that literature nevertheless had its own importance, as during the first half of the sixteenth century Germany was the principal center of the development of both mathematical and descriptive geography. This science, presaged by the cartographic and astronomical work of Georg Peuerbach (1423–1461), his pupil Regiomontanus (1436–1476), the voyager and globemaker Martin Behaim (1459–1507), and Martin Waldseemüller (1470–1518), was largely of a theoretical nature. Of the men just named, only

Martin Waldseemüller can rightly be classed as a geographical author, for his *Cosmographiae Introductio* (St. Dié, 1507), was an essay on geography designed to accompany his great map of the same year; it included in its text Vespucci's *Quattuor navigationes* and is, moreover, famous for inadvertently misnaming two continents. However, this German school of geographers had its greatest exponents in Peter Apian (1501–52) and Sebastian Münster (1489–1552). Apian was an astronomer and a mathematician; in his *Cosmographicus Liber* (Landshut, 1524; subsequently edited by the great Flemish mathematician, Gemma Phrysius, under the simpler title of *Cosmographia*) he based the whole science on mathematics and measurement, following Ptolemy in making a distinction between geography (the study of the earth as a whole) and chorography (the study of specific areas). His work may best be described as a theoretical textbook; for a hundred years it was a standard source.

Münster, on the other hand, was a disciple of Strabo: he paid no regard to the mathematical basis of geography, but simply gave an exhaustive description of the world, country by country. His interests were strongly in the productions of the various regions, and in the manners and customs of the inhabitants. His *Cosmographia Universalis* (Basel, 1544), is therefore a descriptive geography pure and simple; it was the most complete work on the subject produced up to that time, and was so definitive that in the century following its appearance it passed through no less than forty-six editions in six languages. Treating geography wholly from a descriptive angle, the work of Münster forms an admirable companion volume to Apian's book, which approaches the subject from a mathematical and scientific one. It is hardly surprising, then, that the two men between them in effect commenced the separation between what were long called mathematical and political geography; the first appealing mainly to scientists, the second to historians.

Of first-hand accounts of travel by Germans, only four demand notice and three of them deal with South America. Nicolaus Federmann in his *Indianische Historia* (Hagenau, 1557), told (through the medium of his clerk) of his journey in search of El Dorado in western Venezuela and the Colombian highlands. Hans Stade of Hesse, in that very popular narrative, *Warhafftige Historia* (Marburg, 1557), related his experiences as a prisoner among the cannibals of southern Brazil; likewise Ulrich Schmidt or Schmidel described his wanderings in the Plate valley with Mendoza and Irala, in his often-reprinted *Warhafftige Beschreibunge* (Frankfurt, 1567). The only German to write at first-hand about the East (other than pilgrimage literature) was Dr. Leonhard Rauwolff of Augsburg, whose botanical researches (1573–1576) took him through the Ottoman Empire and Mesopotamia, and resulted in his *Beschreibung der Reyss in die Morgenländer* (Lauingen, 1582). These four men were probably the only Germans of the Renaissance to leave accounts of travel "off the beaten track": the forte of the Teutons in geographical literature, as has just been emphasized, lay in other directions.

That there was interest among the reading public in travel as well as in the more theoretical aspects of geography is evident from the popularity of collections of voyages. As early as 1508 the *Paesi* had been printed in Nürnberg as *Newe unbekanthe Landte und ein Newe Weldte in kurtz Verganger Zeythe erfunden*, and in 1532 Simon Grynaeus had published in Basel the first edition of his popular *Novus Orbis*, a book which contained the *Paesi* narratives with the addition of Varthema, Marco Polo, and Peter Martyr. Far more famous, however, were the delightful productions of the family of de Bry, Flemings settled in Frankfurt, who toward the end of the century conceived the grandiose scheme of publishing a series of lavishly illustrated folios dealing both with America and the Orient. De Bry's stately *Grand Voyages*, produced in thirteen parts in Frankfurt between 1590 and 1634 is indeed the cornerstone of every library of Americana, containing as it does Hariot's account of the Roanoke colony; the accounts of the French in Florida; the narratives of Stade and Schmidel; Benzoni's book (which takes up three parts); the voyages of Drake, Cavendish, Quiros, Spilbergen, Schouten, and many others; accounts of Virginia by Captain John Smith and Ralph Hamor; and various other narratives and descriptions by many contributors. The *Petits Voyages* are in twelve parts, ranging in date from 1598 to 1628: they deal with Africa, Asia, the East Indies, and the Northeast Passage. In spite of the name of the series, the volumes therein are sizable folios, albeit somewhat shorter than the magnificent books that make up the *Grands Voyages*. Included therein are Lopes' *Congo*, Linschoten's work, accounts of the early Dutch voyages to the Orient, such as those of Houtman, Neck, and Spilbergen, and also de Veer's narrative of the Arctic voyages of Barents. They are all lavishly illustrated and replete with maps.

Another series, and one of even greater historical import, was started at the close of the sixteenth century by Levinus Hulsius, a native of Ghent who, like the de Brys, had settled in Frankfurt. In 1598 he published the first volume of a collection of twenty-six voyages, printed in the more convenient quarto size. His interests were largely Dutch and English, and because of its convenient format and its wealth of illustrations, his enterprise proved so popular that its publication extended until 1663, when it totaled no less than sixty-nine volumes. Hulsius' achievement of this worthy purpose makes an appropriate close to two centuries of geographical literature.

As citizens of the Low Countries working in Germany, the de Brys and Hulsius form a link between Germany and Holland, so that a glance at the records of travel by Dutchmen is next in order, Holland came late into the field of navigation and discovery, latest in fact of all the nations destined to have a colonial future. Therefore her geographical writings come near the very end of the Renaissance; yet she produced several geographical writers of note, at least one of whom, Jan Huyghen van Linschoten, was of the very greatest importance.

As noticed above, Linschoten had spent several years in India, where he had displayed an avaricious thirst for acquiring knowledge of the East. He had also resided for some time in the Azores and had accompanied Barents on the first two voyages to the Arctic. Like Hakluyt he was a propagandist; he wanted to stimulate Holland to overseas enterprise. This aim is not especially evident in his writings, which are more of a descriptive and navigational character; but as a promoter of projects he must have been very active in the 1590's. His famous work is the *Itinerario* (Amsterdam, 1596), the fruit of his own experience and his deep study, intended, as it was, as a definitive practical textbook for his countrymen. The book is divided into three sections. The first part concerns his own experiences in India, together with a full description of that country. The second part contains a collection of routes to India and America, translated from the manuscripts of Spanish and Portuguese pilots; it is especially rich in details of routes beyond Malacca, including the East Indies and Chinese waters, and it was by this compilation that Linschoten rendered the greatest service to his countrymen. The third part consists of a coast pilot and descriptive geography of Africa and America, taken from Duarte Lopes, Peter Martyr, Oviedo, and de Lery, and like the second part it was of practical use to the Dutch navigators. Thirty-six plates and plans, together with six large maps, complete a work without which no Dutch skipper ventured to sea. As a traveler, as a writer, and as a pleader for overseas expansion, Linschoten remains the leading geographical figure in Renaissance Holland.

Narratives of Dutch voyaging began to appear at the turn of the century, and concerned the East Indies, the Arctic, and the Dutch circumnavigations. The first Dutch voyage to Sumatra and Java is commemorated in Cornelis Houtman's *Verhael vande Reyse by de Hollandtsche Schepen gedaen naer Oost Indien* (Middleburg, 1597), while the voyage of Neck and Warwijk gave rise to a pleasantly illustrated and interesting book ascribed to the former, *Journael ofte Dagh-Register* (Amsterdam, 1600). Both these works were reprinted by de Bry and Hulsius, and were early translated into English for the edification of the East India Company. Most heroic of the early Dutch voyages were Barents' three valiant attempts to penetrate the Northeast Passage. Gerrit de Veer, a survivor of the second and third expeditions, wrote a truly wonderful account of these ventures in his *Waerachtighe Beschryvinghe* (Amsterdam, 1598), in which he recounted in stirring prose the hardships of the terrible winter spent in the Arctic wastes. Likewise the various Dutch voyages through the Straits of Magellan were described in popular narratives. Van Noort's circumnavigation resulted in the well-illustrated *Beschryvinghe vande Voyagie om den geheelen Werelt Cloot* (Amsterdam, 1602), which went through several editions; it is especially interesting because of its descriptive passages on Japan, and the engravings of Japanese shipping and natives must be among the earliest done in Europe.

Such an event as the discovery of Cape Horn naturally aroused much interest, and Schouten's story of his passage around the Horn was told in his *Diarium . . . Itineris* (Amsterdam, 1619). His shipmate Jacob le Maire, who died on the return, left a journal which was printed with the account of another famous Dutch circumnavigator, Joris van Spilbergen. The vivid narrative of the latter's passage of the Straits and his piratical cruise along the west coast of South America is told along with Le Maire's relation in *Oost ende West-Indische Spiegel* (Leyden, 1619), a book attractively embellished with maps and plates. In fact, in writing of Dutch maritime literature of the period, it is impossible not to emphasize the large part that engravings play in the attractiveness and utility of the volumes. Holland was at that time the center of the most active cartographic school in Europe, exemplified by Mercator and Ortelius, and also had an able group of native engravers. Dutch geographical books of the Renaissance (under which head we may perhaps include those of de Bry and Hulsius) are distinguished by a lavishness of illustration and cartography which sets them apart, in a higher sphere of attractiveness, from productions of a similar nature of other countries.

TUDOR GEOGRAPHICAL LITERATURE

Having progressed through Continental Europe in our study, we at last find ourselves in a country whose literature of travel and discovery may be said to rival that of Spain and Portugal. England had little geographical literature worthy of the name until after the middle of the sixteenth century, but in the ensuing seventy-five years she developed to perfection a special variety of this literature — the collection of accounts of travels and voyages. It is true that other nations had produced collections of explorations and discoveries: Italy had the *Paesi* and Ramusio; Germany had Grynaeus, the de Brys, and Hulsius. But the English collections of Eden, Hakluyt, and Purchas were not only more complete than any that had preceded them; they also had a purpose in view, in that they were propagandist pleadings for the creation of a greater England overseas. In the case of the other nations, travel literature followed

expansion: the great chronicles of Barros, Castanheda, and Braz Albuquerque were published when Portuguese power was even beginning to
decline, while Oviedo y Valdes produced his history after Mexico had
been conquered and when Pizarro was already in Peru. But Hakluyt's
activity took place on the eve of the formation of the East India Company and the settlement at Jamestown. Linschoten, it is true, was a very
active force in Holland, but his advocacy of a Dutch empire is hardly
patent in his writings. Of the various types of national travel literature,
therefore, it may be said that England's alone was aimed explicitly at
stimulating expansion. It is this quality, coupled with the epic greatness
with which the material is handled, which places the English collections
of voyages on a par with the Portuguese chronicles.

England came late into the picture, both with respect to exploration
and travel literature. The first work of even passing geographical interest to be written by a Tudor Englishman was *A New Interlude and a
Mery of the Nature of the IIII Elements* (London, *circa* 1519), a lecture
in verse, disguised as a play, on natural science, by John Rastell, Sir
Thomas More's brother-in-law. Rastell himself had attempted a voyage
from Bristol to the New Found Lands in 1517, but had got no farther
than Ireland; he was therefore keen on the new discoveries, and in the
cosmographical section of his whimical, doggerel poem he described the
land found by the Cabots more than two decades earlier. It is to Rastell's
credit that even at that early date he realized the continental nature of
North America, and it is a fair implication that through his interlude he
was trying to provoke support for a further American voyage.

Another early milestone appeared in 1527, when Robert Thorne wrote
his celebrated letters to Henry VIII and Dr. Edward Lee, Henry VIII's
Ambassador to Spain, advocating the use of the northern passages for
English commerce with the East Indies. These two letters, known as *The
Book of Robert Thorne*, circulated for more than half a century in manuscript, and were finally printed in Hakluyt's *Divers Voyages* (1582).
In 1541 Roger Barlow, a close friend of both Thorne and Sebastian
Cabot, translated Enciso's *Suma de Geographia*, a vigorous rendition,
destined to remain in manuscript for four centuries; and about ten years
later William Thomas, Italophile and Marian martyr, rendered into English the travels in Persia of the Venetians Barbaro and Contarini from
the Aldine edition of 1545. This slight catalogue shows how sporadic and
widely separated these early efforts were: a cosmographical play; a letter
favoring the northern passages; a translation of a Spanish geographical
manual; and another of a Venetian mission to the Middle East — these
four works spread over a generation, and only the first printed in its
author's lifetime.

It may in truth be said, then, that no real study of the progress of

Renaissance geography was published or even written in England in the
first half of the sixteenth century, and for the general reading public who
had no access to foreign books the stage portraying the great discoveries
was invisible. The year of grace 1553 may be taken as the symbolic date
when the curtain was lifted; for in that year Willoughby sailed in his
attempt to reach China by the Northeast Passage, and Wyndham made
his voyage to the Guinea Coast of West Africa; in that year, too, Richard
Eden published the first really serious geographical work to be printed
in England.

Richard Eden was a young Cambridge graduate, who was in William
Cecil's employ, and who was a friend and admirer of the aged Sebastian
Cabot. From boyhood he had been interested in geography, and he early
conceived the design of breaking the long silence which had prevailed in
England on the subject — thereby enlightening his countrymen about
the exploits of other nations in the new lands. His first work was slight
and experimental, but was an enormous step in the right direction. Published as *A Treatyse of the Newe India*, it was a translation of that part
of Sebastian Münster's *Cosmographia* that dealt with the Columbian and
Vespuccian voyages, Magellan's circumnavigation, and the early exploits
of the Portuguese in the East. As such, it brought the names of Columbus, Vespucci, Magellan, and Albuquerque before the British reading
public for the first time, and slight as it was, it held rich promise for the
literature which was to follow in the reigns of Elizabeth and James. Eden
had a sound, critical feeling for his subject, and two years later he brought
out a work far more authoritative, fuller, and more useful. This, *The
Decades of the Newe Worlde, or West India* (London, 1555), was the
first collection of voyages in English. It included, at least in part, the
histories of Peter Martyr, Oviedo y Valdes, and Lopez de Gomara, as
well as the Pigafetta-Magellan narrative; an account of the Cabot voyages, several descriptions of Russia, and finally, as stop-press news, an
account of the first two English voyages to West Africa. Doubtless the
outstanding accomplishment of this book was to present for the first time
in England a substantial corpus of information on the great discoveries,
revealing at the same time the major writers on the subject. But this was
not all: in Eden's preface was outlined for the first time the advocacy of
a British colony in North America. With the publication of Eden's *Decades*, therefore, we may say that England fully awoke to the new day;
the fact that the world had changed so materially was at last made
evident.

This collection was Eden's great achievement, although he lived on
to translate the useful navigational manuals of Martin Cortes from the
Spanish (1561) and of Jean Taisnier from the French (1576), and died
in the latter year on the eve of completing a considerably expanded

second edition of the *Decades*. It was left to his disciple Richard Willes to finish the work, which as *The History of Travayle in the West and East Indies*, was published in 1577, its publication doubtless being timed with an eye to Frobisher's voyages to the Northwest Passage. For this reason it included much new material on Asia, such as Varthema's travels, Pereira's description of China, and Maffei's account of Japan, as well as narratives of English journeys (such as Jenkinson's) in Russia and Central Asia. As a result, in Willes' edition Cathay and the way thither were for the first time made real to the English reader, just as Eden's first edition brought forward America as a reality for the first time to the Tudor public.

Eden was a pioneer; he was not as great a figure as Hakluyt, but it was he who started English geographical literature on its course. And his suggestion of overseas expansion burgeoned into positive advocacy and argument among his successors. This propaganda literature is well exemplified in Sir Humphrey Gilbert's *A Discourse of a Discoverie for a New Passage to Cataia*, a powerful plea for the Northwest Passage printed in London in 1576, although written about ten years before and circulated extensively in manuscript in the intervening decade. More than any other piece of literature this was responsible for the impulse behind the Frobisher voyages. This thesis was reiterated in John Davis' earnestly sincere *The Worlds Hydrographical Description* (London, 1595). And everywhere behind the scenes in the period was the mysterious figure of John Dee. During this time he was engaged in a massive work, which thus far has not in its entirety seen the light of day, or unfortunately never shall — *General and Rare Memorials Pertayning to the Perfect Arte of Navigation*. Only the first part was published, the *Pety Navy Royall* (London, 1577), which sets forth the advantages of having a fleet of ships in permanent commission and suggests means whereby such a scheme could be financed, a prerequisite of the policy of expansion which Dee was advocating. The second part of the work, entirely navigational, has been completely lost; the third part, apparently political, was finished but was burned as politically dangerous. Only the bulk of the fourth portion survives in manuscript in the British Museum — "The Great Volume of Famous and Rich Discoveries" (Cotton MS., Vitellius C. vii); a treatise on Renaissance exploration, known to Hakluyt and Purchas, which still awaits the attention of some assidious editor. This last part, as well as the first, displays Dee's pleading for overseas enterprise; its general purpose is to show how the English might bring home the fabled riches of Cathay and the wealth of Ophir.

One of the best ways of making one's plans in a given field is to find out what the other man has been doing, and in the earlier part of Elizabeth's reign there were three excellent translators who made it their task to publish worth-while travel narratives from the French and Spanish. First of these was Thomas Hackett, a well-known Elizabethan publisher, who translated accounts of the French Huguenot colonies in Florida and Brazil. To him we owe the English versions of Jean Ribaut's *The Whole and True Discovrye of Terra Florida* (London, 1563), translated from the original manuscript which did not appear in a French edition until the nineteenth century; Nicholas le Challeux's *Last Voyage . . . into Terra Florida* (London, 1566) and André Thevet's *The New Founde Worlde, or Antarctike* (London, 1568). These books may well have been planned to encourage English colonization of the American seaboard; Thevet's book was in any case considered so useful that it was included in Frobisher's nautical library. Translations from the Spanish were done by two retired merchants of the Spanish trade, who were both happily possessed of considerable literary talents. One, John Frampton of Bristol, had been seized and tortured by the Inquisition while on a voyage to Lisbon and Cadiz; eventually he made his escape and revenged himself on Catholic Spain by translating various standard geographical texts for the benefit of the more aggressive of his countrymen. Among these translations were Monardes' book on botany, rendered under the picturesque title of *Joyfull Newes out of the Newe Founde Worlde* (London, 1577); the American section of Enciso's geography as *A Briefe Description of the Portes . . . of the Weast India* (London, 1578); Bernardino de Escalante's *A Discourse of the Navigation . . . to the Realmes of the East* (London, 1579); *Marco Polo*, along with *Nicolo de Conti* (London, 1579); and Pedro de Medina's *The Arte of Navigation* (London, 1581). The other translator, Thomas Nicholas, had lived in the Canary Islands; like Frampton he had fallen foul of the Inquisition, and when he got to England he put before the reading public the stories of the conquests of Mexico and Peru, in translations of Lopez de Gomara's *Historie of the Conquest of the Weast India* (London, 1578), and Zarate's *History of the Discoverie and Conquest of Peru* (London, 1581). Only one work was translated from the Portuguese in this period: Nicholas Lichefield rendered into English the first book of Lopes de Castanheda's *Historie of the Discoverie and Conquest of the East Indias* (London, 1582), and dedicated it to Sir Francis Drake. Lichefield may have been a pen name of Nicholas himself.

Meanwhile in 1580 another translation had appeared, done by a young Anglo-Italian at the instigation of an unknown and youthful enthusiast of geography. The book was Jacques Cartier's *The Two Navigations and Discoveries*, the translator was John Florio and the inspirer of the project was Richard Hakluyt.

Born in London about 1552 of an old family in Herefordshire, Hakluyt was educated at Westminister School and Christ Church, Oxford, where he took holy orders. Thereafter, he came strongly under the spell of his cousin, Richard Hakluyt of the Middle Temple, a lawyer whose hobby was geography, and who had established an important place for himself as a consultant geographer. The elder's teachings did not fall on barren soil, for his younger namesake dedicated his life to the propagation of geographical knowledge, always with the idea in mind of arousing Englishmen to enterprise overseas. With a prophetic enthusiasm for the possibilities of a future British Empire, the younger Hakluyt throughout his life stressed two especially favored areas: eastern North America and India. This is unquestionably why his first product was the instigation of the translation of Cartier's voyages to Canada. Two years later he brought out a publication on the same North American theme, *Divers Voyages Touching the Discoverie of America* (London, 1582), a collection of the records and writings of the Cabots, Robert Thorne, Verrazano, the Zeni, and Jean Ribaut. In this precious little quarto the conscious purpose of the editor is revealed by the common subject of the narratives. Two years after its publication Hakluyt wrote a wholehearted plea for American colonization in the *Discourse on the Western Planting*, a powerful exposition, circulated in manuscript but not printed for another three centuries (1877).

Hakluyt's knowledge of the field was further widened by his residence in Paris from 1583 to 1588 as chaplain to the English ambassador; here he learned much of the maritime enterprises of other nations, and found that the English were reputed for their "sluggish security." While in Paris he published a complete and revised Latin edition of Peter Martyr's *Decades* (1587), a work translated by Michael Lok (Frobisher's backer) in 1612. All this time he was tirelessly active in gathering materials for his great collection — the collection of English voyages to date, which was designed to stimulate Englishmen to even greater exploits. After his return to England and the year after the defeat of the Armada, the first edition of his monumental work appeared, the one volume *The Principall Navigations, Voiages, and Discoveries of the English Nation* (London, 1589). England had been at least from the fifteenth century a maritime nation; from the later days of Henry VIII she had been a naval nation; she was now about to become a colonial nation. Richard Hakluyt, by chronicling the first two phases through individual narratives, strove to promote the third phase. The plan of the *Principal Navigations* was Ramusio's with improvements and modifications; Hakluyt showed himself the better editor and the better archivist, while in addition he was a consultant geographer with a mission in life. It is not to be wondered at, therefore, that the first edition of the *Principal Navigations* transcended anything that had gone before, though it in turn was surpassed by the second edition. The first edition was divided into three parts: the first dealt with the Levant Company, early travels in the Near and Middle East, and the early voyages to

West Africa; the second concerned the search for the Northeast Passage, the travels in Russia and Central Asia of Jenkinson and his successors; the third part narrated exploits in the Western Hemisphere, such as the voyages of Hawkins and Frobisher, Hariot's account of the Roanoke colony, promotion literature of Gilbert and Peckham, and the great voyages of Drake, Davis, and Cavendish.

That Hakluyt's first edition was magnificent one cannot deny; but there was still much more information which he had not included, and there was so much travel by Britons in the ensuing decade that the volume was soon out of date. Throughout the 1590's, therefore, the indefatigable editor set himself to the formidable task of expanding the collection and bringing it up to date; an undertaking which may be appreciated by the fact that the first edition contained about 700,000 words, while the second contained about 1,700,000. At length, in 1598 the first volume of the second edition of the *Principal Navigations* appeared, to be followed in the next two years by the second and third volumes (1599, 1600). This was indeed Hakluyt's monumental masterpiece, and the great prose epic of the Elizabethan period. In design it was similar to the first edition: the first volume concerned voyages to the north and northeast; the second volume, to the south and southeast; the third volume, to America. All sections were expanded; the first two were approximately doubled and the American part was almost tripled. Much that was new and important was included: the travels of Newbery and Fitch, Lancaster's first voyage, the new achievements in the Spanish Main, and particularly Raleigh's tropical adventures. At first sight the expanded work appears a vast, confused repository, but closer examination reveals a definite unity and a continuous thread of policy. The book must always remain a great work of history, and a great sourcebook of geography, while the accounts themselves constitute a body of narrative literature which is of the highest value in understanding the spirit and the tendencies of the Tudor age.

The three-volume *Principal Navigations* was Hakluyt's *magnum opus*; never again did he attempt anything so ambitious. But parallel with the *Principal Navigations* he was carrying out a work of almost equal value — that of translation. Very little non-English material was included in his collection; but that much of the travel literature produced abroad would be of the utmost importance in England was obvious to his keen insight. Hence from the time of Florio's *Cartier*, for almost thirty years, he was causing translations to be made (and on occasion making them himself) of what seemed to him to be definitive books of lasting utility. While in Paris he had translated Laudonnière's *Florida* (London, 1587); the next year he engaged Robert Parke to translate Mendoza's *China* (London, 1588); and in 1597 a clerical friend, Abraham Hartwell, translated Lopes' *Congo* at Hakluyt's suggestion. Most active of Hakluyt's translators was William Phillip, whose forte was Dutch travel literature. To him we owe the English *Linschoten* (London, 1598), Houtman's account of the first Dutch voyage to the East (also 1598), and de Veer's narrative of the Barents voyages (London, 1609). The picturesque John Pory, associated with both the Levant and Virginia, translated Leo's *Africa* (London, 1600), adding much new material of his own. Other disciples of Hakluyt doing similar work were William Walker, who translated the account of Neck's voyage from the Dutch in 1601, and a Frenchman named Erondelle, who Englished Lescarbot's *Nova Francia* (London, 1609). Hakluyt himself possibly translated Galvão's *Discoveries of the World* (London, 1601), and also de Soto's *Virginia Richly Valued* (London, 1609), while Michael Lok rendered Hakluyt's own edition of Peter Martyr into English in 1612. These translations, then, are part and parcel of Hakluyt's activity; they presented the foreign side of Renaissance travel, as the *Principal Navigations* presented the English side; and both were intended for the use and the inspiration of Englishmen. Hakluyt's activity may therefore be judged by its results, for without the collected voyages and the translations, the vital spark of expansion might well have been lacking. He was indeed the greatest literary figure among British empire-builders.

After his death in 1616 his work was continued by Samuel Purchas, a rather uninspired clergyman with the gift of tireless energy. Purchas in 1625 published his *Hakluytus Posthumus, or Purchas His Pilgrimes, Contayning a History of the World in Sea Voyages and Land Trauells by Englishmen and Others*, a vast work incorporating much of Hakluyt along with accounts of the recent voyages of the East India Company and of the colonization of Virginia, as well as a great deal of translation. The *Pilgrimes* consists of four huge volumes, though the fourth edition (1626) of Purchas' *Pilgrimage*, being exactly the same size, is often catalogued as its fifth volume. Purchas' collection is indeed a vast treasure of geographical history and is, of course, a source of the highest importance.

However, the unifying theme that runs through Hakluyt's *Principal Navigations* is absent, and it is hard for the average reader to see the wood for the trees. Possibly this is due to the vastness of the material, and in part to the fact that Purchas had not the editorial genius of Hakluyt; but in any case the propagandist pleading was not so necessary, since by 1625 the British Empire had been fairly solidly founded in Virginia and India. Unquestionably Purchas was not made to Hakluyt's measure, and he has naturally suffered by comparison. But he was no mean figure in his own right, and students of English literature and history should be grateful to such men as Sir William Foster who have but recently shown this very useful literary personage in his proper stature. Without Purchas much of the record of early English expansion would have been lost (especially as regards the voyages to the Orient); thanks to his industry and ability as a garnerer and collector a great amount of vivid and valuable narrative has been saved and is in print. Samuel Purchas deserves well of posterity.

So much was incorporated in the encyclopedic collections of Hakluyt and Purchas that the separately published records of English travel, especially before 1600, seem few in number and relatively slight; also striking in several cases is the time lag between the ventures themselves and the printing of the narratives. First of all stories of English voyages to appear by itself was John Hawkins' account of the tragic venture of San Juan Ulúa: *The Troublesome Voyadge . . . to the Parties of Guynea and the West-Indies* (London, 1569), an extremely rare little work, which is well supplemented by the narrative of another survivor, long a Spanish prisoner: Job Hortop's *The Travailes of an English Man* (London, 1591). Frobisher's voyages must have aroused interest on a national scale, and several relations, in prose and verse, have come down to us, of which the most interesting is George Best's *A true Discourse of the Late Voyages of Discoverie, for the Finding of a Passage to Cathaya* (London, 1578). There were also noteworthy accounts of the third voyage by Dionyse Settle and John Ellis (the first published in London in 1577, the second in 1578).

Admirers of Sir Francis Drake had to wait far longer to read the separate accounts of his more theatrical exploits. Not until 1626 did Philip Nichols recount the stirring deeds of the Panama raid of 1572–73 in *Sir Francis Drake Revived*, while the separate publication of the story of the circumnavigation was delayed until *The World Encompassed by Sir Francis Drake* appeared in 1628. On the other hand, the venture of 1585 received almost contemporary attention in Walter Bigges' *Discourse of Sir Frances Drakes West Indian Voyage* (London, 1589), a small volume embellished with the celebrated maps by Battista Boazio; and the last and fatal voyage of Drake and John Hawkins is narrated in Sir Henry Savile's *A Libell of Spanish Lies* (London, 1596).

One of the most graphic and readable of all Tudor narratives is *The Observations of Sir Richard Hawkins in his Voiage into the South Sea, 1593* (London, 1622), a dramatic story of a gallant failure, written with strong descriptive power and imagination. Another book of high literary merit is Sir Walter Raleigh's *The Discoverie of the Large, Rich, and Bewtiful Empire of Guiana* (London, 1596), while the ensuing voyage by Captain Keymis is told in the latter's very informative *A Relation of the Second Voyage to Guiana* (London, 1596). Another narration of this region, written with considerable urbanity, is Robert Harcourt's *A Relation of a Voyage to Guiana* (London, 1613).

Raleigh's earlier interest, the Roanoke Island colony, gave rise to a classic account by a brilliant young protégé of Sir Walter's, celebrated alike as a mathematician and a free-thinker. This was *A Briefe and True Report of the New Found Land of Virginia* (London, 1588), by Thomas Hariot, who had visited Virginia with the first colonists in 1585–86. For years after the failure of the colony little was done in the matter of North American enterprise besides coastal reconnaissances. Two of these voyages produced quite remarkable narratives, however. Gosnold's venture to Cape Cod and Martha's Vineyard resulted in John Brereton's *A Briefe and True Relation of the Discoverie of the North Part of Virginia* (London, 1602), while Waymouth's voyage along the coast of Maine gave rise to James Rosier's *A True Relation of the Most Prosperous Voyage . . . in the Discovery of the Land of Virginia* (London, 1605). So important are these two books, historically and geographically, that the stalwart old Americanist, Henry Stevens of Vermont, christened them "the verie two eyes of New England Historie."

As a result of the planting of the first permanent English colony in North America at Jamestown in 1607, a very considerable body of writing arose — personal narratives, promotion literature, sermons, and trivia. In these publications the name of Captain John Smith is prëeminent, not only because he was one of the principal actors, but also because he was possessed of a literary skill and fluency which made him the self-appointed historiographer of the infant colony. When the settlement was but a year old he produced the earliest account of it: *A True Relation of Such Occurrences and Accidents of Noate as Hath Hapned in Virginia since the First Planting of that Collony* (London, 1608). This was followed by the much fuller *A Map of Virginia: With a Description of the Countrey* (Oxford, 1612), in which Smith collaborated with William Symonds to produce an excellent picture of the geography and colonization of early Virginia. Before passing on to Smith's *magnum opus*, two important works by other men should be mentioned. Alexander Whitaker's *Good Newes from Virginia* (London, 1613) is an interesting first-hand narrative by the parson who married Pocahontas and John Rolfe; and Ralph Hamor's *A True Discourse of the Present Estate of Virginia* (London, 1615) gives a quaint description of that marriage, as well as much additional information about the settlement.

Smith had meanwhile turned his attention further up the coast, to what had been hitherto been called "the North Part of Virginia," and in 1616 he published *A Description of New England*, the result of his coastal survey of Massachusetts and Maine. In consequence of this reconnaissance and of the book, he was invested with the title of Admiral of New England. This work was followed by two pieces of promotion literature: *New Englands Trials* (London, 1620), and *Advertisements for the Unexperienced Planters of New England* (London, 1631). Virginia was not forgotten, however, and in 1624 he published his authoritative if some-what self-centered masterpiece, *The Generall Historie of Virginia*, which remains one of the prime works on America. This highly important and definitive publication is well supplemented by *The True Travels, Adventures, and Observations of Captaine John Smith* (London, 1630), in which his adventurous career is related in stirring prose.

England's enterprise in the East resulted in no work of the size or importance of Smith's *Generall Historie*, although the early voyages of the East India Company gave rise to several narratives of considerable merit. Lancaster's voyage for the company is well recounted in the anony-mous *A True and Large Discourse of the Voyage of the Fleet to the East Indies* (London, 1603), while the story of the men left in Java and brought home by Middleton is vividly told in Edmund Scott's *An Exact Discourse . . . of the East Indians* (London, 1606). Scott's narrative was immediately preceded by the account of Middleton's expedition, *The Last East-Indian Voyage* (London, 1606) — a narrative of quite superior merit and interest. The fortunate insistence of the directors of the East India Company that detailed logs of every voyage be kept resulted in a splendid collection of marine journals of the early voyages, still preserved in the India Office Library. Perhaps the most important of these manu-scripts are those of the voyages of Captain Floris to Bengal and Siam (1611–1615) and of Captain Saris to Japan (1612–1613), as well as the logs of Captain Best (1612–1614) and Captain Downton (1614–1615), both of whom vanquished the Portuguese in naval actions off Surat and did much thereby to secure a foothold for the company on the Indian mainland. These four logs have been edited by the Hakluyt Society in a most scholarly fashion: they are plain, vigorous accounts that qualify as "sea literature" pure and simple.

In the late Elizabethan and early Jacobean period a number of very respectable classics of personal travel were written by Englishmen, largely concerned with the Mediterranean area and the Levant. These narratives fall into a well-defined group, marked by their character, their unusual literary merit, and the fact that they cover much the same ground. Since most of the authors have been discussed above in previous chapters, it is unnecessary to rehearse their careers and travels, though emphasis should be placed on their writings. Of these wandering littera-teurs, by all means the most conscientious was Fynes Moryson, whose peregrinations throughout Europe and the Near East are chronicled in an encylopedic manner in his ponderous and thorough *Itinerary* (London, 1617). Supplementing Moryson's thorough account of the Ottoman Empire are the *Travels* of John Sanderson (edited by the Hakluyt Society, 1931). Sanderson was a merchant who lived in Constantinople almost continuously for upwards of twenty years (1584–1602), during which time he traveled throughout Asia Minor and visited the Holy Land. Then there is the naïvely illiterate journal of Thomas Dallam (Hakluyt Society, 1893), the English organ-builder who went to Constantinople in 1599 to install a gadget-filled organ in the seraglio of Mohammed III. Evidently most popular among the printed accounts of the time were the rather slight narratives of travel in Syria and Palestine by Henry Timberlake, *A True and Strange Discourse of the Travailes of Two English Pilgrimes* (London, 1603, and many later editions), and by William Biddulph, chaplain to the English merchants at Aleppo, *The Travels of Certaine Englishmen into Africa, Asia, and to the Blacke Sea, Finished 1608* (London, 1609 and 1612).

Tom Coryate, of course, wrote the whimsical but authoritative guidebook and account of travel, the *Crudities* (London, 1611), although this concerns only his walking trip to Venice. Coryate's narrative of his travels in the Levant has suffered terribly from the editorial zeal of Samuel Purchas, who made drastic excisions; while Tom's two publications from India (*Thomas Coriate Traveler for the English Wits*, London, 1616, and *Mr. T. Coriat . . . sendeth greeting: from Agra*, London, 1618), charming though they are, are merely news-letters. It is a great loss that Coryate was not vouchsafed to return from India, for he would undoubtedly have written a work on his Eastern travels which might even have outdistanced the *Crudities*. We are, however, left with a tale of thrilling adventure and hardship in the Near East and the Mediterranean area in the writings of the dour Scot, William Lithgow. His classic *A Most Delectable and True Discourse of a Peregrination in Europe, Asia . . .* first appeared in London in 1614, but went through at least five editions, being constantly added to, as Lithgow made more travels. Compared with this somber, though rough-and-tumble Caledonian, the scholarly and courtly George Sandys seems to reflect urbane dignity itself. This is evident from the narrative of his travels in Turkey, Palestine, and Egypt: *A Relation of a Journey Begun Anno Dom. 1610* (London, 1615), a handsome and well-illustrated folio, filled with classical allusions and Latin quotations.

Passing from the Levant to the Middle East, we find English travel literature beginning with the mighty journeyings, printed in Hakluyt, of Anthony Jenkinson to Turkestan and Persia (1558–1563), by which knowledge of the Oxus, of Bokhara, of the western Caucasus, and of the Sophy's court at Kazvin was put before the Tudor public. Jenkinson's successors in the hazardous trans-Caspian trade to Persia likewise had their narratives edited by Hakluyt, but the record of the very important journey of John Newbery through Iraq and then back through Persia, from one end of the country to the other (1580–1582), first was printed in the pages of Purchas. That interest in Persia and in the picturesque adventurers who went there held an important place on the literary stage is evident from the sizable literature about the Sherley brothers, of whom much the best account is William Parry's *A New and Large Discourse of the Travels of Sir Anthony Sherley* (London, 1601). This very graphic narrative is greatly to be preferred to Sir Anthony's own turgid self-justification: *His Relation of His Travels into Persia* (London, 1613), a book too tedious for the general reader. That the Sherleian adventures were popular with Londoners is shown by the tract *The Three English Brothers* (London, 1607) by Anthony Nixon, the celebrated Elizabethan pamphleteer; and the imaginative, but quite dull play by Day, Rowley, and Wilkins, *The Travailes of the Three English Brothers* (London, 1607). A work of more solid value, dealing with Persia, Robert Sherley, and John Mildenhall, is John Cartwright's *The Preachers Travels* (London, 1611) — an interesting volume by a pioneer sight-seer in that region. Another absorbing book about Southern Asia is the vigorous narrative of the shipwrecked mariner, Captain Robert Coverte, who traveled overland from Surat to Aleppo: *A True and almost Incredible Report of an Englishman that Travelled by Land Throw Many Kingdomes* (London, 1612). It relates its author's reception by the Emperor Jahangir, and his tedious journey across India, Afghanistan, and Persia, and as such is one of the best examples of a travel journal that the period produced.

Relatively little was published separately about India during the reigns of Elizabeth and James, although several vivid and important narratives of travel in India appeared in the collections of Hakluyt and Purchas. These, out of respect to their authors, should be allowed to stand by themselves. Perhaps the best of these is the vigorous relation of Ralph Fitch, one of the greatest of English travelers, whose wanderings (1583–1591), recounted in Hakluyt, took him from golden Goa to the court of the Great Mogul, and from Bengal to the fabulous Burmese metropolis of Pegu. The interesting story of William Hawkins, the first representative of the East India Company at the court of Jahangir (1608–1613), is included in Purchas, as is the narration of Hawkins' agent in Surat, William Finch (1608–1611). The mission of Hawkins' more official and more successful follower is described in the excellent journal of Sir Thomas Roe (1615–1618; Hakluyt Society, 1899), a very readable account of that diplomat's visit to India and his passages with the Great Mogul at Agra and Ajmere. This is well supplemented by the prosy narrative of Roe's chaplin, Edward Terry (first printed in condensed form in Purchas and later published as *A Voyage to East-India*, London, 1655), a work which in the quaint metaphor of his fellow-cleric, Purchas, is "a good farewell draught of English-Indian liquor." Not only India itself, but also southern Arabia and the East Indies are the subjects of the very important journal of John Jourdain (1608-17), a narration by one of the most useful of the company's servants, who had a long and distinguished career in the East (Hakluyt Society, 1905). China does not figure in first-hand accounts of Tudor and early Stuart travel, but in the letters of William Adams (published as *Memorials of the Empire of Japan* by the Hakluyt Society, 1850), and in the diary of Richard Cocks, cape merchant in the English factory at Hirado (1615–1622; Hakluyt Society, 1822), we are left with records of absorbing interest of two of the first Englishmen in Japan.

Africa, unlike Asia, has little in the way of English accounts of travel in this early period: perhaps a mere handful of relations are all that call for comment. Good, vigorous, first-hand accounts of the Guinea voyages of Wyndham and Lok appeared as far back as the 1555 collection of Eden, and two later Guinea ventures gave rise to the remarkable poems of Robert Baker (printed only in the 1589 Hakluyt), which because of their surprising dramatic power, their general theme of hardship at sea, and their foreboding mystical romanticism strangely anticipate Coleridge's *Ancient Mariner*. In prose there is the stirring record of Andrew Battell, long a prisoner of the Portuguese in Angola, and a fugitive among the savage Jaggas in the interior (printed in Purchas and republished by the Hakluyt Society, 1901). The valuable *The Golden Trade* (London, 1623) by Richard Jobson is a narrative of English enterprise on the Gambia, designed to encourage further exploitation of that region.

One may therefore regard English travel literature of the Renaissance as having reached its climax in the great collections, with a strong supporting cast of translations and separate narrations of personal travel. Throughout, the literary standard is high, while the place of this literature in the history and culture of the nation may be gauged by the fact that it was the expression of the impulse, and the narrative of the expansion, which gave rise to the British Empire. As such, this literature is equal to that of Spain and Portugal.

The effect of the corpus of geographical literature on the Renaissance mind is so far-reaching that a brief analysis is not easy. In 1400 the educated European knew nothing of the existence of an America and knew little enough about Asia and Africa; in 1600 he knew a great deal. It was as if a curtain had been raised, revealing the greater part of the earth's surface; and the revelation was made almost entirely by means of the printed book. Returning mariners doubtless told their tales to small gatherings, but the way in which the bulk of the people became conscious of the world outside the old *oikoumene* was by means of the *Columbus Letter*, the *Paesi*, the collections of Ramusio and Hakluyt, and similar works — in other words, through the geographical writings of the fifteenth and sixteenth centuries.

These writings assumed a different pattern in different countries, and this factor may give us an indication of the effect on the European public. Portugal excelled in her chronicles; Spain was perhaps outstanding for her specific accounts; England was unrivaled for her collections. Of the lands that played a lesser part, Italy produced Ramusio and an interesting group of individual travelers, while Germany was from the start the home of scientific geography, and Holland, through her engravers and cartographers, popularized the new lands by the publication of picture books that will always have a great appeal. In Portugal, where colonial expansion was the great national interest of the day, geographical literature *was* the national literature: we have only to think of Barros and Camoens to realize that. In Spain, where the intensity of the same movement was less, but still great, geographical literature looms large, but does not quite occupy the monopoly that it does in the sister kingdom. In Italy and France that literature was on a secondary level, but there was undoubtedly an avid reading public, and the influence of travel books is evident in general literature — for example in the works of Fracastoro and Giordano Bruno in Italy, and of Rabelais and Montaigne in France. A direct development of geographical literature, particularly in France (and also in England) was the "extraordinary voyage," which in the hands of men like Swift and Voltaire furnished the vehicle for satire destined to have definite political consequences. As regards Germany, the influence of geographical literature is less evident, but such humanists as Sebastian Brandt, Willibald Pirkheimer, and Ulrich von Hutten all emphasized it, and German geographical scholarship certainly dates from the works of Martin Waldseemüller, Peter Apian, and Sebastian Münster. In England, of course, Hakluyt's *Principal Navigations* was the great prose epic of the expansion in the Elizabethan period, and almost every serious work from More's *Utopia* to Bacon's *New Atlantis* and Robert Burton's *Anatomy* betrays the inspiration of travel literature; that inspiration is equally obvious in belles lettres and drama and is evidence of the place it occupied in English thought.

One may hazard the conclusion, then, that the geographical literature of the Renaissance not only was the means of spreading the news of the discoveries, but was also of great importance in the life and letters of the times. It may in fact have been of far more importance than has hitherto been acknowledged or appreciated, since it has not previously been surveyed as a unit in the history of literary culture. Some of it might indeed fall below the generally accepted canons of pure literature: it may have been this reason which has left the subject an orphan among literary historians; but by and large geographical literature of the period of the great discoveries has not received nearly the meed of praise which seems its due.

BIBLIOGRAPHY

In this bibliography I have sought to include only books of proven value, and whenever possible, the latest books on the subject. Older works, once considered standard but now supplemented by more definitive writings, I have generally omitted — with many exceptions, of course. Modern popular books, particularly those of the modern "popular biography" type, I have left out, with such exceptions as Miss Sanceau's excellent volumes. And in the case of men like Columbus, about whom countless books have been written, the list is highly selective. Should this method of compiling a bibliography appear too draconic, it is only fair to add that most of the books mentioned herein have bibliographies of their own, and often very complete ones. Since the bibliography is divided according to the chapter division of the text, in the interests of brevity I have included each title only once: a repetition of Hakluyt's *Principal Navigations* in almost all chapter bibliographies, for example, would appear to serve no useful purpose. Nor have I attempted to include the endless list of magazine articles and contributions to learned journals pertinent to our subject, but for those anxious to explore such byways *The Geographical Journal* (published by the Royal Geographical Society from 1830 to the present) and Petermann's *Geographische Mitteilungen* (Gotha, 1855–1945) are most suitable for their purpose. Both publications are fully indexed.

Several basic series of books may be mentioned, which among them cover virtually every phase of the subject. These include the publications of the Hakluyt Society, the Argonaut Press, the Broadway Travellers, and the Pioneer Histories (all English); the Cortes Society (American); and the Linschoten Vereeniging (Dutch). References to most of the publications in these series appear in this bibliography.

Attention must likewise be called to the lavishness of production and the high standard of scholarship which characterize almost all of the modern Portuguese books dealing with historical geography, which makes them an extremely valuable contribution to the field.

Original materials occur in many library collections throughout America and Europe, while secondary material may be found in most of the large libraries.

GENERAL WORKS

Baker, J. N. L. *A History of Geographical Discovery and Exploration*. London, 1937. Perhaps the best general survey for the history of travel.

Bullon, E. *Los Geografos en el Siglo XVI*. Madrid, 1925.

Dickinson, R. E., and O. J. R. Howarth. *The Making of Geography*. Oxford, 1933. A short but excellent survey of the whole field.

Friederici, G. *Der Character der Entdeckung und Eroberung Amerikas durch die Europäer*. 3vols. Stuttgart, 1925–1936. One of the most important German contributions.

Galvãno, Antonio. *The Discoveries of the World; From Their First Original unto . . . 1555*. Edited by C. R. Drinkwater Bethune. London: Hakluyt Society, 1862.

Gillespie, J. E. *A History of Geographical Discovery (1400–1800)*. New York, 1933. A concise sketch.

Günther, Siegmund. *Das Zeitalter der Entdeckungen*. Leipzig, 1919.

Hamy, E. T. *Recueil de voyages, XIII–XVI siècles*. Paris, 1908.

Harlow, Vincent T., ed. *Voyages of the Great Pioneers*. London, 1929. An important and interesting group of contributions.

Heawood, Edward. *A History of Geographical Discovery in the Seventeenth and Eighteenth Centuries*. Cambridge, 1912. A masterly and definitive treatise, beginning, however, in the latter part of the Renaissance.

Henning, Richard. *Terrae Incognitae*. 4 vols. Leyden, 1936–1939. A very important and valuable survey, including many original texts, of classical and medieval exploration up to the very end of the fifteenth century.

Keane, J. *The Evolution of Geography*. London, 1899.

Keltie, John S., and O. J. R. Howarth. *History of Geography*. London, 1913. Excellent.

Kretschmer, Konrad. *Geschichte der Geographie*. Berlin, 1912.

La Roncière, Charles de. *Histoire de la découverte de la terre*. Paris, 1938. A popular, well-illustrated volume.

    Histoire de la Marine française. Paris, 1934. The official history.

Leroi-Gourhan, André, ed. *Les Explorateurs célèbres*. Paris, 1947. Portraits and biographical sketches of seventy famous explorers.

Navarrete, Martin Fernandez de. *Colección de los viajes y descubrimientos que hicieron por mar los Españoles desde fines del siglo XV*. 5 vols. Madrid, 1825–1837.

Newton, Arthur P., ed. *The Great Age of Discovery*. London, 1932. A series of essays by various contributors.

Parry, J. H. *Europe and a Wider World, 1415–1715*. London, 1949. An excellent concise history of overseas expansion.

Ruge, Sophus. *Geschichte des Zeiltalters der Entdeckungen*. Berlin, 1881. A standard work, of very fine scholarship.

Segundo de Ispizua. *Historia de la geografía y de la cosmografía con relación a los grandes descubrimientos marítimos realizados en los siglos XV y XVI por Españoles y Portugueses*. Madrid, 1922.

Sykes, Sir Percy. *A History of Exploration*. London, 1950. A semi-popular survey, especially good for Asia.

Synge, Margaret B. *A Book of Discovery*. London, 1912. A boy's book, but a very excellent one.

Uzielli, G., and P. Amat di S. Filippo. *Studi biografici e bibliografici sulla Storia della Geografia in Italia.* Rome, 1882.

Winsor, Justin, ed. *Narrative and Critical History of America.* 8 vols. Boston, 1884–1889. Still absolutely indispensable.

1

THE BACKGROUND
CLASSICAL AND MEDIEVAL

(See also the bibliography for Chapters II and III.)

Babcock, W. H. *Legendary Islands of the Atlantic.* New York: American Geographical Society, 1922.

Beazley, Sir Raymond. *The Dawn of Modern Geography.* 3 vols. Oxford, 1897–1906. The greatest work on medieval geography. Definitive and indispensable.

Bovill, E. W. *Caravans of the Old Sahara: An Introduction to the History of the Western Sudan.* London, 1933. A highly interesting book on a little-known subject.

Bunbury, Sir E. H. *A History of Ancient Geography.* 2 vols. London, 1883. Still the classic work on the subject.

Burton, H. E. *Discovery of the Ancient World.* London, 1932.

Cary, M., and E. H. Warmington. *The Ancient Explorers.* London, 1929.

Charlesworth, Martin P. *Trade Routes and Commerce of the Roman Empire.* Cambridge, 1926.

Collis, Maurice. *Marco Polo.* London, 1950. Concise and very good.

Duhem, Pierre M. *Les Systèmes du monde de Platon à Copernic.* 5 vols. Paris, 1913–17. Encyclopedic.

Heyd, W. von. *Histoire du commerce du Levant au moyen âge.* 2 vols. Leipzig, 1936. Extremely useful for the Levant and Middle East.

Kimble, George H. T. *Geography in the Middle Ages.* London, 1938. An excellent one-volume study by the present Director of the American Geographical Society.

La Roncière, Charles de. *La Découverte de l'Afrique ou moyen âge.* 3 vols. Cairo, 1925–1927. A splendid book, of great value.

Lelewel, J. *La Géographie du moyen âge.* 5 vols. Brussels, 1852–1857. Rather out-of-date, but still a classic.

Letts, Malcolm. *Sir John Mandeville: The Man and His Book.* London, 1949. *Mandeville's Travels, Texts, and Translations.* London: Hakluyt Society (in press).

Mandeville, Sir John. *The Buke of John Maundeuill.* Edited by Sir George Warner. London: Roxburghe Club, 1889. A lavish edition of the Egerton text.

Newton, Arthur P., ed. *Travel and Travellers of the Middle Ages.* London, 1930. Valuable essays contributed by various scholars.

Polo, Marco. *The Book of Ser Marco Polo.* Edited by Sir Henry Yule and Henri Cordier. 2 vols. London, 1921. Still the standard edition.

Polo, Marco. *Marco Polo: The Description of the World.* Edited by A. C. Moule and Paul Pelliot. 2 vols. London, 1938. Contains a census and analysis of Polo MSS, including the recently discovered Toledo MS.

Prutz, Hans G. *Kulturgeschichte der Kreuzzüge.* Berlin, 1883.

Schoff, Wilfred. *The Periplus of the Erythraen Sea.* London, 1912.

Tarn, William W. *Greeks in Bactria and India.* London, 1938.

Thomson, J. Oliver. *History of Ancient Geography.* Cambridge, 1948. A definitive work.

Tozer, H. F. *A History of Ancient Geography.* London, 1935.

Warmington, Eric H. *Greek Geography.* London, 1934.

Wright, J. E. *Geographical Lore in the Time of the Crusades.* New York: American Geographical Society, 1925. A mine of information.

Yule, Sir Henry, and Henri Cordier, eds. *Cathay and the Way Thither, Being a Collection of Mediaeval Notices of China.* 4 vols. London; Hakluyt Society, 1913–1916. The travels of Polo's successors.

CHAPTER

2

SOME FREE-LANCE TRAVELERS

OF THE EARLY RENAISSANCE

(See also the blibliography for Chapters I, IV, XVII.)

Atiya, Aziz S. *The Crusade in the Later Middle Ages.* London, 1938. Contains a brilliant survey of pilgrim travel and a full bibliography.

Barbaro, Josafa and Ambrogio Contarini. *Travels to Tana and Persia,* ed. Lord Stanley of Alderley. London: Hakluyt Society, 1873.

Davies, H. W. *Bernhard von Breydenbach and His Journey to the Holy Land, 1483–4.* London, 1911. A sumptuous bibliographical study.

Longhena, Mario. *Viaggi in Persia, India et Giava di Nicolo di Conti, Girolamo Adorno e Girolamo di San Stefano.* Milan, 1929.

Major, Richard H., ed. and trans. *India in the Fifteenth Century.* London, Hakluyt Society, 1858. Includes the accounts of Conti and Santo Stefano.

Polo, Marco. *The Most Noble and Famous Travels of Marco Polo.* Edited by N. M. Penzer. London: Argonaut Press, 1929. Includes Frampton's Elizabethan translation of Conti.

Prescott, H. F. M. *Friar Felix at Large.* New Haven, Connecticut, 1950. A very humanized account of the pilgrimage.

Röhricht, Reinhold. *Deutsche Pilgerreisen nach dem Heiligen Lande.* Innsbruck, 1900. Standard.

Tafur, Pero. *Travels and Adventures of Pero Tafur (1435–39),* ed. Malcolm Letts. London: Broadway Travellers, 1926.

Varthema, Ludovico di. *The Itinerary of Ludovico di Varthema of Bologna, from 1502–1508.* Edited by Sir Richard Carnac Temple. London: Argonaut Press, 1928. The best edition of Varthema, comprising the translation made for the Hakluyt Society in 1863.

Von Harff, Arnold. *The Pilgrimage of Arnold von Harff, Knight.* Translated and edited by Malcolm Letts. London: Hakluyt Society, 1946.

CHAPTER

3

HENRY THE NAVIGATOR
AND THE AFRICAN VOYAGES

(See also the bibliography for Chapters I, IV, VIII, XVII.)

Atlas de Portugal ultramarino e das grandes viagens portuguesas de descobrimento e expansão. Lisbon, 1948. Contains 110 maps.

Azurara, Gomes Eannes de. *The Chronicle of the Discovery and Conquest of Guinea.* Translated and edited by Sir Raymond Beazley and Edgar Prestage. 2 vols. London: Hakluyt Society, 1896–99.

Baião, Antonio, with Hernani Cidade and Manuel Murias. *Historia da Expansão Portuguesa no Mundo.* 3 vols. Lisbon, 1937–1940. A monumental publication of great value.

Beazley, Sir Raymond. *Prince Henry the Navigator.* London, 1895. In the "Heroes of Nations" series.

Blake, John W. *European Beginnings in West Africa, 1454–1578.* London, 1937. A definitive study of Guinea in the early days.

Blake, John W., tr. and ed. *Europeans in West Africa, 1450–1560.* 2 vols. London, Hakluyt Society, 1942.

Branquinho da Fonseca, ed. *As grandes viagens portuguesas.* Lisbon, n.d.

Cortesão, Armando. *Subsidios para a historia do descobrimento da Guiné e de Cabo Verde.* Lisbon, 1931.

Cortesão, Jaime. *The National Secret of the Portuguese Discoveries of the Fifteenth Century.* Trans. by W. A. Bentley. London, n.d.

Crone, G. R., tr. and ed. *The Voyages of Cadamosto, and Other Documents on Western Africa in the Second Half of the Fifteenth Century.* London: Hakluyt Society, 1937. One of the best books for the period.

Dinis, Antonio Dias. *O V Centenario (1446–1946) do Descobrimento da Guiné Portuguesa a Luz da Critica historica.* Braga, 1946.

Eannes de Azurara, Gomez. See Azurara.

Fontoura da Costa, A. *As portas da India em 1484.* Lisbon, 1935. Advancing the theory of Cão's discovery of the Cape of Good Hope on his first voyage.

Fortunato de Almeida, J. *Historia de Portugal.* 6 vols. Coimbra, 1922–1929.

Gonçalves Viana, Mario. *As viagens terrestres dos Portugueses.* Porto, 1945.

Livermore, H. V. *History of Portugal.* Cambridge, 1947. The best general history in English.

Magalhães Godinho, Vitorino, ed. *Documentos sobre a expansão Portuguesa.* 2 vols. Lisbon, 1945.

Major, Richard. *Life of Prince Henry the Navigator.* London, 1868.

Marques, João M. da Silva. *Descobrimentos portugueses.* Volume 1 and Supplement. Lisbon, 1944. Completed only to 1460.

Oliveira Martins, J. P. *The Golden Age of Henry the Navigator.* London, 1914. A rather controversial work, by no means favorable to Henry.

Peres, Damião. *Historia de Portugal.* 7 vols. Barcelos, 1928–1935. The celebrated Barcelos history, lavsihly ilustrated and produced.

Historia dos descobrimentos portugueses. Porto, 1943. A splendid book.

Prestage, Edgar. *The Portuguese Pioneers*. London: Pioneer Histories, 1933. The best survey in English of the African voyages.

Sanceau, Elaine. *Henry the Navigator*. London, n.d.

CHAPTER

4

THE PORTUGUESE IN THE ORIENT

(See also the bibliography for Chapters II, III, VIII, XIII, XVII.)

Adams, William. *See* Rundall, Thomas.

Alaux, Jean Paul. *Vasco da Gama: ou l'epopée des Portugais aux Indies*. Paris, 1931. Good for the illustrations.

Albuquerque, Afonso de. *Cartas*. Edited by Bulhão Pato and Lopes de Mendoça. 6 vols. Lisbon, 1884–1915. The standard corpus of Albuquerque documents.

[Albuquerque, Afonso (Braz) de.] *The Commentaries of the Great Afonso Dalboquerque*. Translated and edited by W. de G. Birch. 4 vols. London: Hakluyt Society, 1875–1883. The standard English edition.

Ayres, Christovam, *Fernão Mendes Pinto*. 2 vols. Lisbon, 1904–1906.

Baião, Antonio, ed. *Itinerários da India a Portugal por Terra (Antonio Tenreiro e Mestre Afonso)*. Coimbra, 1923.

Ballard, Admiral G. A. *Rulers of the Indian Ocean*. London, 1928. Especially interesting from the naval angle.

Botelho da Sousa, Alfredo. *Subsidios para a história militar-marítima da India*. 2 vols. Lisbon, 1930–48.

Boxer, C. R. *Fidalgos in the Far East, 1550–1770*. The Hague, 1948. A very interesting volume, dealing with Macao and Japan.

Breve discurso em que se conta a conquista do Reino de Pegu. Barcelos, 1936.

Cambridge History of India. 4 vols. Cambridge, 1922–1937.

Campos, J. J. A. *History of the Portuguese in Bengal*. Calcutta, 1919. Important and interesting.

Campos, Moreira. *Francisco de Almeida, Vice-Rei da India*. Lisbon, 1947.

Collis, Maurice. *The Grand Peregrination*. London, 1949. The travels of Mendes Pinto.

The Great Within. London, 1941. A delightful book, containing a chapter on Matteo Ricci.

The Land of the Great Image. London, 1943. The experiences of Friar Manrique in Arakan.

Correia, A. C. G. da Silva. *Historia da colonizacão portuguesa na India*. Vol. 1. Lisbon, 1948.

Cortesão, Armando, ed. *The Suma Oriental of Tomé Pires, and the Book of Francisco Rodrigues*. 2 vols. London: Hakluyt Society, 1947. This book is also of great value in the history of cartography.

Danvers, Frederick C. *The Portuguese in India; Being a History of the Rise and Decline of Their Eastern Empire*. 2 vols. London, 1894. An exhaustive history of Portuguese India to the Nineteenth Century.

Du Jarric, Pierre. *Akbar and the Jesuits*. London, Broadway Travellers, 1928.

Ficalho, Francisco. *Viagem de Pero de Covilhan*. Lisbon, 1898.

Fonseca, J. N. de. *Historical Sketch of the City of Goa*. Bombay, 1878.

Gama, Vasco da. *Roteiro da primeira viagem (1497–99)*. Edited by Fontoura da Costa. Lisbon, 1940.

Gonçalves, Julio. *Os Portugueses e o Mar das Indias*. Lisbon, 1947.

Greenlee, William B., tr. and ed. *The Voyage of Pedro Alvares Cabral to Brazil and India*. London: Hakluyt Society, 1938. Very important.

Hart, Henry H. *Sea Road to the Indies*. New York, 1950. An interesting volume, chiefly concerned with Vasco da Gama.

Hümerich, Franz. *Die erste Deutsche Handelsfahrt nach Indien, 1505–6*. Munich, 1922. This concerns the German agents with Almeida.
Vasco da Gama und die Entdeckung das Seewegs nach Ostindien. Munich, 1898.

Jayne, Kingsley G. *Vasco da Gama and His Successors, 1460–1580*. London, 1910. One of the best books in the field.

Kammerer, Albert. *La Découverte de la Chine par les Portugais au XVIème Siècle*. Leyden, 1944. In the "T'oung Pao" series.

Lagoa, Visconde de. *Grandes e humildes na epopeia portuguesa do Oriente*. 2 vols. Lisbon, 1942–43.

Ley, Charles D., ed. *Portuguese Voyages, 1498–1663*. London: Everyman's Library, 1947. A useful and handy collection.

Lupi, Eduardo de Couto. *A Empresa Portuguesa do Oriente: conquista e sustenção do senhorio do Mar*. Lisbon, 1943.

Maclagen, Sir Edward. *The Jesuits and the Great Mogul*. London, 1932.

Maynard, Theodore. *The Odyssey of St. Francis Xavier*. London, 1936.

Pieris, P. E. *Ceylon: the Portuguese Era, Being a History for the Period 1505–1658*. 2 vols. Colombo, 1913–1914. Important.

Pinto, Mendes. *The Voyages of Mendes Pinto*. Edited by A. Vambery. London, 1891.

Ravenstein, E. G., ed. *The Journal of the First Voyage of Vasco da Gama, 1497–1499*. London: Hakluyt Society, 1898. The *Roteiro*, well edited.

Rundall, Thomas, ed. *Memorials of the Empire of Japan in the XVI and XVII Centuries*. London: Hakluyt Society, 1850. The letters of William Adams.

Sanceau, Elaine. *Indies Adventure: The Amazing Career of Afonso de Albuquerque*. London, 1936. Vivid, interesting, and reliable.
Knight of the Renaissance: D. João de Castro. London, 1949. A good sequel to *Indies Adventure*.
O Caminho da India. Oporto, 1948.

Sewall, R. *A Forgotten Empire*. London, 1900. The history of Vijayanagar, including the narratives of Paes and Nuniz.

Slater, Arthur B. *Departed Glory: The Deserted Villages of India*. London, 1937. Includes Goa and Vijayanagar.

Stanley of Alderley, Lord, tr. and ed. *The Three Voyages of Vasco da Gama . . . . . from the "Lendas da India" of Gaspar Correa*. London: Hakluyt Society, 1869.

Sykes, Sir Percy. *A History of Persia*. 2 vols. London, 1930.

Vasconcelos, Frazão de. *Pilotos das navegações portuguesas dos séculos XVI e XVII*. Lisbon, 1942.

Whiteway, Richard S. *The Rise of Portuguese Power in India, 1497–1550*. London, 1899. A definitive survey.

Wilson, Sir Arnold. *The Persian Gulf*. London, 1928.

CHAPTER

5

THE COLUMBIAN VOYAGES

(See also the bibliography for Chapters VI, IX, and XVII. The literature about Columbus is so vast that only the key books are included.)

Columbus, Christopher. *Raccolta di documenti e studi pubblicati dalla R. Commissione Columbiana pel quarto centenario dalla scoperta dell' America.* 15 vols. Rome, 1892–1894. The all-inclusive corpus of Columbian material.

Columbus, Ferdinand. *Le histoire della vita e dei fatti di Cristoforo Colombo.* Edited by Rinaldo Caddeo. 2 vols. Milan, 1930.

Harrisse, Henry. *Christophe Colomb.* 2 vols. Paris, 1884.

Jane, Cecil, ed. *Select Documents Illustrating the Four Voyages of Columbus.* 2 vols. London: Hakluyt Society, 1930–1933.

Jane, Cecil, ed. *The Voyages of Christopher Columbus.* London, Argonaut Press, 1930. Contains the full Journal of the First Voyage.

Kretschmer, Konrad. *Die Entdeckung Amerikas.* 1 vol. text; 1 vol. atlas. Berlin, 1892. The atlas contains superb reproductions of early maps.

Lollis, Cesare de. *Cristoforo Colombo nella legenda e nella storia.* Rome, 1923.

McClymont, J. R. *Vincente Añez Pinzón.* London, 1916.

Magnaghi, Alberto. *Amerigo Vespucci.* 2 vols. Rome, 1924.

Markham, Sir Clements, tr. and ed. *The Journal of Christopher Columbus . . . and Documents relating to John Cabot and Gaspar Corte Real.* London: Hakluyt Society, 1893.

The Letters of Amerigo Vespucci. London: Hakluyt Society, 1894.

Morison, Samuel Eliot. *Admiral of the Ocean Sea.* 2 vols. Boston, 1942. This promises to remain the standard work on Columbus for all time.

Portuguese Voyages to America in the Fifteenth Century. Cambridge, Massachusetts, 1940.

Nunn, G. E. *The Geographical Conceptions of Columbus.* New York: American Geographical Society, 1924. A very useful, though technical, study.

Pohl, Frederick J. *Amerigo Vespucci: Pilot Major.* New York, 1944. An excellent biography, if rather too enthusiastic.

Thacher, John Boyd. *Christopher Columbus: His Life, His Work, His Remains.* 3 vols. New York, 1903–1904. Still extremely useful. Contains reprints and translations of much original source material.

Varnhagen, Francisco de. *Amerigo Vespucci.* Lima, Peru, 1865.

Vignaud, Henri. *Améric Vespuce, 1451–1523.* Paris, 1917.

Histoire critique de la grande enterprise de Christophe Colomb. 2 vols. Paris, 1911. Vignaud's theories are now rather "dated" but are still interesting.

Winsor, Justin. *Christopher Columbus.* Boston, 1891.

CHAPTER

6

THE CONQUISTADORES

(See also bibliography for Chapters V, IX, and XVII.)

Alvarado, Pedro de. *An Account of the Conquest of Guatemala in 1524*. Edited by S. J. Mackie. New York: Cortes Society, 1924.

Anderson, C. L. G. *Life and Letters of Vasco Nuñez de Balboa*. New York, 1941.

Cortes, Hernando. *The Letters of Hernando Cortes*. Edited by J. Bayard Morris. London: Broadway Travellers, 1928.

Crow, J. A. *The Epic of Latin America*. New York, 1946. An excellent survey of South American history.

Cunninghame Graham, R. B. *Pedro de Valdivia*. London, 1926.

The Conquest of New Granada. London, 1922.

Diaz del Castillo, Bernal. *The True History of the Conquest of New Spain*. Edited and translated by A. P. Maudslay. 5 vols. London: Hakluyt Society, 1908–1916. A wonderful source for the conquest of Mexico.

Helps, Sir Arthur. *Conquerors of the New World*. 2 vols. London, 1848–1852. *The Spanish Conquest in America*. Edited by M. Oppenheim. 4 vols. London, 1900–1904. The best edition of this standard work.

Kelly, J. E. *Pedro de Alvarado, Conquistador*. Princeton, N.J., 1932.

Kirkpatrick, F. A. *The Spanish Conquistadores*. London: Pioneer Histories, 1934. Probably the best single volume on the subject.

Madariaga, Salvator de. *Hernán Cortés, Conqueror of Mexico*. London, 1942.

Markham, Sir Clements. *The Conquest of New Granada*. London, 1912.

Markham, Sir Clements, ed. *Reports on the Discovery of Peru*. London: Hakluyt Society, 1872.

Means, Philip A. *Fall of the Inca Empire, and Spanish Rule in Peru, 1530–1780*. New York, 1932.

Spanish Main: Focus of Envy, 1492–1700. New York, 1935.

Merriman, Roger B. *Rise of the Spanish Empire*. Cambridge, Massachusetts, 1918.

Newton, Arthur P. *The European Nations in the West Indies, 1493–1688*. London: Pioneer Histories, 1933. Excellent for the history of the Antilles.

Pizarro, Pedro. *Relation of the Discovery of the Kingdoms of Peru*. Translated and edited by P. A. Means. 2 vols. New York: Cortes Society, 1921. Very important for the conquest of Peru.

Prescott, William H. *History of the Conquest of Mexico*. Various eds. *History of the Conquest of Peru*. Various eds.

Sanchez, Alonso, B. *Fuentes de la historia Española e Hispano-Americana*. 3 vols. Madrid, 1927–1946.

Wagner, Henry R. *The Discovery of New Spain in 1518 by Juan de Grijalva*. Berkeley, California: Cortes Society, 1942.

The Rise of Fernando Cortes. Berkeley, California: Cortes Society, 1944.

CHAPTER

7

EASTERN SOUTH AMERICA

(See also the bibliography for Chapters VI and XVII.)

Acosta, José. *Descobrimiento de la Nueva Granada.* Bogotá, 1942.

Arcinieges, German. *Knight of El Dorado.* New York, 1942. The life of Quesada. *Germans in the Conquest of America: A 16th Century Venture.* New York, 1943.

Capistrano de Abreu, João. *O Descobrimento do Brasil pelos Portugueses.* Rio de Janeiro, 1929.

Cardim, Fernão. *Tratados da terra e gente do Brasil.* Rio de Janeiro, 1925. A modern edition of an early classic.

Cunninghame Graham, R. B. *The Conquest of the River Plate.* London, 1924.

Dominguez, Luis L., tr. and ed. *The Conquest of La Plata, 1535–1555.* London: Hakluyt Society, 1889. Includes the accounts of Schmidel and Cabeza de Vaca.

Federmann, Arnold. *Deutsche Konquistadoren in Südamerika.* Berlin, 1938.

Gandavo, Pero de Magalhães. *The Histories of Brazil.* Edited by John B. Stetson. 2 vols. New York: Cortes Society, 1922.

Haebler, Konrad. *Die überseeischen Unternehmungen der Welser.* Leipzig, 1903. A very important work.

Hantzsch, Viktor. *Deutsche Reisende des 16ten Jahrhunderts.* Leipzig, 1895. This includes the German expeditions to South America.

Harcourt, Robert. *A Relation of a Voyage to Guiana.* Edited by Sir Alexander Harris. London: Hakluyt Society, 1928.

Harlow, Vincent T., ed. *The Discoverie of Guiana, by Sir Walter Ralegh.* London: Argonaut Press, 1928. The introduction includes an excellent essay on the quest for El Dorado.
Ralegh's Last Voyage. London: Argonaut Press, 1932.

Leite, Duarte. *Descobridores do Brasil.* Oporto, 1931.

Lery, Jean de. *Histoire d'un voyage faict en la Terre du Brésil.* Paris, 1880. A narrative of the Huguenot settlement.

Marcondes de Sousa, Thomas. *O descobrimento do Brasil.* São Paolo, 1946.

Markham, Sir Clements, ed. *Expeditions into the Valley of the Amazons, 1539, 1540, 1639.* London: Hakluyt Society, 1859.

Medina, José Toribio. *The Discovery of the Amazon.* Translated and edited by B. T. Lee and H. C. Heaton. New York: American Geographical Society, 1934. The standard account of Orellana's voyage.

Rubio, Julian M. *Exploración y conquista del Rio de la Plata, siglos XVI y XVII.* Barcelona, 1942.

Simon, Pedro. *The Expedition of Pedro de Ursua and Lope de Aguirre in Search of El Dorado.* Edited by Sir Clements Markham. London: Hakluyt Society, 1861.

Staden of Hesse, Hans. *The True History of His Captivity, 1557.* Edited by Malcolm Letts. London: Broadway Travellers, 1929.

CHAPTER

8

AFRICA IN THE SIXTEENTH CENTURY

(See also the bibliography for Chapters III, IV, XII, and XVII.)

Almada, Alvares d'. *Tratado breve dos rios de Guiné, 1594.* Edited by D. Köpke. Oporto, 1841.

Alvares, Francisco. *Narrative of the Portuguese Embassy to Abyssinia during the Years 1520–27.* Edited by Lord Stanley of Alderley. London: Hakluyt Society, 1881.

Axelson, Eric. *South East Africa, 1490–1540.* London, 1940. A very important book. It contains the Antonio Fernandes narrative, and a useful guide to Portuguese libraries.

Battell, Andrew. *The Strange Adventures of Andrew Battell in Angola.* Edited by E. G. Ravenstein. London: Hakluyt Society, 1901.

Castanhoso, Miguel de. *The Portuguese Expedition to Abyssinia in 1541–43.* Edited by R. S. Whiteway. London: Hakluyt Society, 1902.

Colvin, Ian D. *The Cape of Adventure.* London, 1912. The Cape of Good Hope throughout history, as told by voyagers.

Cortesão, Armando, and Sir Henry Thomas. *The Discovery of Abyssinia by the Portuguese in 1520.* London: British Museum, 1938.

Delgado, Ralph. *História de Angola, 1482–1648.* 2 vols. Benguela, 1948.

Gomes de Brito, Bernardo, comp. *História trágico-marítima.* Edited by Damião Peres. 6 vols. Oporto, 1942–1943.

Hamilton, Genesta. *In the Wake of Da Gama: The Story of Portuguese Pioneers in East Africa, 1497–1729.* London, 1951.

Jobson, Richard. *The Golden Trade.* Edited by C. G. Kingsley. London, 1932. Gambia in the early seventeenth century.

Kammerer, Albert. *La Mer Rouge: L'Abyssinie et l'Arabie depuis l'antiquité.* 3 vols. in 7 parts. Cairo, 1929–1949. The second and third volumes concern the Portuguese in the sixteenth century. A magnificently produced publication of great value.

Lima, Americo Pires de. *Explorações em Moçambique.* Lisbon, 1943.

Mesquita Perestrelo, Manuel de. *Roteiro of South and Southeast Africa.* Edited by Fontoura da Costa. Lisbon, 1939.

Pacheco Pereira, Duarte. *Esmeraldo de Situ Orbis.* Translated and edited by G. H. T. Kimble. London: Hakluyt Society, 1937. The famous coast pilot of West Africa.

Penrose, Boies, ed. *Robert Baker: An Ancient Mariner of 1565.* Boston, 1942.

Perestrelo. *See* Mesquita Perestrelo, Manuel de.

Rey, Charles F. *The Romance of the Portuguese in Abyssinia, 1490–1633.* London, 1929.

Sanceau, Elaine. *The Land of Prester John.* London, 1944. The Portuguese in Abyssinia.

Theale, George McC. *History and Ethnography of South Africa.* 3 vols. London, 1907.
History of Africa south of the Zambesi. London, 1896.
The Portuguese in South Africa. London, 1896. Theale's books are all authoritative.

Theale, George McC., ed. *Records of South Africa.* 9 vols. Cape Town, 1901. Vol. VII contains a translation of dos Santos's *Ethiopia Oriental.*

Tracey, Hugh. *Antonio Fernandes, Descobridor do Monomotapa, 1514–15.* Lourenço Marques, 1940.

Welch, Sidney R. *South Africa under King Manuel.* Cape Town, 1946.

Wyndham. H. A. *A Family History, 1410–1688.* Oxford, 1939. Includes the Wyndham voyage to Guinea.

CHAPTER

9

THE EARLY EXPLORATION OF NORTH AMERICA

(See also the bibliography for Chapters VI, XIV, and XVII.)

Barbeau, Marius. *The Kingdom of Saguenay.* Toronto, 1936. Contains a notice of Cartier's relations with Rabelais.

Biggar, H. P. *Precursors of Jacques Cartier.* Ottawa, 1911.

Bishop, Morris. *Odyssey of Cabeza de Vaca.* New York, 1933.

Bolton, Herbert E. *Coronado, Knight of Pueblos and Plains.* New York, 1949.

Bourne, E. G. *Narratives of the Career of Hernando de Soto.* 2 vols. New York, 1922.

Brebner, John B. *The Explorers of North America, 1492–1806.* London: Pioneer Histories, 1933. A fine general history, covering Spanish, French, and English travelers.

Cartier, Jacques. *The Voyages of Jacques Cartier, published from the Originals.* Edited by H. P. Biggar. Ottawa, 1924.

Castenheda, Pedro. *Jornada de Cíbola.* Boston, 1896. Coronado's expedition.

De Soto, Hernando. *The Discovery and Conquest of Terra Florida.* Edited by W. B. Rye. London: Hakluyt Society, 1851.

Hakluyt, Richard. *Divers Voyages Touching the Discovery of America, Collected in 1582.* Edited by John Winter Jones. London: Hakluyt Society, 1850.

Harrisse, Henry. *The Discovery of North America.* London, 1892. Still useful, with fine cartographic and biographical sections.

Hallenbeck, Cleve. *The Journey of Fray Marcos de Niza.* Dallas, Texas, 1950.

Hodge, F. W., and Lewis, T. H. *Spanish Explorers in Southern United States, 1528–43.* New York, 1907.

Lowery, Woodbury. *The Spanish Settlements within the Present Limits of the United States, 1513–61.* New York, 1901.

Maynard, Theodore. *De Soto and the Conquistadores.* New York, 1930.

Murphy, Henry C. *The Voyage of Verrazano.* New York, 1875.

Ober, F. A. *Juan Ponce de Leon.* New York, 1908.

Parkman, Francis. *Pioneers of France in the New World.* Various eds.

Wagner, Henry R. *California Voyages, 1539–41.* New York: American Geographical Society, 1925.
Spanish Voyages to the Northwest Coast of America. San Francisco, 1929.
The Spanish Southwest, 1542–1794: An Annotated Bibliography. Berkeley, California, 1924. A remarkably useful book.

Williamson, James A. *The Voyages of the Cabots.* London: Argonaut Press, 1929. The definitive work on the subject.
Winship, George P. *Cabot Bibliography.* London, 1900.
   Sailors' Narratives of Voyages along the New England Coast. Boston, 1905.
   The Journey of Francisco Vazquez de Coronado. San Francisco, 1933.

CHAPTER

10

MAGELLAN AND HIS SUCCESSORS

(See also the bibliography for Chapters XII, XIII, and XVII.)
Beaglehole, J. C. *The Exploration of the Pacific.* London: Pioneer Histories, 1934. Invaluable.
Bourne, E. G. *Discovery, Conquest, and Early History of the Philippine Islands.* Cleveland, Ohio, 1907.
Burney, Admiral James. *A Chronological History of the Discoveries in the South Sea.* 5 vols. London, 1803–1817. A remarkable book.
Calvert, Albert F. *The Discovery of Australia.* London, 1902.
Collingridge, George. *The Discovery of Australia.* Sydney, 1895.
Denucé, Jean. *Magellan: La Question des Moluques et la première circumnavigation du globe.* Brussels, 1911.
Denucé, Jean. *Pigafetta: Relation du première voyage autour du monde par Magellan, 1519–22.* Antwerp, 1923.
Guillemard, F. H. H. *The Life of Ferdinand Magellan and the First Circumnavigation of the Globe, 1480–1521.* London, 1890. Still the best life of Magellan in English.
Lagoa, Visconde de. *Fernão de Magalhães.* Lisbon, 1938.
Major, R. H., ed. *Early Voyages to Terra Australis.* London: Hakluyt Society, 1859.
Markham, Sir Clements, tr. and ed. *Early Spanish Voyages to Magellan's Strait.* London: Hakluyt Society, 1911.
Mendaña, Alvaro. *The Voyage of Mendaña to the Solomon Islands in 1568.* Edited by Lord Amherst of Hackney and Basil Thomson. 2 vols. London: Hakluyt Society, 1901.
Morga, Antonio de. *The Philippine Islands* (1609). Translated and edited by Lord Stanley of Alderley. London: Hakluyt Society, 1868.
Quiros, Pedro Fernandez de. *The Voyages of Pedro Fernández de Quiros, 1595 to 1606.* Translated and edited by Sir Clements Markham. 2 vols. London: Hakluyt Society, 1904.
Rainaud, Armand. *Le Continent Austral.* Paris, 1893.
Robertson, James A. ed. *Magellan's Voyage around the World.* Cleveland, Ohio, 1906. A well-edited reprint of Pigafetta.
Sarmiento de Gamboa, Pedro. *Narratives of the Voyages of Pedro Sarmiento de Gamboa to the Straits of Magellan, 1579–80.* Translated and edited by Sir Clements Markham. London: Hakluyt Society, 1894.
Spilbergen, Joris van. *East and West Indian Mirror.* Edited by J. A. J. de Villiers. London: Hakluyt Society, 1906.

Stanley of Alderley, Lord, ed. *The First Voyage Around the World by Magel-*
lan. London: Hakluyt Society, 1874. The accounts of Pigafetta and
others.

Stevens, Henry N., ed. *New Light on the Discovery of Australia, As Revealed*
by the Journal of Captain Dom Diego de Prado y Tovar. Translations
by G. F. Barwick. London: Hakluyt Society, 1929.

Wood, G. Arnold. *The Discovery of Australia.* London, 1922.

CHAPTER

11

THE SEARCH FOR THE NORTHERN PASSAGES

(See also the bibliography for Chapters IX, XII, XIII, and XVI.)

Baffin, William, *The Voyages of William Baffin, 1612–1622.* Edited by Sir
Clements Markham. London: Hakluyt Society, 1881.

Bond, Edward A., ed. *Russia at the Close of the Sixteenth Century.* London:
Hakluyt Society, 1856. Includes Giles Fletcher and Sir J. Horsey.

Christy, Miller, ed. *The Voyages of Captain Luke Foxe of Hull, and Captain*
Thomas James of Bristol. 2 vols. London: Hakluyt Society, 1893.

Crouse, Nellis M. *In Quest of the Western Ocean.* New York, 1928.

Davis, John. *The Voyages and Works of John Davis, the Navigator.* Edited by
A. H. Markham. London: Hakluyt Society, 1880.

Hudson, Henry. *Henry Hudson the Navigator.* Edited by G.M. Asher. London:
Hakluyt Society, 1860.

Quinn, David B., ed. *The Voyages and Colonising Enterprises of Sir Humphrey*
Gilbert. 2 vols. London: Hakluyt Society, 1940.

Smith, Charlotte Fell. *John Dee, 1527–1608.* London, 1909.

Stefansson, Vilhjalmur. *The Three Voyages of Martin Frobisher in Search of*
a Passage to Cathay and India by the North-West, A.D. 1576–8. 2 vols.
London: Argonaut Press, 1938. A superb edition.

Veer, Gerrit de. *The Three Voyages of William Barents to the Arctic Regions.*
Edited by Koolemans Beynen. London: Hakluyt Society, 1876.

CHAPTER

12

THE AGE OF DRAKE

(See also the bibliography for Chapters VIII, IX, XIII, XIV, XVI.)

Cambridge History of the British Empire. Vol. I. Cambridge, 1929.

Clowes, Sir William Laird, ed. *The Royal Navy: A History.* 2 vols. London,
1879–1898. Contains chapters by Sir Clements Markham and H. W.
Wilson on voyages and discoveries.

Corbett, Sir Julian. *Drake and the Tudor Navy.* 2 vols. London, 1917. The
traditional classic on Drake, now somewhat dated.

The Successors of Drake. London, 1900.

Dudley, Robert. *The Voyage of Robert Dudley to the West Indies and Guiana in 1594.* Edited by Sir George Warner. London: Hakluyt Society, 1899.

Markham, Sir Clements, ed. *The Hawkins' Voyages.* London: Hakluyt Society, 1878.

Monson, Sir William. *Naval Tracts.* Edited by M. Oppenheim. 5 vols. London, 1902.

Nuttall, Zelia, tr. and ed. *New Light on Drake: A Collection of Documents Relating to His Voyage of Circumnavigation, 1577–80.* London: Hakluyt Society, 1914.

Oppenheim, M. *A History of the Administration of the Royal Navy, 1509–1660.* London, 1896.

Rowse, A. L. *Sir Richard Grenville of the Revenge.* London, 1937.

Taylor, E. G. R. *Late Tudor and Early Stuart Geography, 1583–1650.* London, 1934.

Tudor Geography, 1485–1583. London, 1930. This and the previous volume form a masterly survey of Tudor geographical theory and writings.

Temple, Sir Richard Carnac, ed. *The World Encompassed by Sir Francis Drake.* London: Argonaut Press, 1926. A well-edited reprint of the 1628 edition of this work.

Tenison, E. M. *Elizabethan England.* 9 vols. London, 1933–1951. Although this is a general history, the author pays great attention to overseas enterprise. The illustrations are superb.

Thompson, Edward. *Sir Walter Ralegh: The Last of the Elizabethans.* London, 1935. Perhaps the best one-volume life of Raleigh.

Wagner, Henry R. *Sir Francis Drake's Voyage around the World: Its Aims and Achievements.* San Francisco, 1926. Excellent.

Williamson, James A. *Hawkins of Plymouth.* London, 1949. A definitive book, supplanting the author's *Sir John Hawkins*, London, 1927.

Maritime Enterprise, 1485–1558. Oxford, 1913.

The Age of Drake. London: Pioneer Histories, 1938. A concise and valuable survey.

Williamson, James A., ed. *The Observations of Sir Richard Hawkins.* London: Argonaut Press, 1933.

Wright, Irene A., tr. and ed. *Documents Concerning English Voyages to the Spanish Main, 1569–80.* London: Hakluyt Society 1932. Contains *Sir Francis Drake Revived.*

Further Documents Concerning English Voyages to the Spanish Main, 1580–1603. London: Hakluyt Society, 1951.

Spanish Documents Concerning English Voyages to the Caribbean, 1527–68. London: Hakluyt Society, 1929.

CHAPTER

13

THE ENGLISH AND DUTCH REACH THE ORIENT

(See also the bibliography for Chapters IV, XI, XII, XIV, and XVII.)

Birdwood, Sir George, and Sir William Foster, eds. *First Letter Book of the East India Company, 1600–19.* London, 1893.

Danvers, F. C., and Sir William Foster. *Letters Received by the East India Company from its Servants in the East, 1602–17.* 6 vols. London, 1896–1902.

Foster Sir William. *England's Quest for Eastern Trade.* London: Pioneer Histories, 1933. A superb work of mature scholarship.
John Company. London, 1926.

Foster, Sir William, ed. *The Embassy of Sir Thomas Roe.* London, 1926.
The Journal of John Jourdain. London: Hakluyt Society, 1905.
The Voyage of Nicholas Downton to the East Indies, 1614–15. London: Hakluyt Society, 1939.
The Voyage of Sir Henry Middleton to the Moluccas, 1604–1606. London: Hakluyt Society, 1943.
The Voyage of Thomas Best to the East Indies, 1612–14. London: Hakluyt Society, 1934.
The Voyages of Sir James Lancaster to Brazil and the East Indies, 1591–1603. London: Hakluyt Society, 1940.

Hunter, Sir William W. *A History of British India.* 2 vols. London, 1899. Unfinished, but fine for the early period.

Jenkinson Anthony. *Early Voyages and Travels to Russia and Persia.* Edited by E. D. Morgan and C. H. Coote. 2 vols. London: Hakluyt Society, 1886.

Keuning, J., ed. *De tweede Schipvaart der Nederlanders naar Oost-Indie onder Jacob Cornelisz van Neck en Wybrant Warwijk, 1598–1600.* The Hague: Linschoten Vereeniging, 1938.

Linschoten, Jan Huyghen van. *The Voyage of Jan Huyghen van Linschoten to the East Indies.* From the English translation of 1598. Edited by A. C. Burnell and P. A. Tiele. 2 vols. London: Hakluyt Society, 1885.

Locke, J. C. *The First Englishmen in India.* London: Broadway Travellers, 1930.

Mollema, J. C. *De eerste Schipvaart der Hollanders naar Oost-Indie, 1595–97.* The Hague: Linschoten Vereeniging, 1935.

Moreland, W. H. *Jahangir's India.* Cambridge, 1925.

Moreland, W. H., ed. *Peter Floris: His Voyage to the East Indies, 1611–15.* London: Hakluyt Society, 1934.
Relations of Golconda in the Early Seventeenth Century. London: Hakluyt Society, 1931.

Satow, Sir Ernest M., ed. *The Voyage of Captain John Saris to Japan in 1613.* London: Hakluyt Society, 1900.

Scott, Sir W. R. *The History of Joint Stock Companies to 1720.* 2 vols. London, 1910–1912.

Stevens, Henry. *The Dawn of British Trade to the East Indies.* London, 1886.

Vlekke, Bernard. *The Story of the Dutch East Indies.* Cambridge, Mass., 1945.

Wood, A. C. *A History of the Levant Company.* Oxford, 1935.

Wright, Arnold. *Early English Adventurers in the East.* London, 1907.

CHAPTER

14

TOURISTS IN THE EAST

(See also the bibliography for Chapters IV, XIII, and XVII.)

Bates, E. S. *Touring in 1600*. Boston, 1911. Europe and the Levant.

Bent, J. T., ed. *Early Voyages and Travels in the Levant*. London: Hakluyt Society, 1893.

Chew, Samuel C. *The Crescent and the Rose*. New York, 1937. A scholarly study of early English travel in the Orient.

Coverte, Robert. *A True and Almost Incredible Report of an Englishman That Travelled by Land Throw Many Kingdomes*. Edited by Boies Penrose. Philadelphia, 1931.

Della Valle, Pietro. *The Travels of Pietro Della Valle in India*. Edited by Edward Grey. 2 vols. London: Hakluyt Society, 1892.

Foster, Sir William, ed. *Early Travels in India, 1583–1619*. Oxford, 1921. Includes Fitch, Mildenhall, William Hawkins, Coryate, etc.

The Travels of John Sanderson in the Levant, 1584–1602. London: Hakluyt Society, 1931.

Howard, Claire. *English Travellers of the Renaissance*. London, 1914.

Hughes, Charles. *Shakespeare's Europe*. London, 1903. Based on Fynes Moryson.

Lithgow, William. *A Most Delectable and True Discourse*. Glasgow, 1906.

Moryson, Fynes. *An Itinerary*. 4 vols. Glasgow, 1907–1908.

Mundy, Peter. *The Travels of Peter Mundy*. Edited by Sir Richard Carnac Temple. 5 vols. London: Hakluyt Society, 1907–1936.

Oaten, E. F. *European Travellers in India during the 15th, 16th, and 17th Centuries*. London, 1909.

Penrose, Boies. *The Sherleian Odyssey*. London, 1938.

Urbane Travellers. Philadelphia, 1942. Moryson, Coryate, Lithgow, Sandys, Cartwright, Blount, and Herbert.

Pyrard, François. *The Voyage of François Pyrard of Laval to the East Indies. . .* Edited by Albert Gray. 2 vols. in 3. London: Hakluyt Society, 1887–1889.

Ross, Sir E. Denison, ed. *The Travels of Anthony Sherley*. London: Broadway Travellers, 1933.

Teixeira, Pedro. *The Journey of Pedro Teixeira from India to Italy by Land, 1604–5*. Translated and edited by W. F. Sinclair. London: Hakluyt Society, 1902.

CHAPTER

15

THE EARLY COLONIZATION OF NORTH AMERICA

(See also the bibliography for Chaps. VI, IX, XII, XVII.)

Andrews, Matthew Page. *The Soul of a Nation*. New York, 1944. The story of early Virginia.

Bishop, Morris. *Champlain: The Life of Fortitude.* New York, 1948.

Bourne, E. G. *The Voyages of Champlain.* 2 vols. New York, 1922.

Brown, Alexander. *The First Republic in America.* Boston, 1898.
    The Genesis of the United States. Boston, 1890. The Jamestown colony.

Champlain, Samuel de. *The Works of Samuel de Champlain.* Edited by H. P.
    Biggar. 7 vols. Toronto: Champlain Society, 1922–1936.

Dionne, N. E. *Champlain.* Oxford, 1926.

Lescarbot, Marc. *Nova Francia.* Edited by H. P. Biggar. London, 1927.

Lorant, Stefan. *The New World.* New York, 1946. The French in Florida and
    the English on Roanoke Island. A beautifully produced book.

Parkman, Francis. *The Jesuits in North America in the Seventeenth Century.*
    Various eds.

Quinn, D. B., ed. *The English Voyages to North America, 1584–1605.* 2 vols.
    London: Hakluyt Society (in preparation).

Smith, Captain John. *Works.* Edited by Edward Arber. 2 vols. Glasgow, 1907.

CHAPTER

16

THE CARTOGRAPHY AND NAVIGATION
OF THE RENAISSANCE

(See also the bibliography for Chapters III, IV, V, VI, VII, IX, X, XVII.)

Alba, Duke of. *Mapas Españoles de America, siglos XV–XVII.* Madrid, 1951.
    Definitive and very sumptuously produced.

Almagia, Roberto. *Monumenta cartographica Vaticana.* 2 vols. Rome, 1944. An
    important work.

Anthiaume, Albert. *Cartes marines, constructions navales, voyages de décou-
    verte chez les Normans, 1500–1650.* Paris, 1916.
    Pierre Desceliers, Père de l'hydrographie et de la cartographie françaises.
    Paris, 1926.

Brown, Lloyd. *The Story of Maps.* Boston 1949. An excellent survey. The au-
    thor emphasises printed maps rather than portolan charts.

Cortesão, Armando. *Cartografia e Cartografos Portugueses dos Seculos XV e
    XVI.* 2 vols. Lisbon, 1935. Absolutely essential.

Denucé, Jean. *Les Origines de la cartographie portugaise et les cartes des Reinel.*
    Ghent, 1908.

Fischer, Joseph, and Franz von Wieser. *The "Cosmographiae Introductio" of
    Martin Waldseemüller.* New York, 1907.

Fite, E. D., and A. Freeman. *A Book of old Maps.* Cambridge, Massachusetts,
    1926. Chiefly Americana. The plates in some cases are faintly printed.

Fontoura da Costa, A. *Roteiros Portugueses.* Lisbon, 1940.

Fordham, Sir H. G. *Maps: Their History, Characteristics, and Uses.* Cambridge,
    1927.

Guillén, Julio. *Cartografía marítima española.* Madrid, 1943.
    Monumenta chartographica indiana. Madrid, 1942.

Humphreys, Arthur L. *Old Decorative Maps and Charts.* London, 1926. Printed
    maps, now in the National Maritime Museum, Greenwich. Good cata-
    logue.

Imago Mundi. 7 Parts (to date). Berlin, London, Stockholm, 1935–51. An invaluable publication.

Jervis, Walter W. *The World in Maps.* London, 1938. Useful for its chronological list of maps and bibliography.

Jomard, E. François. *Les Monuments de la géographie.* Paris, 1862.

Kretschmer, Konrad. *Die Entdeckung Amerikas. Atlas.* Berlin, 1892.

Kunstmann, Frederich. *Atlas der Entdeckung Amerikas.* Munich, 1859. A justly famous work, which has given its name to at least four early maps.

Lagoa, Visconde de. *Atlas de Fernão Vaz Dourado.* Oporto, 1946.

La Roncière, Charles de. *La Carte de Christophe Colomb.* Paris, 1924. The monograph that touched off a very acrimonious controversy in cartographic circles.

Müller, Frederick. *Remarkable Maps of the XV, XVI, and XVII Centuries.* 6 parts. Amsterdam, 1894–1897.

Muris, Oswald. *Der Behaim-Globus zu Nürnberg.* Berlin, 1943.

Nordenskiöld, Baron A. E. *Facsimile-Atlas to the Early History of Cartography.* Stockholm, 1889. Indispensable.

Periplus: An Essay on the Early History of Charts and Sailing Directions. Stockholm, 1897. Indispensable.

Nunn, G. E. *The Mappemonde of Juan de la Cosa.* Jenkintown, Pennsylvania, 1934. A theory that the La Cosa Map was made later than 1500.

Outhwaite, Leonard. *Unrolling the Map.* London, 1935. Popular.

Ravenstein, E. G. *Martin Behaim: His Life and His Globe.* London, 1908. A valuable book, useful also for its account of Cão's voyages.

Santarem, Visconde de. *Atlas.* Paris, 1849. *Supplement.* Paris, 1854.

Essai sur l'histoire de la cosmographie et de la cartographie. 3 vols. Paris, 1849–1852. The first important work to be written on early maps and still good.

Stevens, Henry N. *Ptolemy's Geography.* London, 1908. A descriptive list of editions now in the Newberry Library, Chicago, Illinois.

Stevenson, Edward L. *Atlas of Portolan Charts* (Egerton MS 2803). New York, 1911.

Maps Illustrating Early Discovery and Exploration in America, 1502–1530. New Brunswick, 1906. A magnificent set of full-scale reproductions of the early cartographic classics.

Marine World Chart of Nicolo de Canerio. New York, 1908. With full-scale reproduction.

Portolan Charts, Their Origins and Characteristics. New York, 1911.

Terrestrial and Celestial Globes. 2 vols. New Haven, Connecticut, 1921.

Stevenson, Edward L., ed. *Geography of Claudius Ptolemy.* New York, 1932. The first edition of Ptolemy in English. Plates are from the Ebner MS in the New York Public Library.

Tooley, R. V. *Maps and Map-Makers.* London, 1949. Very useful.

Vascano, Antonio. *Juan de la Cosa.* Madrid, 1892.

Wagner, Henry R. *The Cartography of the Northwest Coast of America to the Year 1800.* 2 vols. Berkeley, California, 1937.

Wauermann, H. E. *L'Ecole cartographique belge et Anversoise du XVIe siècle.* 2 vols. Brussels, 1895.

Wertheim, Alexander. *Old Maps and Charts.* Berlin, 1931.

Wieder, F. C. *Monumenta Cartographica.* 4 vols. The Hague, 1925–1933. Largely seventeenth century.

Wroth, Lawrence C. *The Early Cartography of the Pacific.* New York: Bibliographical Society of America, 1944. A definitive work.

NAVIGATION

Anderson, Roger C. *The Rigging of Ships (1600–1720).* London, 1927.
  The Sailing Ship. London, 1926.
Barbosa, Antonio. *Novos subsidios para a história da ciencia nautica portuguesa da epocha dos descobrimentos.* Oporto, 1948.
Bensuade, Joaquim. *Histoire de la science nautique portugaise.* 7 vols. Lisbon, 1914–19. Facsimiles of the early eds. of navigational books.
  L'Astronomie nautique au Portugal a l'époque des grandes découvertes. Berne, 1912.
Caravelas, naus, e galés de Portugal. Oporto, n.d.
Cantera, Francisco. *Abraham Zacut.* Madrid, 1935.
Castro, João de. *Roteiros.* 3 pts. Lisbon: Agencia Geral das Colonias, 1940.
  Tratado da sphaera, da geographia. Lisbon, 1940.
Clowes, G. S. Laird. *Sailing Ships: Their History and Development.* 2 pts. London: Science Museum, 1931–1936. Excellent.
Fontoura da Costa, A. *A marinharia dos descobrimentos.* Lisbon, 1933. A very important work.
Guillén, Julio. *La carabela Santa Maria: Apuntes para su reconstitución.* Madrid. 1927.
Gunther, R. W. T. *The Astrolabes of the World.* 2 vols. Oxford, 1932.
Hewson, J. B. *A History of the Practice of Navigation.* London, 1951.
Marquet, F. *Histoire générale de la navigation.* Paris, 1931.
Meigs, J. F. *The Story of the Seaman.* Philadelphia, 1924.
Morais e Sousa, L. de. *A sciencia nautica dos pilotos portugueses nos séculos XV e XVI.* 2 vols. Lisbon, 1924.
Oliveira, João Braz de. *Os navios da descoberta.* Lisbon, 1940.
Quirino da Fonseca. *A caravela portuguesa.* Coimbra, 1934.
Stevens, John R. *An Account of the Construction and Embellishment of Old-time Ships.* Toronto, 1949.
Villiers, Alan. *Sons of Sinbad.* London, 1940. The classic work on Arab dhows, by a yachtsman who shipped on one.
Viterbo, Marques de Sousa. *Trabalhos nauticos dos Portugueses nos séculos XVI e XVII.* 2 vols. Lisbon, 1890–1900.
Wroth, Lawrence C. *The Way of a Ship: An Essay on the Literature of Navigational Science.* Portland, Maine, 1937. Invaluable.

CHAPTER

17

THE GEOGRAPHICAL LITERATURE
OF THE RENAISSANCE

(Other references occur throughout the bibliography and in the text.)

Anselmo, Antonio J. *Bibliografia das obras impressas em Portugal no século XVI.* Lisbon, 1926.

Arber, Edward, ed. *The First Three English Books on America*. Birmingham, 1885. The works of Richard Eden are here reprinted.

Atkinson, Geoffroy. *La Littérature géographique française de la renaissance*. 2 pts. Paris, 1927–36. A definitive bibliography.

Les Nouveaux Horizons de la renaissance française. Paris, 1935.

Les Relations de voyages du 17e siècle et l'évolution des idées. Paris, 1924.

Baginsky, P. B. *German Works Relating to America, 1493–1800*. New York, 1942.

Barros, João de, and Diogo do Couto. *Da Asia*. 24 vols. Lisbon, 1778–1788. (New ed. of Barros' four Decades, Lisbon, 1945.)

Bell, Aubrey. *Diogo do Couto*. London, 1924.

Gaspar Correa. London, 1924.

Luis de Camoens. London, 1923.

Portuguese Bibliography. London, 1922.

Portuguese Literature. Oxford, 1922. An excellent survey.

Beristain de Souza, J. M. *Biblioteca Hispano-Americana Septentrional*. 5 vols. Mexico, 1947.

Böhme, Max. *Die grosse Reisesammlungen des 16e Jahrhunderts*. Leipzig, 1904.

Boxer, C. R. *Three Historians of Portuguese Asia: Barros, Couto, and Bocarro*. Macao, 1948. Short, but full of information.

Braga, Theophilo. *Camões, epoca e vida*. Oporto, 1907.

Burton, Sir Richard. *Camoens: His Life and His Lusiads: A Commentary*. 2 vols. London, 1881.

Callender, Sir G. A. R. *Bibliography of Naval History*. London, 1924–25.

Cambridge Bibliography of English Literature. Volume I, section entitled "Books of Travel."

Cambridge History of English Literature. Volume IV, chap. iv, "The Literature of the Sea"; chap. v, "Seafaring and Travel." By C. N. Robinson and John Leyland.

Camoens, Luis de. *The Lusiads of Camoens*. Translated by Leonard Bacon. New York, 1950. The latest translation, and certainly one of the best. With valuable notes.

Cawley, Robert R. *The Voyagers and Elizabethan Drama*. Boston, 1938.

Unpathed Waters: Studies in the Influence of Voyagers on Elizabethan Literature. Princeton, 1940.

Cole, G. W. *A Catalogue of Books Relating to the Discovery and Early History of North and South America, owned by E. D. Church*. 5 vols. New York, 1907. The Church books are now in the Huntington Library.

Correa, Gaspar. *Lendas da India*. 4 vols. Lisbon, 1858–1860.

Cox, E. G. *A Reference Guide to the Literature of Travel*. Seattle, 1935.

Faria e Sousa, Manuel de. *Asia Portuguesa*. 6 vols. Lisbon, 1945–1947.

Fontán y Lobé, J. *Bibliografía colonial: Contribución a un indice de publicaciones africanas*. Madrid, 1946.

Gallois, L. *Les Géographes allemands de la renaissance*. Paris, 1890.

Goes, Damião de. *Crónica do Serinissimo Senhor Rei Dom Manoel*. 4 vols. Coimbra, 1926.

Gomara, F. L. de. *Historia General de las Indias*. 2 vols. Madrid, 1922.

Hakluyt, Richard. *The Principal Navigations, Voyages, Traffiques, and Discoveries of the English Nation*. 12 vols. Glasgow: James MacLehose and Sons, for the Hakluyt Society, 1903–1905. Contains Professor Raleigh's brilliant essay on English voyages of the sixteenth century.

Hantzsch, Viktor. *Sebastian Münster; Leben, Werk, und wissenschaftliche Bedeutung.* Leipzig, 1898.

Las Casas, Bartolome de. *Historia de las Indias.* Edited by Gonzalo de Reparaz. 3 vols. Madrid, 1927.

Leonard, Irving A. *Books of the Brave.* Cambridge, Massachusetts, 1949.

Lopes de Castanheda, Fernão. *Historia do descobrimento e conquista da India pelos Portugueses.* 4 vols. Coimbra, 1924–7.

Lynam, Edward, ed. *Richard Hakluyt and His Successors.* London: Hakluyt Society, 1946. The centenary volume of the society.

Machado, Barbosa. *Bibliotheca Lusitana.* 4 vols. Lisbon. 1741–1759.

Maggs Brothers. *Bibliotheca Asiatica et Africana.* Catalogue 519. London, 1929. *Bibliotheca Brasiliensis.* Catalogue 546. London, 1930. *Seventy-five Spanish and Portuguese Books, 1481–1764.* Catalogue 589. London, n.d.

Manuel II, King of Portugal. *Early Portuguese Books, 1489–1600, in the Library of H. M. the King of Portugal.* 3 vols. London, 1929–1936. A superb work on early Portuguese literature and bibliography, written by Manuel II, who was a distinguished scholar.

Manwaring, G. E. *Bibliography of British Naval History.* London, 1930.

Martyr, Peter. *Decades.* Translated by F. A. MacNutt. 2 vols. New York, 1912.

Means, Philip A. *Biblioteca Andina: The Chroniclers of the 16th and 17th Centuries Who Treated of the pre-Hispanic History and Culture of the Andean Countries.* New Haven, Connecticut, 1928.

Medina, J. T. *Bibliotheca Hispano-Americana (1493–1810).* 7 vols. Santiago, Chile, 1898–1907.

Mendes dos Remedios. *Historia da literatura portugueza.* Lisbon, 1908.

Moses, Bernard. *Spanish Colonial Literature in South America.* New York, 1922.

Nuñes, Leonardo. *Crónica de Dom João de Castro.* Edited by J. D. M. Ford. Cambridge, Massachusetts, 1936.

Oliveira Martins, J. P. *Camões e a Renascenca em Portugal.* Lisbon, 1910.

Oviedo y Valdes, G. F. de. *Historia general y natural de las Indias.* ed. J. A. de los Rios. 4 vols. Madrid, 1851–55.

Palau y Dulcet, A. *Manual del Librero Hispano-Americano.* 7 vols. Barcelona, 1923–27.

Parks, George B. *Richard Hakluyt and the English Voyages.* New York: American Geographical Society, 1930. Most useful.

Prestage, Edgar. *The Chronicles of Fernão Lopes and Gomes Eannes de Zurara.* London, 1928.

Purchas, Samuel. *Hakluyt Posthumus or Purchas His Pilgrimes.* 20 vols. Glasgow: James MacLehose and Sons, for the Hakluyt Society, 1905–1907.

Sencourt, Robert. *India in English Literature.* London, 1926.

Stillwell, Margaret B. *Incunabula and Americana, 1450–1800.* New York, 1931. An invaluable bibliographical study.

Taylor, E. G. R., ed. *The Original Writings and Correspondence of the two Richard Hakluyts.* 2 vols. London: Hakluyt Society, 1935.

Ticknor, George. *History of Spanish Literature.* 3 vols. Boston, 1849.

Underhill, J. G. *Spanish Literature in the England of the Tudors.* New York, 1899.

Wright, Louis B. *Middle-class Culture in Elizabethan England.* Chapel Hill, North Carolina, 1935.

INDEX